Too Ill to Talk?

User involvement and palliative care

Neil Small and Penny Rhodes

London and New York

First published 2000
by Routledge
11 New Fetter Lane, London EC4P 4EE

Simultaneously published in the USA and Canada
by Routledge
29 West 35th Street, New York, NY 10001

Routledge is an imprint of the Taylor & Francis Group

© 2000 Neil Small and Penny Rhodes

Typeset in Goudy by
HWA Text and Data Management, Tunbridge Wells
Printed and bound in Great Britain by
University Press, Cambridge

British Library Cataloguing in Publication Data
A catalogue record for this book is available from the British Library

Library of Congress Cataloging in Publication Data
Small, Neil
   Too ill to talk? : user involvement and palliative care / Neil Small
   and Penny Rhodes.
      p. cm.
   Includes bibliographical references and index.
      1. Palliative treatment. 2. Physician and patient. 3. Patient
   participation. 4. Primary health care. I. Rhodes, Penny J. II. Title

   R726.8 .S586 2000
   352.1′75--dc21

00-055815

ISBN 0-415-23316-X (hbk)
ISBN 0-415-23317-8 (pbk)

Too Ill to Talk?

User involvement has become an important part of health policy initiatives during the last decade, but how realistic is the concept and do all users want to be involved? This book brings the voices of people with serious illness, and those caring for them, into the debate about how far health and social care services can reflect the views of users.

Opening with a useful overview of the literature on user involvement, the book goes on to look at the policy and professional context within which user involvement is undertaken, in particular user involvement in palliative care. In this section, the authors discuss two key concepts – palliative care and empowerment – and analyse the role of self-help groups and new information and communication technologies in this context. The last section of the book focuses on the detailed narratives of people coping with three life-threatening illnesses – cystic fibrosis, multiple sclerosis and motor neurone disease – and in this way the views and experiences of the 'user' are brought into play to critique current policy and practice.

Too Ill to Talk? addresses a current health services issue in a refreshingly critical manner. It challenges the assumption that user involvement is either easy to achieve or that it is necessarily welcomed by all parties. It will be valuable reading for students on health studies courses, health professionals and policy makers in health and social care.

Neil Small is Professor of Community and Primary Care, University of Bradford.
Penny Rhodes is a Research Fellow, Bradford Health Authority.

Contents

Acknowledgements   vi
List of abbreviations   viii

1   Introduction   1

2   User involvement: selected review of the literature   18

3   Palliative and community care   56

4   Multiple sclerosis: 'we all live in hope'   94

5   Motor neurone disease: 'just a little bit of hope'   125

6   Cystic fibrosis: 'as normal a life as possible'   155

7   Conclusions   211

Bibliography   222
Index   245

Acknowledgements

At the heart of this work are interviews with people who have multiple sclerosis, motor neurone disease or cystic fibrosis. We are grateful to those who agreed to be interviewed by us. We also interviewed some members of their families and had a number of contacts with volunteers and with professionals involved in caring for people with these conditions. Without the generosity of these people, who gave their time and shared their thoughts and experiences, we would not have been able to proceed.

We received help from members of the Multiple Sclerosis Society; Jan Hatch and, in particular, Ann Crossley played an important part. Likewise the Motor Neurone Disease Association helped. Tricia Holmes and, in particular, Jane Connell were key to our making progress. Dr Rosie Jones, Director of the MS Research and Resources Unit at Bristol Royal Infirmary and Ian Robinson, Director of the Centre for the Study of Health, Sickness and Disablement at Brunel University offered advice when we were at an early stage in our thinking.

In relation to cystic fibrosis many clinical nurse specialists expressed an interest in the project and helped to facilitate other contacts. In particular, we would like to thank Jean Pounceby, author of the *Coming of Age* project, Louise Hickey and Jonathon Farrell of the Association of Cystic Fibrosis Adults and Peter Kent, Director of the Rainbow Trust (formerly Director of Family and Adult Support Services for the Cystic Fibrosis Trust).

We benefited from an Advisory Group made up of Marian Barnes of Birmingham University, Caroline Glendinning from Manchester University, David Gibbs of the Derbyshire Coalition for Independent Living, Joyce Dainton, Stephanie Strange and Sue Huskins. Thanks also to Andrew Nocon of Leeds University. In the design stages for the research that forms the core of this work we are grateful to Professor David Clark (Sheffield University) for the central role he played.

Some of the ideas we present have been used in conference presentations and the reaction to them has helped us refine our thinking. Ideas have been discussed with colleagues and we are grateful for their support. The proposal to develop the research into a book was reviewed by anonymous experts and their constructive criticisms helped shape our progress.

The research project this book draws on was funded by the Joseph Rowntree Foundation. They support a wide range of projects, some with a research and some with an innovative development focus, which they hope can contribute to both policy makers and practitioners. We acknowledge both their generosity and patience. Specifically, at JRF, Alex O'Neil has been a continuing source of support and advice.

All these people notwithstanding, the views expressed, and the conclusions reached, are decidedly those of the authors and not necessarily those of any of the above.

Abbreviations

ACFA	Association for Cystic Fibrosis Adults
ACHCEW	Association of Community Health Councils of England and Wales
ACS	Age Concern Scotland
ACT	Association for Children with Terminal conditions
AIDS	acquired immune deficiency syndrome
ALS	amyotrophic lateral sclerosis
ARMS	Action for Research into Multiple Sclerosis
BMA	British Medical Association
CF	cystic fibrosis
CFF	Cystic Fibrosis Foundation
CFS	chronic fatigue syndrome
CFT	Cystic Fibrosis Trust
CHCs	community health councils
CMC	computer mediated communication
CVS	Council for Voluntary Services
DHA	district health authority
FASS	Family and Support Service
GP	general practitioner
HIV	human immuno deficiency virus
ICTs	information and communications technologies
IPPR	Institute for Public Policy Research
IRC	Internet-related chat
IV	intravenous
JCCs	joint consultative committees
LMCA	Long-term Medical Conditions Alliance
MND	motor neurone disease
MNDA	Motor Neurone Disease Association
MP	Member of Parliament
MS	multiple sclerosis
MUDs	multiple user domains
NHS	National Health Service
OPCS	Office of Population Censuses and Surveys
OT	occupational therapist

PBP	progressive bulbar palsy
PMA	progressive muscular atrophy
RAGE	Radiotherapy Action Groups Exposure
SSD	Social Service Department
UKCC	United Kingdom Central Council for Nursing, Midwifery and Health Visiting
US	United States

1 Introduction

This is a book about user involvement. Its starting point is the experience of a small number of people living with one of three medical diagnoses: multiple sclerosis (MS), motor neurone disease[1] (MND) and cystic fibrosis (CF). How far do these people wish to be involved in the sorts of care they receive? What has been their experience, as service users, in shaping their day-to-day care? Do they want to contribute to the debate about overall service provision for people living with the same diagnosis as theirs? If they do want to contribute have they been able so to do? Is user involvement high on a person's agenda when they are living with a serious illness? Or, is user involvement best understood as something to do with the assumptions and practice of the health and social care system and the politicians and professionals who shape it?

User involvement has been high on the political agenda for some time, although it has appeared under different guises and has had many contingent meanings. Much of what follows will concentrate on questions of policy. We will not assume that user involvement is an unqualified good. Perhaps it is just another way for those in power to justify and legitimise their position (Nettleton 1995). Perhaps it makes unwelcome demands on people whose priorities are not those of the policy makers.

We will also consider professional practice. People living with chronic or terminal illness are likely to encounter a lot of professionals. Some of these give higher priority to communication and involvement; some are better at it than others. User involvement should be a professional concern and we will consider its practice implications.

Policy and practice provide the necessary, but not sufficient, context for user involvement. What is also needed is understanding, access and will on the part of the users themselves. Consequently, we will consider the phenomenological world of our potential service users. How is their everyday world made up and what meaning do they attribute to events within it (Berger and Luckmann 1967)? How are problems they come across understood and how is this understanding translated into problem solving activity (Bauman 1978)? What is the relationship between these understandings and the body of professional opinion and political orthodoxy they encounter?

It is also possible that a concern with user involvement is best understood if we see it as illustrative of a more general change in society, and particularly in the way health and social care is perceived. Frank (1995) describes the times we live in as postmodern, and here there is 'an ethic of voice, affording each a right to speak her own truth, in her own words' (Frank 1995: xiii). We will return to consider what Frank means and to ask how important this is at various points in what follows.

Our choice of illnesses

Our choice of illnesses has been precipitated by a number of factors. Much excellent work in illness narrative has been undertaken in relation to chronic illnesses. Autobiographical work has emerged from responses to living with terminal illness. For example, both cancer and acquired immune deficiency syndrome (AIDS) have provided the illness context out of which the existential encounter with the possibility of premature death has been explored (Small 1998a). Our three illnesses offer an opportunity to build on this work. Together they embrace the chronic, the progressive and the terminal. They engage with predominantly different age groups: CF younger, MS in adulthood and MND in older age. Overall they impact on men and women in similar numbers. They include a spread between the therapeutic optimism associated with CF, a continuing sense of uncertainty about the progression of MS and the predominate, but not universal, sense of a remorseless decline with MND.

The specific circumstances of our chosen illnesses allow us to consider their impact on the body and to look at that in terms of the possibilities for user involvement. Frank asks 'Do I *have* a body, or *am* I a body?' (Frank 1995: 33). For him illness stories are embodied, they are told not just about the body but through it. Our chosen illnesses can, and do, have a profound impact on the body and indeed they can even inhibit the capacity for speech, making Frank's conflation of the body and the story more piquant than it would be for many illnesses.

All three conditions are served by vigorous voluntary organisations which both offer services and lobby health and social care policy makers and service providers. We are interested in the potential role for such intermediate organisations and see our chosen areas offering illustrative examples of wider relevance.

Narrative

We seek to encompass the individual and the social dimensions of user involvement by drawing on narrative, the way people talk about their life after their diagnosis and the way those people closest to them talk about care. People establish narrative reference points between themselves and society. These narratives are 'bounded by and constructed in relationship with various individual people and organisations' (Williams 1984: 181). Williams argues that: 'Narrative reconstruction is an attempt to reconstitute and repair ruptures between body, self, and world by linking-up and interpreting different aspects of biography in order to realign present and past and self with society' (Williams 1984: 197). If this is so then the facilitation of narrative reflection in the research interview can not only constitute a gift from the respondent to the researcher but can assist the respondent's reconstructive endeavours (Small 1998).

Narratives of illness display complex causal models, for example: 'The person without cancer can afford to be more dogmatic about cancers and is likely to think in stereotypes. The closer he comes to dealing with the disease the less clear-cut and more complex the explanations may become' (Linn *et al.* 1982: 838). These complex models can also show wide differences even between individuals with the same illness diagnosis and with ostensibly similar life situations. Something of the richness of this difference is captured in Frank's stance towards published non-fictional accounts of illness. He argues that:

> Far from claiming that most people experience illness as the author does, publication implies an opposite claim: the subjectivity articulating this illness experience is worth reading because it is singular. The claim of publication is that the reader may have had the same illness experience as the author, but the reader has not experienced it in the same way.
>
> (Frank 1997: 135)

Of course the narrative can differ depending upon who it is delivered to. Public accounts can simply confirm the sense of the 'approved' while private accounts can derive from an experiential world in which body dysfunction and personal despair intrude (see West 1990). Further, the accounts of the same experience as told by the people themselves and by their carer, even as part of the same discussion/ interview, can embrace different discourses and understandings.

Here it is the singularity of narrative that we offer as illuminating aspects of the person's life. We also can focus on differences between the public and private and between the person with the illness and their carer. This is not a work in which we claim our stories as representative; they are illustrative of some of the complex issues that touch upon user involvement. We agree with the summary of the value of life stories and illness narratives provided by Monks and Frankenberg:

> [they] are increasingly valued tools in the investigation of personal experience and its shaping within larger social and cultural frameworks. Their particular value has been said to lie in the breadth of contextualization (identified at various levels and across different domains) and in the insight they provide into how illness functions as an idiom for discussing and defining more general societal and cultural concerns. They may also be set critically against clinical and other accounts, and in addition their temporal aspect has provided a medium for understanding the processual character of the phenomenology of illness and disability.
>
> (Monks and Frankenberg 1995: 107)

That interface between the personal, social and cultural helps us highlight, in the context of this work, hypotheses about both the likelihood of user involvement and possible barriers to it. Although in what follows we do, to a certain extent, separate policy concerns from the narrative of those people living with our chosen illnesses, we recognise that there is a much more reciprocal, reflexive relationship between policy and lived experience. For example, a policy and/or clinical decision about what drug can be prescribed may impact on the sense a person has about the health care system acting in their best interests. Consequently it helps shape their contact with professionals. It may set them at odds with what they see as an indifferent or hostile health service. It may convince them they have less of a future to look forward to. It is likely that any dispute about the availability of a drug will mean a considerable amount of their time is spent either worrying about the drug's absence or agitating for its prescription. The availability of the drug beta interferon for people with MS is a case in point and is discussed in our MS chapter.

The narrative approach in considering chronic illness and life-threatening illnesses of many sorts has been shaped by the contributions of Kleinman (1988) and Frank (1995). Our approach shares Frank's recognition that, 'The ill person who turns illness into story transforms fate into experience' and 'becomes a witness to the conditions that rob others of their voices' (Frank 1995: xi–xii). It also is offered within the rationale Kleinman presents when he says:

> Illness narratives edify us about how life's problems are created, controlled, made meaningful. They also tell us about the way cultural values and social relations shape how we perceive and monitor our bodies, label and categorize bodily symptoms, interpret complaints in the particular context of our life situation; we express our distress through bodily idioms that are both peculiar to distinctive cultural worlds and constrained by our shared human condition.
>
> (Kleinman 1988: xiii)

Key features of the narrative

There are some aspects of the experience of living with, and responding to, MS, MND and CF that are common to other chronic or life-threatening illnesses and some that appear to be particularly highlighted in the conditions we have focussed on. In policy terms we have to engage with the impact of conditions that combine the possibility of high need but have a relatively low incidence in any given geographical area. Planning and policy making that concentrates on needs assessment across populations may act to the detriment of people with these sorts of conditions. We will explore the potential for tension between a model of health that is based on public participation and one based on user involvement. It may be that a utilitarian, or an aggregated, approach to need acts against the best interests of the people we focus on.

In terms of the characteristics of the illnesses themselves there are two defining factors. First is the frequent presence of physical deterioration and premature death. Second is a prevalent sense of uncertainty. Each of these factors, we will argue, creates challenges in terms of developing a user involvement agenda. We hypothesise that engagement with a user involvement agenda presupposes a future orientation. It is also, we think, facilitated by some sense of knowing what you can expect. We will illustrate, in what follows, the disruption to a person's sense of self and to their place in society created by diagnosis and then by a series of other transitions that may be faced: not being able to walk, not being able to eat unaided, not being able to talk as before and so on. For many a steady state is not reached, nor is a secure sense in which one can forecast even the very near future. The result is a present orientation and everyday life characterised by a series of evolving challenges.

The physical impact and the uncertainty are experienced in a social context. That social context, and a person's sense of self, shape the experience of the illness through a complex, nuanced and reflexive relationship. In this introductory section we will comment on three aspects of this relationship that will recur in our subsequent chapters. They replicate the major dimensions in the biographies of people with chronic illness described by Corbin and Strauss (1987):

- The body
- Disruption of the life course (Corbin and Strauss had a category of 'self')
- Time

In addition we will comment on ways the social role of the ill have been conceptualised. Specifically, we will consider questions as to the 'appropriate' moral role society requires of them.

The body

Kelly and Field (1996) remind us of the body's role in chronic illness. It is the point at which self is in touch with itself, it is the point of immediate salience for self, and a point of reference for external labels. Biological facts become social facts because others respond to the person in terms of their physicality. They also act as limiting factors on social action for the sufferer. 'No amount of euphemism or politically correct discourse can distract from the centrality of the public and physical difference. It cannot be socially constructed out of existence' (Kelly and Field 1996: 251).

But if difference cannot be socially constructed out of existence there remains a very strong element of social construction to engage with. The physical symptoms associated with our chosen conditions often produce impairment. It is the social context within which people with impairment live that produces disability. Disability can be defined as: 'The disadvantage or restriction of activity caused by a contemporary social organisation which takes no or little account of people who have physical impairments and thus excludes them from the mainstream of social activities' (UPIAS 1976: 3–4). Oliver has argued that: 'far from being an appendage, disability is an essential part of the self. In this view it is nonsensical to talk about the person and the disability separately' (Oliver 1990: xiii).

Much research has served to perpetuate an individualistic view of disability and to locate its concerns within a functionalist and interactionalist paradigm.

That is, it concentrates on the place of disability in society, specifically in terms of its function, or it looks at roles and socialisation. Such approaches can undermine the significance individuals give to the conditions within which they live and the meanings they embrace (see Barton 1996). People with our conditions may need intimate bodily care – eating, bathing, and going to the toilet. They may experience challenges to mobility and to normal forms of communication. These needs are not social constructions, they are embodied. But their becoming disabilities, or the meaning they have in the context of personal and social relationships, is created at the interfaces of the individual and the social (see Parker 1993). Our narrative approach allows for these significances and meanings to emerge in all their diversity and reflexivity. But it also means that we have to engage with the possibilities of being critical of a social model of disability, summarised above. We will consider both the body and the role of individual agency. To what extent does the physicality of our chosen illnesses define the experience? What role does individual choice play in the experience of disablement?

Disruption of the life course

'Serious illness is a loss of the "destination and map" that had previously guided the ill person's life' says Frank (1995: 1). We have identified uncertainty as one of the defining characteristics of the illnesses we are considering. We will see in our narrative accounts both an omnipresence of uncertainty and variation in its form. Sometimes the uncertainty is a product of the varied progression of the disease, as with MS. Sometimes it is because of the developments in treatment, as with CF. Sometimes it is both. What stance towards the opportunities for the future is realistic amidst such uncertainty? There are precedents readily available that underline a sense that medicine cannot provide a route from uncertainty. Sometimes advances in treatment make earlier pessimistic assessments redundant for many, as has been the case with HIV in the West. Sometimes early promise results in little longer-term impact, as has been the case with many apparent breakthroughs in cancer treatment. There are also residual, folk beliefs that the individual has to consider alongside medical knowledge and much anecdotal 'evidence', for example that you should fight illness, that 'if you give up you die'. The resulting scenario is one in which there is not only the trauma of the diagnosis but also the strain of not knowing the reliability of the prognosis given. A doctor specialising in HIV-related illness told how some of his patients would eagerly await his return from international conferences thinking he might have brought information about a cure in his briefcase (Small 1993). Now doctors in many areas tell of their patients coming with news of the latest bit of treatment innovation or therapeutic optimism gleaned from the Internet.

The literature in relation to chronic illness, in the main using narrative accounts, has to be framed within this context of change and uncertainty when we look at our chosen illnesses. That literature includes an examination of the disruption of the normal life course (Bury 1982) and of the way individuals make sense of the course and progression of their illness (Brody 1987). There is also work that identifies how a redefinition of normality or competence as social actors occurs with some people (Gerhardt 1996) and other studies that report a sense of the disintegration of self-image when confronted with chronic illness, a disintegration often not simultaneously countered by the emergence of a valued new self-image (Charmaz 1991). Work by Parr *et al.* on aphasia describes a change that is more tentative: 'The person's sense of identity and status become fragile and vulnerable. People who develop aphasia temporarily lose their bearings. Their past becomes untenable and their future becomes uncertain' (Parr *et al.* 1997: 112).

There is, though, a sense that one way of coping with illness is to display strength of character. This includes taking responsibility for one's own health (Blaxter 1996) and emphasising inner strength and support from close networks (Ong *et al.* 1999). That people live with their illness in a family context as well as a societal one is underlined in work by, for example, Bluebond-Langner (1989 and 1996). Her focus on families where one person has cystic fibrosis emphasises how much these families are like other families. The presence of CF does not mean that their *raison d'être* is of something being wrong but rather it is of 'living life as it is'.

Bluebond-Langner's rich picture of family life and CF, and her sense of stressing the things shared with other families, raises the question of the extent to which the diagnosis of chronic or terminal illness, in itself, prompts an ontological break for the person so diagnosed. There are other possibilities. First the break may be epistemological rather than ontological, that is it relates to the way that we have knowledge of the external world and it has knowledge of us rather than relating to our being or essence. The world may see us differently, indeed we may also see it as a different place, but we may really think we are, at heart, the same people we always were. An analogy may be to look at the difference between having children and getting older. When you have your first child you see society differently and you are seen differently. You also become a different person to the one you were before – at the very least you become a parent! When you get older you see society differently and are seen differently, but at heart you think you are the same person you always were! Is being diagnosed with a terminal or chronic illness like having children or like getting older? Or is terminal illness like having children and chronic illness like getting older?

It may not be useful to construe change using terms like 'breaks'; rather we can look to the complex idea of liminality in illness. Turner (1974) called intervals between structural positions liminal. Murphy *et al.* suggest that the life histories of people with disabilities may be: 'dramatised in a rite of passage frozen in its liminal stage ... (their) ... state of being is clouded and indeterminate' (Murphy *et al.* 1988: 238–41). Price (1995) calls that period between terminal diagnosis and death a liminal one in that many individuals live neither fully in, nor fully out, of the social world. In this stage they can, in Monks and Frankenberg's words, fall: 'ambiguously between sickness and wellness, living and dead, participation and exclusion' (Monks and Frankenberg 1995: 109).

Frankenberg (1986) sees liminality as periods of novelty or antistructure where the routine constraints of daily life are relaxed. He believes such stages are 'not only lived' but 'simultaneously performed' (1987: 133). As one listens to the narrative of those people with MS, in his and Monks' 1995 study, any sense of a linear flow from past to future has to be modified to include periods of self-reflection and reorientation. These separate periods of conventional structure. Thus, liminality emphasises expressive functions and can sit between periods of a life that appear very different in kind.

We need to consider if the particular circumstances of the illnesses we concentrate on mean that, unlike many other illnesses, the identity of the person is predominantly encompassed by the role of 'person with this disease'. More generally we can see that one lives with illness. The medical is only one component amongst many in the ill person's everyday experience. While this might seem obvious, much academic scholarship considering illness has been captured by a 'medicocentrism' (Frank 1997) and consequently gives too much weight to one part of a person's life, the ill part. One effect of this has been to overemphasise the sense of a life with illness as one structured around dramatic moments. In many peoples' accounts their lives are better depicted as a series of ongoing developments, of change accruing via the accumulation of small adjustments.

Time

We have noted above that time features as one of three major dimensions in the biographies of people with chronic illness described by Corbin and Strauss (1987). Their interest in time lies in the way an accommodation can be sought between biographical time, which flows from the past, through the present to the future, and 'clock time' which must be juggled to accommodate the different demands the person with the illness is subjected to. Some people locate their illness within the biography of their lives; some appear to be trapped in the day-to-day; illness becomes their major life focus and biographical time slips from their grasp.

Monks and Frankenberg (1995) have taken the dimensions of Corbin and Strauss and have looked further at the balance in the lives of a group of people with MS. What is devoted to the self and what is devoted to the body and the disease? In practice the balance shifts according to the individual and according to the point in the experience of the illness one considers. This is not surprising given the considerable variation in the manifestation of the illness not just between individuals but also between different points within any individual's life. But we will see in our detailed narratives that such variation is characteristic of illness as something that exists in the interplay between body, society and state of mind, and is rarely dominated by any one factor. Even at times of the most extreme manifestations of illness on the body the person can put this aside in accounting for the gestalt of their lived experience. There is a literature that reports people near to death, and with complex and severe symptomotology, assessing their quality of life as good (Hornquist *et al.* 1992).

Here, in relation to time, we have an area in which we can hypothesise that the person with MS, MND or CF may have a different sense of future orientation and a clearer sense of an ontological split between their life before diagnosis and after as compared with people diagnosed as having chronic, but non-life-threatening, illness (although with CF it may be the family that has that sense of split).

Some of the things described by Davies in her study of people diagnosed as HIV positive may have relevance here. She argues that they have a 'provisional existence' (Davies 1997: 561) imposed upon them. She quotes Ortega y Gasset (1953): 'life is an operation, which is done, in a forward direction. We live towards the future because to live consists inexorably of doing, in each individual life making itself' (quoted in Davies 1997: 562).

But with diagnosis the orientation towards the future changes, there is a break, normal life ends. 'The routine sense of lived time is reversed and the experience of the present is likely to become an end in itself, rather than simply a means to an end (one's future life), the reality of which has become increasingly uncertain' (Davies 1997: 562).

She quotes van den Burg (1972):

> The beginning of every serious illness is a halt. Normal life ends. Another life takes its place. One suddenly becomes uncertain about things most taken for granted: faith and integrity of the body, one's role in other peoples' lives and their role in one's own life, and faith in the future ... The horizon of time is narrowed. The plans of yesterday lose their meaning and importance. They seem more complicated, more exhausting, more foolish and ambitious than I saw them the day before ... the past seems saturated with trivialities. It seems to me that I hardly ever tackled my real tasks.
>
> (van den Berg 1972: 28)

Davies identifies three forms of temporal orientation towards long-term HIV positivity:

- living with a philosophy of the present
- living in the future
- living in the empty present

The first orientation allows some possibility for living with the potential for growth. The second is an orientation of active-denial in which the diagnosis is not allowed to ruin the plans a person has previously had. It includes a refusal to entertain the possibility of the imminence of death. The third orientation allows one to hang on to the present, although with a radically reduced sense of the possible. Davies relates this orientation to the sorts of security Tillich associated with a prison (Tillich 1952: 66). The individual doesn't plan or commit because they are afraid of disappointing themselves, afraid of failing. This orientation also includes an increased focus on the past, a desire to have things as they used to be.

Davies sees in the first and third orientations a possibility of formulating some sort of positive meaning (Lifton 1968), an ability – borrowing Frankl's terms (1984: 161) – to adopt a tragic optimism, to say yes to life, albeit in the third orientation to do so with a reduced sense as to what one is saying yes to. There are shared concerns here with the reflexive project of the self characteristic of postmodern times and summarised by Bauman (1992). Here we get two alternative forms of postmodern self. One he describes as having momentary identities, identities for today. These are primarily concerned with self-interest but this can encompass others who are included 'until further notice'. The alternative form of postmodern self is of 'being for the other', that is: 'The self is understood as coming to be human in relation to others, and the self can only continue to be human by living *for* the other' (Bauman 1992: 167). Bauman is here fashioning a postmodern ethic that will be exemplified in the everyday choices made by people. But these choices are made within the constraints of the prevalent social forces acting upon us. We will go on to look at the way moral agendas have been constructed out of encounters with illness.

Moral agendas

One aspect of the formulation of positive meaning lies in the need to appear a creditable and worthy individual. This need is both socially constructed and indicative of the shifting agenda of the self, introduced above.

Historically much sociological literature has equated illness with deviance and health with conformity. Parsons (1951) for example seemed to see health as a functional prerequisite of society, with illness a failure to keep well. Interaction-alists retained this dichotomy although they saw people being first labelled as ill and illness behaviour then following (Williams 1998: 436). Critics of these sociological approaches, and the others that have followed them without really questioning their theoretical assumptions, suggest they have not pursued knowl-edge and understanding as it is viewed from 'below'. Rather, they have contributed facts that have underlined a prevalent individualistic way that illness has been defined, understood and responded to (see Oliver 1996a).

Here we want to develop an understanding of the relationship between illness and deviance as it relates to moral concerns. Specifically, a user involvement agenda appears to incorporate the danger that an ethical imperative to be involved will become part of the construction of the appropriate social role of the ill. This risks becoming part of what Foucault has described as disciplinary power. A discourse of personal responsibility constructs the acceptable bounds of behaviour and shapes the individual as a subject, in this case constructing the morally acceptable sick (Foucault 1982). This is not only an imposition on the sick but also interferes with the opportunity for those not sick to act altruistically. If people are expected to exercise responsibility for their own care via user involvement, both insofar as it immediately affects them and more generally as it affects those with the same diagnosis, then others can step aside. Thus, we can see how a user involvement agenda has resonance for the social contract and how we construe our relationship with 'the needs of strangers' (Ignatieff 1984).

Frank (1997) has explored the moral life and the moral agency of the sick person. In so doing he argues that we should move beyond the Parsonian tradition in which the sick role establishes the normative expectations of compliance, of the moral expectation of the patient that they return to health and that the physician facilitates that return. This sick role is further consolidated by a societal injunction to be a 'good' patient, compliant and grateful and with a sober optimism, not to be too 'gung ho' positive as to suggest denial or ingratitude or too pessimistic or withdrawn to upset others.

Frank argues that illness is, for some, an opportunity for achievement, albeit an achievement they might have thought they could do without:

> ... the achievement of the personal resolve to go on living with the continued excavation of complex suffering. Perhaps this resolve is what survivors of critical and chronic illness mean when they say, as so many do, that while they are not glad they had cancer, they do appreciate some of the changes that cancer has brought to them as persons.
>
> (Frank 1997: 144–5)

Further it may be possible to become 'successfully ill'. In Frank's terms that is to learn about the world and ourselves and to act on what we learn. For example we might seek a defining role in the process of seeking healing. We might add to this the possibility of becoming successfully ill through acting on behalf of others, through altruistic behaviour. Even if you don't have a future orientation for yourself, do you have a sense of a family, a collective, a community, or a group future that you can contribute to? For Frank, storytelling by the ill person is '*for* another just as much as it is for oneself' (Frank 1995: 17). It is a manifestation of what he identifies as a postmodern ethic that 'must be sought in the everyday personal struggles of people ... who are trying to make moral sense of their suffering and who are witnesses to sufferings that go beyond their own' (Frank 1995: 19). This prompts the question, how far are models of the self and futurity like Davies (summarised above) too individualistic?

This moral agenda exists within the context of a broader political and ethical debate and it is to this that we now turn.

Needs and wants

In considering user involvement we have to engage with one of the most fundamental questions, the King Lear conundrum, that is the relationship between needs and wants (see Ignatieff 1984). Lear, having given away his kingdom to two of his daughters, tells them he needs his retinue. They tell him he can rely on being cared for by them, they will meet his needs. But his retinue are not just there to provide for his food and clothing; they also bring with them a sense of dignity, autonomy and confidence, things integral to Lear's sense of self-respect. The daughters classified the retinue as wants and not needs and, as such, gave them a lower status and were not prepared to countenance them. Lear saw their refusal as ingratitude and disrespect – and the tragedy of the play unfolds.

If we translate such a situation to the present day we can see that there has to be some way of mediating between wants and needs, and that mediation will require reference points that involve both the individual and society. But who should be involved in the decision-making process and what should the balance of power be between the individual and the collective voice? Further, needs are complex in that many of them are socially constructed and hence variable. Maslow (1968) distinguished between survival and growth needs. What is necessary for survival may not change that much over time: food, warmth, shelter, and some sort of human contact. But in Western societies at least, there is in addition to the category of survival needs another category that is best described as 'the provision of essentials'. This category does shift because it relates to the general level of resource in society and it is centrally relevant to the identification of what people assume they must have to be a part of that society.

The mediation between wants and needs and the assessment of what is essential to be included in society has been, is and will remain a central political issue. For example, after its election in 1997, the Labour government chose to place combating social exclusion at the centre of its social policy agenda. The policy sought a nuanced analysis of the many factors that foster inclusion. It incorporated the argument that simply giving money, through welfare payments, was not sufficient to create that sense of inclusion. This is also something of a wants and needs argument and includes the possibility of a collective assertion of what fosters inclusion that might be at odds with an individual's own assessment.

In recent years the guiding force in social policy and welfare provision has been utilitarianism, the greatest good for the greatest number. This has been conflated into a market orientation in which it was assumed that if one gave people some avenue to exercise choice then they would be both involved and empowered. But this is a crude understanding of what markets do. Markets also generate inequality, envy and competition. Adam Smith, often invoked as the guiding historical spirit of markets, saw them as places that needed individuals able to exercise a stoical self command; they were places that needed moral sentiments. They were not just a route to enhance the wealth of nations (Mannion and Small 1999: 259).

Since 1997 this dominance of the market has been modified. The benefits of public participation in planning have been invoked as an alternative way to seek policy making informed by the wishes of people. These wishes are often interpreted from the results of opinion polls or the deliberations of focus groups. But public participation of this sort is also essentially utilitarian. It does not assure the fair treatment of those people whose needs might be considerable but whose numbers are small. Further, assuming that what is best for most is the thing that should be done ignores the problems in what philosophers call consequentialist thinking. These problems are that you can't measure consequences accurately and certainly can't foresee them all when you initiate action; you ignore the argument that the question 'Is it fair?' should preceded the question 'Does it work?' and you side-step questions of distributive justice, that is the impact of an intervention on inequality.

If you don't have a utilitarian approach then what? In many areas of health and social care you get the decisions of experts, more or less clouded by vested interests. But in our chosen area, as in so many others, we do not know who the real experts are. Do we elevate one sort of knowledge – the scientific for example – over the lived experiences of the person with a particular illness? How do we counter-balance the intrusion of self-interest? How do we resolve the disparity of investment parties to a decision may have? For example it may be of very central importance to a person that they receive a particular drug treatment but of only marginal significance to a prospective prescriber. But the relative social power of the participants makes it likely that the latter's view will prevail.

If we put utilitarianism in questions of resource allocation and paternalism in the negotiation of everyday contacts alongside health and social care systems then we have problems in thinking about the context in which individual service users seek to have their views translated into action. We need to shift the basis of the argument. One way to do that is to look to the work of John Rawles (1972). Doyal and Gough offer this analogy as a way into understanding Rawles' position: 'a child (is) told to slice a cake fairly by ensuring that she will not know in advance which piece she herself will receive' (Doyal and Gough 1991: 128).

There is, in this, something of a return to a 'social contract' approach. Each person in this Rawlsian situation will be concerned to protect the least well off, as they may find themselves belonging to this group. Hence the rights of the least privileged group will always be optimised. Two things follow that will be of significance in the argument we will develop about user involvement. First, everyone is to have the same rights to liberty and to a place in civil society. Second, Rawls argues that any changes that effect everyone should disproportionately advantage the least well off.

What has to be added is an equal opportunities proviso and a recognition that there is also an underlying imperative not to do anything that reduces individual dignity, confidence and autonomy. Without self-respect, Rawls argues, 'All desire and activity becomes empty and vain, and we sink into apathy and cynicism' (Rawls 1972: 440).

We are now getting nearer to a formulation that illuminates some of the key questions we will explore in what follows. Ignatieff identifies four areas of concern.

- It is not just what is given that is important, but the manner of that giving. It is the way people listen, the care they take when they lift you, the sensitivity to your fears and grief. 'Respect and dignity are conferred by gestures such as these. They are gestures too much a matter of human art to be made a consistent matter of administrative routine' (Ignatieff 1984: 16).
- It is the extent to which one sees what one receives as a right or as a gift. Should one feel entitled or grateful for the favours of others?
- Respect for each individual's needs may be incompatible with treating everyone equally.
- There must be a place for responding to those needs we have that are not located in ourselves.

It is as common for us to need things on behalf of others, to need good schools for the sake of our children, safe streets for the sake of our neighbours, decent old people's homes for the strangers at our door, as it is for us to need them for ourselves. The deepest motivational springs of political involvement are to be located in this human capacity to feel needs for others.

(Ignatieff 1984: 17).

An overview of user group activity in the UK

We have noted above the evident political commitment to promoting user involvement and we have also acknowledged some of the challenges that have to be overcome in its pursuit. There are also some dangers in adopting a focus on user involvement and we have commented on these. In this section we will make introductory comments on the way user groups have organised to have a say in health policy and service delivery. We will go on to comment in more detail on user groups in palliative care and particularly in MS, MND and CF in subsequent chapters.

While there might have been a shift in the willingness of policy makers and service providers to acknowledge the validity of the user voice, we must see this in the context of a change in the willingness of the public to question the authority of previously acknowledged experts. This is a change associated with a shift within and beyond modernity. But a move towards user involvement has not simply emerged or been given, it has been won. There have been concerted efforts over decades, often by particularly disadvantaged people, to change the culture of care (Sang 1999). That user involvement is higher on the agenda is in large part their achievement. It is an incomplete achievement, of course, until we can be sure that involvement leads to impact.

Issues around childbirth, the role of carers and mental health services were of key importance in shaping the service user movement in the UK. Those pursuing user involvement in these areas have been joined by people with HIV and by cancer groups (see Gott *et al.* 2000 and McLeod 2000) and also by more generic organisations – the Long-Term Medical Conditions Alliance, for example. The LMCA are replicating a US initiative, the 'expert patient programme', involving, and run by, people with arthritis. This will extend to other conditions and indeed the British Liver Trust are developing similar approaches (Moore 2000: 71). Advocacy has grown from its beginnings with people with learning difficulties, multiple disabilities and enduring mental health needs and is now undertaken in relation to a wide range of needs (Atkinson 1999). There are groups that include both professionals and users – ASH, MIND and MENCAP, for example – and generic consumers organisations such as the Consumers Association, the National Consumer Council, the Consumer Congress and more specifically with a central health remit the College of Health and the Patients Association. There is very much a spectrum in terms of how far these groups are user led. For example, in relation to mental health, Survivors Speak Out, Mindlink and the UK Advocacy Network have been developed and are run by service users, or former service users, themselves whereas generic groups like the Patients Association do not have a large grassroots membership (Hogg 1999a: 13).

There are umbrella groups such as Cancerlink, which launched a declaration of rights of people with cancer in 1990. These rights included 'to be told in a sensitive manner and to share in all decision making about my treatment and care in honest and informative discussions with relevant specialists and other health professionals' (Cancerlink 1990). Cancerlink, at this point, was drawing on the experience and views of 450 cancer support and self-help groups around the country, a network it continues to support (see Bradburn *et al.* 1992). On occasions, in relation to cancer services, a policy initiative can have a beneficial impact on user involvement. The rolling forward of the Calman Hine reforms (Department of Health and Welsh Office 1995) has been accompanied in Trent Region by an accreditation programme which includes, as one of its criteria, scrutiny of the extent to which user views have been sought and acted upon (Gott *et al.* 2000). Hence from unlikely sources progress comes. Unlikely because of the lack of user representatives on the group that drew up the Calman Hine Report and the lack of attention the group gave to issues like psychological and social support for people with cancer (Hogg 1999a: 12).

There are groups with a specific focus, like the Consumers Advisory Group on Clinical Trials, initiated by cancer patients, or Radiotherapy Action Groups Exposure (RAGE), a pressure group formed by women irreversibly injured by radiotherapy for breast cancer (Sikora 1994). McLeod (2000) reports on self-help support groups for older women with secondary breast cancer. There are groups designed to bring together a wide range of views to contribute to the NHS policy process, such as the Standing Advisory Group on Consumer Involvement in the NHS. There are specific groups within government charged with seeking user views, such as the Service First Unit in the Cabinet Office (Service First Unit 1999), and £2.5 million has been allocated by the Department of Health to fund a research programme on public involvement in NHS decision making (Department of Health 1998d). Internationally there has also been an increase in interest in user involvement (see Kahssay *et al.* 1998).

Summary

In this introduction we have sought to locate questions about user involvement in a broad context. We believe that user involvement is not simply a technical, administrative or procedural question. It is not just a policy issue. Nor is it simply a matter of individual inclination. Considering user involvement allows us to interrogate the relationship between the citizen and the state in the context of the citizen living with a particular illness. As such it illuminates questions of meaning, at the level of the individual, and questions of power at the level of the state and the professions.

So the possibilities for, and the nature of, user involvement are shaped by the institutional and policy context and their interface with individual agency. How far do people want or feel able to be involved? We have suggested that there are some dimensions of the individual experience that we have to question:

- How far does wanting to plan for oneself imply that one has a future orientation?
- Do the heavy demands of the present and particularly the impact of ill health on the body, drive out the possibilities of devoting much time or energy to the future, or to the concerns of others?
- Does the presence of uncertainty militate against planning?
- Does a person feel taken over by their illness, is there a sense of a break in their lives, a pre- and post-diagnosis person? Or are there periods of time in which they feel uncertain about themselves, after which a shift to a new sense of self occurs?
- Is illness seen as offering new moral agendas? Does becoming successfully ill have a resonance with the people we consider?
- Can an imperative to be involved be an imposition and a burden? What does it do to altruism?

We then shifted the emphasis and considered how we reconcile needs, wants and scarce resources in our society. The dilemma for the conditions we concentrate on is that they can be characterised as high need/low incidence. As such they are not automatically likely to be well served by the prevalent utilitarianism in welfare. We considered some of the alternatives to a policy of pursuing the greatest good for the greatest number because, we argued, this contains a risk to minorities. One alternative is to let the professionals decide, and there remains a strong policy and practice attraction to this. Another approach is to look towards social contract and justice models. Here we invoked Rawls and considered the central questions raised by Ignatieff. This moves us beyond defining principles of participation or involvement to look at the sort of template we might set up that does not create splits between users, professionals, and the indifferent. In so doing we can consider an approach where questions of how we meet the needs of strangers is a measure of our civilisation.

We concluded this introduction by looking at the development of self-help groups and in so doing we underlined how user involvement has been won and not been given in many settings.

Plan of the book

In what follows we seek to interrogate narratives in the context of policy and practice and critique policy and practice with the insight of the narratives. We will first consider the literature on user involvement and then go on to look at the policy and professional context within which user involvement is undertaken. In particular we will examine user involvement and palliative care (care when the intention is no longer curative). We continue with three substantive sections each concentrating on a single condition. There are some experiences that are shared between our chosen diagnoses and there are some policy and practice concerns common to all. We have tried not to be too repetitive while recognising that readers may have a special interest in one of the conditions we discuss and hence each chapter needs a coherence and comprehensiveness of its own. We have though concentrated our discussion of new information technologies (which we consider to offer considerable potential to developing user involvement) in our CF chapter. This, in part, explains its greater length. We have also discussed theoretical concerns in more detail in our MS chapter and would suggest that much of this discussion is also relevant to MND. We have not replicated this discussion there.

Our substantive chapters draw centrally on interviews with people living with the condition and with those caring for them. The approach is a narrative one; stories are told and through these the reciprocal relationship between the individual and society is explored, as is the way the narrative is used to realign present, past and future. The narrative can also be used to contrast this experience with that offered by others, for example by professionals writing about these conditions or by health and social care staff reflecting on what they do.

The narratives, in the main, are not discourses about user involvement. They are reflections about the way people have experienced the services they have had and how they think things could be better. More than that they strive, in Radley's words, for 'some experiential coherence'. In the introduction to his edited collection on *Worlds of Suffering* Radley describes how individuals, in accounts of their illness, seek to, 'render suffering and uncertainty tangible and, at least, subject to anticipation if not prediction' (Radley 1993: 5). But we find, in the specific circumstances we consider, that while people can seek to make their experience tangible, it does not mean they also seek to anticipate what will come next. The narratives we present illuminate that sense of future orientation and a belief in the capacity of acting in the world that we hypothesise are crucial for user involvement. But they also show the reluctance to look beyond the present and make choices about meaning and response in a situation where one wishes one had never had to make a choice at all.

Notes

1 In North America MND is known as amyotrophic lateral sclerosis (ALS) or as Lou Gehrig's disease. Lou Gehrig was one of baseballs major stars who was diagnosed at age thirty-six and died two years later.

2 User involvement

Selected review of the literature

The World Health Organisation states that people have a right and a duty to participate in the planning and delivery of their own health care and includes participation within its definition of primary health care. 'Primary health care is essential health care based on practical, scientifically sound and socially acceptable methods and technology made universally accessible to individuals and families in the community through their full participation …' (World Health Organisation 1978: 3).

The *Priorities and Planning Guidance 1996–97* for England and Wales specified giving 'greater influence to users of NHS services and their carers' as a medium-term goal. This was reiterated in the Guidance for 1998–99: 'The involvement of local people, including users and carers, in developing local services, is critical to the development of responsive services which command their confidence' (Department of Health 1997a, Annex para. 10). User involvement is firmly on the national and international agenda.

In this chapter, we will consider the nature of user involvement, the distinction between consumerism and empowerment, the roles envisaged for user involvement within health and social care policy, the nature of public participation, and the specific contribution that service users can make to service planning and provision.

The nature of user involvement

Throughout the literature, the term 'user involvement' has been used somewhat loosely to describe varying degrees of involvement and participation in the planning, design and delivery of services by the people who use them. Although there is general agreement about the need for clarity of terms, different definitions and conventions are in widespread use (Gilbert 1995). Most people distinguish between different levels of involvement. Hamilton-Gurney (1993), for example, suggests that involvement, consultation and participation represent a hierarchy of increasing commitment to an active user voice. Involvement is seen as a loose, umbrella term for any area where consumers are brought into the decision-making process at any level; consultation demonstrates a more explicit intention to obtain user views; whereas participation is defined as a more active process, drawing on a wider definition of the term as 'partnership'.

A number of studies (e.g. Hoyes *et al.* 1993; Goss and Miller 1995) have used a modified version of Arnstein's (1969) 'ladder of citizen participation'. In their research into user empowerment in community care, for example, Hoyes *et al.* (1993) drew up a 'ladder of empowerment':

HIGH   Users have the authority to take decisions

   Users have the authority to take selected decisions

   Users' views are sought before decisions are finalised

   Users may take the initiative to influence decisions

   Decisions are publicised and explained before implementation

LOW   Information is given about decisions made

Although Arnstein's approach is useful in placing power at the centre of the process of participation, its linear form has been criticised for failing to accommodate the range and complexities involved in the relationship between service providers and the community, or to take into account different types of service user and, in the context of the NHS 'market', the different stages of the purchasing cycle (Peckham 1993).

Sullivan (1994) distinguishes between *participation*, used to describe the highest level of activity undertaken by people currently using services, and *public engagement*, bringing the wider community into questions of democratic interest, thus allowing a distinction between current users and the wider community of taxpayers and potential users.

Participation can be analysed along at least three dimensions: the type of participant; the function of participation; and the way power is apportioned (Peckham 1993; Hallett 1987). According to Peckham (1993), there are different and competing interpretations of what is meant by participation and differing expectations depending, for example, on whether one is a politician, user, carer, purchaser or service provider. Included among non-users of health care services are those who are currently well but who may need services in the future; those who need services but do not receive them; and those who are in need of health care but are unable or unwilling to use existing services (ibid.). Taylor *et al.* (1992) identify five different categories of service user: direct users; indirect users, such as carers; potential users; excluded users; and proxy users, such as care managers, the voluntary sector, the 'community'. Although useful in highlighting the possibility of different perspectives, the category of 'proxy user' lumps together a wide variety of people and perspectives and does not distinguish between the 'community' and the individual user who is part of the community (Peckham 1993).

Hallett notes that, where users 'tend to stress participation as a means of increasing power or influence over planning and service delivery', service providers are more likely to see

> the role it can play in providing legitimation for particular policies or projects and securing a degree of public acceptance or support, or as an extension of their own power since a visible and articulate user voice can be useful in publicising and defending services.
>
> (Hallet 1987: 6)

Whether people viewed collectively are termed consumers, clients, users or customers, Gilbert (1995) notes, depends on the role in which they are cast by the systems in which they operate. A useful distinction is drawn between a commercial/economic approach, in which consumers exercise individual choice in a market-driven system, and a political model, in which users are given a *voice* in a system which ensures their participation (Saltman 1994). Consumers are able to exert power both through their initial choices and their ability to change from one product or service to another. Hirschman (1970) distinguishes between 'exit', which refers to the power that consumers can exert over providers through the possibility of transferring their business elsewhere, and 'voice', which refers to the ability of consumers to exert influence over a service provider, for example by seeking a change or modification in the service. Whereas 'exit' is broadly compatible with a market approach, 'voice' accords with a more 'democratic' approach whereby service users, or the wider public, might seek to influence the overall pattern of services (Nocon *et al.* 1995; Taylor *et al.* 1992).

For Saltman (1994), the patient as consumer remains the compliant *object* of the service delivery system, in contrast to the patient as decision-making user, who takes the role of *subject*. It is the transition of the patient from passive object to active subject of care which, in Gilbert's view, is at the heart of patient empowerment (Gilbert 1995).

The term *empowerment* is generally equated with the stronger forms of involvement, although, as Saltman (1994) has observed, empowerment means different things to different people. Where professionals may consider it something which is in their gift to bestow or withhold, service users are more likely to see it as active involvement on their own terms. 'By empowering patients', Gilbert writes:

> we want to produce people who know where they are going, who will treat them, when, and for what reason; people who have access to information but absolute confidence that their own information stays within the care team; people who feel they are part of a dialogue, but have access to support and redress if dialogue breaks down.
>
> (Gilbert 1995: 34)

The aim, in Liddle's words, is to enable patients to feel 'confident, competent and in control' (Liddle 1991).

Barnes and Walker (1996) draw a primary distinction between a bureaucratic model of service organisation and an empowerment model. Whereas a bureaucratic model is service or provider oriented, inflexible, provider-led, power concentrated, defensive, conservative and input orientated, an empowerment model is user orientated, responsive, needs-led, power sharing, open to review, open to change and outcome orientated. Where the bureaucratic model encourages dependency, the empowerment model 'emphasises the interdependent status of service users as citizens requiring assistance but with the right to autonomous decision making' (Barnes and Walker 1996: 379). The Conservative Government's consumerist approach was still predominantly service centred (Beresford and Croft 1993) and, according to Barnes and Walker (1996), accorded more closely with the bureaucratic than the empowerment approach. The marketisation of the public sector, they maintain, is an insufficient basis on which to empower service users. The approach of the new Labour government, although seeking to revoke many of the health service reforms of the previous administration (Department of Health 1997b), remains essentially consumerist (Rhodes and Nocon 1998).

Although empowerment remains a contested concept, there have been few attempts to define it (Barnes and Walker 1996) and its practice is unevenly developed, with both geographical disparities and inequality in the extent to which different groups of service users have been able to exert an influence (Braye and Preston-Shoot 1995).

In an attempt to define the concept, Barnes and Walker (1996) list eight principles of empowerment:

- empowerment should enable personal development as well as increasing influence over services
- empowerment should increase people's abilities to take control of their lives as a whole, not just increase their influence over services
- the empowerment of one person should not result in the exploitation of others: either family members or paid carers
- empowerment should not be viewed as a zero sum: a partnership model should provide benefits to both parties
- empowerment must be reinforced at all levels within service systems
- empowerment of those who use services does not remove the responsibilities of those who produce them
- empowerment is not an alternative to adequate resourcing of services
- empowerment should be a collective as well as an individual process; without this people will become increasingly assertive in competition with each other

User involvement in healthcare policy

A policy of 'user involvement', by which health service managers were required to pay greater attention to the wishes and views of individual service users and carers as well as to the views of the wider public, emerged as a contemporary policy initiative in the UK National Health Service (NHS) during the 1990s. The introduction of market principles into the NHS (Department of Health

1989a) cast recipients and potential recipients of health care in the role of consumers. The dominant conception of service users was therefore that of consumers and the notion of consumer choice underpinned a number of policy initiatives, including *The Patient's Charter* (Department of Health 1991) and the publication of hospital performance tables. It was also the driving principle behind the document *Local Voices* (NHS Management Executive 1992) which exhorted health service managers to consult with their local populations.

The Patient's Charter

The Patient's Charter was, arguably, the most forthright of the initiatives to promote the rights of patients as consumers by laying out a set of standards which patients could expect from the health service. In Gilbert's view, the Charter was 'the most important mechanism for patient empowerment to emerge from the reformed NHS' (1995: 24). Its value, however, was far from universally accepted. Critics pointed to the lack of consultation about standards with either patients or service providers and to the potential for widespread dissatisfaction caused by the combination of a high political profile and public expectations raised beyond providers' capacity to deliver improvements (Gilbert 1995). Later developments, such as the approach of the primary care version (Department of Health 1993a) and local community care charters (Department of Health 1994b), adopted a more flexible, bottom-up approach. A more fundamental criticism, however, sees consumer rights as illusive in the absence of resources directly linked to the exercise of choice (Barnes and Walker 1996; Saltman 1994; Winkler 1987).

The Patient's Charter rights are aimed at patients as a group and do not necessarily address the particular needs of people from minority groups who often number among the least articulate and most vulnerable in society. Condition- and service-specific charters may help to safeguard users of specific services but more general needs are often less well addressed (Gilbert 1995). People with a sensory or physical impairment, mental distress or learning disabilities, for example, are often among those least empowered (Ahmad and Atkin 1996; Begum and Fletcher 1995; Davis 1993a). Their needs are not only less likely to be adequately addressed but their rights to services are in greater danger of being abused. Advocacy schemes and patients' councils have been one means of finding out what users need by listening directly to them (Ferguson 1997; Lindsay 1997; Morgan 1997; Rust 1997). Historically, people from minority ethnic groups have been poorly served but progress in meeting their specific needs has been slow (Ahmad 2000; Ahmad and Atkin 1996; Chan 1994; Smaje 1995).

Local Voices

The focus of the document *Local Voices* was on consultation by health authorities with their local populations. Unlike *The Patient's Charter* which was concerned with individual consumers, *Local Voices* aimed to achieve greater public participation in the planning process. It recommended eleven techniques for doing this: public meetings, local voluntary groups, focus groups, health forums, rapid appraisal, community initiatives, telephone hotlines, surveys of public opinion, patient satisfaction surveys, one-to-one interviews and complaints procedures, but warned against 'over-reliance on any one method' (NHS Management Executive 1992).

Prior to the publication of *Local Voices*, public consultation was rare. Whitehead (1992), among others, drew attention to the fact that decisions about changes in funding formulae, which channelled more resources to some parts of the country than others, and the removal of entitlement and access to NHS services for vulnerable groups, for example long-term, non-acute health care for elderly people, were typically taken without recourse to any public consultation. A subsequent evaluation by the NHS Executive of progress on *Local Voices* found that 21 per cent of health authorities could be categorised as 'good', in that 'they had consulted widely, involved local people ... made tangible changes to plans and contracts ... and established arrangements for feeding back decisions'. The remainder had made little progress and 22 per cent were categorised as 'unsatisfactory' (NHS Executive 1994a: 10).

Reasons for focus on user involvement

The focus on user involvement has been traced to a need to impart legitimacy to a system suffering increasingly from democratic deficit (Coote 1996; Harrison *et al.* 1997; Wistow 1993). Among a number of contributory factors were the gradual erosion of the local democratic credentials of health authorities and other NHS institutions (Harrison *et al.* 1992; Hunter and Harrison 1997), and the dismantling of the old bureaucracies and their reconstitution into smaller organisations. Legitimacy was further weakened by the introduction of the internal market and a competitive market ethos, rising costs and demands for health care requiring more explicit prioritisation and rationing of services, and an increasingly critical questioning of 'old style' professional paternalism (Harrison *et al.* 1997). According to Khan, 'it cannot be a complete coincidence that the upsurge of interest in involving the public in decision-making has coincided with a period of significant fiscal retrenchment' (Khan 1998: 32). Local authority representation was removed from health authorities following the 1989 white paper (Department of Health 1989a). Harrison *et al.* (1992: 135) pointed out that:

> ... the new DHA [district health authority] is supposed to champion the people's needs, but lacks any representative element that might legitimise its role in speaking for those needs. On the contrary, DHAs are in danger of being merely 'ivory tower' contracting bodies governed by a small group of managers and non-executive members, many of whom have come into the NHS from business backgrounds.

Although *Local Voices* provided clear policy guidance to purchasers and commissioners on the need to take account of local people's views, it cannot be seen as sufficient in itself to secure public participation because those responsible for its implementation were neither explicitly nor implicitly accountable to the public

(Barnes and Walker 1996; Davis and Daly 1995). The case of a leukaemia patient denied a second round of costly and painful treatment by her local health authority highlighted the need for central policy clarification. Calling for a parliamentary debate in its leading article following the case, the *Health Service Journal* commented:

> ... purchasing managers will ponder how difficult rationing makes their working lives. It calls into question the fundamental legitimacy of their very organisations; what scope have their local populations for influencing and challenging their decisions?
>
> (cited in Gilbert 1995: 39–40)

A similar point was made in a report from the Institute for Public Policy Research (IPPR) (Cooper *et al.* 1995) which argued that, although health authorities are now understood to have responsibility for complex ethical issues of political sensitivity, their present constitution does not give them a mandate to make such ethical and politically contentious judgements. Furthermore, the emphasis on management and business experience in health authorities may be equipping them for only part of the job. However, even the return of local authority representation would not guarantee local authority non-executive members any greater weight than their unelected counterparts, since the decision-making process remains dominated by professional and managerial interests (Barnes and Walker 1996; Jordan *et al.* 1998). The IPPR study argued that rationing should not be left to doctors whose primary responsibilities are to individual patients and who are therefore not best placed to plan community-wide services (Cooper *et al.* 1995). But, although managerial influence may have increased at the expense of professionals (Harrison and Pollitt 1994), managers may be no more likely to consult users than professionals. Evidence from ombudsmans' cases suggested that there were many managers who believed that consultation delayed necessary decisions and users who felt powerless and believed that their views were ignored (Hogg 1995).

At an individual level, the emphasis on consumerism and patient choice was seen as a counter to the professional power and authority which were perceived to be primary impediments to organisational change (Harrison and Pollitt 1994). While an individualist approach to health care may not necessarily weaken the decision-making power of professional or managerial staff, the introduction of customer choice, nonetheless, presented the possibility of consumer authority coming into direct conflict with professional authority (Barnes 1997). The whole edifice of professionalism on which such authority is legitimated – the training, qualifications, membership of peer associations, peer regulation and supervision – was thereby undermined (*ibid.*).

The 1997 white paper

A primary objective of the white paper *The New NHS: Modern, Dependable* was to rebuild public confidence in a service which had been radically restructured under the previous administration and whose democratic mandate had been progressively weakened (Health Care UK 1996/97). Equally important was the need to rebuild staff morale. The election of a new government in 1997 was welcomed enthusiastically by a workforce alienated and demoralised by eighteen years of relentless organisational change and ensuing uncertainty, the introduction of the disciplines of the internal market and consequent undermining of the traditional values of welfare. The health service reforms of the previous administration forced a move away from lifetime professional careers under national terms and conditions of service to time-limited contracts with locally determined pay and conditions; 'professional solidarity' was undermined by professionals working for rival providers forced into competition with each other, and an expectation to support the corporate image and refrain from public criticism led to conflicts between allegiance to employers and to professional bodies (Harrison and Pollitt 1994). Towards the end of the Conservative administration, morale in the NHS had sunk dangerously low, with difficulties of staff retention and recruitment in many areas (Audit Commission 1997; Snell 1998). A second objective of the white paper was, therefore, to regain professionals' goodwill and support by reinvesting them with an authority which, previously, many felt had been challenged and undermined (Rhodes and Nocon 1998).

The white paper was thus concerned both to address the problem of public legitimacy and to court the goodwill of health professionals. The result has been a potential weakening of users' voice by a conflation of user involvement with public participation and the investment of health professionals with the authority to define users' needs for them (*ibid.*). Although it gives some acknowledgement to the potential contribution of service users to local health service planning, there is no specific discussion of how this might be achieved. The white paper contains no real discussion of users' distinctive role and gives no direction or guidance as to how that role might be enhanced by building on past experiences and avoiding past failures. In consequence, there is a danger that, as other priorities take precedence, it will not be included on local agendas as a separate issue needing special consideration (*ibid.*). Given the vehemence of Labour's past critique of Tory market reforms, we might have expected this to have extended to a critique of the conceptual underpinnings of their policy of user involvement. However, far from a critique of the past construction of service users as consumers, the white paper retains an implicit commitment to the consumerist ethos.

The emphasis is on broad public accountability and participation, and a variety of measures to enhance public involvement are set out, including:

- involving the public in developing the Health Improvement Programme
- ensuring that Primary Care Groups have effective arrangements for public involvement
- publishing agreed strategies, targets and details of progress against them
- participating in a new national survey of patient and user experience (para. 4.19)

Furthermore, all NHS Trusts will be required to open up their board meetings to the public (para. 2.23) and to ensure that board membership is more representative of the local community (para. 6.39). New ways of securing informed public and expert involvement in decisions about local service planning are to be explored and a clear set of principles for decision making and criteria for ensuring that due process is observed are to be drawn up (para. 4.20). Primary Care Groups will be required to have clear arrangements for public involvement, including open meetings (para. 5.15). Finally, Health Action Zones will offer opportunities to explore new ways of involving local people (para. 4.19).

The second area which is likely to have a serious impact on the potential for service users to have an independent voice is in the authority of health service professionals to speak on their behalf. Service users' independent and distinctive voice appears to have been largely subsumed within the newly reinstated authority of professionals to speak for them (Rhodes and Nocon 1998).

Where, previously, many professionals felt sidelined from health service decision making (Harrison *et al.* 1992; Martyn 1998), under Labour they are to be rehabilitated in a central role (para. 6.31) and a series of measures is set out to ensure staff involvement. By empowering health professionals, the Government clearly believes that not only will services become more responsive to patient needs (para. 2.6) but public confidence will be increased (para. 6.37). Where, in the 1990s, managers were exhorted to become 'Champions of the People' (NHS Management Executive 1992), it is now health professionals who are being recast in that role (Rhodes and Nocon 1998). The white paper is peppered with references to the belief that professionals are best placed to represent patient interests: '… decisions about how best to use resources for patient care are best made by those who treat patients – and this principle is at the heart of the proposals in this white paper' (para. 1.22). There is little room for the view that patients themselves might be best placed to articulate their own wishes and needs and thereby to contribute to the discussion. The underlying assumption seems to be that input from individual service users and carers can be adequately interpreted by practitioners on the basis of personal interactions between patients and staff: 'Of course, service quality is essentially determined at local level, through the personal interaction between NHS staff and patients' (para. 7.4).

Even while recognising that professional and other staff may well be service users at various times, their contribution to service planning is likely to rest primarily on their occupational roles; this cannot be a viable substitute for consulting with service users directly. Pressures on resources are always likely to occur, and an ability to take account of the opinions of all interested parties (including different groups of service users) is essential when determining priorities. Although this will not resolve difficult problems of equity or definitions of need, the decision-making process will be more transparent when participants' various opinions are made explicit. The emphasis, Miller noted:

> is on the way in which a process of open discussion in which all points of view can be heard may legitimate the outcome when this is seen to reflect

the discussion that has preceded it, not on deliberation as a discovery procedure in search of a correct answer.

(Miller 1993: 77)

At a national level, the white paper makes a number of provisions for the partici-pation of service users' representatives on newly proposed national bodies, such as the National Institute for Clinical Excellence and the Commission for Health Improvement (paras. 7.12, 7.14). However, the experience of the advisory group for *The Patient's Charter*, whose members complained of being ignored when its report came to be written, provides a salutary lesson in pointing up the difference between a consultative and advisory role and a genuine partnership in the sharing of executive powers (Butler 1999). More recently, twelve leading charities walked out of a government consultation group on welfare reform on the grounds that their contribution was being ignored and none of their recommendations had been accepted. There was a general feeling that their presence was simply to give the forum credibility and that their participation was interpreted as a sign of support for Government policy (Brindle 1999). Criticisms have also been voiced at a local level in relation to the new Primary Care Group boards, where the lack of explicit direction about the inclusion of service users suggests an element of tokenism (Smith and Dickson 1998; Wood 1999).

The primary mechanism for tapping users' views is to be a new national survey of patient and user experience (para. 8.10). According to the white paper, 'the survey will give patients and their carers a voice in shaping the modern and depend-able NHS' (para. 8.10). However, as a means of giving users a voice, a national satisfaction survey is a rather blunt and inflexible instrument which is likely to constrain users' comments to predetermined questions and areas of interest (McIver and Meredith 1998; Carr-Hill 1992) and, in view of the need to standard-ise questions for the purposes of comparisons between different parts of the country, is unlikely to be sufficiently sensitive to local needs and conditions (Miller 1995). Furthermore, it is not clear what weight users' views will be given or exactly how they will feed into policy decisions. It is, perhaps, more likely that the survey will be used as a management tool for assessing service performance than as a means to give service users a genuine voice in shaping services (Rhodes and Nocon 1998).

User involvement in community care

Official rhetoric has tended to equate consumerism with empowerment: how-ever, the two strands were given different emphasis in different documents. Where *Working for Patients* (Department of Health 1989a) described a consumerist model for the NHS, *Caring for People* (Department of Health 1989b) established a more participative approach (Gilbert 1995) which set out to enable people to 'achieve maximum independence and control over their own lives'. At the individual level, it set out a framework for active participation by service users and carers in the assessment process and design of care plans; at the collective level, local authorities were required to consult their local populations on their plans for the provision of community care services. Subsequent guidance issued by the Social Services Inspectorate took this a step further by suggesting that 'the empowerment of users and carers' required 'a change in attitude and approach by managers and practitioners at every level that amounts to a new organisational culture':

> Instead of users and carers being subordinate to the wishes of service-providers, the roles will be progressively adjusted. In this way, users and carers will be enabled to exercise the same power as consumers of other services. This redressing of the balance of power is the best guarantee of a continuing improvement in the quality of service.
>
> (SSI/SWSG 1991: 9)

In consequence, the emphasis on local relevance and user input in the development of Community Care Charters (Department of Health 1994b) was very different from the approach adopted by *The Patient's Charter* (Department of Health 1991) (Gilbert 1995). However, neither the 1990 NHS and Community Care Act nor the ensuing policy guidelines contained any concrete proposals for user involvement or empowerment (Barnes and Walker 1996) and, in the absence of clear guidelines, professionals' opinions often continued to dominate (Davis *et al.* 1998; Lewis and Glennerster 1996).

Rodgers (1994) suggests that, whereas user involvement in the NHS was based on consultation, in social service departments the focus was on empowerment. Certainly, compared with secondary care initiatives in the NHS, which rarely extended beyond surveys of satisfaction with existing services, community care services sought to develop client- or user-led initiatives (Gilbert 1995). This does not mean, however, that user involvement was working in community care, whereas it was not in the health services. Although there are some good examples of projects in community care which involved users at the individual level of needs assessment and care planning (e.g. Goss and Miller 1995; SSRG 1997), practice still lags a long way behind the ideal (Davis *et al.* 1998; Myers and MacDonald 1996). In Barnes and Walker's view, far from being a genuinely user-centred approach, care management is often little more than an administrative tool for cost containment (Barnes and Walker 1996). Although the 1990 Act required social service departments to consult with users and carers about their community care plans, there was far less emphasis on input to individual care planning (*ibid.*).

This distinction is similar to that in the NHS where health authorities were encouraged to consult local people about priorities for health service development (NHS Management Executive 1992) but it was left to individual professionals to decide the extent to which they involved patients in decisions about their health (Barnes and Walker 1996). Despite the rhetoric, the reforms of the 1990 Act, Barnes and Walker argue, were based more on a narrow market ideology than a model of citizen empowerment:

The 1990 Act was never intended to achieve empowerment as we have defined it. Instead, there were much more limited goals of increasing service responsiveness with some user involvement following the model of market consumers, rather than recognition of the citizenship rights of public service users.

(Barnes and Walker 1996: 390)

The 1998 white paper

Like its sister paper *The New NHS: Modern, Dependable*, the social services white paper *Modernising Social Services* builds on the Conservatives' legacy of consumerism and individual choice, yet with a new stress on responsibilities as well as rights (Rhodes and Nocon, forthcoming). The passive welfare recipients of the past are to be recast as active welfare consumers. Although the Government places emphasis on the accountability of services to users, the *quid pro quo* of that is that individual users are expected to take greater responsibility for their own well-being – as epitomised in the emphasis on paid work over reliance on welfare. An implicit distinction is drawn between the responsible and irresponsible service user. In the NHS, too, there is increasing emphasis on the responsible use of services. Yet, it is difficult to see how the tension between the Government's goal of social inclusion and its stress on responsibility can be reconciled (Rhodes and Nocon, forthcoming). Will the 'irresponsible', for example, be punished by exclusion? And what will be the consequences for the project of user involvement if certain people are excluded from becoming service users or relegated to a second-class service?

In both white papers the focus is on consumer satisfaction and reliance on customer surveys. Quality, regulation and performance indicators remain the managerial tools through which standards will be maintained and consumers protected. The consumerist emphasis is highlighted in the wish to achieve greater transparency in decision making and in the provision of information. In both cases, though, the effect is the development of more user-friendly services rather than user involvement *per se*. A further key component is the availability of choice. User voice is to be achieved through consultation with service users and the wider public. This is presented as a means of ensuring greater accountability. However, the underlying emphasis is on informing managers of the public's or users' views rather an extension of the democratic rights of citizens to determine the shape of services (*ibid.*).

At stake are the disputed identities of citizen and consumer (Barnes 1999). In both white papers user involvement is justified in terms of its instrumental value in making services more sensitive to people's needs, improving efficiency and cost-effectiveness rather than any intrinsic right of people to have an active say in their own care. From an instrumental perspective, the process of involvement is less important than the outcome. However, the inherent weaknesses of this approach become obvious where users call for changes which professionals find unhelpful or unacceptable. An illustration of user involvement in the social services white paper, for example, portrays the benefits in terms of customer satisfaction and cost savings (para. 2.50). Would the same example have been used, one wonders, if the service user in question had wanted a more expensive service?

Local variation in the availability and quality of services was a feature of provision under the previous administration, encouraged by the introduction of market principles and competition between service providers. The new white papers, by contrast, are strongly underpinned by principles of equity and aim to achieve a national service characterised by fair access and consistent quality. The NHS white paper sets out to replace the internal market with a system of provision labelled 'integrated care'. Consistency and fairness are to be secured through the establishment of a framework of national standards (para. 1.22) and are allied with a parallel concern with 'improving public health and tackling inequalities' (para. 1.20). Similar aims are expressed in the social services white paper, where the themes of regulation and control are even more pronounced. The emphasis is both on reducing local inconsistencies, in particular the very considerable differences – and inequities – in charging policies for social care around the country (para. 2.31), and on rectifying past failures of social services to protect their users from harm. In particular, attention is drawn to a system of local accountability which has failed to ensure adequate standards.

Inevitably, the stress on central direction and guidance diminishes the scope for local autonomy. Welfare provision is to be implemented within clear national frameworks. Within these constraints, the project of public involvement may have more to do with generating understanding and ownership and with sharing responsibility for the difficult and politically sensitive decisions facing managers in a climate of stringent financial restraint, and less with enhancing local self-determination in relation to welfare services (Rhodes and Nocon, forthcoming).

Where the two white papers begin to diverge is in the different emphases given to public participation and user involvement. Despite a common concern with issues of public legitimacy and accountability, a crucial difference is that, whereas social services are held accountable via the local democratic process, there is no comparable local democratic mandate for the NHS. While the emphasis of the NHS white paper on alternatives to the electoral process represents an attempt to make good a perceived 'democratic deficit', in the case of social services the problem is not so much one of 'democratic deficit' as the perceived failure of the local democratic machinery to ensure adequate accountability and safeguard the interests of users. The white paper notes, for instance, that it will no longer be 'acceptable for elected members to claim that they are shocked when evidence emerges of serious service failures' (para. 7.29). The solution it suggests is for both greater central direction – as seen, for example, in the publication for the first time of joint national priorities for health and social care (Department of Health 1998c) – and the reform of local government (Department of the Environment, Transport and the Regions 1998; Clarke and Stewart 1998). Greater accountability is to be achieved through increased clarity, information, transparency of decision making and regulation.

In part, the lower profile of public participation in the social services white paper reflects differences in public perceptions of service usage (Rhodes and Nocon, forthcoming). Being a user of the NHS is still widely seen as a universal right and most people do use NHS services, even if they subscribe to private provision as well. Not everyone, however, sees him- or herself as a potential user of social services. However much the white paper may proclaim that 'social services are for all of us' (para. 1.1), most people see themselves as outside the categories of service user listed in the white paper. The majority of users are poor, unfortunate or seen as unworthy in some way (Philpot 1998). As many as 80 per cent have incomes at or below income support level and, crucially, in light of the moral language of the white paper, are not working and not seeking work. The public view of social services may, thus, serve only to reflect existing stigmas. Arguably, whereas most people consider themselves to have a stake in the NHS, fewer are concerned with the details of social services.

One reason for the greater acceptance of user involvement in social services is that, unlike the NHS, where the illusion persists of the patient as the passive recipient of services, the technologies of social care are more obviously the result of co-production between service provider and user. Although user involvement receives little explicit attention in the social services white paper and the concept itself is not discussed, it remains an implicit underlying theme. One specific manifestation of commitment to the principle of user involvement lies in the announcement that direct payments are to be extended to older people. Such payments, currently available to adults under 65, enable service users to control the services they use. For some older people, at least, the white paper does therefore indicate the possibility of greater involvement in deciding the sorts of services to be provided and how they should be delivered.

Social services staff have never been held in the same public esteem as doctors and nurses and, in many senses, can be seen to be carrying out society's dirty work (Hugman 1991). They have also been more vulnerable to the criticisms, from disabled people in particular, of professional paternalism (Davis 1993a). These themes run throughout the white paper, which notes that some service users have been inadequately protected from those who were supposed to care for them and criticises those who 'provide what suits the service rather than what suits the person needing care' (para. 1.4). As a result, where health services staff are to be given a central role in shaping services with the remit to speak on patients' behalf, the emphasis in the social services white paper is on regulation and control, with measures to protect clients from incompetence and malpractice. While health professionals' role in relation to users is to be strengthened, the opposite is true for social services staff.

In sum, although the white papers go some considerable way towards strengthening the machinery of wider public participation, many authorities still view public consultation as an optional add-on to decision-making processes (Khan

1998) and user involvement as a potential resource which they can manipulate to their advantage (Harrison *et al.* 1997; Pickard *et al.* 1995). Service users remain firmly locked in the role of consumers. The emphasis in the white papers is on the provision of more user-friendly services rather than genuine empowerment.

Criticisms of the consumerist approach

The consumerist model has been challenged on several counts. The *Charter* approach, it has been argued, suggests that people acquire rights to health services through payment of taxes rather than by virtue of community membership. According to Montgomery (1992: 101), for example, the onus for change is on the health services: 'the standards impose duties on officials, but do nothing to empower patients. As such, they are more a management tool than an enhancement of the position of patients'.

As a result, managerial energies have been directed to patients as consumers, reflecting, in Saltman's view, 'a fundamentally different understanding of the role of the patient than does the direct decision-making about appropriate providers made by the patient as *user*' (1994: 208). Many management initiatives, including customer care training for staff and patient satisfaction surveys, were therefore designed less to empower patients than to increase the market share of organisations (*ibid.*).

The consumerist model assumes that the primary values to the consumer are variety and the opportunity to exercise choice. According to the market rhetoric, the operation of market forces will exert an upward pressure on quality as consumers choose only those goods or services of the highest quality. The underlying assumption is that people make rational choices based on personal self-interest and the aggregation of these individual choices determines priorities for service provision. In certain situations, however, users may value choice less highly than confidence in services and the ability to influence them to be responsive to their own particular needs and circumstances (Barnes and Prior 1995).

Secondly, competition between service providers, far from enhancing overall service quality, may exert a downward pressure on quality as providers strive to undercut one another. Variety may be reduced as only those goods and services least costly and most in demand are provided. Consumers with minority interests and needs may therefore lose out to the majority (Barnes and Walker 1996).

Critics of this approach have pointed out that users of health services are not true consumers. In practice, patients have little opportunity to exercise real choice (Barnes and Prior 1995; Gilbert 1995; Winkler 1987). As Blaxter (1993) has observed, a true market would require the consumer to have:

- adequate information and a practical range of alternatives
- competence to make rational choice
- the opportunity to exercise choice
- readiness to make quality comparisons
- protection by legal rights and possibility of redress

Within the context of the NHS, these conditions are rarely met in their entirety. Individuals' choices are constrained by geographical differences in access to services, the inherently powerless position of the patient at the time when choice is most necessary, the gap in knowledge between patient and service provider, and uncertainty about what constitutes the best 'product choice' in many situations (Gilbert 1995; Winkler 1987).

One of the few opportunities for patients to exercise any market choice is in choosing their general practioner (GP) but, as Gilbert (1995) notes, even this is only possible in urban areas with more than one accessible practice. Taylor (1984) questions whether patients are in a position to evaluate the skills or competence of their GP: 'They cannot evaluate doctors the way they do blenders or auto-mobiles.' The only thing they can evaluate, she suggests, is 'whether they instinct-ively feel that the man or woman across the desk is a "good doctor" (Taylor 1984: 210). If patients can be said to have had a choice, it was exercised indirectly: by GPs, if they were fund-holders, or by commissioning agencies, if they were not. Although fund-holding has now been abolished under changes announced in 1997 (Department of Health 1997b), the power of GPs in Primary Care Groups or Primary Care Trusts to choose a hospital or consultant will not change. Other practical obstacles to patients exercising their rights as consumers include primary care policies which prioritise local purchasing and limit referrals to more distant service providers.

A more fundamental critique is of the consumerist approach itself. As Barnes and Prior (1995) have observed, if the context of choosing is divorced from the contexts in which power in society is exercised, increasing choice cannot in itself be a means of empowerment. Choice will be of little value if none of the options are appropriate. Far from empowering service users, the necessity to choose can create confusion and stress, irreconcilable dilemmas, risk and a sense of inadequacy (*ibid.*). Preferences may remain at an abstract level; for example people may simply want to get better rather than demand a particular intervention. For many, the information required to make a choice is not available, and the imposition of a choice may be an added and unnecessary burden (Williams and Grant 1998). In addition, by concentrating on individuals' needs, the consumer approach fails to recognise the role of public services in addressing the collective needs of society (Barnes and Prior 1995; Buck 1996). According to Buck:

> The NHS is witnessing the co-evolution of two potentially conflicting movements: the attempt to allocate health resources according to their best use for society, and the introduction of ideas which stress individual choice but which neglect the consequences for others.
>
> (Buck 1996: 20)

It has been suggested that consumer choice tends to mould demand to the products being marketed, and to interpret need in terms of the services available rather than as user-defined need (Barnes and Wistow 1992). People may have preferences which they do not regard as appropriate and therefore do not articulate (Williams and Grant 1998). Further, the emphasis on individual choice and responsibility for choice may encourage a victim-blaming culture in which individuals are held accountable for their own poor health (Donahue and McGuire 1995). The dangers of an approach which attempts to balance rights to services with responsibilities are clear.

In sum, not only do the conditions of health and social-service use fail to reflect those of a true market but consumerism imposes responsibilities on people which may not be welcome and which they may find difficult or impossible to fulfil. The point is underlined in an extract from an Australian Consumer Association publication:

> Patients are consumers no less than supermarket shoppers or users of other services. The same principles apply: know what you want, shop around, and if the service is unsatisfactory, take your business elsewhere or seek redress.
>
> (Quoted in Lupton *et al.* 1991: 20)

This raises the question of why people should have to be so active in trying to achieve those goals and whether it is feasible or practicable to impose the role of consumer on people who are physically or mentally ill (Williams and Grant 1998). These questions are of especial concern when people are very ill or dying.

Choice and empowerment

Barnes and Prior (1995) analyse the conditions of public service use along the dimensions of coercion, predictability of outcomes, frequency of use, significance (life or death, or peripheral), and participation (user as passive recipient or active co-producer) and suggest that it is the way in which these particular dimensions of service use combine in any specific instance that will indicate whether choices are likely to be experienced as empowering or otherwise by potential users. Choice, they suggest, is likely to be disempowering if:

- there is no information, or poor information, on which to base decisions
- people have no influence over the options available from which they are invited to choose and their possible actions are restricted to the range of options presented to them
- they have no grounds for confidence that what is offered will meet their needs
- people are inexperienced or unskilled in making choices
- people find themselves in crisis situations where a speedy response is necessary to avoid or minimise harm
- when it creates a dilemma that people feel inadequate to deal with
- public services are required to intervene in people's lives against their will

On the other hand, choice can be important: when services are required to meet very personal needs; where the relationship between provider and user is critical;

and where services are interactive with individual users, for example where they make certain demands of them. In these circumstances, the dimensions of choice which are likely to be valued include: the nature of the service, the type of person who provides it, and when and where it is provided (*ibid.*).

In some circumstances, Barnes and Prior conclude, confidence, security and trust may be more appreciated than the opportunity for choice. Focusing on choice, they suggest, brings limited benefits and can disempower people, whereas user empowerment is more likely to be achieved through user 'voice' and giving users a collective say in policy making.

Patients as consumers

Legal redress

An important condition of the consumer model is protection by legal rights and the possibility of redress. In matters of civil liability, however, British courts have tended to allow doctors to set their own standards (Gilbert 1995) based on a medically defined concept of patients' welfare. Despite widespread challenge to this tradition of benevolent paternalism, there has been little evidence of change (Gilbert 1995). Publicity over so-called 'right to die' cases, for example, has underlined the fact that relatives have no right legally to veto doctors' decisions in such cases (Dyer 1996). Whilst warning against a confrontational assertion of rights likely to damage individual doctor-patient relationships, Teff (1994) advocates a shift away from the paternalistic model to a 'therapeutic alliance' which places greater emphasis on patients' rights (cf. Winkler 1987).

Access to information

Access to information has been identified as one of the essential requirements for the exercise of choice as a consumer (Blaxter 1993). On the whole, people want information about their condition and treatment (Meredith *et al.* 1996; Sandy *et al.* 1996), and may feel better (or, at least, less unwell) if they are given more information and feel more in control (Brody *et al.* 1984). Within the field of palliative care, this issue has been the subject of long standing debate to which we will return in a subsequent section. The balance of power between doctor and patient is crucial, both in terms of access to information and in the extent to which the patient is prepared or permitted to act autonomously in the context of the consultation (Gilbert 1995). However, studies have shown that there is a general preference for letting doctors decide, which increases with age and severity of illness (e.g. Fallowfield *et al.* 1994). The right to decline to participate in decision making should, therefore, be respected. In a review of studies of doctor-patient communication, Gilbert concluded:

> The message from this important body of work is clear: the doctor's own manner contributes to the amount of information requested and given. The

provision of information, and an active patient role in the consultation, may be linked to better outcomes.

(Gilbert 1995: 19)

Others have pointed out that the giving of information is more of a process than an event (Robinson *et al.* 1996; Wynn-Knight 1996). The way in which this process is managed by both professional and patient will have important consequences for an agenda of user empowerment. This is especially pertinent where strategies for managing information flow constitute one of the main ways in which people cope with living with a life-limiting illness. People need to be able to control information flow in ways and at a pace that they feel able to handle. In many situations, patients do not have this control. One such area is likely to be the difficult issue of informed consent to treatment.

Informed consent

This was the subject of a British Medical Association (BMA) conference on medical ethics (BMA 1998) where doctors reported that, although hospitals had instituted procedures for talking patients through the treatments they were about to have, these were often ignored in practice (Boseley 1998). Many doctors believe that they are being forced to inflict unwanted and complicated information on patients, often at a time when they are least able to evaluate it. An article in *The Guardian* cited the case of a woman of 75 who was about to undergo a biopsy on a suspected brain tumour. Her surgeon proceeded to list all the possible side effects.

'He warned me that I might lose my sight, have a stroke or have to have emergency brain surgery. It was only five minutes before the operation and I really did not want to hear all these things. He obviously felt that he had to warn me in case I sued him. He gave me the information to protect himself, not to help me.'

(Ferriman 1998: 8)

The issue of consent can be especially fraught in relation to the recruitment of patients to randomised controlled trials of medical treatments. As one doctor explained:

'When patients are trying to cope with a recent diagnosis of cancer, it is such an emotionally distressing time that the last thing that they need is a complicated conversation about the shortcomings of the existing treatments and the fact that their treatment is going to be determined by the flip of a coin.'

(Ferriman 1998: 8)

The Internet

The doctor-patient relationship is being radically changed by the 'information explosion' made possible by the new technologies of electronic, computer-mediated communication. Increasing numbers of people are turning up at their doctor's surgery armed with the latest information on their condition gleaned from the Internet. It is now possible to trawl websites of patient groups for treatment options, drop into chat rooms and message boards to exchange experiences with fellow sufferers, pick up the latest research findings from medical journals previously accessed only through medical libraries, order your own prescriptions, even have virtual consultations and second opinions from doctors or complementary therapists who inhabit the Web. This unfettered access to health information is set to undermine traditional power relationships between doctors and patients (Bower 1999). According to Lynn McTaggart, founder of the patient lobby group, What The Doctors Don't Tell You, 'The Web is the ultimate subversive medium. It allows people information they couldn't have got before' (quoted in Bower 1999: 14). Access to information gives people the confidence to engage in genuine dialogue with their doctors and this confidence can spread to other areas of their lives (Catti Moss, chairwoman of the Royal College of General Practitioners, quoted in Bower 1999).

Yet, there is also a downside. The information overload posed by the Internet can make matters even more stressful for some people (Brosnan 1999). An electronic search on pain relief, for example, yielded over 420,000 entries (Bower 1999). Sifting through this information deluge and knowing what to discard can be overwhelming. Nor is it easy to distinguish good from bad information. 'On the Internet anyone can wear a white coat and there is no easy way of judging the quality of online data, or the *bona fides* of anyone offering advice' (Bower 1999: 14). In 1998, German researchers reported that of ten free and seven charging cyberdocs consulted about a fictitious, potentially life-threatening rash needing immediate treatment, only seven replied and only five gave accurate advice (cited in Bower 1999). A further issue is the problem of commercialism, with many sites peddling dubious cures. Even conventionally available sources of information have been found to be suspect. A survey by the King's Fund found that most patient information is poor and that much is inaccurate, misleading or biased, even when written by doctors (Coulter 1998). Experts recruited for the study found potentially harmful errors and omissions in leaflets, videos and telephone helplines routinely offered to patients.

Clinical guidelines

Exchange of experiences with other Internet users can serve to highlight differences in practice between different practitioners and differential access to services in different areas. A recent attempt to address this problem of geographical and inter-practitioner variability has been the introduction of clinical guidelines. However, some doctors fear that the introduction of standardised practice may be used more as a management tool than a means for improving outcomes for patients (Harrison and Pollitt 1994) and, secondly, that, in offering better outcomes to the many, choice may be restricted for those whose preferences or circumstances do not conform to professionally defined norms (*ibid.*).

Performance targets

The emphasis on performance targets has led to the greatest investment of resources in areas where 'success' can be readily measured, such as waiting lists. As a result, the subjective elements of patients' experiences of ill health and treatment have been routinely excluded from studies of outcome (Gilbert 1995). Attempts to obtain patients' views of care have tended to concentrate on process measures, or what Pound *et al.* (1994: 73) have described as 'the hotel aspects of health care or the personal qualities of staff'.

Despite the slow pace of change, however, the definition of outcome has begun to include patients' own assessment of their health and evaluation of the care and services they receive (Davies *et al.* 1993). This process has been facilitated by the development of multi-dimensional health status profiles which are designed to assess patients' own response in different dimensions to the outcome of care (Gilbert 1995). In the field of palliative care, where cure, by definition, is not an expected outcome, attention has been increasingly focused on quality-of-life measures.

Quality

Another potential force for change has been the provision of quality standards in contracts. This is likely to be most effective where there has been consultation with patients about what the standards should be (Rigge 1994). However, as Gilbert (1995) points out, the best-intentioned purchasers have only been able to invest small change in the pursuit of quality for its own sake. Without that investment, many providers find themselves so hampered by traditional poor practice that they cannot release sufficient staff time and resources to effect improvements. In Gilbert's view, 'The NHS has acquired the language of quality, but efficiency targets and short-term performance goals mean that effective action and genuine commitment rarely keep pace with the rhetoric' (1995: 26).

Audit

The method that has gained greatest currency has been the introduction of audit. However, it has been the arguments in favour of audit as a professionally dominated activity which have held sway. *Working for Patients* states that 'the quality of medical work should be reviewed by a doctor's peers' (Department of Health 1989a: para. 5.8). Although this view is still widely supported within the medical profession (Moore 1997), it has been subject to increasing criticism (e.g. Dunning and Needham 1994; Moore 1997; Rigge 1995, 1997a). Nevertheless, until recently, clinical audit has been allowed to develop without central direction or local accountability. Doctors have decided which treatments are to be subjects for audit and kept the results secret. Many audits have been poorly carried out and, even when successfully completed, lines of accountability were often so confused that poor standards could be concealed or left unchanged (Hopkins 1996). In practice, many doctors still resisted, avoided or refused to undertake clinical audit or to act on its results (Moore 1997). The House of Commons Public Accounts Committee found, in 1996, that 14 per cent of GPs and 17 per cent of hospital consultants effectively did no audit and that only a third of the projects which did take place led to any change in clinical practice (*ibid.*).

While there now appears to be a clear political will to pursue audit, it took a major scandal to push the Government into confronting the medical profession. In the wake of the heavily publicised disciplinary enquiry into the conduct of two doctors who continued to operate on babies despite much higher than national average mortality rates, plans were announced to produce preliminary clinical indicators which would allow patients to judge their local hospital in relation to death rates after operations, heart attacks and fractured necks (Department of Health 1998a). Further clinical indicators then followed (*The Guardian* 11 June 1998). From 1999, all hospital doctors were required to participate in a national audit programme appropriate to their specialty or subspecialty externally endorsed by the new Commission for Health Improvement (Department of Health 1998a). Within Primary Care Groups, formally introduced programmes of clinical governance, based on peer scrutiny, are becoming increasingly influential.

Patient involvement in audit programmes, however, has followed a more uneven path. In 1994, the Department of Health issued guidance which required service providers to 'develop mechanisms to ensure successful patient/carer input to clinical audit and processes'. EL(94)20 set out in its code of practice for clinical audit the need to 'respond to the views of local patients and patient advocacy groups' (NHS Executive 1994b). Many doctors serving on audit groups and committees, however, were still hostile to the involvement of lay people (Dunning and Needham 1993; Kelson 1995). Patients have little say in what should be audited, and lay people involved in audit face hostility, marginalisation, lack of support and training (Rigge 1994). Moreover, lack of agreement over who can be a representative user may preclude any consumer involvement for fear of appearing tokenistic (Kelson 1995). An investigation of consumer involvement in the South and West Regional Health Authority, for example, found only minimal attempts to involve service users in audit other than patient satisfaction surveys (Barnard 1998). Yet many people believe that service users have a potential role in every stage of the audit cycle: selecting the study topic, setting criteria and standards, monitoring, disseminating findings and implementing change (Joule 1992; Rigge 1994, 1997b).

The integration of patients into clinical audit has been made easier by the development of multi-dimensional health status profiles which assess patients' own response in different dimensions to the outcome of care (Gilbert 1995). Yet, as Davies *et al.* (1993) observed, despite widespread statements of commitment to continuous quality improvement, most organisations still concentrated on one-off measurement or piecemeal monitoring of outcomes. 'Amid the jargon we are all getting used to – patient-focused care, shared decision making, graduated patient care, and so on', according to Marian Rigge of the College of Health, 'there is a danger of thinking the rhetoric has become reality' (Rigge 1995: 26).

Consumer audit

The most popular approach to consumer audit, satisfaction surveys, has been widely criticised (Nocon 1997; Thomas 1996; Carr-Hill 1995; Williams 1994). According to one commentator, 'Satisfaction questionnaires are like a management drug. They give you a temporary high, but they distort your vision of reality and you should stop taking them' (Rudat, Director of Health Research at MORI, quoted in Moore 1996: 30). Dixon (1993) raises three major objections:

- maximising patient satisfaction is not a principal aim of the health services
- there is no guarantee that high satisfaction means good-quality care
- satisfaction is unlike other health care outcomes in that is not measured as a change from a 'before' to an 'after' state

An alternative approach, developed by the College of Health (1994), uses a range of qualitative methods to obtain the views of service users and potential users who have been unable to obtain services. According to the College, 'those best placed to inform about access, process and outcome – some of the key elements of clinical audit – are patients themselves' (College of Health 1994).

Complaints

A central plank of the consumerist approach is the ability to complain and the expectation that complaints will be acted on. NHS complaints procedures have been criticised for being cumbersome and unwieldy. Professionals see themselves as subject to arbitrary attack from increasing numbers of demanding patients, while patients consider the system to be stacked against them in principle and in practice (Gilbert 1995).

A number of measures have been introduced to strengthen the process. A set of recommendations for reform was produced in 1994, which included: review panels for unresolved complaints; the extension of the Health Service Commissioner's role to clinical matters; informality and good communication; and the appointment of dedicated staff (Department of Health 1994). *Acting on Complaints* (Department of Health 1995), a new complaints procedure based on these recommendations, was implemented in April 1996. In response, there has been greater emphasis on informal discussion and conciliation and many hospitals have appointed Patients' Representatives. The new system unifies complaints about hospitals, community and family health services. It is meant to be 'simple and streamlined' and about 'listening to the concerns of patients and their relatives, acting positively to put matters right when they have clearly gone wrong, and improving the quality of service which the NHS provides by learning the lessons from complaints' (Dillner 1997: 16). Yet, in some instances, it still leaves much to be desired in practice (Buckley 1997; Dillner 1997). Although many have embraced its spirit, others have reacted defensively (Dillner 1997). Inevitably, this higher profile will encourage more people to complain but, if the level of complaints is taken as an uncomplicated indicator of quality, providers will be reluctant to introduce changes to their complaints handling (Gilbert 1995).

User involvement and research

In 1991, the Director of Research and Development in the NHS gave a commitment to involve consumers at all stages of the research process. In 1996, the new Director, observing that 'more might have been done ... the process has been uneven', was moved to set up a Standing Advisory Group (NHS Executive 1998). The Group's first report was launched at a conference in January 1998 (*ibid.*). The report explained its use of the term 'consumer' rather than 'user' or 'lay person' by its applicability to consumers as patients and potential patients, carers, organisations representing consumers' interests, members of the public who are the targets of health promotion programmes and groups asking for research because they believe they have been exposed to potentially harmful circumstances, products and services.

Active involvement in the research process can take place in any or all of the stages, from setting the research agenda, through commissioning and undertaking research to disseminating the results. Simply having consumers present at research meetings can have a powerful effect – they remind researchers of the purpose of their work (*ibid.*). Consumer involvement in maternity, HIV/AIDS and cancer care has resulted in particular emphasis being given to information and support (Oliver and Buchanan 1997), but there have been few examples of consumers having a say in how research is prioritised, undertaken and disseminated. Consumer involvement in research has been described as an area 'without an evidence base' (NHS Executive 1998: 5). Examples of ways in which consumers have been involved in NHS research and development include: research on service delivery, where the National Cancer Alliance (1996) has looked at the extent to which cancer services take into account the views of consumers; development of guidelines, where service users at the Lynda Jackson Macmillan Centre for Cancer Support have helped to produce guidelines for the communication of 'bad news' (Walker *et al.* 1996).

However, there remains considerable resistance to the idea of involving consumers in research. Arguments against their involvement include: the contention that clinicians can act as proxies for patients; that those service users who do participate are unrepresentative of the majority of users leading to the danger of unrepresentative users having undue influence; that users themselves will see it as tokenism and refuse to become involved; pressure for rapid results means that there is not enough time for consumers to play an effective role; consumers will not understand technical information; and scepticism that consumer involvement would make a difference to the outcome. Such scepticism has some grounds in past experience: for example, when North Thames Regional Health Authority commissioned the College of Health to research consumer and voluntary sector priorities for research and development, none of the priorities so identified were adopted by the Region.

Despite the lack of progress in the past, the lack of commitment to involving consumers, lack of knowledge about what involving consumers would entail, absence of an action plan, and lack of consideration of the impact of wider organisational changes in the NHS, there has been some recent movement. In 1996, the Patient Partnership Strategy and the Patients' Subgroup of the Clinical Outcomes Group were established (NHS Executive 1996) and the second conference of the advisory group, Consumers in NHS Research, was held in January 2000.

Public participation

According to Adonis (1998), there are three concurrent agendas for public involvement:

- to enhance democracy by grafting new forms of direct democracy and consultation on to existing representative democracy
- to improve decision making through contributions from representative forums of ordinary citizens
- to enlarge citizenship

The key characteristics of true participation, according to a contributor to a seminar to the inaugural launch of the Public Participation Programme, include: consensus building, sharing information, creating dialogue, independent support or facilitation (Public Involvement Programme 1998). Participation, therefore, should not be confused with representation and consultation which are 'authority-led, encourage dependency and impose constraints on citizenship' (Public Involvement Programme 1998: 5).

A report published by the Institute for Public Policy Research (Cooper *et al.* 1995) points out that people have a dual relationship with the NHS – as patients, concerned about what happens to them when they use the service; and as citizens, with a broader interest in what happens to the wider community. These two interests may conflict – not least in decisions about the allocation of finite resources. Questions about the direction of health policy and the pursuit of health gain, the report claims, ought not to be treated as purely managerial or clinical matters, since they are essentially political questions which need to be settled with political legitimacy. The same principle applies to decisions about the rationing of health care (Cooper *et al.* 1995).

According to Øvretveit (1995), the three key functions of healthcare commissioners are:

- assessment of population health status and need
- evaluation of effectiveness of treatment and cost-effectiveness of services
- 'social value prioritising'

Gilbert (1995) argues that the areas most amenable to tackling through public engagement are the functions associated with public health: needs assessment and prioritisation. Lupton and Taylor (1995: 23), for their part, record a range of objectives among commissioners who engage in public participation '... to inform the public about health issues and concerns; to establish accountability to, and credibility with, local communities; and to seek feedback on current services and future needs'.

The essential purpose of public participation, it can be argued, is to inform purchasing, both by identifying needs and priorities and by monitoring the effectiveness of services purchased. The aim is to achieve what Øvretveit (1995) characterises as 'justifiable commissioning' – commissioning as a service to the public. Purchasers need to '... seek guidance about prioritising decisions in a way which upholds its [i.e. the purchasing authority's] purpose in the eyes of the public as a service to them' (Øvretveit 1995: 124).

The difficulty authorities have in prioritising services, especially where judgements have to be made about the relative value of services with no obvious bases for comparison, has been noted by Ham (1993). Authorities often made greater progress in assessing priorities within service areas than across them. Ham comments that, 'given that there are no right answers in the priority-setting debate, an important justification for the decisions that are made is that they have been arrived at as a result of due process' (Ham 1993: 436). The same challenges face Primary Care Groups (and Trusts) as they seek to set their own priorities, albeit within national frameworks and health authority Health Improvement Plans.

The difficulty lies in defining 'due process'. Ham suggests that 'given the complexity of some of the choices that have to be made, it may be that an investment in informing and educating the public about the issues involved is needed before citizens are asked to list priorities in rank order' (Ham 1993: 438).

People's responses to questions about priorities for services vary not only with their understanding of the issues but with the way in which questions are phrased (Bowling 1993). Pollock and Pfeffer (1993) argue, therefore, for greater consideration of ethical issues in designing and implementing consultation exercises. They comment that 'investigators experience no pressure to consider whether the public understands the different interests that drive these various undertakings and the purposes to which the findings might be applied' (Pollock and Pfeffer 1993: 27).

A useful set of guidelines is provided by Sullivan (1994) who urges commissioners to be:

> honest with the public about what is being asked of it and what people can expect to influence. This includes ensuring that people understand the timescale involved – that is, whether they are being asked to influence short- or long-term changes.
>
> (Sullivan 1994)

Another key factor is sensitivity to the norms, values and cultures of different communities and an understanding of where and how to approach different members of each community.

Hoffenberg (1992) warns that, whilst determining priorities is a legitimate arena for public involvement, rationing – defined as 'the deliberate withholding of certain services due to costs or lack of facilities or staff' – should be 'a policy decision, one that is taken by the Government or a health authority, not the public' (Hoffenberg (1992: 182). In the interest of equity and transparency, he argues, services should be withdrawn *en bloc*. The alternative, of reducing the amount of care available within a given service, leaves doctors shouldering the burden of deciding which patients not to treat and the public not knowing what level of service any individual can expect. It does, however, have the political advantage of leaving rationing in the murky realm of clinical judgement (Saltman 1994).

According to Lupton and Taylor (1995), the outcome and focus of public participation activity tends to depend on which part of the organisation has initiated it. They comment that:

> If public health takes the lead, it is likely to concentrate on work with local communities in the identification of health needs and priorities ... Where the lead role is with quality assurance, the focus is more likely to be on work with direct service users and the development of feedback and monitoring mechanisms.
>
> (Lupton and Taylor 1995: 23)

Conditions central to effective development of public participation are identified as:

- where there is senior management understanding of and practical commitment to public involvement, and where identified senior managers have a clear responsibility for working at the strategic level to ensure its effective integration into commissioning
- where there is access to staff with sufficient skills and confidence to undertake public involvement activity and to develop credibility with outside organisations
- where there is a positive organisational culture for public involvement and effective mechanisms for making good use of the knowledge of specialist staff and ensuring the messages from consumers and the public are fed into the organisation

A similar list is provided by Donaldson (1995):

- an organisation-wide strategy for involving patients and carers as individuals, and as groups
- a long-term plan that enables trust and an infrastructure to be built up
- training and support for staff at all levels of the organisation, recognising that it is a long-term learning process for health service staff and users
- dedicated NHS staff to develop projects and links with the community
- resources for community groups to develop their experience and skills
- build in evaluation from the start

However, difficulties arise when:

> the organisation, driven … by national requirements, requires instant action and clearly identifiable outcomes. This tends … to skew their work towards the superficial and short-term, so missing opportunities for the development of more substantial and ongoing forms of public involvement.
>
> (Lupton and Taylor 1995: 22)

Other issues may be given priority, with constant organisational change playing a part in the disruption of good, but less urgent, intentions on public involvement (*ibid.*). A survey of health authorities' strategy plans found that, although much was said about involving the public, little was actually achieved (Redmayne 1995). Although commissioning plans talked about user involvement, few gave any details about the methods they intended to use (Donaldson 1995).

Some authorities are beginning to experiment with longer-term initiatives. Leeds Health Authority carried out focus group work and an annual postal survey of 2,000 people and North Bedfordshire, Bradford, and Kirklees and Calderdale Health Authorities set up standing panels drawn from the local population of between 500 and 2,500 people (Donaldson 1995). Kirklees and Calderdale found that most panel members were confused about the nature of a health purchaser's role. In consequence, the authority engaged in a leaflet campaign to raise awareness (*ibid.*). Elsewhere, communications and public relations initiatives have tended to centre on the media and one-off initiatives, such as public meetings.

Standing and interactive panels

A standing or research panel is a large sample of a local population (from 500 to 3,000 participants) used as a sounding board by a public sector organisation to track changes in opinion over time. Members are recruited by post or by telephone. Panels have a standing membership, a proportion of whom will be replaced regularly and who will be consulted at intervals. Participants are asked regularly about different issues over a period of time (Stewart 1996).

Interactive panels are a variant of the standing panel, which also have a standing membership that may be replaced over time, but consist of small groups of people meeting regularly to deliberate on issues. Examples include health panels composed of twelve members of the public and meeting three or more times a year to discuss topics set by a health authority. A number of health panels meet for each authority, and each discuss the same topics to provide some confidence in the results (*ibid.*).

The role of community health councils

Gilbert (1995) suggests that the role of 'honest broker' may be effectively fulfilled by community health councils (CHCs), providing that they are adequately resourced. Avon Health, for example, paid Bristol and District Community Health

Council for a two-year project to investigate how far it was possible to involve local people in purchasing decisions. Areas chosen for the initiative were characterised by high rates of ill health and social and economic deprivation (Donaldson 1995). The Institute of Public Policy Research (IPPR) report *Voices Off* calls for CHCs to be overhauled, with income, premises and membership independent of the NHS, and rights to be informed, to inspect hospitals, and to demand that senior NHS executives report to them (Cooper *et al.* 1995).

Not all, however, agree. A correspondent to the *Health Service Journal*, for example, called for the scrapping of CHCs on the grounds that they are ill-equipped to deal with complex health care issues and systems; volunteers receive no remuneration, are inadequately trained and poorly regulated. The letter concluded with the warning that over-reliance on the CHC model can have the effect of diverting NHS bodies from more imaginative communications with the public (Craig 1997a). Others have pointed out that CHCs' 'independent' status is compromised by the fact that some members have health service backgrounds, are local councillors or social services committee members (Craig 1997b). According to Manero,

> 'The nub of the problem' is that, whereas the official view sees CHCs as an adjunct to the NHS and evaluates their effectiveness in terms of their usefulness to the NHS, CHCs do not belong to the NHS but to patients and the communities they serve, most of whom have never heard of them.
> (Manero 1997: 17)

A report, jointly commissioned by the NHS Executive, NHS Confederation and Institute of Health Services Management (Department of Health 1998b), calls for a radical reshaping of CHCs on the grounds that they lack democratic legitimacy and are often seen to be unrepresentative of their local communities. The newly constituted CHCs would focus on reviewing the contribution of health and local authority services to the public health of local people, auditing policies to assess their impact on health, and inspecting health facilities (*ibid.*).

Citizens' juries

As we have seen, obtaining a representative view from the public can be extremely difficult and the methodology of ranking lists of treatments and services can be criticised as superficial in relation to the complexity of the decision to be made (Bowling 1996). In an attempt to develop a more sophisticated technique for involving the public in these difficult decisions, the Institute of Public Policy Research and Local Management Board have experimented with the model of citizens' juries based on the experience of the US and Germany over the past twenty years (Stewart, Kendall and Coote 1996). Typically, a jury consists of between twelve to twenty members, selected at random or chosen to reflect the general socio-economic make-up of the area, who are asked to address a question or questions on a matter of policy or planning. Over a period of days, they hear evidence from expert witnesses, ask questions, and engage in deliberation and discussion among themselves before making their conclusions public. Their conclusions are compiled in a report which is submitted, subject to jurors' approval, to the commissioning body.

In the UK, citizens' juries have been used to debate a number of issues, ranging from broad questions, such as how priorities for purchasing health care should be set (Opinion Leader Research, IPPR 1996), to more specific questions, such as services for people who are dying (IPPR 1996). In the latter case, the jury rejected the four models proposed by the health authority and commissioned its own independent expert to put forward alternatives (*ibid.*).

There are two models for citizens' juries: a 'deliberative' model involving broad, open-ended questions where the jury is engaged in a process of guiding policy makers and offering feedback and opinion from the local community; and a 'decision making' model, where the jury adjudicates on a 'live' issue involving a clear set of options and where a statutory body has found it difficult to reach a decision using standard procedures. Both models contribute to the democratic process and the latter might improve the legitimacy with which controversial decisions are made (Stewart 1996).

Advocates of the jury model believe that, contrary to received wisdom, citizens' juries show that, given sufficient time and information, ordinary citizens can assimilate complex information and arguments and are capable of addressing complex policy questions. Citizens' juries provide an alternative to public meetings which, too often, can degenerate into rabble rousing which inhibits discussion and turns protest into anger. However, as their organisers point out, they are not a substitute for other forms of citizen involvement; rather, they constitute one element in a repertoire of techniques (Coote and Lenaghan 1997).

Strategies of public involvement, such as citizens' juries, are based on a model of representative democracy which can exclude those deemed to be unrepresentative or biased. In Lenaghan *et al.*'s view, 'to retain impartiality, it may be necessary to vet jurors to ensure that none has a vested interest' (Lenaghan *et al.* 1996). Where the debate is restricted to issues of resource allocation and priority setting, service usage may be thought to disqualify people on the grounds of vested interest. In selecting juries, a primary concern is that members are representative of their local community and stringent efforts are made to achieve this (White 1996). However, any number of criteria for achieving representativeness could be employed and the views of certain groups, such as travellers, young people and people from ethnic minorities, are often overlooked. This concentration on representativeness, which is promoted as one of the jury system's greatest strengths, may also prove to be one of its greatest weaknesses. As one commentator observed, 'If the jury is truly representative, what justification would any authority have for rejecting its advice?' (Westland, quoted in Thompson 1997: 23). The problem is that no jury of between twelve and twenty citizens can ever be considered 'truly representative'. True representation is an all too elusive goal whose very elusiveness can be used to obstruct participation and devalue unpalatable views.

A further problem is that, although the commissioning body is expected to publicise the jury and its findings and to follow its recommendations or explain why it chooses not to, there remains the dilemma of what happens if the jury's recommendations are ignored (Thompson 1997).

Other approaches

Deliberative opinion polls straddle the gap between citizens' juries and ordinary opinion polls. They are able to reach a larger number of people than juries and, whereas opinion polls give a sample of the general public's immediate views, deliberative polls are designed to elicit a more informed opinion from ordinary citizens (Stewart 1996).

Deliberative polls involve 250 to 600 participants. A base-line survey of opinion and demography is carried out. The participants of the poll are then recruited to resemble the wider group both in terms of demography and attitude. Participants are recruited in advance and the briefing often begins before the event by means of written information. Polls last between two and four days, during which time participants deliberate in smaller groups and compose questions to be put to experts and politicians in plenary discussion groups. Changes in opinion are measured before and after and incorporated in a report.

Other approaches include community issues groups, which are a combination of the focus group and citizens' jury and aim to capture the energy, reach and cost-effectiveness of a focus group combined with the potential depth of a jury. Groups consist of between eight and twelve people who meet for two to three hours on several occasions to discuss designated issues in depth. Each meeting is designed to build on discussions of the previous one and begins by revisiting the previous discussion (Stewart 1996).

Consensus conferences usually consist of between ten and twenty volunteers, recruited through advertisements, and last three to four days, preceded by one or more preparatory weekends. Conferences are open to the public, illustrating the transparency of the process. The panel control the content and key aspects of the whole process and produce an independent report. The aim, as their name suggests, is to seek common ground on an issue (*ibid.*).

The role of service users

Despite the requirement of *Local Voices* for 'ongoing involvement' 'throughout the purchasing cycle' (NHS Management Executive 1992), involving service users is more likely to be limited to the quality assurance aspect of the commissioning function, on the grounds that people currently receiving a service can judge its quality more competently than the wider public, whose interests lie more in its availability (Gilbert 1995). Their experience gives them authority to highlight both shortcomings and gaps in provision. Health-related self-help groups, community health councils and organisations such as the Patients' Association, Long-Term Medical Conditions Alliance and Patients Influencing Purchasers Project have led calls for users to participate on both fronts (Moore 1997; Rigge 1995, 1997b). Among others, Sullivan (1994) distinguishes between reactive consultation, in which service users are asked to respond to a predetermined agenda, and proactive consultation, which enables users to have a potentially much wider influence on service planning and delivery. The need for cultural sensitivity in reaching out to small groups of users is vital to securing successful participation, whether by groups of users or the wider public.

The views of some service users are much easier to elicit than others, leading to over-reliance on the opinions of the most articulate and vocal groups. In the field of palliative care, people with breast cancer or AIDS are generally more assertive in expressing their views than people with other life-threatening conditions. This risks the twin dangers of 'decibel diplomacy', where the views of the most vocal and articulate dominate, and 'the tyranny of the majority', in which the interests of the many predominate over the interests of the few (Barnes and Walker 1996). In Barnes and Walker's (1996) view, both politicians and officers in health and welfare services have responsibilities to seek out those 'quiet voices' which, too often, are not heard. Barnes and Walker's (1996) primary concern is with frail older people. Others have pointed to the need to involve people with mental health problems (Lindow 1991), learning disability (Cambridge and Brown 1997), homeless people and people from minority ethnic groups (Bewley and Glendinning 1994). The primary concern of the present study is with those people with life-limiting conditions whose needs may be considerable but whose absolute numbers in the population are low. People who are not in receipt of services (who may be in need but are unaware of the services available, have been refused services, or for whom appropriate services do not exist) are often excluded from discussions. In the context of the present study, for example, discussions about the extension of hospice services to groups with a diagnosis other than cancer have been largely confined within the professional sphere.

Attempts to elicit service users' views have usually been limited to process issues, such as 'hotel' facilities and waiting times, rather than more technical aspects of care which are deemed beyond users' understanding (Williams and Grant 1998). Where views have been sought, questions of technical accuracy have rarely been to the fore; rather, the explicit aim has been to improve future compliance with clinical care (Ballard 1990; Rashid *et al.* 1989; Savage and Armstrong 1990) and it is in these terms that user involvement initiatives have been justified (CCUF LINK 1993). The collation of users' views has, thus, been treated as a means to the end of improving patient compliance in meeting clinical need rather than having validity and importance in its own right. Such an approach not only fails to recognise users' rights to express their views but also excludes from consideration those views which do not have a bearing on aspects of compliance. However, given the monopolistic position of the NHS, people frequently have little alternative other than to put up with unsatisfactory aspects of the service and will continue to use services and comply with treatments despite their dissatisfaction (Williams and Grant 1998).

Williams and Grant relate this failure to recognise both service users' right to express their views and their independent validity to the domination of clinical need over what they term 'people centredness'. In their view, the NHS can be characterised as addressing 'disease' to the exclusion (or sometimes at the expense) of 'illness', in other words, abnormalities in biological structure and function as opposed to people's subjective experience (*ibid.*).

Paradoxically, illness and impairment have been seen as a reason for excluding people from consultations. In a survey of forty-two voluntary organisations, for example, Robson *et al.* (1997) reported that respondents commented that the nature of the disability or condition of their users inhibited participation in meetings. Among problems raised were that users could be fatigued, stressed or too emotional or, through ill health, be less effective at decision-making; might not have the level of literacy required for committee papers; would have difficulties in travelling; or might lack motivation or be institutionalised.

The issue of representation

A central issue in discussions and developments around user involvement is that of representation. According to Beresford and Campbell, 'The issue of representativeness has become a focal point for the expression of conflict, and stressing the unrepresentativeness of service users has become one way in which service providers seek to win it' (Beresford and Campbell 1994: 316).

Representation is presented as a technical and access problem where the concern is to obtain a reliable, accurate, complete and unbiased picture from service users. The search is for the elusive 'representative' or 'typical' view rather than recognition of the multiplicity of users' views and that every view has validity in its own right. As one disillusioned service user commented: 'If a piece of nursing practice is bad and devaluing, does it become less so because my organisation only has fifty-two members, and even less so because they are all over 63 and come from Hendon?' (Campbell 1990, quoted in Beresford and Campbell 1994: 319).

One consequence is that users invited to participate feel demeaned, devalued, undermined and excluded by having their views regularly challenged on the grounds of being unrepresentative (*ibid.*). By questioning whether or not service users are truly representative, service agencies are able to question the validity of what they say. Alternatively, users may feel pressured to present a representative view when they do not feel qualified to do so. Historically, service users have been largely excluded from contributing to service planning and delivery. The mere fact of becoming involved may therefore be seen as making people 'unrepresentative'. People who do get involved are often treated with suspicion and dismissed as politically motivated or unrepresentative activists (*ibid.*; Harrison *et al.* 1997; Jordan *et al.* 1998). A further issue relates to the problem of 'spoiled identity', which occurs when people become stigmatised by virtue of their service usage, allowing policy makers and service providers to appeal to dominant expectations, assumptions and stereotypes in dismissing the legitimacy of their views (Beresford and Campbell 1994; Harrison *et al.* 1997).

Experience has shown that questions of representativeness assume greatest importance when users' views threaten or challenge the status quo. An appeal to questions of representation therefore becomes the means by which users' views can be effectively neutralised or excluded (Beresford and Campbell 1994; Harrison *et al.* 1997; Lindow 1991). This is reinforced by the forms of user involvement employed by service agencies involving structures based on allocated places for user representatives. Thus, while their discussion raises fundamental questions about the nature of representation, their practice, as Beresford and Campbell (1994) point out, is typically based on traditional formal representation.

A related issue has been the tendency to conflate user involvement with general public participation. Again, a dominant concern has been with questions of representation. Some have suggested that service users have vested interests which disqualify them from contributing to public consultation exercises, other than as members of the public. However, in focusing on geographical communities, communities of interest or concern may be neglected (Stewart 1996). In particular, it is important for the views of low-incidence, high-needs groups and unpopular or minority user interests to be heard and recognised. In any case, the remit of user involvement is wider than questions of resource allocation and priority setting: it also has an important contribution to make in relation to issues of service quality and the definition of desired outcomes (Rhodes and Nocon 1998). As in any consultative exercise, the most appropriate target group will depend on the aims of the consultation and the issues to be addressed (Coote and Lenaghan 1997; Khan 1998).

Focus on the question of whether or not an individual service user or group of users is 'typical' of a community of users denies the heterogeneity of users. For many service users' groups, the alternative of sending delegates with a democratic mandate to represent members' views is often an unrealistic option. Few organisations of service users have the resources or infrastructure to canvas members' views. Resource and organisational constraints are most severe where people are geographically scattered and have problems of communication and mobility. Such people are most likely to be excluded from both user involvement initiatives and exercises in general public participation. Issues of representation, whether in terms of statistically representative samples or democratic representation, are even more challenging and unlikely to be fulfilled. For these groups, in particular, the quest for true representation is an elusive goal which inhibits rather than enhances efforts to involve people.

Partnership

A major theme in the new NHS (*The New NHS: Modern and Dependable*) and social services (*Modernising Social Services*) white papers is the concept of partnership between health and social services and voluntary agencies. However, the history of collaboration and joint planning initiatives in terms of the involvement of service users is chequered (Nocon 1994). Joint consultative committees (JCCs) offered a legal mechanism for consultation between health and social service agencies,with the voluntary sector having a statutory right to take part. JCCs, however, were criticised for merely rubber-stamping decisions which had been taken elsewhere (Ham 1986). In other areas, the machinery of JCCs was abandoned in favour of joint commissioning groups, usually set up for a specific project or area of work. Groups may be free-standing or sub-groups of the JCC structure. Where service users have been invited to take part, it has usually been at the lower levels of the decision-making structure: rarely have they been involved in strategic decision-making groups at the level of senior management. The main purpose of these consultative groups has been to raise issues rather than to act as forums for decision making.

Users' views have generally been represented by voluntary groups rather than directly. Some local authorities have appointed a specific member of staff to facilitate consultation with voluntary groups, the main impetus being the requirement to consult over community care planning. It is often the same few vocal and active individuals who are consulted and become ubiquitous members of consultation groups. Others seem to show little interest in the consultative process or are prevented from taking part by transport or caring responsibilities. Many of those with what Barnes and Walker (1996) term 'quiet voices' lack the confidence or skills to take part. In the process of gaining the relevant skills, however, there is a danger that some service users will simply become co-opted to the agenda of the statutory agencies (Forbes and Sashidharan 1997).

This brings us to a further tension in New Labour's agenda. At the 1999 Charity Fair, serious doubts were expressed about relations with government and the proper role of modern charity (Brindle 1999). In the opinion of one participant,

> It's becoming increasingly obvious that the Government's 'partnership' with the voluntary sector means the sector becoming a delivery agent for its programme ... The amount of campaigning work, or even exemplar work, is being further and further eroded. It's all very, very funder led.
>
> (Mike Eastwood, Director of the Directory of Social Change, quoted in Brindle 1999: 23)

Speaking at the National Council for Voluntary Organisations annual conference in 1999, the Prime Minister said: '... government cannot achieve its aims without the energy and commitment of others – voluntary organisations, business and, crucially, the wider public' (quoted in Etherington 1999: vi). With a government keen to promote the image of inclusivity and consensus, it may not be easy for users' organisations to engage in overt criticism and thereby risk being seen as unco-operative and unwilling to engage constructively in the collective project (Woolf 1999; Brindle 1999b; Etherington 1999). The question of criticism becomes especially acute where the government also seeks strong, central control of the agenda and has the resources with which to ensure conformity. The issue is not simply one of reliance on the statutory sector for resources but of the ways in which voluntary organisations' capacity to serve as independent advocates is compromised by their role as service providers (White 1999). Here, we are seeing replicated at a national level some of the dangers of incorporation and marginalisation experienced at the local level (Bewley and Glendinning 1994). One way around the dilemma would be a clear separation of service provider and advocacy functions. Already, some grassroots members, dissatisfied with what they perceive to be the paternalistic stance of their parent organisations, have broken away to form their own independent, disabled-run organisations: Muscle Power, for example, is a breakaway from the Muscular Dystrophy Society. The difficulty for such groups is that, while their aim is to stress abilities rather than disabilities, it is the image of disability as personal tragedy that attracts charitable giving. Compared with their much wealthier parent bodies, organisations run by disabled people tend to be underfunded and struggling. They are also much less likely to be invited to participate in user involvement initiatives than their more high-profile counterparts (Beresford and Campbell 1994; Forbes and Sashidharan 1997). Evidence from local consultations suggests that local authorities have tended to exclude user-run advocacy groups in favour of the more traditional charities (Beresford and Campbell 1994).

In some ways, the role of pressure groups was more clearly defined under the previous administration, where the political climate was more conflictual than consensual. Pressure for change, some argue (e.g. Forbes and Sashidharan 1997), has come primarily from outside participatory debates and structures. The crucial questions, however, are the extent to which such pressure can be translated into change and whether, in some circumstances, a participatory approach would be more effective. The risks of mere token consultation or of co-option to an official agenda underline the importance of sustaining an independent oppositional voice, and highlight the dangers of an all-embracing policy of user involvement which stifles other forms of commentary from outside statutory organisations (Rhodes and Nocon, forthcoming).

Limited success

Progress in user involvement over the past decade has been patchy. During the Conservative administrations of 1979 to 1997, public sector agencies were in a state of constant change, leaving little energy to devote to issues of user involvement. Despite the promises of the official rhetoric, user involvement often took a low priority compared with other concerns (Lupton and Taylor 1995). The latest local government reorganisation and the establishment of unitary authorities set in train a further period of upheaval likely to disrupt established consultative mechanisms but with limited resources to develop replacements or alternatives (Craig and Manthorpe 1996).

The rhetoric of the reforms following the 1989 white paper was to improve patient choice but many believe that the reality was to improve operational processes and control costs. This was often at the expense of patient choice, which was reduced through the curtailment of GPs' referral freedom. Although purchasers have embarked on public consultation projects, patients' views have had little, if any, effect on major decisions. Patients still have very little choice and decisions are taken on their behalf by doctors or managers (Moore 1996). Furthermore, there was widespread confusion between the *Patient's Charter*, which was about rights for people at the point of use, and *Local Voices*, which was concerned with wider public involvement (Donaldson 1995). The reforms announced in the 1997 NHS white paper were mainly concerned with ensuring service legitimacy through enhanced public participation rather than with the direct involvement in decision making of service users.

Most commentators seem to agree on the principle of increasing the involvement of service users in decisions about their own treatment and care and in consultations about service planning and delivery. There is less agreement about the means, with the most trenchant criticism levelled at the attempt to introduce the principles of consumerism into welfare provision. According to this criticism, it was the central rationale – the construction of service users as consumers in a market – rather than the policy of user involvement itself, which underlay many of the failures of implementation in the past.

Discouraging outcomes are attributable not just to a failure to involve users but to the forms of user involvement adopted (Forbes and Sashidharan 1997) and an unwillingness on the part of managers to recognise the legitimacy of users' views (Harrison *et al.* 1997; Rhodes and Nocon 1998). Commentators have pointed to the risks of tokenism, service users becoming co-opted onto managers' agendas, and collaborative models of involvement which suppress critical questioning (Beresford and Campbell 1994; Forbes and Sashidharan 1997; Lindow 1994). Such was the fate, for example, of patient and user councils, originally set up as a 'state-endorsed model of action in hospital self-advocacy groups', but often co-opted by the system itself, with workers employed by health authorities rather than directly by ex-patients and with advisory groups 'above' the user group (Lindow 1994). Pressure for change has therefore often come largely from outside participatory debates and structures (Forbes and Sashidharan 1997). Some commentators have questioned the value of the whole user involvement enterprise and suggest that a more profitable approach would be to focus on securing legally enforceable procedural rights for users (*ibid.*). Others see greater scope for change in community-based initiatives with wider popular appeal (*ibid.*).

It has been argued that a definition of users which is specifically linked to the particular experience of service usage marginalises what users themselves want (Forbes and Sashidharan 1997), limits definitions of need to the narrow perspective of what services can provide (Barnes and Wistow 1992), excludes those who have been denied or are unable to access services (Osborn 1992), and fails to acknowledge the unequal power relations that underlie service transactions between the agency and users (Forbes and Sashidharan 1997) A generic definition as 'user' conceals the diversity of user experience and the heterogeneity of users and obscures other sources of disadvantage and discrimination, such as gender, class, disability and race (Croft and Beresford 1992; Forbes and Sashidharan 1997).

Where user groups have engaged in challenge, health service managers have been able to dismiss their legitimacy by reference to their unrepresentative nature and/or unsatisfactory character as formal organisations (Beresford and Campbell 1994; Harrison *et al.* 1997; Jordan *et al.* 1998). Harrison *et al.* (1997) note that managers have appeared to support user involvement as a means of securing legitimacy for their decisions while, at the same time, evading the consequences of challenge.

Nevertheless, there have been a number of initiatives which have aimed to involve users in service planning and delivery. GPs' patients have been involved in focus groups on specific aspects of primary care, as well as in broader-ranging patient participation groups or consultations on practice plans (Department of Health 1997c). The King's Fund Nursing Development Unit has undertaken projects on user involvement in oncology services, rehabilitation, mental health advocacy and choices for people with learning difficulties (Copperman and Morrison 1995). Consumer audits have been carried out by the College of Health as a complementary approach to clinical audit (Rigge 1994) while, elsewhere, service users have been involved in the clinical audit process itself (Barnard 1998). Mental health service users have conducted interviews with other users as part of monitoring the care programme approach (Ford and Rose 1997). Focus groups of patients have been involved in developing protocols for clinical trials in breast cancer care (Bradburn *et al.* 1995) and pilot projects under the Patients Influencing Purchasers initiative have involved people with long-term medical conditions in service planning, development and monitoring (Lewthwaite 1996).

The examples of user involvement are many and varied and there is no single 'best' model. What is needed is a commitment to the principle that users have a right to be involved in shaping the services that are designed to meet their needs. The rhetoric of the NHS reforms of the 1990s placed the involvement of service users in service planning and delivery firmly on the policy agenda and opened a window of opportunity for the development of many new initiatives.

If user involvement and public participation are to be anything more than cosmetic exercises in public relations, there is a need for direct and transparent mechanisms that translate consultation into genuine partnership and sharing of powers, a genuine willingness to engage with challenge and a preparedness to implement sometimes radical change. User involvement is more than simply lobby politics by sectional interests. It is more than mere political expediency to comply with prevailing fashionable notions of participatory democracy. Users possess a unique and specific expertise based on experience. They also have a right, based on the principle of active citizenship, to be fully involved in shaping the services which directly affect their lives.

3 Palliative and community care

What is palliative care?

Palliative care is holistic care offered to people when the intention is no longer curative. Historically, specialist palliative care developed out of an increasing refinement of symptom control, particularly pain control, in clinical settings in the 1950s and 1960s. Many of these advances were then taken up and further developed by the modern hospice movement, which developed after the opening of St Christopher's Hospice in Sydenham, London in 1967. Palliative medicine is now a recognised specialism and there are higher qualifications for nurses in palliative care. By the 1990s one could identify three key features of the contemporary practice of palliative care:

- a developing sophistication in symptom control
- an emphasis on quality of life
- a continuing priority to see patients' needs holistically, including physical, psychological and spiritual needs and with a concern for the family context and continuing needs of carers

However, the national pattern of provision appears patchy and unequal (Addington-Hall 1998; Addington-Hall and McCarthy 1995b; Neale 1991) and is heavily skewed towards services for people with cancer. Provision for many people with terminal illness is heavily dependent on the voluntary sector, with the state adopting, in some cases, a merely residual role. Many services are allocated on the basis of diagnosis and predicted survival time. However, neither approach is a reliable means of rationing services (Rhodes and Shaw 1998). First, accurate diagnosis is often notoriously difficult to achieve and many people, through mis-diagnosis or late diagnosis, will be denied services to which they are entitled. Secondly, it is not only difficult to predict survival time but it may not always be in the patient's best interests to attempt to do so. Finally, this approach is likely to leave many people in equal or greater need without adequate support (*ibid.*). The arguments most usually put forward in its defence are that current techniques and strategies for caring for the terminally ill may not be appropriate for those dying from non-malignant disease and, secondly, that current services would be 'swamped' should they be opened to all those who might need them. Neither argument has been adequately tested in practice (George and Sykes 1997).

Nevertheless, there are grounds for optimism. Over recent years, there have been moves nationally to broaden the scope of palliative care on three levels: first, a movement away from the exclusive association of palliative care with terminal care; second, a move away from seeing palliative care as the exclusive preserve of cancer care; and, third, a growing concern with differences in access to and use of services. All three have implications for the consideration of access to services for people: in different stages of illness; with differing diseases and conditions; and from differing ethnic and socio-economic circumstances (Rhodes and Shaw 1998).

These trends have been given recent impetus in national policy. The Calman–Hine Report, *A Policy Framework for Commissioning Cancer Services* (Calman and Hine 1995), breaks the association between palliative care and terminal care and calls for palliative services to be offered to people earlier in their illness (para. 4.5.1). This not only broadens the scope of palliative care but extends it to people who would previously have been denied services because they had not been given a terminal prognosis. The report also stresses the importance of the integration of palliative care with all cancer treatment services. The 1997 white paper *The New NHS: Modern and Dependable* takes this a step further by suggesting that the Calman–Hine model could be extended to services for people with other conditions (para. 7.9).

The 1997 white paper, with its repeated emphasis on fair access to services, contains a number of elements likely to have an impact on the provision of palliative care services. The call for partnership between health services, local authorities and voluntary organisations encourages greater co-ordination of services to people in the community. Already, social services departments are beginning to recognise palliative care as a distinctive area of need and to include it as a separate item in community care plans. This, and the enhanced role given in the white paper to primary care teams, provides an opportunity for a shift in emphasis away from physical care and crisis intervention towards a more holistic approach. Together, they promote the better integration of health with social care services and enable community professionals to take a more proactive role in identifying needs.

Why user involvement in palliative care?

Two broad categories of purpose underlie initiatives to increase user involvement in service provision:

- to improve the quality of services by making them more sensitive or responsive to the needs and preferences of those who use them
- to extend the capacity of users to participate in decisions about the design, management and review of services (Barnes and Wistow 1992)

Whereas the first of these focuses on enhancing service quality, the second is more concerned with issues of legitimacy and empowerment. Empowerment applies at both an *individual* level – to redress the balance of power between patient and professional and to enable people to have a greater say in their own treatment and care – and at a *collective* level – to increase the participation of users of services in decisions about their design, management and review or, as citizens, in wider consultations about services and priorities. On both counts, people who are seriously debilitated by chronic or life-limiting illness may find themselves disempowered and excluded.

Why might it be important for people to be involved in decisions about the provision of care towards the end of their lives? One important reason is the rapidly changing policy context. Major changes have taken place in the way that health and social care is structured and supported by the state. As the purchasing function of both local authorities and health authorities has been enhanced, it has become necessary to develop needs assessment in order to plan and prioritise. Integral to that needs assessment is the importance of seeking the voice of users in community care planning and in evaluating the services provided (Heslop 1995). At the same time, services provided in acute hospitals have been changing, with moves towards shorter periods of treatment. This has been prompted by cost imperatives, by the development of new techniques and treatments, and by the expressed preferences of many service users to receive treatment, when possible, in their own homes.

A further area of change likely to have considerable impact on this group of people has been the development of continuing healthcare policies. In 1994, health authorities were required to review their policies for continuing nursing and other health care needs, draw up criteria for eligibility for continuing NHS care, and establish procedures for review and appeal where decisions of eligibility were in dispute. This was confirmed in Circular HSG(95)8/LA(95)5. Local policies were to be confirmed and implemented from April 1996. An early review of a sample of final documents, however, indicated a number of areas of disquiet (Henwood 1996). Of particular concern were discharge arrangements for people likely to die in the near future. The guidance on NHS responsibilities for continuing health care recognised the needs of patients who finished acute treatment or inpatient palliative care in a hospital or hospice but who were likely to die in the very near future. In such circumstances, patients should be able to choose to remain in NHS-funded accommodation (Department of Health 1995b: HSG(95)8). Despite a letter circulated in February 1995, which emphasised the need 'to ensure sensitive discharge practice for this group of patients while recognising that clinical prognosis in many cases will be imprecise' and that 'any time limits should be applied flexibly in the light of individual circumstances', there was wide variation between authorities and some had set time limits of as little as two weeks (DH 1996b: 7).

The most heated public discussion around terminal illness, however, has focused on the issue of euthanasia. The House of Lords Select Committee reported in 1994 and the debate continues (Bosely 1998). Several doctors have been prosecuted for allegedly assisting in the suicides of terminally ill patients (*The Guardian* 1998b, 1998c). A more informed discussion about the nature of services for people with terminal illness and about their quality of life is needed but this cannot be achieved without seeking and then communicating their views.

Within this changing context, it is important to consider the needs of those people who have lived with complex physical conditions and who are now in the final stages of life. While all around them the nature of service delivery changes, they, and their carers, are faced with many challenges as to how they might live this last part of their lives and how the services they receive might best meet their requirements.

The hospice movement

One area of planning and service delivery which has a history of actively seeking to involve service users and their carers is the hospice movement. In its post-war history in the UK it has gone through major change from being a service based on the provision of residential care to being one that offers, where possible, care in the home. It is now facing three important challenges. First, it has had to adapt to the new market in health and social care. Hospice provision was protected from the market by the allocation of ring-fenced monies until April 1994 when these were withdrawn. Secondly, there has been an increasing emphasis on the provision of domiciliary and respite care. Many hospices have extended the range of services they offer in line with these developments and some of the newer hospices do not provide inpatient care. However, these changes seem to have been responses primarily to market pressures or professional initiatives rather than to consultation with service users.

The third challenge was made in a 1992 joint report of the Standing Medical Advisory Committee and Standing Nursing and Midwifery Advisory Committee. This called for an expansion of hospice provision beyond the established service to people with cancer. Department of Health policy guidance EL(96)85 states: 'Provision of care with a palliative approach is to be included in all contracts for services for those with cancer and other life threatening diseases' (Department of Health 1996).

Other groups to whom hospice provision might be extended include those with cerebrovascular disease, which may leave people severely disabled and needing domiciliary support and palliative care, and people with cardiovascular disease, who may have long illnesses that require symptom relief. Multiple sclerosis, cystic fibrosis, motor neurone disease, chronic respiratory disease and AIDS are also areas where hospice provision and palliative care could be further developed. For some people, the same team will offer care through a person's life until death. In other cases, specialist palliative care services will become increasingly evident in the final stages of illness.

These developments have provoked a heated debate among palliative care specialists as to whether it is appropriate to try to extend the ethos and services of palliation developed in the hospice movement for patients dying of cancer to other groups and, if so, how this might best be achieved (Discussion at 'From evidence to practice', Conference, Sheffield, March 1997; Hicks and Corcoran 1993; George and Sykes 1997; Addington-Hall 1998). To date, these discussions have been largely confined within the professional arena and there has been little consultation with people using hospice or other palliative and community care services or with potential users of these services.

Few people with a diagnosis other than cancer die in hospices or even have access to hospice or specialist palliative care services (Addington Hall 1997; Eve *et al.* 1997). Where there is no marked terminal phase, patients and their carers may be denied the services of palliation and holistic care extended to cancer patients and their carers (Addington Hall 1998). Most of their care is received in other settings, through the primary care team or in hospital, where the approach tends to be more individual, reactive and post hoc than the more collective, active and anticipatory approach of the hospice.

The reluctance of some hospital staff to confront the inevitability of death (McSherry 1996; Mills *et al.* 1994; Ramsay 1995) can lead them to resort to heroic interventions, even at inappropriate times and especially in the case of children (personal communication from staff at Acorns Children's Hospice, Birmingham). This was graphically described by a respondent in a study by Calnan:

> They'd do a lot for their patients. They'll fight and fight and fight until the bitter end but it's gone too far and they've left a person behind ... I mean the person as a person has been forgotten.
>
> (Calnan 1988: 315)

Staff reluctance is matched by an institutional reluctance, evident both in the ethos of aggressive, interventionist treatment and in the transfer of dying patients to other settings in order to prevent bed-blocking. Hospitals do not have a strong tradition of involving families and carers as partners in care and the emphasis on cure and short-term provision leaves little room for the development of an alternative ethos and culture perhaps more appropriate for the care of the dying. With the patient's death, the relationship is usually terminated and bereavement support and aftercare is rarely a service that is offered.

The exclusion of people whose needs are high, but whose overall numbers in the population are low, from debate or discussion about services risks either assigning their needs a low priority compared with those of larger groups whose members are more articulate or simply assuming their needs to be equivalent. People who are very sick or dying are among the least able to communicate their needs and wishes and, therefore, among the most vulnerable in society to neglect and exclusion. In a system founded on a consumerist model, where individuals seek to maximise their own need satisfaction without reference to others with similar needs or to groups who might be making competing demands on services, priorities will be set in favour of the majority and the most vocal: the survival of those services least in demand and least economical to provide will inevitably be threatened (Barnes and Walker 1996). The losers will be those with 'quiet voices', 'those whose needs are complex and shared with few others; and those who can command little public support and sympathy' (*ibid*: 385).

Involving users in planning care services during the last stages of life allows them to have a voice in this rapidly changing policy and practice environment. Shifts in community care, in the nature of acute care, in the range of hospice intervention and in the development of palliative care are occurring: indeed, they are at a point of major change. User views need to contribute to the debate about the best place and best way to offer care for dying people.

The roles of health and social services authorities

People with chronic and terminal illnesses may receive care and services from a range of agencies outside hospices, including health and social services, independent and voluntary providers. These services may be provided voluntarily, purchased directly by the patient or his or her family, or purchased on the patient's behalf by a range of agencies, including health authorities, primary care groups and social services. Such services may or may not be identified as being specifically for people in a particular diagnostic group or stage of their lives. Health service providers, for example, tend to view palliative care services as exclusive to people who are in the late stages of terminal illness, with the major part of provision allocated to people with cancer. The services provided or purchased by social services departments, such as home care, short-term breaks, equipment and adaptations, on the other hand, are often considered part of generic provision and are not separately identified for people who are terminally ill. In addition, services are normally allocated on the basis of distinctive client groupings, distinguished by age, physical impairment, mental health problems or learning difficulties, which cut across palliative care needs.

The requirement to differentiate social care from health care needs can be particularly difficult in the case of people with palliative care needs. The trend since the 1960s towards what has been called 'the medicalisation of death' has meant that care of the dying has largely been confined within the health service sphere. However, extension of the concept of palliative care beyond the control of physical symptoms to embrace psychosocial needs has led to the development of a holistic, multidisciplinary approach which fits uneasily within a system of care which has multiple providers of services and separate administrative systems for the purchase of health and social care. Social services departments as such have seldom played a part in the development of palliative care services, although, over the past few years, specialist palliative care social work has developed within the voluntary sector. Many hospices, for example, now employ their own palliative care social workers.

Health and local authorities are required to consult with each other and with service users when developing service plans. Different approaches and views about both the need to consult and the means of consultation, however, mean that, from the perspective of service users or potential users, there is no single or obvious route for consultation. Overcoming these difficulties would require:

- joint recognition of people with chronic and terminal illnesses who are approaching the ends of their lives as a distinctive group
- joint recognition that the issues which concern this group straddle agency boundaries
- the development of machinery for joint consultation with service users and potential users of services

There has been some progress towards this with the establishment of Joint Palliative Care Strategy Groups and joint consultations in the drawing up of continuing health care policies and social services' community care plans. However, the extent of collaboration varies between agencies and there is little evidence of the participation of service users (Rhodes 1996). The focus on palliative care, although it has undoubtedly achieved much in highlighting the needs of people who are dying in the context of health services, may distract attention from the need to view service provision for this group as an issue of wider inter-agency concern.

Evidence from a survey of health authorities and social services departments in the Trent region of England (Rhodes 1996) found that, despite a professed commitment to the principles of user involvement, few managers and service commissioners had made an effort to consult users of palliative care services or people with chronic or long-term illnesses in general when assessing needs or planning services. Reasons included: the low priority, openly admitted by some informants, accorded to palliative care services in relation to other services; the low numbers involved, especially in the case of people with multiple sclerosis, motor neurone disease or cystic fibrosis, the three specimen groups examined in more detail in this study; and the complexity of involving people who could be at a difficult stage of their lives. As we have argued, the lack of consultation with users highlights the vulnerability of low-incidence groups with high levels of need who do not possess a strong 'voice'. The difficulties involved in consultation, the lack of tested approaches, and the time and costs involved in any consultation effort all militate against consultation and make it even more attractive to rely on professionals' views. However, such views cannot be accepted as genuinely reflecting the views, needs or wishes of service users themselves.

There is some evidence that professionals may shield very sick patients from involvement in research projects and consultative exercises which seek to elicit people's views and experiences of services and care (Parkes 1995). Some commentators have even argued that 'dying' places a special frame of reference around people which should exclude them from qualitative research (de Raeve 1994). Others have suggested that vulnerable people should only be involved if they can be shown to derive some benefit (Lasagna 1970). However, the potential harms and benefits are not always apparent at the outset of a study and this is particularly true of qualitative research that is exploratory in nature (Beaver, Luker and Woods 1999; Raudonis 1992). Opposing views appeal to a moral imperative to conduct research with dying people and their carers since it is only in this way that areas of unmet palliative care needs can be identified and addressed (Mount *et al.* 1995) and appropriate services evaluated and developed (Seymour and Ingleton 1999). There may be a conflict of professional and patient opinion in deciding what is in the patient's best interests (Beaver, Luker and Woods 1999). But, although it may be argued that patients should be allowed to make their own decisions about whether or not to participate, the danger in any initiative to involve service users, whether in research or other participatory exercises, is that they will feel coerced or morally obliged to take part against their personal inclinations.

Methodological problems

There are major problems in developing user involvement in this area. First, it is often not apparent when the final stage of life has been reached. The change from aggressive therapy to palliative care, or the first involvement of a hospice, might be signs of entry to such a stage but, even then, the boundary may not be clear. Secondly, the length of time a person is considered to be terminally ill and in need of palliative care will vary according to the nature of the illness and, within illnesses, there will be considerable individual variation. Thirdly, to put things bluntly, there will be other preoccupying agendas for some people at this stage of life. Fourthly, and of particular importance, the nature of the final illness might make any communication of wishes or needs difficult.

It might be that user involvement has to be pursued in advance of treatment needs or by proxy. In advance, it would need to be included in the overall way user views were sought and utilised in developing care for those with disabling and degenerative conditions. By proxy, there would need to be a route by which carers or advocates could make views heard that included the views of the person who is dying. Alternatively, it might be that organisations representing people with specific conditions could be used as proxies.

Obtaining views in advance

Here, we move into the difficult realm of living wills and advance directives. Aside from the complex ethical questions around the issue of euthanasia and physician-assisted suicide, there are numerous difficulties, not least of which is the question of whether the person writing the will or issuing the directive can speak for the person he or she becomes when it is due to come into effect (Dworkin 1993; Parker 1997; Russon 1997). We know from various studies that people can change their minds as their circumstances change and, in particular, their health deteriorates (e.g. Hinton 1994). A second important question is that of who is going to carry out the directive and whether or not it is, indeed, ethical to place this burden on another person (Lewis 1996). Although some have argued that better palliative care services would mean such measures would no longer be necessary (Bernat 1997; Twycross 1996), the issue has become the subject of growing debate (Parsons and Newell 1996; Oxenham and Boyd 1997; Balfour Mount 1996; Billings 1996).

Common responses of people diagnosed with degenerative illnesses are to deny the seriousness of their condition both to themselves and to others (Illman 1997; Monks and Frankenberg 1995) and to take 'one day at a time' (Bluebond-Langner 1996; Monks and Frankenberg 1995). Under these circumstances, attempts to engage people in discussions about their future needs may be likely to fail. Many people's energy, both individually and collectively, is taken up with keeping up to date with the latest medical advances (Cardy 1993). A concern with issues of terminal care appears to be low on the agenda of both individuals and the national organisations which represent them (Robinson *et al.* 1996; Cardy 1993). Encouraging a debate about palliative care as more than just terminal care and something which can be offered from the point of diagnosis onwards would engage with both denial and developing treatment literacy.

As people with degenerative conditions become progressively more impaired, their needs will inevitably change and so too will the range and nature of services they require. Many people are not only reluctant to think about a future of declining health and progressive impairment but lack the knowledge which comes from experience with which to anticipate their future needs. It may be dangerous to rely too heavily on the capacity of people to speak for those who are more ill or impaired than they are or even for themselves when their condition deteriorates.

Consultations about services are likely to involve only those most able to participate and to exclude people who are seriously ill or impaired. As a result, changes in service provision may be implemented in accordance with the views of those consulted but to the detriment of other service users or even of themselves when their condition deteriorates. One consultative exercise involving the patients of a unit for younger disabled people, for example, found that people who were relatively well were likely to be critical and reluctant to use a hospital respite care service, whereas others, whose condition was more advanced, regarded it as a form of insurance, a service which would be available when their carers were no longer able to cope at home (personal communication).

Obtaining views by proxy

A second alternative is to consider the use of proxies.

Professionals as proxies

The White Paper *The New NHS: Modern and Dependable* gives health professionals an important role as patient advocates and suggests that professionals are the best placed to articulate patients' needs. However, we know from many studies (e.g. Barnes and Wistow 1992; Heritage 1994; Twigg and Atkin 1994) that professionals, carers and users may hold different, and sometimes conflicting, views. Of particular relevance in the context of the present study, professionals tend to place a lower value on people's quality of life (Spence 1984) and to assess the severity of symptoms differently from patients (Abbott, Dodd and Webb 1995; Pounceby 1997).

Disabled people have fought long and hard for the right to an independent voice in defining their own needs (Davis 1993b). Professionals' presumption to speak on disabled people's behalf is often experienced as patronising and demeaning (Davis 1993a) and the 'social model' of disability promoted by many disabled people's organisations stands in direct opposition to the 'medical model' which has informed professionals' views (Barnes and Mercer 1996; Shakespeare 1996).

> We reject the whole idea of 'experts' and professionals holding forth on how we should accept our disabilities, or giving learned lectures about the 'psychology' of disablement. We already know what it feels like to be poor, isolated, segregated, done good to, stared at, and talked down to – far better than any able-bodied expert.
>
> (UPIAS 1976: 4)

A 'medical model' based on the techniques of life-saving and cure may have little to offer people who are dying, whose chief 'medical' needs are for symptom relief. It was its opposition to this 'medical model' and its promotion of an alternative 'holistic' and non-interventionist approach which gave the modern hospice movement its primary identity (James and Field 1992).

Carers as proxies

Similarly, carers may not always be good judges of a patient's needs and wishes. Evidence from the field of cancer research suggests that carers are likely to overestimate physical discomfort at the expense of psychological and spiritual distress (Field *et al.* 1995; Higginson, Priest and McCarthy 1994; Higginson, Wade and McCarthy 1990). Carers and patients may have differing and, sometimes, conflicting interests (Grande *et al.* 1997; Twigg and Atkin 1994). Carers, for example, may feel unable to cope with a person's suffering and may ask for greater pain control (Lewis 1996) whereas the patient may prefer to be suffering and conscious than sedated and 'out of it'. Sedated patients may simply be less trouble-some (Sone 1997). It is unwise to assume that what is good for the patient is necessarily good for the carer or, vice versa, that what is good for the carer will also be good for the patient. The potential for users and carers to hold differing views and have differing needs has recently been acknowledged in the Carers' (Recognition and Support) Act 1995. Although the Act recognises that carers have separate and legitimate interests of their own, it is important to consider the ways in which service provision may generate conflict between direct service users and family carers (Twigg and Atkin 1994) and to recognise that carers may suppress their own needs and wants when asked to speak on behalf of those they care for (Barnes and Walker 1996; Grande, Todd and Barclay 1997).

The potential for conflicts of interest between carers and those they care for can become especially acute in situations of great distress. As one carer asked:

> When sufferers are physically and mentally incapacitated and unable to communicate, who can tell how much understanding remains and what their wishes and feelings are? It is easy to write them off as having no quality of life, but how can we be sure they do not still find life worth living?
>
> (Lewis 1996: 3)

At such times, it may be extremely difficult to disentangle the carer's own desire for relief from a genuine concern for the ill person's suffering. Lewis, talking about his dying wife, commented, 'In the moments when I considered it would have been a kindness to end her life, it was probably because, selfishly, I was finding her suffering unbearable' (Lewis 1996: 3).

Organisations

A distinction is frequently made between organisations run on behalf of disabled people, where non-disabled people presume the right to speak in their interests, and organisations run by and for disabled people themselves (Oliver 1996c). Although there have been some changes in recent years, many of the national organisations serving people with degenerative illnesses fall into the former category. Common criticisms include insufficient attention paid to the views of ordinary members and the portrayal of people with the condition or impairment as victims of personal tragedy in order to generate sympathy and attract funds. Until recently, their interests were largely expressed by others who presumed to speak on their behalf – by families and carers, professionals and other well-meaning people (Davis 1993a, 1993b). The last few years have seen a gradual change in approach in response to the co-ordinated critique of disabled academics and service users who have counterposed an alternative 'social model' of disability (e.g. Abberley 1987; Oliver 1990; Barnes 1991, 1992).

> Where disability had been treated as if an individual problem that stemmed inevitably from a person's impairment, this is reinterpreted as a socio-political issue. The central concern is the impact of disabling barriers and hostile social environments. The way forward has been to reconceptualise disability as a complex system of social oppression or institutional discrimination.
>
> (Barnes and Mercer 1996: 7)

The critique by the movement for disabled people has had considerable impact in enabling people to have a greater say both in control of their own lives and the organisations purportedly set up to serve their interests. However, there are especial problems for organisations serving people with severe degenerative conditions. First, there is the disruption caused when active members become too ill to participate; secondly, people who are very sick or incapacitated may have to rely on proxies to represent their interests. This is especially pertinent to the present study where it is those who are most ill and least able to participate or to articulate their needs and wishes who are likely to be among those most concerned with issues of palliative and terminal care. In addition, there seems to be a certain reluctance on the part of some people to associate with others with the same condition who are more ill or incapacitated than they themselves are (Robinson et al. 1996). The common approach of 'taking one day at a time' and of 'not looking too far ahead' may similarly inhibit informed discussion.

There is also a certain tension between the positive portrayal of disabled people as active citizens and the issue of concern to the present study – engaging people's involvement in debates about palliative and terminal care. The social model of disability has been criticised for being more appropriate to people with a static impairment than to people with degenerative conditions and for failing to accommodate the biological imperatives of pain and illness. The argument oscillates between those who believe that the inclusion of impairment in the account of disability will undermine the political force of the social model (e.g. Oliver 1996c; Shakespeare 1996) and those who maintain that the individual experiences of disabled people run counter to the exclusion of the pain, fatigue and depression that often goes with impairment and chronic illness (e.g. Crow 1992, 1996; French 1993).

Although few would claim that the social model can explain all aspects of disability, its dominance in debate may have suppressed discussion of other important aspects of the lives of many disabled people, notably their experiences of impairment.

> Yet our insistence that disadvantage and exclusion are the result of discrimination and prejudice, and our criticisms of the medical model of disability, have made us wary of acknowledging our experiences of impairment. Impairment is safer not mentioned at all.
>
> (Crow 1996: 58–9)

Indeed, this does seem to be close to the position adopted by some commentators:

> … the hegemony of the individual model of disability may have begun to be challenged by the social model, but it has not yet replaced it. Hence, engaging in public criticism may not broaden and refine the social model; it may instead breathe new life in the individual model with all that means in terms of increasing medical and therapeutic interventions into areas of our lives where they do not belong.
>
> (Oliver 1996c: 52)

> The achievement of the disability movement has been to break the link between our bodies and our social situation, and to focus on the real cause of disability, i.e. discrimination and prejudice. To mention biology, to admit pain, to confront our impairments, has been to risk the oppressors seizing on evidence that disability is 'really' about physical limitation after all.
>
> (Shakespeare 1992: 40)

Organisations founded on the social model of disability may therefore be unable to offer an adequate 'voice' to people whose most pressing concerns may be excluded from discussion.

A more fundamental issue for the present study is the difficulty people have in confronting their likely prognosis (Illman 1997; Cardy 1993). This leads some people to avoid situations which might force them to confront the possibility of declining health and death in the future and selectively to filter out information which alludes to it (Bluebond-Langner 1996). Although distancing and avoidance seem to be important means of coping for many (Illman 1997; Quinn 1996; Robinson *et al.* 1996), they can also prevent people from being able to plan for their future or prepare themselves for the decline which may overtake them. A further issue is the reluctance of some people with degenerative illnesses to associate themselves publicly with the illness or to join local groups and national organisations as active members (Gallup 1996; Robinson *et al.* 1996; Lewthwaite, Patients Influencing Purchasers Project, personal communication).

Many single-issue groups have created alliances with interested professionals to work together to secure resources for their particular cause. This has sometimes had the result that medical definitions have predominated concerning the types of resources and research that are needed. Not only has this fed into the continuous search for the miracle cure but it has compromised the capacity of the group to act as an advocate for members who wish to oppose professionals (Marian Barnes, personal communication).

The main thrust of the activities of the charities set up for people with degenerative conditions has been fundraising for medical research into new treatments and the search for a cure (Cardy 1993). This reinforces a 'medical model' of disability and its characterisation as a personal tragedy, since it is this portrayal which is most successful in attracting donations. Unlike organisations 'of' disabled people, such bodies were not set up to promote the collective voice of people with a particular impairment or condition. In many cases, such people are not represented on committees or boards and premises are inaccessible. Social support, advocacy, lobbying and campaigning on specific issues were rarely more than secondary functions to the primary aim of raising money for medical research (White 1999).

Individual empowerment

A fundamental question of the current study is how to empower people who are chronically sick or terminally ill to take greater control over their own lives, especially in the final stages. Choice may not be a sure route to empowerment (Barnes and Prior 1995; Barnes and Walker 1996) but it can be an important element. As a person with motor neurone disease said recently, 'Choice is a thing which disablement tends to rob you of – but not entirely' (Jackson 1997: 4).

The dimensions of choice

In the context of public service use, Barnes and Prior (1995) suggest that whether or not people are likely to experience choices as empowering will depend on a combination of factors identified as: coercion; predictability of outcomes; frequency of use; significance, and extent of, participation.

Coercion

The distinction between coercion and free choice is often confused and indistinct, especially in the field of palliative care. In the extreme case, a person may be unconscious or so severely incapacitated that he or she is unable to express a choice. To protect people's wishes, there is, perhaps, a need to put into place some sort of framework to enable advanced planning – living wills and advanced directives being the most commonly discussed options. Coercion may be overt, such as when people are refused services or forced into accepting them against their will. Examples might include decisions to cease curative or life-prolonging treatments or enforced admissions to hospital or nursing home. People who, in the eyes of others, are not able to look after themselves adequately may be coerced into accepting services.

Coercion is often far more subtle. The withholding of information, for instance, may limit people's ability to make choices about their treatment and care. In one recently reported case, a nurse had avoided answering a patient's direct question about her prognosis and had subsequently found herself avoiding the patient in order to withhold the truth (Parker 1997). Clause 5 of the United Kingdom Central Council for Nursing, Midwifery and Health Visiting (UKCC) Code of Conduct requires the nurse to 'work in an open and co-operative manner with patients and their families respecting their involvement in the planning and delivery of care'. In Parker's view:

> All patients have a legal right to information about their condition and any patient who asks for this information is entitled to honesty. There is, of course, a possible conflict between nurses and relatives about giving information, but the nurse is ultimately accountable to her patient.
>
> (1997: 38)

Yet some professionals continue to act in the belief that it is not always in the best interests of the patient to divulge information, especially where the information will destroy hope (*ibid.*). People denied information about their illnesses cannot plan and make choices based on adequate assessments of their likely future needs. Similarly, where resources are limited, service providers sometimes argue that it is inappropriate to provide information about services which would only raise patients' and relatives' expectations unrealistically (personal observations). In this way, people may be constrained to accept interventions and services, or the lack of them, through ignorance of possible alternatives.

Despite (or, perhaps, because of) the emphasis within much palliative care on an holistic approach and the family as the 'unit of care', it is often difficult to determine who is the focus of care and whose interests are being served by a particular intervention or non-intervention. Where choices about treatment or care are a possibility, who actually makes the choice or whose choice prevails is often difficult to determine. Decisions are often the outcome of complex and subtle negotiations between professionals, carers, relatives and patients, and people may be manoeuvred into making particular choices or decisions without their full awareness (Parker 1997).

Predictability

A useful distinction has been drawn between 'search goods', whose likely qualities or effects can be discovered prior to use, and 'experience goods', whose qualities can only be appreciated in the process of use (Barnes and Prior 1995, following Walsh 1991). Many of the services of palliative and community care fall into the latter category. As will become clearer in the present study, opportunities to obtain information about the likely effects of a service in advance of the decision to use it, even at second hand, are limited. In addition to the inability of dying people to pass on their experience, as people become progressively less able to maintain their social contacts when their health deteriorates and/or caring responsibilities increase, they become more and more isolated and invisible within their local communities (Young and Cullen 1996; Skilbeck *et al.* 1997; Rhodes and Shaw 1998).

Frequency

The use of a particular service may be sufficiently frequent to enable the user to develop expertise and experience in the outcomes the service can deliver. However, it is unlikely that many people will have prior experience of the treatments and services offered during the terminal stages of their lives. Despite calls for palliative care to be offered earlier (Calman and Hine 1995), it is usually only available in the last stages of a terminal illness (Rhodes and Shaw 1998). In addition, people with conditions other than cancer are less likely to be offered palliative care services (Harris 1990; Cowley 1990; Addington-Hall 1998; Addington-Hall *et al.* 1997; Rhodes 1999). In consequence, they have little on which to base judgements and are heavily reliant on professionals to advise them.

Significance

The last part of life, in particular the process of dying and manner of death, may give shape to a person's entire life (Dworkin 1993). In Garrard's words, 'People's lives have a certain individual shape, determined, at least in part, by how they choose to live them. The endings of these lives can fit, or alternatively distort, that overall shape' (Garrard 1996: 94). The significance of the palliative care and other services a person may or may not receive may therefore go beyond the immediate confines of the final months or weeks and make a difference to the significance of the whole of the person's life. Partly for these reasons, Garrard goes on to argue that:

> palliative care is very high value indeed, second only in importance to life saving ... In palliative care, we are dealing with the whole of the rest of the patient's life, and the provision of adequate care is of correspondingly great importance.

> (Garrard 1996: 93)

It may also have a significant impact on carers' health status (Fakhoury, McCarthy and Addington-Hall 1997), bereavement and the memories of the bereaved (Young and Cullen 1996; Rosenblatt 1995). Because the ultimate outcome is death, where interventions or care are botched, poor or inadequate, there is no possibility of restitution or compensation.

Yet, it is the very association of palliative care services with death and dying which causes many people to both fear and shun them. We know from other studies that many people are reluctant to use hospice services because they associate the name and the building with the process of dying (Shaw *et al.* 1998). Similarly, older people may be reluctant to be admitted to certain nursing homes because of the associations with their former function as poor houses.

Participation

Participation refers to the extent to which successful outcomes depend on the active involvement of the user as a co-producer of the service rather than as a passive recipient. Participation may be an important element of some palliative care services, such as music, art or relaxation therapy, but in some forms of symptom control, such as pain relief, patients may simply be passive recipients. At the extreme, they may be unconscious and unable to communicate their wants and needs except through others' interpretations.

Circumstances which may compromise the consumer approach

People are likely to feel disempowered when they lack adequate information on which to base their decisions. Choice *between* services or about whether or not to accept a service depends on having information about different options, and on having additional information about significant differences between services in terms of their essential characteristics and/or their effectiveness (Barnes and Prior 1995). However, patients rarely have adequate information on which to make informed choices. Often information is available on occasions that are already stressful rather than at times and stages to suit the patient's frame of mind (Cardy 1993). Even where patients do have adequate information, they may be unlikely to be able to act on it because they are too ill, do not have the practical resources, or the choice is not open to them anyway. 'Where choice amounts to little more than treatment or no treatment, this intervention or no intervention, can it really be considered choice?' Cardy asks.

> Far more sophisticated frameworks of consideration should become the norm, especially ... where the patient may be physically very dependent, where communication may be very difficult, and where the social and medical needs of the immediate caregiver may also be a major consideration.
>
> (Cardy 1993: 7)

Given that an important aim of much public service provision is to target those people most in need (Barnes and Walker 1996), where provision is limited, the luxury of choice between services is likely to be a hollow promise. Among people with cancer, access to specialist palliative care services is highly uneven (George and Sykes 1997). Those dying from other conditions, as we have already noted, are even less likely to be offered specialist services (Addington-Hall 1997, 1998; George and Sykes 1997). Where people cannot manage by themselves or informal caring arrangements break down, admission to a nursing home may be presented as the only option. An evaluation of an early hospital discharge and admission prevention scheme found not only that many patients and their families were unaware that they may have a choice in the matter but that professionals were reluctant to acknowledge that patients should be given a choice (Research Officer, Wandsworth Social Services, personal communication).

A common theme emerging from studies of users of public services is the poverty of available information which makes access to any service difficult to achieve (Barnes and Prior 1995). However, knowledge of the available options will only be of limited value in enabling patients and their families to plan this last part of their lives if they do not have basic information about the nature of their condition and likely prognosis. Yet, these are areas where the communication of appropriate information is often least well accomplished (Parker 1997; Russon 1997; Faulkner 1995). It may involve degrees of awareness and complicated strategies of collusion, avoidance and dissembling between patient, family members and professionals: some people may 'know'; others may not; different people may 'know' to differing degrees and may interpret their knowledge in different ways (Faulkner 1992).

Much has been written about the difficulties of 'breaking bad news' and the problems which can ensue when this is done clumsily or inappropriately (e.g. Faulkner 1995, 1998; Walker *et al.* 1996; Franks 1997). The failure of professionals to communicate adequately with each other can result not only in conflicting information and advice being passed on to families and patients but people being unaware of what information has been given to whom and by whom. People have differing abilities to assimilate information and there will be times when they are more ready and more able to accept and assimilate certain types of information than others (Faulkner 1996).

Although 'open awareness' between patients and professionals is generally promoted as the most desirable approach (Faulkner 1996), professional guidelines are not necessarily always followed in practice (Parker 1997). Some warn against assuming that 'open awareness' is necessarily the best approach in all cases (Illman 1997; Kellehear and Fook 1991; Fulton *et al.* 1996). Collusion between profess-ionals and family members in protecting a person from 'bad news' often results from a desire to protect the patient from distress, to avoid disruption of family relationships when bad news is broken, or to keep the patient happy for as long as possible (Faulkner 1996). Typically, both colluder and patient avoid any allusion to the prognosis in an attempt to protect each other (*ibid.*). Families may engage in forms of tacit communication and understanding which outsiders may fail to appreciate. Yet families where the prognosis is not openly acknowledged and discussed may be characterised as exhibiting pathological 'denial' or 'collusion' by professionals (Kellehear 1990).

Choice may be experienced as disempowering if people have no grounds for confidence that what is offered will meet their needs (Barnes and Prior 1995). The aim of palliative care is to improve quality of life even though there may be little that can be done to arrest or delay the disease process. Quality of life may involve staying in one's own home for as long as possible and home-based techniques for symptom control are becoming more important. However, a general reverence for 'high-tech' hospital medicine may lead some people to mistrust the efficacy of home-based techniques and those with less common conditions or particularly distressing symptoms may have little faith in the skills of non-specialist staff (Skilbeck *et al.* 1997; Robinson *et al.* 1996). Without appropriate knowledge and information, people may be unskilled in making relevant choices.

Many palliative care decisions are made at times of crisis when people may be too ill or distraught to exercise their rights. The compartmentalisation of services and separation into different specialities may mean that patients and carers experience services as disjointed and disruptive. At a time when they are likely to be most incapacitated and least able to express their wishes, people may be forced to receive into their homes and to accept intimate care from a succession of strangers (Young and Cullen 1996). One study identified as many as twenty-five professional and voluntary groups that could potentially be involved in palliative care (Blyth 1990). The need for outside help may, at times, conflict with the need to preserve independence, dignity and familiar aspects of life (Grande, Todd and Barclay 1997). At worst, people may find themselves forcibly transplanted from a familiar environment into a strange setting. Although it is recognised that patients value continuity of care and the trust and confidence which develops from a personal relationship with their carers, continuity is a benefit which patients rarely enjoy. Crucial changes, such as a transfer from hospital to community services or from hospital or home to a nursing home or hospice, often take place when patients are least able to cope with change, and continuity may be most valued. The priority for most people is likely to be prompt help in which they feel confident, with minimum disruption and obtrusiveness.

Finally, the opportunity for choice may engender profound dilemmas associated with the dangers of making the 'wrong' decision. Where death may be imminent, as in organ transplant decisions for people with cystic fibrosis, such choices may, quite literally, be life or death decisions. Faced with 'impossible' choices, people may 'choose' to abdicate responsibility and to place the onus of decision making on a trusted professional. Experience with patients with cancer has shown that many people form a relationship of trust with a particular doctor who then becomes their principal guide on what is termed 'the cancer journey'. Alternatively, they may seek to escape the decision by engaging in diversionary activities. Canadian research suggests that searching for alternative therapies may be a way of escaping the responsibility of being in control: the action of searching could prevent conclusive decision-making about cancer treatments or cancer acceptance (Montbriand 1995).

Two of the most important dimensions of the consumer approach are *exit*, the opportunity to leave a service or to change to an alternative provider, and *redress* in the case of a service failing to meet accepted standards. For people in the last stages of their lives, neither option may be available. The possibility of leaving a service or changing to an alternative provider depends on the availability of alternatives. There are also likely to be costs. The effort of moving and of growing accustomed to a new service and new staff may be considerable. People may also fear being labelled as 'trouble makers' or not being accepted back should the new service fail to meet their expectations. Even where alternative options are possible, people may be too ill and the effort of change too great and/or they may have too little time left to make an alternative choice. Where there is no option of 'exit', decisions about appropriate services and providers will be crucial. In addition, many commentators (e.g. Gilbert 1995; ACHCEW 1993) have highlighted the difficulties people have in obtaining an adequate hearing and compensation in cases of negligence or incompetence. For those in need of terminal care who do not receive it, no compensation is possible, although relatives may sue for compensation for failures in care.

When choice may be important

Place of death

An area of potential choice open to people in the late stages of terminal illness is the decision about where to die. Yet, while most people appear to prefer to die in their own homes (Addington-Hall *et al.* 1991; Townsend, Frank and Fermont 1990; Dunlop, Davies and Hockley 1989), most die in hospital. Unpacking the circumstances of individual deaths may help to shed light on the issue. A contributory factor may be inadequate symptom control in the community and patients' and/or carers' sense of greater security in hospital. Community services may be insufficient to support a home death. Carers may not be able to face the possibility of having to witness the death of a loved one on their own or of living in the house or even sleeping in the bed in which the person has died (Rhodes and Shaw 1998). Very often, informal caring relationships break down in the last few days or even hours before death and many admissions to a hospital or hospice occur in this period (Shaw *et al.* 1998; Hinton 1994; Boyd 1993).

To some extent, place of death will depend on a person's socio-economic circumstances (Cartwright 1992, Simms *et al.* 1997), especially whether or not he or she is living alone, and on the nature of the illness, for example whether it involves a slow decline or death occurs after an acute exacerbation which requires hospital admission. It will also be influenced by the approach to palliative care of the particular speciality or consultant under whom he or she falls. Specialist domiciliary services developed for care of the dying over the past twenty years have been focused around cancer, and home-based palliative care in many other specialities is relatively underdeveloped. The option of choice may not even be presented and, if it is, there may be insufficient resources to sustain it. These issues are explored in more detail in later chapters.

A further issue is whether the decision is to return home from hospital or to leave home and go into hospital. To what extent is the choice between a passive option to remain where one is and an active decision to move? Some people may be discharged from hospital to die against their wishes, while others are refused admission through a shortage of beds. To what extent is place of death a choice and, if so, whose choice – the patient's, relatives' and carers', or professionals'?

The availability of alternative options is an important factor. Only a small percentage of people, for example, die in a hospice or even have access to specialist palliative care services (Eve *et al.* 1997; Addington-Hall 1998). Most hospices operate restrictive admissions policies and limit access by diagnosis, age and geographical area. Even for those who fall within these criteria, access may be constrained by geographical distance to the nearest hospice facilities.

Ceasing treatment

A second area in which there is opportunity for potential choice is in decisions about when to cease curative or life-prolonging treatment. Such decisions may be intensely traumatic but may also be important decisions about quality of life. In many cases, however, patients are not told or are unaware of the transition and may continue to believe that they are receiving curative or life-prolonging treatments although doctors' objectives are purely palliative (Parker 1997).

Euthanasia is not a legally endorsed option in this country, yet terminally ill people may still have some degree of control over the length of their lives. The philosophy of much hospice care emphasises quality of life, defined in terms of minimal intervention. By opting for hospice care, people may accept tacitly an emphasis on symptom control over life-prolonging treatment. In hospital, on the other hand, the opportunities for patients to express a choice are likely to be fewer, with treatments administered or withdrawn without patients' full understanding of the implications and, sometimes, even without their knowledge (Parker 1997; Billings 1996; Boseley 1998). A survey of over 400 doctors in the Netherlands, where voluntary, physician-assisted euthanasia has been decriminalised since 1998, found evidence of life having been ended without the explicit, concurrent request of the patient (van der Maas *et al.* 1996; Jochemsen and Keown 1999).

A vigorous debate about the alleged practice of so-called 'slow euthanasia', in which patients are given progressively increased doses of morphine or other pain-control drugs in order to induce a painless death, has been conducted in the pages of the specialist palliative care journals (Billings 1996; Mount 1996). Although some people may wish for such a painless death (Billings 1996), there is a danger that professionals and carers may collude in effecting this without the patient's consent, even though they may genuinely believe that they are acting in his or her best interests. As we have already noted, studies have shown that professionals and carers tend to assess patients' quality of life differently from patients themselves and to place a lower value on their lives (e.g. Spence 1984). In a situation of intense pressure to avoid bed-blocking, and where performance is evaluated in terms of speed of patient throughput, the dangers of potential abuse are very real.

As we have seen, the opportunity for choice may not always be empowering in the sense outlined by Barnes and Walker (1996). Other aspects of service provision and care may sometimes be more important. In many circumstances, people may value continuity more than the opportunity for choice. Continuity and stability generate familiarity, confidence, security and trust. Yet, at a time when these may be most important to people, when they are losing control over their bodies and their lives, these are aspects of care which are often the most likely to be disregarded or threatened. Empowerment is more than simply providing the opportunity for choice. It is about having a say and having one's views respected and acted on, retaining self-respect and dignity, feeling confident, secure and in control at a time when one may seem to be losing control. As Barnes and Prior (1995) note, public services are often used in conditions which are likely to be experienced by users as risky, confusing and uncertain. This implies that, at the point of consumption, values such as confidence, security and trust may be more appreciated by users than the opportunity for choice. User empowerment, they suggest, is more likely to be achieved through mechanisms that aim to increase the effectiveness of user 'voice', by enhancing the capacity of users to influence public service provision, than through extending consumer choice.

Collective empowerment

A number of questions or dilemmas arise in relation to the collective empowerment of people with palliative care needs:

- What role do single-condition or impairment organisations have to play compared with larger alliances? In the context of the market and priority setting, low-incidence groups may find themselves in competition with each other for scarce, specialist resources. Might there be strength in greater collaboration? Or might there be a danger that a focus on common needs would lose sight of more particular needs?
- How can people organise at a local level when their numbers are extremely low?
- How can people be engaged in discussion if they are reluctant to become engaged?
- How can people who are very ill or have mobility and/or communication difficulties be enabled to take part? One way forward might be telephone and/or computer link-up. Ought we to be developing these approaches now in anticipation of more widely available technological advances? But, in the meantime, what about those who do not have access to these resources?

Alliances

By focusing on single conditions, illness- or impairment-specific organisations have been criticised for preventing disabled people from recognising their common situation and common oppression:

> Our own history has taught us this in the way in which we have been classified and segregated by our impairments and the way in which single impairment organisations have failed to provide an adequate basis for collective self-organisation amongst disabled people in the past.
>
> (Oliver 1996: 51)

The movement of disabled people has emphasised their common concerns in the context of common oppression (Oliver 1996a, 1996c; Shakespeare 1996; Abberley 1987). In advocating a move away from single condition groupings, it has appealed to strength in numbers and avoiding the fragmentation and competing interests which result from separation (Campbell and Oliver 1996). This has stimulated an ongoing debate about the ability of the collective to accommodate successfully people with very wide-ranging needs and interests (Barnes and Mercer 1996). To what extent, for example, will a focus on common concerns result in the submergence of particular needs?

Specialist palliative care services have been largely organised around single diseases. Most of the developments have been in the field of cancer. AIDS, which shares many of the characteristics of cancer, especially in a marked terminal phase, presented a major challenge to existing palliative services. However, the predominant response, especially in the earlier days, has been the provision of separate services (Layzell and McCarthy 1993). For people with other illnesses, access to specialist palliative care services may depend on the approach of their particular medical speciality and of individual practitioners. One of the aims of the current study was to explore the extent to which people with illnesses other than cancer share common needs and concerns. To what extent is it appropriate or possible to extend provision and discussion to the needs of people with other illnesses whose numbers are much lower? Without a strong 'voice', there is clearly a danger of their more specific needs and concerns being submerged by those of the majority.

Shakespeare (1993) asks whether the claim for disabled unity, and the denial of a role to non-disabled people, is undermined by the fact that disability is not a unitary concept and the experiences of people with different impairments will differ markedly. Although recognising that 'it is important not to ignore differences between impairments, despite the tendency of writers to gloss over difference in favour of the totalling and unifying role of oppression' (*ibid*: 255), in Shakespeare's view, it is 'social oppression [which] is the most immanent aspect of [disabled people's] experience' (*ibid*: 255) and which forms the basis for collective identity and collective action.

The formation of a collective identity is necessary to the growth of group consciousness. 'Only when [people] see that their problems are shared by others like them, the group', writes Klein, 'can they attribute the source of their concerns to social conditions, such as discrimination, and look to political solutions' (Klein 1984: 2). In her analysis of the women's movement, Klein identifies a three-stage process in the development of a political consciousness: first, affiliation through group membership and sharing of interests and concerns; secondly, a rejection of traditional definitions for that group's status in society; and, finally, the conversion of personal problems into political demands (*ibid.*). People with complex physical conditions and life-limiting illness, however, may fall at the first hurdle. Collective organisation may be hindered by geographical isolation, mobility and communication difficulties, unpredictable and fluctuating illness, and exclusion from the networks and media which help to enable people to come together. According to Shakespeare:

> it may be more difficult for people with impairments to identify as disabled, as socially oppressed, than it is for women, blacks, or gays. The oppression is couched in terms of paternalistic support and charity. The dominance of professionals is wellnigh total. The very real element of physical impairment restricts activity, and reinforces 'natural' explanations of disability.
>
> (Shakespeare 1993: 256)

For these reasons, the movement of disabled people fails to reach out to the total constituency of disabled people and appeals primarily to the 'relatively active, relatively young, middle-class elements' (*ibid.*). For people for whom illness and impairment are more intrusive and likely to assume greater prominence in their lives, the movement's 'social model' and attendant political consciousness may be more difficult to embrace. Thus, although it might offer scope for the development of a collective critique of existing palliative care provision and an emergent political consciousness, it has been unable to reach out to many of those for whom such a discussion might be most relevant. If, within the movement of disabled people, the downplaying of the role of impairment may exclude those who identify via their particular impairment, how much more so might this be the case within the field of palliative care?

Shakespeare notes that:

> the possibilities of people with various impairments coming together in a political struggle are reduced by the tendency of medicine and welfare to divide up arbitrarily the constituency: to separate the old from the young, to segregate people with different physical conditions, who nevertheless share similar social experiences.
>
> (Shakespeare 1993: 256)

In the field of palliative care, a powerful force for fragmentation comes from the charities, each representing the interests of different groups and competing with each other for public support. The large and successful cancer charities which dominate have shown little interest in adopting a more inclusive approach and thereby, perhaps, diluting their public appeal. On the whole, the major charities have been characterised by an inward focus rather than an outward-looking, proselytising stance. In part, this is a product of an increasingly competitive fund-raising environment; in part, it is a reaction to the fear and stigma with which cancer and AIDS have been regarded by the rest of the world. In addition to notions of contagion and associations with death and dying, people with HIV/AIDS have the stigma of moral opprobrium. Paradoxically, although seen as worthy causes and attracting substantial public donations, hospices are shunned as places of death and dying. There has therefore been little impetus either for the dominant organisations to embrace or extend their mission to other groups or for others to want to associate with them.

The organisation of medicine and health services similarly militates against collaboration and the formation of alliances, with different specialities each competing for scarce resources and jealously guarding their specialist status. The relatively new discipline of palliative care has the potential to cut across these competing interests and groupings. However, the barriers to interdisciplinary collaboration are strong and palliative care is still seen by many as an extension of oncology, with little relevance to other diseases and little relevance beyond terminal care (Fordham *et al.* 1998).

Nevertheless, there have been some promising developments. First, there has been a growing discussion amongst disabled people of issues concerning illness and impairment and attempts to dismantle the divide which has been erected between illness and disability (Barnes and Mercer 1996; Crow 1992, 1996; French 1993). Secondly, within the field of palliative care, alliances have been established outside the spheres of cancer and HIV/AIDS. Examples include the Long-Term Medical Conditions Alliance (LMCA), Neurological Alliance, and Association for Children with Terminal Conditions (ACT) and their families.

Self-help groups

Most of the literature on the role of self-help groups in the field of palliative care refers to cancer self-help groups. Self-help groups are made up of people who have personal experience of the same problem or life situation. They are run by and for their members and may have little or no help from professionals (Urben 1997). They are usually voluntary and have a small group structure (Johnson and Lane 1993). A review by Liz Urben (1997) from Cancerlink, an umbrella organisation for cancer self-help groups, listed their main functions as the provision of emotional support, the sharing of information and ways of coping based on personal experience, and the offer of direct assistance to members, enabling them to live positively with the best possible quality of life (*cf.* Cella and Yellen 1993; Stuart 1994). In part, the development of self-help groups represents a questioning of the relevance of the biomedical model of illness to the subjective reality of the individual's experience (Fulton *et al.* 1996). Many groups were specifically established to offer an alternative, independent and distinctive approach. However, there was little emphasis on advocacy, campaigning or input into health service planning and delivery. Consultation and dialogue with statutory service providers was not an objective and relationships were often antagonistic. In fact, many professionals were dismissive of the value of these alternative approaches (*ibid.*). Importantly for the prospect of user involvement in the current policy climate, members of self-help groups 'do not see themselves as customers or consumers: health and social care are not commodities to them' (Gott *et al.* 2000). Nevertheless, groups have the potential to influence planning, delivery and evaluation of services at a strategic level from a perspective grounded in their own experience-based understanding of their disease (Zola 1987; Gray *et al.* 1995).

Consultative exercises which have included disability and condition-specific organisations have been strongly criticised for including only organisations 'for' disabled people and excluding those run by disabled people themselves (Oliver 1996c). However, the issue is not simply one of exclusion but of the nature and character of many self-help groups. In a review of the relationship between self-help groups and professionals, Wilson (1994) found that very few had been formally involved in community care or health service planning, although some had had informal opportunities to influence how services were provided. None of the groups saw campaigning or influencing services as their main task and some took no part in this (*ibid.*). By engaging in these activities, some groups would clearly be changing their character and function and, in the process, perhaps losing some of their independence from statutory services and their appeal to members. The issue is one of the extent to which it is justifiable to expect groups to engage in activities which do not fall within their primary aims and functions. Wilson (*ibid.*) found that some groups resented being diverted from their original aims or the commandeering of their limited time and energy.

Urben (1997: 26) suggests that 'self-help groups can help to reduce the sense of isolation that someone with cancer may feel' and that 'attending a group can help to overcome the feeling of stigma they may be experiencing'. In the case of other conditions such as cystic fibrosis and multiple sclerosis, however, some people may be reluctant to join self-help groups because they do not want to be publicly associated with the condition. Even in the case of cancer, self-help groups are not necessarily representative of the population of people with cancer. The *Directory of Cancer Self-Help and Support* (Cancerlink 1998), for example, lists 155 breast cancer groups but only four for testicular cancer, two for colorectal cancer and none for lung cancer. For some cancers, the small numbers involved may prohibit effective involvement. In the case of lung cancer, a combination of social class profile and burden of illness may account for the low level of involvement (Gott *et al.* 2000). By contrast, the high numbers of self-help groups among people with breast cancer has been attributed to a legacy of self-help and mobilisation arising from the feminist movement and also to the legitimate levels of optimism which now accompanies breast cancer treatment (*ibid.*). Fewer men than women attend cancer self-help groups and people from minority ethnic groups are also under-represented (Urben 1997).

According to Fulton *et al.* (1996), groups frequently develop their own 'objective' reality about the circumstances of their experiences. Some support groups, for example, develop a repository of knowledge about alternative therapies. Not only will their reality differ from that of many professional health carers, but their ability to cater adequately for the needs of potential members will be limited. 'Often such groups do not provide adequate support for individuals who believe they are beyond any form of acute or alternative therapy and simply seek emotional support during the terminal period of their illness' (Fulton *et al.* 1996: 1, 354).

The influence of the 'social model' of disability can be detected in the attempts of some groups to assert a positive self-portrayal to counter the negative imagery of the past. Yet, as some people living with AIDS have found, these efforts can belie their own experiences. Fulton *et al.* (1996) recount how one man left a support group because he was exasperated by the constant portrayal of living with AIDS as a 'growth experience'. His predominant experience had been one of constant illness and grieving for the death of many friends, his inability to work and maintain a normal lifestyle and the general drudgery of daily living, rather than a spiritually enriching experience. This instance highlights the difficulties of any group trying to cater for people whose needs will vary not only with their individual biographies and circumstances but their experiences of illness and the progression of their disease.

A survey of cancer self-help groups carried out by Cancerlink in 1992 found that, although the majority of groups were started by someone with cancer, or a relative of someone with cancer, at least 40 per cent had some form of professional involvement (Urben 1997). Although the involvement of professionals might be thought to compromise a group's independence, this does suggest that self-help groups in this area may be difficult to initiate and sustain without additional support and facilitation (*cf.* Lindsay 1997). There are clear implications for the prospect of developing self-help groups among people with chronic and life-limiting conditions other than cancer, since professional energies and resources are heavily skewed towards people with cancer. Most research has reported on groups run with professional facilitators, such as nurses or social workers (Urben 1997), with very little carried out on self-help groups without this input (Hitch, *et al.* 1994).

One review found that professionals provided an often crucial means of access to self-help groups (Wilson 1994). A concern of group members was that potential members might be unaware of a group's existence or of what it offered. Professionals, on the other hand, said that they lacked reliable information about groups and a strong sense of responsibility for clients or patients often led them to be selective in the giving of information. On some occasions, professionals exhibited overt hostility towards certain groups. By contrast, groups believed that the decision of whether or not to participate should be left to the individual.

A further issue, which is certainly an area of difficulty for cancer self-help groups (Urben 1997) and is likely to be common to any group of people with a terminal illness, is the group's response to death and its effect on other members. Groups develop their own ways of acknowledging the death of a member and will vary in their ability to deal with dying and bereavement as part of their group task. Few of the cancer groups referred explicitly to the role of death (Urben 1997) or were as open in their approach as the group described by Tyler (1994):

- We believe as a group in: not avoiding the subject of illness and cancer and that there is always hope; the acceptance of death can often enhance the quality of living.

- When we meet as a group, the group tries to be positive and express hope, but not at the expense of avoiding talking about death and endings, as well as about living, when there is a need to discuss these issues.

(Tyler 1994)

Although the numbers of people with specific cancers may not be high, the numbers with some form of cancer are considerable compared with the numbers of people with other life-limiting diseases. In any one health authority area, there may be too few people with a particular disease to make the setting up of a local self-help group a feasible enterprise.

Many people will be too ill or have mobility and/or speech difficulties which severely limit their ability to attend meetings or to communicate using conventional methods. Arrangements to accommodate their needs will be beyond the resources of most self-help groups without additional support. Telephone conferences (Thornton and Tozer 1995) or computer link-up may avoid the need for face-to-face meetings but require resources beyond those of most members. Despite these difficulties, one group (Muscle Power, a national organisation of people with neuromuscular impairments) has managed to provide each of its committee members at least with a personal computer. A dedicated site on the Internet has become an increasingly important source of personal link-up and information exchange for people with a wide range of illnesses and conditions. But, although computer links are likely to become even more important in the future, they run the risk of creating a well-informed elite who are in regular contact with each other and a relatively ill-informed and disempowered, albeit decreasing, majority who do not have access to the Internet.

Self-advocacy groups

The growth since the 1980s in self-advocacy groups, and in cancer self-advocacy groups in particular, has been most marked in North America where it is has been closely linked to the growth of self-help groups and with consumer and activist movements more generally (Bradburn and Maher 1995). The increasing politicisation of groups has been attributed to a number of factors, including: the 'market place' organisation of health care and rise in consumerism; increasing information and awareness among citizens; the influence of the media; the unequal power relationships between patients and professionals; conflicts between lay and professional perspectives; and competition for scarce resources which has led to cancer becoming a political issue (*ibid*.; Chesler 1991).

One of the most successful projects has been the National Breast Cancer Coalition (NBCC) which, following in the footsteps of AIDS activists, has established a strong patient voice based on 'survivor politics'. According to this view, people affected by AIDS or breast cancer are not the victims of disease so much as survivors who gain self-respect and a sense of autonomy through speaking for themselves. Combined with feminist politics, this has enabled breast cancer activism to become a powerful force. In 1992, pressure from the lobbying activities of the NBCC resulted in $214 million being diverted to breast cancer research from the USA defence budget (Bradburn and Maher 1995).

In Europe, many of the national cancer societies have encouraged and supported the development of patient support groups. In the UK, Cancerlink supports locally based cancer self-help groups through a regular newsletter, training and advice. A potential role as self-advocacy groups, however, remains underdeveloped. A notable exception and example of how advocacy can operate at a local level to influence health care providers has been the collaborative venture between the psychosocial oncology team at Mount Vernon Hospital, a regional cancer treatment centre in Middlesex, and a network of locally-based cancer self-help groups. The groups meet regularly at the hospital and group representatives work closely with health professionals (*ibid.*).

Developments in the UK have generally been characterised by collaboration between patient advocacy groups and sympathetic health professionals (*ibid.*). Examples include the National Cancer Alliance, launched in 1993 to bring together health professionals, patients and relatives to seek improvements in cancer treatment and care (newsletter of the National Cancer Alliance 1995) and the Radiotherapy Action Groups Exposure (RAGE), referred to in Chapter 1.

Bradburn and Maher (1995) list the benefits of advocacy group activity as legislative changes resulting from lobbying activities, research funding, improvements in cancer care services, and 'the personal satisfaction of feeling empowered and in control'. The dangers of the UK approach, however, lie in the risk of groups developing too cosy a relationship with health care professionals and thereby losing their independence.

According to Bradburn and Maher, 'patient advocacy groups need a network of informed and active members. Maintaining a strong and independent voice relies on a grassroots structure quite unlike that found in healthcare bureaucracies' (Bradburn and Maher 1995: 17).

In the field of cancer, this grassroots structure is supported by the national organisation Cancerlink and draws for its membership on a large pool of potential members, including many 'cancer survivors' who have both the resources and energy to engage in active campaigning. These favourable conditions are unlikely to hold for other life-limiting diseases with not only a much lower incidence but lower proportions likely to be well enough to become active members of local groups. Moreover, the assertive 'survivor politics' found among advocacy groups in North America may have less relevance to people with non-malignant, degenerative and/or life-limiting disease. The rise of self-advocacy groups in North America and the success of powerful lobbying organisations such as the NBCC signals a further danger of pressure group politics, where the strongest and most powerful voices are able to influence policy and secure resources often at the expense of less well-organised and less vocal groups.

Professional initiatives

A distinction can be made between attempts to influence service planners emanating from outside service structures and user involvement initiatives generated from within (Forbes and Sashidharan 1997). Self-help and self-advocacy groups straddle the divide with varying degrees of professional involvement. Internally generated initiatives rarely extend beyond places allocated to representatives from voluntary organisations on consultative or strategy groups. Examples of more imaginative projects to involve frail and socially isolated service users directly include the Fife Users Panels Project and the Wakefield 'Talk Back' scheme. Both were collaborative ventures with the charity Age Concern.

The Fife Users Panels Project

Although there have been very few initiatives to involve seriously ill people in decisions about service delivery and planning, there are examples of advocacy projects working with individual frail older people (Ivers 1994). Chances to have some say in decisions affecting them are increasing for older people in service or communal settings but, as yet, there are few opportunities for the majority still living in their own homes to become involved (Thornton and Tozer 1994). On the whole, collective action has presupposed the involvement of fitter older people (*ibid.*). A notable exception is the Fife Users Panels Project, developed by Age Concern Scotland (ACS), involving older people whose frailty means they are unable to leave their homes without assistance.

> Whilst a major aim of the project was to develop a mechanism through which frail older people's voices could be heard and could influence service planning and provision, it sought to do this in a way which enabled development in older people themselves, and within the groups established to enable them to meet together.
>
> (Barnes and Walker 1996: 386)

Seven panels were established during the initial three-year period of the project. The panels were distributed throughout Fife to enable geographical access and to include older people in rural and urban localities and from different socio-economic groups. Potential members were identified by social and health service providers, through ACS networks and by existing panel members. Criteria for membership were that people were users or potential users of community services, normally (though not exclusively) living on their own, and over 75 years of age. The aim was for each panel to comprise six to eight people, although actual numbers have varied over time. Each panel met monthly, supported by three ACS staff.

The Fife model has provoked discussion about the extent to which the panel participants can be expected to 'represent' the views of others, given the comments of some statutory agency staff about their failure to consult more widely to obtain the views of other service users. Although the panel members were considered to be typical of others in similar situations, they were not expected to 'represent' other older people (Barnes, Cormie and Crichton 1994; Barnes and Walker 1996). The focus of the project was on the empowerment of older people whose frailty often means that a representative role is not practical. Indeed, Barnes and Walker (1996: 384) argue that it would be 'unreasonable and unrealistic to expect those whose frailty and isolation has led to their use of services to act as representatives, seeking out and reflecting the views of others in similar situations'.

From the other side of the coin, the Fife panel members did not believe that their own perspectives and views could be adequately expressed by other older people who were younger and fitter. This raises the difficult question of whether people with a particular illness or impairment can speak for those who are more ill or impaired than they are or even for themselves when their condition deteriorates.

Like the cancer self-help groups referred to above, the Fife groups experienced a high rate of attrition resulting from the deaths and deteriorating health of members. However, unlike the cancer groups, the organisers did not believe that this has had a serious impact on the morale of members (Joyce Cormie, Fife Development Officer, Age Concern Scotland, personal communication). Older people who have lived the full, expected span of their lives may be able to confront the prospect of death with greater equanimity than those whose lives will be cut short by illness and who may feel 'cheated' of a full life span.

The Wakefield 'Talk Back' Project

An alternative to the Fife approach, which brought frail older people together, is the Wakefield 'Talk Back' Project which engaged volunteers to visit people in their own homes (Willis 1999; Age Concern 2000). Older people's views about the 'sort of assistance they feel they need to help them get the most from life' was recorded in diary form. Although, unlike the Fife model, the 'Talk Back' project made no provision for the sharing of experiences and exchange of views, it was potentially able to reach a larger number of people. Neither project could offer participants any guarantee that services would be changed in line with their recommendations:

> We are not able to promise that those taking part will be able to receive the help they feel they need. However, we expect that our findings will help Wakefield Metropolitan District Council to plan their services for older people. This should mean long-term improvements in services to people over 75.
> (Age Concern 1997: 4)

However, the Fife panels did enable members to present their views directly to service planners who attended panel meetings and the findings from the Wakefield consultations were considered during the formulation of the subsequent Community Care Plan (Age Concern 2000).

Information and communication technologies

The rapid development of electronic information and communication technologies (ICTs) and increasingly sophisticated enabling technologies, such as speech aids, is likely to have wide implications for people with serious, debilitating illnesses and palliative care needs, especially those with communication and mobility difficulties and those who are socially isolated and geographically dispersed. The Internet can provide people with life-threatening or life-changing illness with new ways of meeting people and making friends, receiving care and support, and gaining access to information and services. People can communicate and share experiences and information with people whom they would never otherwise meet; in particular, people with rare conditions can communicate with and learn from others.

Electronic sources of professional information include: online directories, databases and websites containing access to information and services, online access to professional advice and guidance, and interactive computer programmes which simulate dyadic communication (Sofka 1997). Examples of websites containing frequently asked questions and medical information include CancerNet, run by the International Cancer Information Centre, and OncoLink, developed by the University of Pennsylvania Medical School. These sites offer information about diagnoses, treatment options, psychosocial aspects, and resources for coping and support (*ibid.*). Similar services, also based in the United States, exist for people with HIV or AIDS. Opportunities are available for computer-mediated discussion with professionals and 'question and answer boards' are designed to allow people to post queries via email for response by experts (*ibid.*).

Electronic sources of lay information include: online support groups, chat groups, news groups and discussion groups, narrative sites, bulletin boards and mailbases. Online support groups and self-help groups provide fora for communicating with other people to share experiences and coping strategies. Some Internet-related chat (IRC) services and support groups simulate conventional support groups by allowing participants to interact with each other in real time. Interactive conversations, using multiple user domains or MUDs, take place at regularly scheduled times. A British example is a chat service for people with chronic fatigue syndrome (CFS). Some people have created websites specifically to share with others their personal experiences of illness or loss. One of the most highly publicised examples of such a narrative site was Timothy Leary's home page prior to his death from AIDS in May 1996, in which he related his efforts to achieve 'hi-tech designer dying'. His descriptions included mental and physical status reports and a menu of his average daily intake of neuroactive drugs (Sofka 1997). An example of a site aimed at a mixed lay and professional usership is the International Alliance of ALS/MND Associations (http://www.alsmndalliance. org). This site provides online information about amyotrophic lateral sclerosis/ motor neurone disease from around the world and encourages patient involvement and the exchange of ideas about good practice and current research.

A number of projects have been initiated to try to co-ordinate the many disparate sources of service and welfare information, including electronic sources. The National Disability Information Project, which ran for three years from 1991, was set up by the Department of Health in England to investigate ways of improving access to information for disabled people, their carers and service providers. A more recent UK initiative, StartHere, which is targeted specifically at the information needs of carers, aims to provide a single, integrated system or 'digital, one-stop shop' which is 'easy, accessible and user-friendly'. It proposes to do this by exploring existing and future infrastructures, making the service available in as many different outlets as possible and accessible in as many different ways as possible. The long-term objective is to provide the service in people's own homes using a 'set-top box', which converts digital signals so that they can be read on a standard television screen. European examples include a project for the inclusion of disabled and elderly people in the development of telematics – a combination of telecommunication and computer technology. A principal aim of the InClude web server is to encourage dialogue between the designers of products and services and their end users (Hyppönen 1997). A second European collaborative project, Action, aims to provide online care information and direct communication between family carers in their homes and professional carers.

Treatment literacy

Information technology offers people the opportunity to become better informed about their illness, make more informed choices about their treatment and care, and engage in genuine partnership with physicians and professional carers. As one person with multiple sclerosis commented: 'If you know you've got the knowledge, it gives you confidence to ask for what you want' (quoted in McKee 1999: 13). This growing treatment literacy, however, can also lead to tensions in the relationship, where the patient appears to be better informed than the doctor or where patients demand new treatments. People living with life-limiting illness tend to focus their hopes on new treatments which hold out the promise of prolonging life, and new drugs or treatments at pilot or full trial stage have begun to attract attention disproportionate to their current value (*ibid.*). Similarly, patients who see a new treatment as their only hope have questioned the ethics of placebo trials. In this 'field of exceptional hope and aspiration' (Cardy 1993), it may be all too easy for unscrupulous commercial interests to exploit patients' hopes by inflated claims about their products in order to stimulate demand.

However, such tensions can help to make explicit the covert rationing of treatments and expose inequalities between the policies of different service providers, thus opening up to public debate decisions which previously had been taken by physicians, managers and planners in private, away from public scrutiny.

Access to information sources on the Internet represents a growing challenge to professional monopolies of knowledge and information and can be seen as part of the self-help movement which has developed in health and community care, facilitating the propagation of alternative therapies and lay perspectives on health and illness that can both challenge and complement professional perspectives.

ICTs offer people opportunities to access information privately without others knowing that they are seeking it or having to explain why they want it. Some North American sites, for example, may facilitate access to materials related to advance directives (Choice in Dying) or contain online libraries related to phys-ician-assisted suicide (DeathNet). Issues of suicide and assisted suicide are openly presented and discussed and right-to-die organisations have posted a mass of information online (Sofka 1997). It is therefore possible to find information about and to discuss with strangers topics which it would not be possible to discuss with either friends and family or with health and welfare professionals. The potential for anonymity allows users to communicate with each other under pseudonyms without having to reveal personal details. Participants can talk with impunity in the knowledge that their real identity is concealed. Moreover, they have greater control over the communication than in face-to-face encounters. They can choose when to log in, when to withdraw, what to read and what not to read.

Input to service planning and access to policy makers

The new information technology offers the potential for people to have an input to policy through electronic links with service planners and providers. Dedicated websites can provide a means not only for disseminating information about services to people in their own homes but for inviting feedback from users on existing services or on proposed changes or new developments. It would also be possible for hospitals and other service providers to invite comments and suggestions by providing computer terminals in outpatient clinics, GP surgeries and other places where service users are likely to congregate.

Experiments in public involvement using electronic media, however, have tended to focus on one-off consultations or debates. Buckinghamshire Health Authority, for example, commissioned a citizens' jury and held a simultaneous discussion on a website to debate the issue of whether or not the Authority should fund treatment from osteopaths and chiropractors for people with back pain (Buckinghamshire Health Authority 1997). Visitors to the site were given informa-tion from the jury and were asked to register and vote on the jury's recommen-dations. The first electronic citizens' jury was run from the Science Museum in London. Several electronic public debates have also been run by UK Citizens Online (IPPR 1998).

The focus has been on high-profile, one-off ventures, such as citizens' juries, rather than ongoing participation and dialogue. Such events demand intensive participation over a period of days and exclude people whose energies are limited through illness or who may be subject to unpredictable and changing conditions which preclude them from committing themselves in advance.

Collective organisation

Through discussion groups, chat lines and other interactive sites, the new tech-nology enables the rapid formation of virtual communities of common interest or concern. In particular, people isolated by geographical distance, illness, mobility or communication difficulties can make contact with others in similar situations and with similar experiences with whom they would not normally meet. Such electronic forums enable people, who would otherwise be excluded, not only to extend their range of social contacts and exchange information but also to identify and discuss issues of common concern. Potentially, they provide a mechanism for the rapid co-ordination of collective action in relaying these concerns to relevant service providers or policy makers, both nationally and internationally.

They also provide the means for the rapid co-ordination of direct action. Although people who are seriously ill may not be able to take part in conventional forms of direct action such as demonstrations, electronic communication gives them the ability to network quickly and cheaply and provides the potential for direct action through, for example, the co-ordination of demands for particular treatments or approaches to care or the boycott of services or providers. Already, people with life-limiting diseases have used informal networks of electronic communication to influence the conduct of clinical trials. Participants in small open trials in one country communicate quickly through friends or relatives to other countries and pressure follows immediately for trials to begin or for new drugs or treatments to be released (Cardy 1993).

The disembodied body

Through the Internet and the development of increasingly sophisticated assistive technologies, people isolated by distance and impairment can establish a social life with a wide number of contacts across the world (McKee 1999; Wired Welfare? 1999). The new technologies enable people to communicate not only with others in similar situations and with similar conditions but also with others without the illness or impairment with whom they would not otherwise have been able to make contact. Through the Internet, individuals can contact other people without the fact of their illness or impairment becoming known to the other party. There are clearly many implications for people with existing or potential palliative care needs. To what extent, for example, do people actively seek to make contact with others with similar impairments or illness experiences and to what extent do they seek to conceal or choose not to reveal their impairment or illness? What are the factors likely to influence their behaviour? And what are the circumstances under which people seek different types of contact? In a recent article in *The Guardian*, a person with multiple sclerosis claimed that one advantage of the Internet is that nobody knows from what she types whether she is in a wheelchair or not: 'I am not prejudged by my appearance' (McKee 1999).

Communication via the Internet may avoid the issue of not wanting to meet others who may be in worse health than you are or not wanting others to see you when you are ill. The anonymity it affords circumvents the problem of having to confront people physically and, in so doing, perhaps confront, the possibility of one's own mortality, deterioration and decline. People may use the Internet to communicate with people whom, otherwise, they may have been reluctant to contact.

Electronic communication may make it possible for people to broach topics of discussion which they would find difficult to raise in face-to-face interaction. It may, for example, be easier to discuss, in the relatively anonymous and disembodied context of the Internet, those all too material bodily subjects which are avoided in other contexts. In other words, communication via the disembodied context of the Internet may facilitate discussions of bodily issues which are inhibited in interactions where people are forced to confront the realities of each other's bodies.

Some cautions and challenges

The new technologies have the potential to enable, to liberate and to broaden the social networks of people whose social horizons may be very limited. They also have the potential to isolate. Precisely because electronic communication avoids the necessity of physical interaction and allows anonymity, the quality of communication is likely to be very different from that in more conventional contexts. The dynamics of interactions are different without non-verbal interchanges and cues. Social relationships and ties made via the Internet are likely to be different in quality from those that have a physical dimension. Where electronic communication comes to supplant face-to-face physical contacts, people whose abilities to engage in the latter are limited may find themselves feeling even more isolated.

The experience of a national telephone helpline on incontinence issues (Shearer 1991) may serve as a salutary parallel in pointing up the potential benefits and dangers of anonymous communication. Although the helpline promoted the discussion of intimate topics not normally possible in other contexts and enabled sufferers to make contact with each other, the very anonymity which facilitated discussion also opened the door to abuse by sexually offensive callers (Helen White, Helpline Organiser, Newcastle, personal communication). The experience of the incontinence helpline signals a clear danger for people with life-limiting illnesses seeking to use the Internet for similar purposes. Their very vulnerability exposes them to potential exploitation on a number of fronts. It may be all too easy to manipulate people who have reached a stage where conventional medicine seems to have little or nothing left to offer. In such situations, people may become victims of scaremongering or have their hopes raised by peddlers of inadequately researched new treatments or 'cures'. On a more benign but potentially equally dangerous level, the possibility of receiving unintentionally inaccurate, misleading or inappropriate information or 'bad advice' may pose a serious threat to people's safety. A brief search can throw up hundreds of health information sources but, although there may be some attempt at internal policing, it is difficult to ensure that the information is accurate and appropriate (Buck 1996). A further danger is that people will discover distressing information about their illnesses without the safety net of a supportive environment. Where people deliberately seek out the information, they may have been able to prepare themselves mentally for the possibility of 'bad news'; where they come across it accidentally, the impact may be devastating.

Some service providers have been quick to seize on the opportunities presented by the new technologies to make changes to the way in which they provide services. An example in the field of palliative care is the National Cancer Institute of Milan's experiment to introduce a computerised, interactive videotelephone system that allows images to be transmitted in real time from the patient's home to the physician at the hospital (De Conno and Martini 1997). But, although service providers have been able to offer users an enhanced service or to extend their services to a wider range of people, they have also been quick to realise the potential for efficiency savings in expenditure on staff time visiting patients (*ibid.*). It has now become possible for much advice and treatment to be provided telematically without those providing the service having to come into face-to-face contact with the recipients of the service. Where the costs of innovation are experienced in terms of reduced human contact, patients may end up the ultimate losers.

Paradoxically, service providers and planners may use the new technologies to further insulate themselves from service users by controlling the flow of information both to and from users. Disembodied comments read on a computer screen may be easier to discount or ignore than the same comments made in face-to-face interaction. Although the channels of communication are potentially wider and more numerous and immediate, they are dependent on those who service them to keep them open and active. Where electronic telecommunications come to supplant rather than supplement more conventional forms of communication, there is a danger that users may find themselves more disempowered than empowered.

As of 1999, only about 10 per cent of the British population had access to the Internet, only a very small minority of whom will be the people who are the subjects of this study. Although the numbers are likely to grow rapidly in the future, full coverage in the short to medium term is an unlikely prospect. Moreover, the technology to access and construct sites on the web is becoming increasingly complex. Although a growing number of consumers may have access to the Internet through low-cost terminals, they may find themselves increasingly restricted not only by the types of programmes and hardware needed to take advantage of new developments but by the level of training required to implement them.

Conclusions

These new technologies have not been used widely in developing new approaches to user involvement and their value in this respect has yet to be fully tested. In any case, users themselves may have other preoccupying concerns at this stage of their lives and may not see involvement in service planning and delivery as a major issue. Self-help groups, certainly, have tended to focus on other areas of concern. This leads us to the broader question of whether it is, indeed, ethical to ask people who have little time left to them to contribute to discussions about services which have an uncertain outcome, where no guarantee can be given that their views will be taken into account, and where any improvement likely to result will be unlikely to occur within their remaining lifetimes. The most important question, perhaps, is whether or not user involvement in this area is a cause worth pursuing, given that service users themselves have not identified it as an issue.

It could be argued that what people who are isolated through frailty or illness may have valued most from the Fife project, for example, was not so much the opportunity to contribute as the opportunity to get out of their homes and to meet other people. Many of the 'Talk Back' participants agreed to take part because they wanted the company (Age Concern 2000). However, there is no doubt that participants valued having a say and feeling that their views and experiences of services mattered. The Fife panel members were generally highly positive about their experience:

> that's been one of the best things that's ever happened to me, is getting to go there so that I could voice my opinion on things and say to them what I think. I feel, you feel you are getting somewhere by doing that and being able to do it, whereas before I couldn't.
>
> (Quoted in Barnes and Walker 1996: 388)

For individuals themselves, empowerment is more than simply giving people the opportunity for choice. As has been argued, the necessity to make a choice in situations of anxiety and uncertainty can be stressful and disempowering . There is no easy definition of empowerment: what may be experienced as empowering by one person may be disempowering to another. Giving people information may help them to plan and make choices but, for some, the costs may outweigh the benefits – where the giving of information destroys hope, for example. We need to be alert to the potential dangers of the promotion of 'open awareness' as a dogmatic policy or to seeing the giving of information as a simple transfer of responsibilities for difficult and complex decisions. Information *per se* is not a route to empowerment. Individuals will differ both in their ability to assimilate and act on the information they are given and their in desire to take control.

Similarly, we need to beware of an over-enthusiastic espousal of user involvement as a policy imperative. People in receipt of services may feel an obligation to participate. Where reliance on services and those who provide care is very great, the sense of obligation may be correspondingly great and people may feel even more uncomfortable refusing. Empowerment includes allowing people to choose not to participate, both in decisions about their own treatment and care and in matters of wider service planning and delivery.

However, people who are very sick or dying are amongst the most vulnerable and most likely to be excluded from consultations. It is not enough simply to assume that they are too sick or to point to the obstacles that stand in the way as a reason for exclusion. In what follows, we attempt to explore both the practical and emotional barriers to involvement both in terms of individual care and, at a strategic level, in service planning and delivery and wider policy debate.

Giving people the opportunity to have a say is not just about making services more sensitive to people's needs and wishes but about giving them the opportunity to contribute to the future, giving them a sense of purpose and meaning to their lives at a time when purpose and meaning may seem to be fading, and the dignity and self-respect of knowing that their views are valued. As a participant in the Wakefield 'Talk Back' project commented: 'It doesn't say that because my body is failing that my brain is too' (Willis 1999: 32).

Yet the opportunity to become more involved may be one that many may not wish to take up. There is a danger that efforts to increase user involvement may be experienced by some people as oppressive. An expectation that people will become actively involved in discussions about service planning and delivery may be experienced as coercive in the same way as the ethos of consumerism in its requirement for people to make active choices about their care.

4 Multiple sclerosis

'We all live in hope'

Consistent with our overall remit we want to explore the nature of individual and collective involvement in service provision for people with MS. But, as we have argued, this has to be put into the context of what policy makers understand and intend vis-à-vis user involvement. It also has to be located in the context of the wishes of the person with MS and the wishes of their carers. In what follows we combine a critical review of literature with the insights gained from interviews with people living with MS, with carers, with specialist doctors and with bereaved relatives. Our intention is to illuminate those aspects of the experience of living with MS, or caring for someone with MS, that informs a user involvement agenda.

Such an agenda was not, usually, an articulated one on the part of the people we interviewed. Rather it featured as a component, sometimes a sub-text, of the everyday experience of living with MS. Much more prevalent than a specific orientation towards user involvement were discussions of how future oriented a person was, how much they felt able to meet and share with others outside the immediate family and friends, and how supported or disempowered they felt by their contact with professionals. In effect we will argue that these three areas set the context for moving forward with user involvement – a future orientation, ease socially and positive experiences around diagnosis and treatment are necessary, if not entirely sufficient, features in generating involved service users.

As we encouraged people to talk their stories ranged over many of the areas reported in existing qualitative research on MS and on other chronic illnesses. As such what follows both illustrates, and critiques, the accumulated observations of others. In total six people with MS were interviewed, as were two carers, two bereaved carers and four specialist workers. Of the people with MS, four were women and two were men and the overall age range was from early 30s to mid 70s.

Robinson *et al.* (1996) note that the people with MS they involved in their study exhibited a sense of not being sure what happened to all the information they gave to others. Further, some people with MS can experience difficulty in communicating and most will be living lives that have complex timetables and multiple demands. Consequently it seems important not to seek to duplicate insights already reported elsewhere. The relationship between researcher and researched is a complex area. Both the motives for seeking information and for giving it are multifaceted. Fallowfield *et al.* (1987) reported that, in carrying out a psychological study of people with breast cancer, respondents found the study itself a helpful extension to their treatment. But the research interview is not overtly a therapeutic encounter and one must be aware that any discussion veering towards this is likely to be outside the professional expertise of most information gatherers (see Clark and Haldane 1990). The complex reasoning concerning why information is sought and given is explored in some detail in Small (1998).

We begin by examining the way user views have been sought so far. Surveys have only recently arrived while personal accounts, either elicited as part of research using qualitative methodologies or presented in autobiographical work, have a slightly longer history. We then consider the possible areas of tension between user and professional views. We go on to look at the extent and the nature of MS, considering in some detail diagnosis and living with the uncertainty of progression. Our interview narratives present a group of people who are fraught with anxieties, dissatisfaction and tentative constructions of meaning, as complex ways of 'knowing' and 'being' take shape. But the narratives also include energetic assertions of personal integrity and social confidence. We see how complex needs call into place multiagency responses. This in itself is problematic when one considers user involvement – where do you direct your attention and whose procedures and language do you learn if you have health, social services and voluntary sector help? We conclude with thoughts about how people have sought to have their voices heard, both as individuals and collectively.

Seeking the views of people with MS

Robinson and colleagues at Brunel University (Robinson *et al.* 1996) point out that seeking the views of people with MS themselves is a relatively recent development in the management of the disease. While there is one study from 1987 (Radford and Trew), almost all the questionnaire studies that have been carried out have been done in the 1990s. This is similar to the situation arising in many health and social care contexts and has to be understood in this wider context.

While there has been this recent discovery of an imperative to consult, or to give the appearance of consulting, there is a longer tradition of first person accounts describing the impact of the diagnosis and subsequent development of MS. Some of these accounts are found in works written by people with MS. Some are writers who use the words of people with MS they have interviewed. Burnfield's book, *Multiple Sclerosis: A Personal Exploration* was first published in 1985 and has been through eight reprints. Graham's book, advocating self-help, was first published in 1981 and has been reprinted four times. She writes in the preface to the second edition:

> I was diagnosed with MS 18 years ago, and like any young person newly diagnosed I was fearful of the future … My wish is that this book will satisfy a sorely felt need, particularly that of the newly diagnosed people all over the world. If doctors are failing to answer this need, then we must do it for ourselves
> (Graham 1982: 13–17)

From Canada, Louise Giroux (1995) has written about her father's and her own MS and Eva Marsh in her autobiographical book (Marsh 1996) engages with the professional literature as she seeks to chronicle her life with MS. She describes a desire to wear 'black patent-leather high heel shoes' as a spur to make herself work harder than ever to overcome (her) 'clumsiness' once more.

We quoted Frank in our introduction as he identified the phenomenon that 'The ill person who turns illness into stories transforms fate into experience' (Frank 1995: xi). These books do that but they also are books that represent individuals seeking to fill a vacuum of unmet need, they are people talking to others like themselves. They are also attempts at engaging in a remedial dialogue with professionals – seeking to educate those who have been ill-prepared to communicate with their patients or to appreciate the real challenges of living with MS. Together, such works of autobiography, or testimony, can be seen as part of a collective narrative for people with MS. They are at one and the same time about making sense of what is being experienced and looking out at the world to see what can be done.

Many writers have looked at the meaning and experience of disability in general and MS in particular: Blaxter (1976), Campling (1981) Robinson (1988b), Forsythe (1979, 1988), Thorne (1993) and Perry (1994) offer examples. Indeed Robinson and his colleagues at Brunel University have assembled, and report on, a wealth of data including many personal accounts lodged in their MS archive.

While these accounts are valuable we must note the problems in making one's voice heard that can come from both some of the manifestations of the illness itself and from the lack of a social infrastructure that allows people with MS to access others. Between 5 and 10 per cent of people with MS will have speech problems. They may also have vision, movement and cognitive difficulties. Some will present with psychiatric symptoms and some with dementia: these may or may not be causally linked to their MS. Most will experience fatigue. A recent survey of people with MS found problems in travel to be the most commonly reported impact (Layward *et al.* 1998). With the possible exception of the last problem, these features of MS are best understood as impairments and should provoke imaginative responses in terms of accessing views and encouraging involvement. They can, though, be seen as disabilities when impairment encounters contemporary social organisation that does not take the steps necessary to facilitate inclusion (Oliver 1990: 11).

The nature and extent of multiple sclerosis[1]

Multiple sclerosis (MS) is the UK's most common neurological condition, affecting directly about 85,000 people. It has been recognised for the past century and a half, having previously been known as disseminated sclerosis. Although considerable research has been undertaken, the exact cause remains unknown.

The most common age for diagnosis is the late twenties to mid-thirties. Onset is rare before the age of twelve and after fifty. Women are disproportionately affected with a ratio between the sexes of three to two. It appears to be a condition most prevalent in temperate climates and is rare in tropical countries.

MS is a chronic condition of the central nervous system, the brain and the spinal cord. The nerves that run from the brain via the spinal column to every part of the body are surrounded by a myelin sheath. It is this that is attacked and becomes inflamed. This inflammation can die down leaving no permanent damage. If the scarring process continues the myelin sheath is destroyed at the point of the attack leaving fibrous scar tissue known as plaques or sclerosis. This process is usually known as demyelination and, as scarring usually occurs in more than one place in the brain and/or spinal cord, the condition is known as multiple sclerosis.

Diagnosis

The process of diagnosis

As will become clear in our subsequent description of people's experience of living with MS, a characteristic feature is that of uncertainty. That uncertainty begins with, and can be characterised by, the process of diagnosis. Uncertainty is also evident in the vagaries of progression.

There is no 100-per-cent conclusive diagnostic test for MS. Indeed, the process of diagnosis is effectively designed to eliminate other potential causes of symptoms. Once all else has been eliminated, what remains must be MS.

Demyelination can affect the motor and sensory nerves effecting movement, touch and sensation. But the symptoms experienced can vary greatly and it is not possible to identify a set pattern. Many of the symptoms experienced – fatigue, changes in sensation, memory and concentration for example – would be easily attributed to other conditions. Some of the more common symptoms include: blurring of vision, double vision; weakness or clumsiness of a limb, altered feelings in arms and legs such as tingling or numbness; giddiness or lack of balance and the need to urinate urgently and/or frequently. Taking a medical history may help locate these symptoms as manifestations of MS. A neurological examination can establish if there are abnormalities in nerve pathways but cannot say what is causing these. Tests of visual and auditory reactions to stimuli, lumbar punctures, x-ray examinations of the spinal cord (Myelogram) and the use of magnetic resonance imaging scanners are all potential diagnostic aids.

The experience of diagnosis

Peoples' experience of the diagnosis process is often negative. As such, at the outset, one can argue a particular perception of the relationship they have with professionals is set in train.

> I had problems with my left hand, I thought I had hurt it. The doctor said it might be that. In the next few weeks I had problems with my legs, my ankle

started to turn over. It wasn't too noticeable at first because my daughter was in a pushchair and so you are leaning against something. My doctor sent me to a neurologist within four or five weeks and I had a lumbar puncture. I never thought about MS. I did know about MS because in the past I had known a couple of people who had it but they were both in wheelchairs and I didn't know the symptoms leading up to it. I just saw them, how they were at that time. How I found out, I was in a ward with people with similar symptoms, the woman opposite I knew had MS. A nurse came to interview her and as she talked about her symptoms: the nurse saw me looking, abruptly stopped and went out of the room and I think it was at moment that I thought 'That's what I've got'. I asked the doctor, he wouldn't commit himself and said many neurological illnesses had similar symptoms.

(Mrs A, aged 48, diagnosed in 1981)

Another person, talking of a time almost ten years later, describes a similar experience:

I'd been ill a long time, long time, before I knew what had happened. The way I found out, the way I was told was done very badly. The first time I had an attack was in 1973, it paralysed me. I was taken to hospital and left like that for seventeen weeks then it came back as suddenly as it went, all my feelings came back, just like that, as quick as it went. Then it happened five years later, it happened the same, paralysed me. They had to do everything for me. It didn't last as long this time. In 1983 again something went in my thumb. I couldn't go to the doctors with a pain in my thumb, I felt stupid. I went to the chemist and then to casualty. The chemist said I might have broken something. I walked in (to casualty) and then went out in a wheelchair. The next day I couldn't move my legs. I was under a broken bone specialist, then a rheumatologist. I was three to four months in hospital, home at weekends. ... After that it was alright. [In 1988] I was rushed to hospital again, same symptoms. I've never walked again. It was very difficult. No one would say what anything was. They didn't know, they said. They just let me get on with it myself. I had no treatment, nothing. They said it was arthritis – really – I was being treated for that. Then my sister, she's a nurse ..., said you aren't getting any better, she said I don't think its arthritis. ... I had been to various specialists. One said to me, I would have to keep off the drink. The nurse was a bit disgusted: 'He should not have said that to you'. More and more tests, a lumbar puncture. They wanted me to see a psychiatrist, I said no. They still think you are imagining all this. Eventually I went back and said 'I want to be told.' He muttered on, 'it's your nerves'. 'You're not telling me I'm imagining this are you?' 'No but something in the brain is not connecting to the nerve ends in part of your body.' And I thought that's to do with MS. And he still didn't, wouldn't say it. Sometime I think that they think if they just turn round and tell you these things that something is going to drastically go wrong. That you are going to do something.

In fact when she was told, some time later, she describes her reaction to the news like this:

> It upset me a little. But knowing what it was I could deal with it, accept it. It was a relief, I knew exactly what I had to deal with. There was a name behind it. In the end I had begun to believe I was going mental, perhaps I was imagining it all.
>
> (Mrs B, age 49, diagnosed, 1990)

These narratives of diagnosis are very important for people. They help define both their own illness identity and the relationship they have with their potential caregivers. While they do reflect some of the real difficulties of a diagnostic process that is based on the elimination of possible alternative explanations, they also appear to reflect a more widespread phenomenon: the shortcomings of the doctor in giving 'bad news'. The result for the patient is, possibly, years of uncertainty and self-doubt – in Mrs B's case seventeen years.

Uncertain progression

Once diagnosed, uncertainty remains a key feature of one of the two patterns MS appears to take. Some people experience relapse and remissions. During a relapse new symptoms may occur or old symptoms reappear. These relapses can be relatively slight or quite severe, they may last from between a few days to many months. It does not seem possible in advance to anticipate their course. Often they occur for no apparent reason, but sometimes they can be triggered by infection, trauma or stress. Further, there may be temporary exacerbations when the appearance of an old symptom occurs for a short period, sometimes for as little as a few minutes, sometimes for as long as a few days. Remissions, marked by the disappearance of symptoms, can last for weeks, months or years.

Some people who start with relapsing-remitting MS have fewer periods with reduced symptoms over time. They are then deemed to have 'secondary progressive' MS. Others will have a first period of symptoms that may be followed by decades without any 'worse' periods. This form of MS is sometimes called 'benign' MS.

> My kneecap kept giving way. They said it was oesteoarthritis and I had half of it removed and that was when I had to have the wheelchair. That's when I found I had MS. I've had no other problems. Just the legs. It's gone from the waist down. If you could give me a new pair of legs I think I would be all right. I had it late in life. I'm now 74 so I got it at 62. He [the doctor] said 'You will be in a wheelchair for the rest of your life'.
>
> (Mrs C, age 74, diagnosed 1985)

The second dominant pattern following diagnosis is termed 'progressive' MS. There are no periods of remission, rather there is a developing number of symptoms over the years.

There has been a gradual deterioration over the years, since 1988. First a stick, then a wheelchair for long distances, then almost all the time. I stopped work in 1992.

(Mr Y, age 59, diagnosed 1988)

There has been a steady progression, the right leg first. I went from a stick to a Zimmer frame to a chair for even short distances. Now it's also total, no legs, no arms, no feet, a catheter.

(Mrs D, age 53, diagnosed 1979)

Peter Cardy, Chief Executive of the MS Society, has identified a belief that MS isn't fatal as being part of the folklore of MS. He points out that Office of Population Censuses and Surveys (OPCS) figures for the UK indicate about 700 deaths a year in which MS is identified as the first cause. He also reminds us that everyone with MS will die with it if not from it (MS: Frontiers in Science and Patient Care and Disease Management Conference, 5–6 May 1998, Birmingham). Although there is no evidence that MS itself significantly reduces the life expectancy of all those affected, it can lead to severe levels of disability and, in such a situation, susceptibility to other illnesses. These, in turn, might be life threatening. The accumulation of other illnesses usually occurs in old age and causal links with MS are difficult to identify. Exploring a link between MS and premature mortality is an important area needing further scrutiny. However, people with MS do not, in the main, consider themselves to be terminally ill.

Treatments

It is not known what triggers the process of scarring. Subsequent treatments are designed to dampen down inflammation; steroids are the most commonly used medication for this. Specific medications can be prescribed to help manage individual symptoms: muscle relaxants to ease cramps or spasms, analgesics to respond to pain. Supportive therapies such as physiotherapy can be important. These treatments are essentially palliative.

The UK has seen a considerable expansion of specialist palliative care in the last twenty years. This has been accompanied by sustained attempts to argue that palliative care is neither just for people with terminal illness nor, more specifically, for people with cancer. But there are still barriers to winning acceptability for modern approaches to palliation and the use of specialist resources for people with MS. The relative lack of progress may be because of the configuration of specialist resources whose rhetoric of inclusion is not matched by their practice. They still are organised around the assumption that they will be responding to the needs of people with cancer. In part it may be a problem properly located with primary care because they do not appropriately refer to specialist palliative care. But it may also be reluctance on the part of people with MS to seek out, or accept, a care approach they may still equate with the dying.

There are drugs which are not curative in the sense that all existing damage to the central nervous system is repaired, and no further symptoms appear, but which do offer the possibility for making a considerable impact on relapse or progression of the disease. The presence of these sorts of drugs contributes to a sense of alternating hope and disappointment characteristic of many people's experience of MS. Most notable of these drugs, in recent years, has been beta interferon but others, Co-polymer-1 for example, come onto the scene at various times. These drugs are invariably of potential benefit to only a part of the MS population. For people with MS, the realisation that they have the 'wrong type' of MS, or that their stage of progression makes them unsuitable for the new drug treatment being optimistically talked about, is a common occurrence. There is also research both to seek a cure and to repair existing damage to myelin. The latter strand of research is known as remyelination.

Many of our interviewees had comments to make about the potential of drugs, and their availability.

After an 'attack' of symptoms Mrs A was prescribed steroids:

It was as if someone had waved a magic wand.

But as time went on,

Steroids were taking longer to have an impact. There were always side effects, a moon face, confusion, hot flushes, but it was worth it.

Mrs A had been going to the local Therapy Centre for eighteen months:

I can't get physiotherapy through the health service in (this town), not many people with MS can. I have physiotherapy (at the Therapy Centre) subsidised so that I only have to pay £2 for a half-hour session. And I have reflexology, which I find really helpful, £6 for an hour.

Talking of beta interferon Mrs B says:

I wouldn't have the chance of having this new drug anyway. They just take so many, don't they. Well I think that is wrong. If there is a new drug out and it is so expensive it shouldn't be that some can have it and some can't. Everyone should have it. Everyone should be given that choice. If it's that expensive, they shouldn't have gone for it anyway.

Beta interferon is not going to be of any help (to us) and others are not on the market yet. We all live in hope … We haven't met anyone who has had it (beta interferon) yet.

(Mr D)

The debate about beta interferon can be seen as illustrative of a more generally changing relationship between consumers, prescribers and producers of drugs. The onset of the HIV epidemic saw some empowerment of people with HIV in the West vis-à-vis drug regimes and protocols (Edgar and Rothman 1991). We now see drug information disseminated over the Internet and the identification of need by potential users, unmediated by professionals. The discovery of a drug for impotence, Viagra, and then the rapid emergence of a demand for it are an example (Cameron 1998). A shift from professionally defined access to data to a more widespread access raises questions about where and how people get information and how they can make a judgement as to it's reliability.

While the Internet is central in the new dissemination of knowledge it offers more for people living with particular illnesses. It can provide an environment in which people can seek contacts and gain support. As such its potential is profound, and it has a special resonance for people whose illness impacts on their mobility or their speech or those for whom illness inhibits physical social contact because of fears of infection. We explore this area in more detail in our chapter on cystic fibrosis.

If uncertainty typifies the MS experience then it is not surprising that there are different stances towards the advisability of speculative treatments:

> I get quite a lot of information at the Therapy Centre. They have newspaper clippings or you hear something new about something someone else has tried. I think there is more of that at the Therapy Centre than at the MS Society because the Therapy Centre seems more geared up to trying anything and everything really whereas the MS Society like to have proof that something is working before they would recommend it. That has always been the case, even when it was ARMS. They seemed to 'go for it' rather than the MS Society, which is more cautious and won't ever commit themselves.
>
> (Mrs A)

Some potential treatments achieve a public prominence. The therapeutic use of cannabis provides a controversial example. Inducing a general feeling of well-being, the most commonly reported experience of cannabis use, can be of value to anyone living with a chronic form of disability. That the benefit of such an effect can be dissipated by an increased drowsiness, unsteadiness and problem with concentration is also widely recognised. More overtly therapeutic effects, a positive impact on spasticity reported in US studies and more serious problems such as hallucinations and confusion, are also debated. The problem is not only the absence of conclusive studies but also the legal status of cannabis. A person with MS can evaluate the evidence and opinion and come to an informed choice but their options to act on that choice are inhibited because of the illegality of the drug.

The history of responses to MS includes stories of treatments some report as beneficial but where the exact mechanism that achieves that benefit is not known. In this sense MS is like many other conditions. Hyperbaric oxygen and steroids are two examples. Hyperbaric oxygen first became popular in the 1970s after encouraging reports from the USA. Early hopes were not sustained by information from subsequent clinical trials. However, some people reported positive effects. Most people with MS will have steroids prescribed for them at some stage. Again it is not clear how they work although it can be hypothesised that they probably act by partly suppressing the immune system or by reducing fluid accumulation around the site of nerve damage.

End-of-life care

As we introduced above, the need for specifically oriented end-of-life care for people with MS is also debated. However for some people such a need is clear. Here, as in other areas of MS care, there are problems in knowledge of, and access to, the most appropriate services. We illustrate these areas by drawing on the recollections of a woman who had cared for her husband (Mr W) from his diagnosis at age 29 to his death five years later in 1994.

> W's MS was very extreme, we didn't know anyone who was as bad as him, so we felt isolated. We never spoke about dying of MS at a young age. We couldn't really talk about it even when he was very ill, although I would have liked to. At the end he was on lots of morphine and didn't seem to know what was happening. I wished we could have talked more about it, dying, we could have if he had let us. Neither of us knew there was a possibility he might die very soon. I was a bit naive. I never believed he would die of MS so soon. People with medical knowledge knew. A couple of the doctors said, 'Have you never heard that MS can be a terminal illness?' I said 'No,' I had thought it was a chronic illness.

Mrs W's mother, Mrs V, had heard about hospice care in a radio programme and together they tried to get care for W at their local hospice.

> Their GP had been very supportive and never hesitated to visit at home but he did say that the hospice would not take W. He didn't want to refer him because he did not want to see us rebuffed. But the Twilight Nurses visited and encouraged us.

Mrs W added:

> The District Nurse said you must push. She said 'They don't usually take MS, they can't tell how long they will linger'… But a consultant [from the hospice] visited and then the home care team to administer the syringe driver and other things.

W died in the hospice. Mrs W now helps as a fundraiser for the hospice. Mrs V comments:

> I can see that it can't take everyone on board. [But I believe] Anybody who is dying should have the facility of hospice if they need it.

In its recent history, the modern hospice movement has emphasised holistic approaches and care by multidisciplinary teams. We have seen above, in the account of the illness and subsequent death of Mr W, how hospice services can help both the person with MS and his or her family. However, most hospices do not admit people with MS as inpatients. In a 1996 survey only 28 per cent reporting that they did admit (Eve and Smith 1996). In 1993 there were 235 hospice inpatient admissions for people with MS; this represents slightly less than 0.05 per cent of total hospice admissions. Reasons for the relatively small numbers are more difficult to ascertain. It might be that this reflects the choice of potential users and carers – they prefer to stay with their existing service providers rather than move to a specialist facility – or they may find their needs for home care are better met elsewhere. It might be because of an absence of appropriate information, people with MS not knowing what sort of contribution hospices could make to areas like control of symptoms, respite care or terminal care. It might be that GPs equate palliative care with cancer and do not consider it an option for people with MS. It may also be that a sense of the unpredictability of progression in MS means both an uncertainty about referral and a concern by hospices that they may be taking on a commitment to care that will last for a considerable time. Much outpatient and home care associated with hospices is carried out by Macmillan Nurses whose remit is to focus, predominantly, on cancer care and, hence, there is an absence of specialist input of the sort they offer in home care also. There also appears to be little usage by people with MS of day care, home care, hospice at home and night-sitting services offered by hospices or specialist palliative care units (Field 1998b).

Uncertainty, unpredictability and action

Our intention here has not been to seek a detailed list of possible treatments but rather to underline the theme of uncertainty that is a dominant characteristic of the experience of living with MS. We suggest that this uncertainty generates the possibility of different paradigms of knowledge for the person to negotiate. Specifically, the scientific/evidence-based paradigm often says we don't know why this works or even if it does work. In such a situation a set of 'folk' beliefs develop. Some are based on what individuals make of the message of experts. Some beliefs are shaped by patterns of peer group experience. All are filtered through an individualised world view based on the idiosyncrasies of one's own experience.

In such a context helping the individual negotiate informed consent or meaningful involvement in, say, planning or evaluating services has to encounter the challenge that many different explanatory and evaluative constructs might exist at the same time. An example is provided by the comments in the Foreword of Judy Graham's book (1981). Dr Patrick Kingsley is critical of the orthodox clinical trial because of its propensity to underestimate improvement. It denies the validity of attributing improvement to intervention if only a small number of people report benefits. The clinical trial paradigm would attribute such improvements to chance. 'The tragedy of this approach is that all MS sufferers are different ... So how can groups be compared? Far better to find out what is causing *your* MS and apply it to yourself, never mind the next person' (Kingsley 1981: 12).

Kingsley's approach will generate a sympathetic response in many people who would argue that even if only a minority benefits from a treatment, in the absence of alternatives, then this treatment ought to be available. Essentially, this approach, critical of a prevalent utilitarianism in medicine, is concerned with needs and rights. One has to engage with intensity of need as well as level of incidence, and with individual utility as well as aggregate experience. Engaging in debates about 'due process' and 'scientific protocol' in conditions of incurable or terminal illness challenge all concerned. While the needs of science can well be understood there is this counter epistemology. People with AIDS argued that scientifically unproven drugs should be made available to those who wished to have them in circumstances of their informed choice. That is, the person who would take the drug (not the person who prescribes it) should have access to the arguments about their efficacy and risk and should decide accordingly. These debates came to the fore given a scenario (then) characterised by an average life expectancy with AIDS that was less than the usual length of time a clinical trial has to run (Edgar and Rothman 1991).

Seeking information

Information about developing treatments and research into curative interventions are widely disseminated by the Multiple Sclerosis Society, in collaboration with nine other relevant charities in the UK. There are also journal publications, for example the International Federation of Multiple Sclerosis Societies publishes *MS Management*. Information is also available on the Internet about work in progress as well as about newly available treatments. There are debates about the efficacy of existing interventions. There are, in addition, a number of guides to living with MS that offer an overview, for example Benz (1988), Sibley (1996), Schapiro (1994) and Povey *et al.* (1997). Other work concentrates on specific aspects of symptoms or impacts, e.g. Segal (1994), or of treatment, e.g. Loder (1996) and Thomas (1995). Fildes (1994) and Fitzgerald and Briscoe (1996) concentrate on diet while Cornell (1996) offers a *Complete Body Manual* including massage, exercise, alternative therapies and nutrition. Van Overstraten (1999) considers the patient's role in the improvement of care, and there are widely disseminated summaries of best practice guidelines in the management of MS (Barnes *et al.* 1999).

The range of treatments, knowledge of them and opinion as to their efficacy are ever changing. The potential exists for an informed patient group to possess up-to-date information that they can bring to any discussion about options with the professionals they encounter. Indeed, a developing scenario of access to reports of ongoing work, world wide, means that for those who pursue it much data and opinion will be known to them that may not be known to any generalist, a general practitioner for example, with whom they come into contact.

It is interesting to note how professional opinion about what to tell people with MS and their family and friends has changed. When the first edition of Matthews' *Multiple Sclerosis: The Facts* was published in 1978 the author expressed the fear that many of the facts of MS might prove to be unwelcome and disturbing to readers. Subsequent experience showed him that fear was unfounded and underlined the benefit many felt from being in possession of such information. By the third edition, in 1993, no such reservations are expressed.

The argument that medical care and treatment is best dealt with via sharing responsibility between patients and professional has a history as long as that of medicine itself. But the balance of that responsibility and the nature of power that underlines it has more often than not been unresolved. Some interesting metaphors emerge: Siegler and Osmond (1979) compared the doctor-patient relationship with that of the elephant and the elephant driver, the mahout.

> The elephant is a strong, powerful and useful creature but, if not managed properly, he can become dangerous for those very reasons. It is essential that the mahout make sure that the elephant does not roll over, or sit in the wrong places, and that a group of elephants are not accidentally stampeded!
> (Siegler and Osmond 1979, quoted in Burnfield 1989: 68)

(It is a quote that is apt whether or not one casts doctors or patients as the elephant!).

Burnfield believes that:

> patients must learn to manage their medical advisers if they are to get the best out of them and doctors need to understand that their job is to serve their patients. A crucial part of this is the way the doctor makes available expert knowledge, at every stage, and the way patients learn to give voice to their needs and expectations.
> (Burnfield 1989: 4)

The presence of information at various stages in a person's life with MS, the criteria for evaluating its usefulness and the welcome to be given to such information as well as its impact on relationships with caregivers are themes explored in various parts of this work. There is now an MS Society Information Sheet titled 'The case for telling the truth'. In a very few persuasive pages it reviews research data, offers a guide to effective communication and talks of the partnership that is at the heart of the care alliance in MS (Burnfield 1989).

But one cannot make a straightforward assumption that information will be generally welcome, let alone sought after. Some people are very keen to find out what they can:

> After his diagnosis, and up to near the end, we did talk about treatments and hopefully about finding a cure and an effective treatment, we grasped onto the hope of that.
> (Mrs W)

I wanted to find out as much as I could, books, asking people, the MS Society.
(Mr Y)

When I knew (I had MS) I found out lots about it. My doctor took me to the MS Society. I had already got in touch with the ARMS Association to find out what it was all about. Now I like to think I can help other people. (Mrs B)

I kept up to date with developments. Beta Interferon is not going to be of any help and other drugs are not on the market yet. We all live in hope. I went to a beta interferon conference in Birmingham last year. It will only benefit remitting/relapsing people and they don't know about side effects. But some people with MS don't really give a damn about side effects if they can get treatment for the MS.

(Husband of Mrs D)

Talking to Mr and Mrs D together allowed for some of the nuanced differences in the need for information, and in future orientation, of even the closest carer and cared for:

Mr D: I've always looked forward … the most important thing is anticipating what you need. People don't think ahead.
Mrs D: Well you don't want to. You don't want to think you will be that dependent on things. It's not a nice thing to have to think about. But when you have you are glad you did.

One can have a future orientation for others if not for oneself. We asked Mrs A if she looked ahead, planned for the future:

Not any more. I used to but now I don't. I haven't done that in a long time. Now I try things day by day. I don't think you can plan for the future, not now I'm at this stage of things. It's very hard work keeping going day by day at times. You can't plan for the future when you have got something like this because you don't know what the future holds for you. You can wish for the future. You can think about what your children will do in the future. You can plan that way. But as far as making plans yourself for the future, no you don't do that.

Attitudes towards systematically seeking information vary from individual to individual, some are not as keen as our interviewees above. Attitudes may also change as time passes:

I didn't find out much about MS. I don't think I wanted to know. People started telling me different things about MS. My Mother-in-law got lots of books from the library but I thought I just don't want to know. I will just take it as it comes. I just tried to forget about it.

(Mrs A)

Later on in her life with MS, Mrs A's approach had changed:

> I try to hear about new treatments, drugs, but its just getting access to the
> information. The *MS Matters* is every month. That's very good because it
> tells you different research. How far research … This thing I read in *MS
> Matters* last month about nasal sprays, that has some effect on T cells in the
> brain, that is quite interesting. And that gives you hope, you need hope and
> that's very encouraging to read information like that, even if it's years away
> at least it's a light at the end of the tunnel and is something to hope for and
> I think that is what you need. It would be nice if someone could come up
> with a miracle wouldn't it?

Meeting others

As well as different views about information both between individuals, between
people with MS and their carers and differences in the same person when newly
diagnosed as opposed to some years later, there are also different attitudes to the
benefits of meeting others with MS. In part this is to do with the management of
identity, that is how people reconcile their view of themselves and their new
status as a 'person with MS'. That identity and status is not fixed and it may be
that the person with MS has to negotiate many changes.

Inevitably our interviews reflect, in the main, a positive view about meeting
and discussing MS, after all our interviewees agreed to see us and their names
were obtained from a branch of the MS Society.

> I joined the MS Society as soon as I was diagnosed. We went to one meeting
> in (1988) but not again until 1995. [The reason for the gap was that] Everyone
> was worse than I was. It didn't distress us. At the time we thought that things
> were going to stay the same as they were, walking with a walking stick. We
> never envisaged it getting any worse. It wasn't that I minded seeing people in
> wheelchairs who were worse than me it was that I thought this wasn't going
> to happen to me. We felt we were there under false pretences. By 1995 when
> I went back I was in a wheelchair by then.
>
> (Mr Y)

> The problem with meetings (of the MS Society) is that older people in
> wheelchairs dominate it. I don't think meetings are the right place for them.
> You just have to put it behind you and go for it.
>
> (Mrs B)

Mrs W, talking of her husband, says:

> When (he) was well he didn't like seeing people who were worse than him.
> Then when he got worse he got worse quickly and was not able to meet, he

didn't get help really from others. He couldn't take part in anything. It was a huge effort at the end.

Mr and Mrs D considered meeting others:

Mr D: You have got to the stage now where you don't want to go to the Society because you are the worst. You have said that more than once.

Mrs D: I feel that I'm the worst now of all the ones that went when we first started that are still going. I'm the worst one that goes. Sometimes I don't want to go. When it comes to some of the things they do ...

Mr D: like eating, because you have to be fed now.

Mrs D: I think it's totally me. They don't care.

Mr D: I think a lot of people with MS tend to become insular, live in their own domains.

Complex needs and multi-agency services

As well as their encounters with doctors, people with MS may have complex physical needs that might best be responded to by other professionals. They may have emotional, social and practical, including financial, needs and they may have what we might call existential or spiritual needs. Of course, in this they are not necessarily different from the rest of the population. But we might hypothesise that, for some, diagnosis or progression in the disease might precipitate a number of these possible locations of need coming together in such a way that each compounds the other – losing a job because of physical incapacity generates financial needs, increases tension at home and so on. We will go on to look specifically at the relationship between stress and both progression and quality of life but here want to concentrate on what a constellation of needs means in terms of service provision and planning.

Medicine

Perhaps the best way to identify some of the challenges of the complex of needs and services is to focus on some areas that have, and do, provide problems for people with MS. There are fewer than 300 neurologists in the UK, a ratio of one per 300 MS patients. Although it is likely that all neurologists will have been involved in diagnosing and managing people with MS at some point in their careers, fewer than thirty would consider it their primary interest (Boggild 1998). A GP, on average, may have three or four MS patients in his or her practice but it is likely that these patients will have widely different needs. The opportunity to build up experience in the management of MS is, therefore, limited. One might argue that in group practices there is a case to be made for one partner specialising in MS (or neurological illness in general) so that sufficient experience and up-to-date knowledge will be available to that practice's patients. The specialisation/generalist debate in general practice goes beyond the group of patients we are

concerned with here. The reorganisation of general practice following the 1997
NHS white paper (Department of Health 1997a) offers an opportunity for specialism within the new organisational structure of Primary Care Groups and Trusts.

The experience of contact with neurologists and with GPs featured in many of
our interviews. Neurologists are principally encountered at diagnosis and we have
presented some of the problems associated with this above. GPs can play a pivotal
role in ongoing care:

> The GP was superb. If you get a GP who knows about it it's brilliant. She was
> the GP MS Advisor for the area. She's retired now. The new one is fine but
> she says we know more about MS than her.
>
> (Mr Y)

> The GP is very good. He has kept abreast of any developments and is always
> interested if we hear of anything, in the way of drugs or anything. He will
> check up and come back to report to us. If he doesn't know he tries to find out.
>
> (Mrs D)

But not all GPs get such a vote of confidence:

> There is no backup from your GP. When my GP told me I had MS he just
> said 'there's no cure for MS, don't go sort of chasing rainbows, don't go looking
> for cures and spending a lot of money on these so-called cures because there
> is no cure'. So just go away basically and forget you have got it. Which is
> what I tried to do. Which you can do when you are symptom free. But it gets
> harder. But there is no backup from the medical profession. I think the thing
> is with doctors, I think they are embarrassed because there is nothing they
> can do. Because they are so used to having people come to them who they
> can make well, you know, give them a tablet to make them better. Then you
> go, and they feel embarrassed and inadequate and they don't quite know how
> to handle it. I don't know what they expect of us really, because I don't
> expect them to cure. I know they can't cure me. I know they can only go as
> far as medical science will let them go so I don't expect them to cure me. But
> it would be nice if they understood that you need them there to listen to you
> and say this could happen or there is such and such in the offing. Just to give
> you a little bit of hope. But they don't.
>
> (Mrs A)

Mrs A went on to talk of one specific encounter with a GP. At the time she was
still able to walk and she asked him what she could expect to happen:

> I'll never forget what he said to me. It was absolutely devastating at the time.
> He said, 'Well, what are you asking me? If you are asking me when you are
> going to be a cripple well I can't tell you.' Those were his exact words. I
> didn't hear anything else he said, all I heard was the word 'cripple' and I
> haven't been back to see him since.

Given the thinly distributed neurologists and the variation in the level of GP knowledge it is not surprising that many MS patients describe how they fall between hospital and community and primary care services. Thompson and colleagues (1997) welcome shifts of health care resources towards community care and see this as one way of tackling the need for more collaboration and joint planning as well as a more timely response from services, particularly in the early stages after diagnosis. In general, shifts towards a primary care-led NHS (the central idea of the 1997 NHS white paper) increase the possibility for the co-ordinating role of a GP being central (Hansell 1995). But not all GPs appear able or willing to take on such a role.

Ways of bridging gaps between services

There have been innovative attempts to offer services that bridge organisational divides. These attempts include services developing from Neurology and Neurorehabilitation Centres. The Walton MS Centre in Liverpool provides one example. Here patient care is co-ordinated by two MS nurse specialists collaborating with two neurologists with a special interest in MS, and another twelve neurologists working from the centre (Boggild 1998). In the Neurorehabilitation Unit at London's National Hospital for Neurology and Neurosurgery a programme has been devised, and put into place, which includes the use of Integrated Care Pathways. This is an approach developed with the aim of promoting patient-centred care (Layton 1993) and can enhance a sense of multidisciplinary collaboration as well as identifying clear plans and highlighting deviations from them. It is, then, both a route that can facilitate patient involvement and an audit tool to see how far that involvement, and the contribution of the staff team, has had the desired impact. Each new admission is allocated to a key worker who co-ordinates discussion with the patient and team about objectives, both short- and long-term. The extent to which these objectives are met is scrutinised regularly and deviations from the plan are examined. Thus objectives are set at this organisational level. This is a secondary end point, in effect, in that it relates to service delivery and not health status. But health status is also closely monitored and correlation sought between service delivery and appropriate primary end points like addressing fatigue or cognitive functioning (Rossiter and Thompson 1995).

In Staffordshire the welfare officer of the Tamworth and Lichfield Branch of the MS Society, Margaret White, has been successful in setting up links between social services and health services such that those newly diagnosed will get better support. She reports horror stories she has heard from those newly diagnosed who said they were told, 'You've got MS, now go home and forget about it,' or, 'You'll just have to live with it.' In her experience, people leave hospital 'uninformed and frightened, with 101 questions running through their mind. When they finally stumble across the MS Society, many say "If only someone had told me earlier."' The Staffordshire project places a person in the hospital where diagnosis is given to give the help a newly diagnosed person needs (*MS Matters* 1998).

There has been some input by the MS Society into auditing services. Rivermead Hospice and the MS Society have collaborated in developing an audit of services for neurological illness for parts of Oxfordshire, for example. There are also User/Carer Forums and panels across health and social services. Such developments appear to be consistent with the 1997 NHS white paper and its general commitment to more collaboration between health, social services and voluntary sector organisations. But, in practice, attempts at multidisciplinary working are not widespread and in many cases examples of joint working are often not really multidisciplinary – they often pull together doctors and nurses, but not others.

Nursing

Support teams of health care professionals exist for a number of chronic illnesses, for example diabetes. But most people with MS do not have access to this type of service. Nor do most hospitals offer a link liaison nurse or therapist to whom patients can self-refer during a relapse. In these circumstances, it is the community nurse who not only plays a major part in meeting needs but also organises access to other services. A community nurse is likely to sit at the centre of a web of services including GPs, physiotherapists, occupational therapists and social workers. Planning in advance presents difficulties for nurses, as for other professionals, in that the pattern of contact with a person with MS is likely to feature lengthy periods in which there is little or no need for help. Then, when someone experiences a relapse, needs can be considerable over a relatively short period of time.

There has been some shift in the way nursing addresses MS. A recent summary in *Nursing Times* sums up the change and the current position:

> Although multiple sclerosis has been thought of in the past as a 'no hope' illness, there is now much that can be done in terms of symptom management. Moreover, new treatments are beginning to offer some hope for disease management. Nurses can be advocates for these patients, providing them with up-to-date information as well as enabling them to gain access to the relevant services. But teamwork is essential if continuity is to be maintained across the disciplines. Referring on and liasing with other multidisciplinary team members are as important as skilled nursing intervention.
>
> (*Nursing Times*, 12 March 1997: 62)

This shift, at least as reported in *Nursing Times*, may have been prompted by changes within nursing, particularly the development of specialisms, by developing treatment regimes for people with MS, or by the gradual impact of the growth of palliative medicine and palliative nursing which prioritises symptom control as a legitimate area of professional activity.

Other specialist services

The care team can include a wide range of people other than doctors and nurses.

Physiotherapy can be one of the most valuable management strategies for people with MS. Physiotherapists can help with general mobility as well as spasticity, balance and upper limb functions. They can advise on the need for aids to help mobility. Some physiotherapists can give specialised help, for example around pain control or continence problems. Occupational therapists can advice on methods to maximise potential for activities of daily living or on ways of achieving the dexterity associated with work or leisure pursuits. Some concerns have been expressed that, although the potential help from both sorts of therapist are clear, many are not specifically trained in the nuances of need associated with neurological problems. Here, we encounter the general problem of supporting specialist services when the population incidence of MS is fairly small and when, as we have discussed above, it is likely that times of high need will be interspersed, in an unpredictable way, with times of low need.

Other specialist services, including dietetics, speech therapy and interventions from outside the normal medical paradigm, like yoga, massage and aromatherapy, are also available to some and are reported as providing significant relief.

Sometimes home care workers can juxtapose the role of helper and friend:

> She helps in every way, day and night. She sees me as her friend. She doesn't see me as a disabled person. She doesn't see me as a person with MS. She sees me as her friend. ... It would be very hard if I had to have a stranger.
>
> (Mrs B)

Sometimes it feels as though there is no-one. Mrs C lives by herself:

> It's nice to be left to yourself. But I could do with some more help ... At the moment [I am] coping. When [I] can't I shall have to sell up and go into sheltered accommodation. But I don't want to do that.

Social work

The spectrum of needs for people with MS includes the social and financial. Social workers can play a key role in helping negotiate with the institutions of the welfare state and they can also, if needed, help with the stresses and conflicts experienced in relationships with family and other carers. Neither of these areas is straightforward. Indeed, problems in each area can be mutually reinforcing. Our interviews revealed some dissatisfaction with both social workers and others involved in offering help. This dissatisfaction often related to organisational matters, a lack of continuity for example. Sometimes it seemed linked to resource constraints. But there was also a sense that some social workers were unsympathetic.

Mrs A had a stair lift to enable her to have access to the upstairs in her house:

> They [the Social Services Department] did not understand that I needed it to get upstairs to my daughter ... the problem with [the Social Service Depart-

ment] is that they listen but they don't hear and act on your wishes. They have a certain set of rules. They just treat you as if you are absolutely stupid. Your first priority is self-preservation, you are not going to do anything to yourself to endanger your own well-being and your own life. You don't need these bits of kids, that's what they are really, the occupational therapists, in my opinion, they just don't know what they are talking about.

The lift was taken out.

Not being able to get upstairs really gets me down. Sitting at the bottom of the stairs, it's like looking up Mt Everest and thinking I'm never going to see that again.

A final call of protest to the Social Dervices Department (SSD) produced the reply:

You didn't kick up enough fuss. We are always having people saying they won't let it be taken out ... I am quite a bolshie person and stick up for my rights but at that particular time I wasn't feeling up to it ... I thought, 'Well, what's the point'.

Mr Y has:

No complaints with the NHS but every time I try to do something with the OTs [occupational therapists] I seem to get trouble. It would help if you always had contact with the same one. Whereas you have to tell your story over and over.

Mrs B had wanted help from the Social Services Department to install a downstairs toilet. They wouldn't, but would install a lift to help her get to the upstairs toilet.

I wanted to think ahead. I had a conservatory and I thought if I couldn't get upstairs I could sleep in there. All I needed was a toilet ... I believe that Social Services and other people who come out, they tell you. They don't listen to you and I'm afraid I can't be told like that. They talk down to you, let's put it like that, as if you were nothing, a nobody, and that is wrong. They can get around easily, they don't understand disabled people so, until it happens to them, they don't understand it. Nobody listens and wants to know your needs.

Mrs W's experiences, on the other hand, were mostly positive:

Social Services carers came in every day. The regular ones were very good, only when it was a relief worker were there any problems. Twilight Nurses came at night, helping him into bed and help with medication, pressure sores, help with dressing. It was well co-ordinated. Sometimes there were meetings at the house to plan; I could be an advocate for him. Hospitals didn't seem to have enough staff to do what was needed. They didn't have the levels of nursing. He was in for a urinary tract infection and a chest infection and got sores and looked dreadful when he came out.

Three further contentious areas help to illustrate some of the challenges faced.

Respite care

Access to appropriate respite care can be important for both people with MS and their carers, as it can for those with other conditions. This is a reality underlined in the 1995 Carers (Recognition and Services) Act. But it is a service much constrained by cuts and resource shortages. A 1997 survey (Carers National Association) found that eight out of ten carers reported not having had an assessment of their needs. Many only asked for help when they reached breaking point. This is generally the experience for carers: the specific experience vis-à-vis MS is that dependency levels in respite care are rising significantly. Many less disabled service users have had respite care cut back or removed altogether from their care packages (Ridley 1997). While it is argued that it is funding shortages that are, at root, the problem, there is some argument that a more flexible interpretation of what constitutes respite care might increase user satisfaction without increasing cost. For example, funding home respite services and family placement would be seen as of great benefit by many people with MS and their carers and it would give them more flexibility and independence. This is an alternative sort of respite care that might prove less costly but that is not pursued because it falls outside the remit of the current financial allocation (Ridley 1997). The pattern of resource allocation also does not meet the observation of the House of Commons Health Select Committee (1996) who state (quoted in Ridley 1997: 8):

> It is potentially counter productive for authorities not to invest in preventative services as this may only lead to the earlier onset of the demand for long-term care, often at a 'crisis point' in the life of an individual needing care.

Funding allocations and priorities do not reflect the measured choice of service users. Indeed, as Ridley reports (1997: 8) 'Users are sometimes given the choice between fewer weeks in the (MS) Society's centre or more weeks in a cheaper, and arguably less suitable unit – user choice but on whose terms?'

Two comments from our interviewees help illustrate some of the problems in reconciling provision and self-perceived need. These problems can be both for the carer and the recipient of the respite care.

> Most respite works on the assumption that the spouse left behind has a rest whereas, in fact, they are fretting most of the time.
>
> (Mr D)

I went to respite care once; I didn't want to go. It wasn't for me. It was geared up for people who were very dependent. You couldn't get on with things yourself.

(Mrs A)

Costs of multiple sclerosis

A consideration of the costs of multiple sclerosis reveals the dangers of over-simplification, but also illustrates some of the problems the person with MS faces if they seek to shape the services they receive. There are four major components to the total annual cost burden of MS: the cost of state benefits; NHS costs; the loss of tax revenue that would have been raised should people with MS have been in waged work; and the costs in terms of the lost earnings for non-professional carers. These lost earnings have been calculated at £395 million (of which 26.3 per cent is attributed to non-professional carers). Annual NHS costs range from £336 to £4,275 per patient, depending on level of disability, and the total annual cost burden is estimated at almost £1.2 billion (Holmes *et al.* 1995). Thinking imaginatively, with these different components in mind, it might be possible to emphasise services to, for example, prolong mobility and therefore delay the point at which people have to give up paid work. Or it might be that one can emphasise care at home so reducing costs of hospital care.

Information about types and level of costs could also be used to help people with MS and carers contribute to decisions about resource allocation. But there are problems. First, the aggregate information offered in these figures embraces so many individual differences that the intrusion of the specific is not easy. Second, although one can see the merits of reviewing costs as a whole, in practice, these costs are born by different parties and one of these may not have an incentive to increase their costs in such a way as to lower the overall total. 'Joined-up thinking', which would look at areas of need and not at professional demarcation to determine the allocation of resources, is an aspiration of New Labour and it is, as yet, too early to see its impact on practice.

Stress

There has been a continued interest in the relationship between MS and stress from the very earliest days. For example, Charcot, the physician who gave MS its name, suggested that emotional shock might play a role in MS aetiology. However, despite much scrutiny, the exact relationship remains unknown. Warren and colleagues have reported studies on the relationship between stress, the development of MS (Warren *et al.* 1982), and its impact on coping with exacerbations (Warren *et al.* 1991). A study published in 1993 identified MS as having the most devastating impact on the individual of any chronic illness. It is a finding probably linked with the age of diagnosis, in one's twenties and thirties, when the resulting dislocation between self-image, personal expectations and a new reality of living with a chronic and possibly worsening illness is most acute (Devins *et al.* 1993).

However one should not assume that diagnosis in older age is ipso facto less profoundly disturbing. Chronological age and life expectations are not exactly correlated.

Our interviewees talked about non-MS-related stress as it links with the onset of symptoms and talked about the continuing presence of stress in their lives:

> The night my husband told me of his affair I felt a complete physical change. It was like someone walking over my body. From that moment on that is when all my problems started to happen.
>
> (Mrs A)

> When my Mum died, I've never been right since. But I've not had stress since, I don't let anything worry me ... I have MS but MS hasn't got me, that's how I look at it. If you have that negative look on it, I think it would have taken me worse than I am. I would have gone downhill. I have that positive outlook.
>
> (Mrs B)

An important dimension in considering stress is the extent and nature of social support the person with MS gets. Indeed, the impact of social support on stress is an important factor influencing patient health outcomes (Ell 1996). At the heart of social support is the family, but here, as with other forms of support, there is the possibility for a dislocation between the patient's view and that of the carer. Research into the relationship between people with cancer and their carers has found that the cancer patient desires emotional but not informational support from the family (Neuling and Winefield 1987) and that efforts by the carer to prioritise a reduction in stress can be unhelpful (Dakof and Taylor 1990). However, the stress the family experiences in, and through, caring has to be addressed and this can be positively influenced by giving information. For example, in research on diabetes and on heart disease a major source of conflict between patient and carer relates to the acceptable level of physical activity the patient can engage in. This sort of dispute has to be addressed via information giving (Carter 1984). But it is not just in information giving that the stresses can be ameliorated. There is also the need to combat the social isolation that many carers experience (Jones and Vetter 1984).

It can be in the loss of status, dignity or privacy that most stress is generated. Mrs A lives at home with her teenage daughter, whom she identifies as her principle carer:

> She finds it a strain at times. Sometimes she has to do quite intimate things. Well, we have changed roles really. She has become the mum and I've become the daughter to a certain extent, at certain times, and that creates problems and I find it a strain at times. I know she finds it difficult ... I had an intercom from downstairs with an extension in my daughter's room. It had a small fault, a broken wire, and Social Services took it away. They gave me a baby

monitor, would you believe, where all I could do ... I have this thing by the side of my bed with 'baby' written on it and my daughter has the other half with 'parent' written on it and she can hear my every move. I was so angry about it.

Counselling

Many conflicts are not readily resolved and, like many other major changes that we face, the availability of counselling can be of help, for example at diagnosis or at times of major change either in symptoms or in life more generally. This help is often provided by counsellors or by social workers. Some of the potential conflicts the latter face are well illustrated in a case discussion presented by George (1998). George presents a woman with MS whose condition was deteriorating. Her arms and legs had ceased to function, she required catheterisation and had a gastrostomy for supplementary feeding. She was not able to speak but could communicate by mouthing words. The social workers at the hospital where she was an inpatient were concerned that she wished to return home where her husband had a drinking problem, where the house was not clean and where there was evidence of the husband's verbal violence to his wife and to other caregivers. Herein lie a number of key issues. First, the patient was able to clearly communicate her wish to go home. But her physical needs were such that her health might have been jeopardised still further if care was erratic or if hygiene was compromised. The hospital and social services organised a care package that included a live-in twenty-four-hour carer and access to specialist day care in the hospital. The hospital social worker involved sums up:

> This has actually proved to be a more robust arrangement than we had before and her health has improved significantly. For one thing, her ability to swallow has improved. The live-in carer has made an enormous difference, even though she has effectively had to take on the husband as well.
>
> (George 1998: 19)

It is a situation that underlines the vulnerability of people who cannot communicate easily. It also shows the potential for conflict between professionals and patients in seeking to define 'in the patient's best interest'.

There must be planning that includes the hospital and home – a typical person experiencing problems with their MS is likely to have to move between sectors. It is also necessary to consider the patient's problems in the context of the family needs.

This holistic approach is not only justified on humanitarian grounds but, as we have seen above, can be justified in a utilitarian way, including a best-use-of-resources argument – even comprehensive home care might be less costly than the alternative of hospitalisation. Any hospitalisation might be delayed or avoided. A secure home environment can reduce anxiety and may make things like swallowing easier (tension is counter-productive in this area) and helping the family may have beneficial effects on its other members. We might note that, in George's example, we do not know what the husband wanted.

The encounter between user and professional views

Robinson and colleagues (1996) note how the professional seeking the user view often comes with a set of predetermined perceptions, a background discipline, that will result in them assessing need in a particular way. In contrast people with MS have very different and diverse experiences and backgrounds. It is likely that questions to them will, first, produce diverse and complex information that will create challenges in terms of interpretation; secondly, it will result in the expression of needs that are not related to resources or to cost-effectiveness. That is, the sorts of needs expressed might be in harmony with one set of shaping parameters of the new welfare state, i.e. consumerism, that are not in harmony with another, i.e. cost-sensitivity.

One can hypothesise two potential conflicts between somewhat ill-matched opponents: homogeneous professional views against diffuse user views, needs linked to knowledge of available resources against needs linked to wishes. But we have to add some riders to this over-simple scenario. First, professional views are only likely to be homogeneous if one takes single professions and views from one strata within them. One can imagine rather different formulations of need if neurologists and, say, social workers were included within a professional formulation. Differences within professions as well as between them are also likely to occur. If one took the views of the top echelon of a profession and contrasted these with those people who had the closest contact with clients views might differ also. (This is a phenomenon that is widely reported and experienced; an alliance is forged between workers and clients whose interests are posed against those of the more removed senior layers of their organisation. One might call it empathy, or, more pejoratively, 'going native)'.

It is also too simplistic to think that all those people with MS will be unable or unwilling to recognise and respond to resource limitations – they have all lived, and continue to live, in the real world and understand its limitations.

Acting in the world

There were some examples amongst our interviewees of individual empowerment and of some engagement with wider issues. Mrs A spoke of the Direct Payments she had received:

> Since July I have had funding for my own care staff. I now have three people who come in at various times. This is funded by the SSD. But I was able to advertise myself, interview them. Pendrills Trust help in advertising, doing wages and other things. The social workers that came to set that up were brilliant. Did everything I asked for.
>
> (Mrs A)

Some interviewees reported involvement with groups engaging with a wide range of problems; other contacts were specifically for people with MS.

> I've been to a 'User Network' meeting and a Counsellor gets up and says how they are going to bear in mind the feelings of the people they are looking after. But there is actually no difference.
>
> (Mr Y)

> I went to a Disability Network Meeting. The meeting room was upstairs and there was a running buffet – what chaos! ... I went to the MS Conference in Birmingham and heard a talk from Professor Giles, a neurologist, I could have listened to him all day. Everyone who has MS should go. I'm getting to know how the services run, because they like to waste money. All local government, all government, likes to waste money. Well they should have me there, I know exactly where to spend it. (Waste) is very unsettling.
>
> (Mrs B)

> I go to meetings, conferences and so on, as a member of the MS Society. I think that is important, to have a voice. To express yourself. They don't always listen, but hopefully one of these days, if you keep chipping away, they might start to listen. I belong to the Disabled Rights Association ... you don't sit there and talk about your problems. So I can't honestly say I know much about other disabled people's problems.
>
> (Mrs A)

The MS Society is generally welcomed, both as an ally in negotiating for, or a direct provider of, services. It also has a role in putting people in touch with each other and with wider issues and debates. In the classified advertisement section of the magazine *MS Matters* (March/April 1998), for example, is this poignant request: 'Single Male, 34, living in North Yorkshire, diagnosed two years ago, I would love to correspond with and meet others in the same position, as I don't know another living soul who has MS. All letters answered.'

The MS Society helps:

> Keep you up to date with developments ... its benefits are sociable. When you are in a wheelchair your social life is very limited. ... [But the] local membership is 280 patients and at monthly meetings we have a maximum of thirty patients and twenty carers.
>
> (Mr D)

> The MS Society has been brilliant to me, they have been very supportive all the way through – with advice, financial help, backup with letters ... the MS Society gives me support and financial support.
>
> (Mrs A)

There are eloquent and forceful voices of people with MS within national organisations, and indeed, internationally via the International Federation of Multiple
Sclerosis Societies whose Chair of the International Committee is Reid Nicholson,
himself a person with MS. At a recent conference, Reid Nicholson drew an interesting distinction between the possible agendas of professionals (he was speaking
specifically of researchers) and of those with MS when he wondered if 'for
researchers, maybe the journey is enough, but for the person with MS, it's only
the destination' (MS Frontiers in Science and Patient Care and Disease Management, Birmingham, 5–6 May 1998).

Perhaps the difference is the investment one has in the subject matter. The
ham and eggs analogy is apposite – that is in preparing this meal the hen is involved
and the pig is committed.[2]

While the destination remains the focus for many people, we have seen above
a realism as to the ability people with MS have to engage with a sense that they
have to live with their MS and not just contemplate its eradication. A part of
that 'living with' involves an engagement with the services they receive and a
consideration of what would improve the quality of their lives. An important
dimension of this engagement involves the MS Society, which both informs and
guides and is, in turn, informed and guided by people with MS as to their needs.
The recently published *Standards of Healthcare for People with MS* (Freeman *et al.*
1997) provides an example. The MS Society held two workshops in which the
views of people with MS and their families and carers, together with healthcare
professionals and volunteers, were encouraged and common problems and gaps
in service provision were identified. They then addressed what they considered
appropriate standards of care. The rationale for this enterprise was summarised in
a comment from Peter Cardy, the Chief Executive of the MS Society: 'The basic
therapeutic and disease management techniques required to ensure that life for
people with MS is not abject misery, but dignified and independent, are long
established' (Freeman *et al.* 1997: 1). However, either through lack of understanding or lack of will, these basic techniques are not in place everywhere. Hence
the need to establish standards that the best may already achieve but which should
'become the common denominator of care for all'.

Standards are linked to four characteristic stages of MS: the diagnostic phase,
the period of minimal impairment, of moderate disability and of severe disability.
They range across a wide spectrum of areas, ones that are identified by our respondents in this chapter. For example information, support and clarity of diagnosis
feature in the first phase, access to treatments and continuity of care as well as
the recognition of the importance of self-management in the second and third
categories and respite and long-term care in the severe phase (Freeman *et al.*
1997).

There are also initiatives in terms of developing minimum standards in MS
that will have an impact across Europe. The European Federation of Neurological
Societies' Task Force identified ten standards which embrace all stages from diagnosis to long-term care; there is no mention of terminal care although the importance

of having multidisciplinary teams is asserted throughout (Barnes 1999). There are no standards or guidelines that relate directly to how far and in what way users should be involved in planning or evaluating services, although the standards identified reflect the accumulated experience of people with MS and their carers as to the needs they have and how these needs could be best met at different points in their MS career.

The pursuit of user involvement via standard-setting could be an important dimension in the overall spectrum of user involvement activity. Saying what should be in place and then seeking some mechanism to monitor achievement offers a route that allows the incorporation of two paradigms, a consultation one and a rights-based approach to user involvement. Its strength relies on both the nature of input and the effectiveness of monitoring. That is, the consultation process needs to be wide ranging and to have enough flexibility to incorporate the opinions of people not necessarily in harmony with that of the majority (or not in harmony with the organisations leading on the standard setting). It also needs to give due regard to the whole range of needs throughout the lifetime of the people with the illness. There is also the need to set up effective monitoring structures and the opportunity to intervene at both the short-term and the more strategic level to ensure that, as services develop, they do so in a way consistent with the agreed standards.

Conclusions

While there have been advances in treatment of MS and in the care regimes that are available there is much still to do. We can see in the material we have reported above, most notably in the interviews we draw on, that the picture is mixed. There is progress in developing standards but we can still encounter reports of experiences that are almost completely negative. A woman caring for her husband, who has MS, recently wrote to the newsletter of the MS Nurse Forum, *Way Ahead*, identifying twenty-five years of 'unbelievable' experiences, especially in the last six years during which his physical condition and cognitive capacities have been increasingly compromised. The particular problems she identifies include unsatisfactory care in hospital; nursing staff with no experience of MS taking no account of her husband's cognitive problems; doctors who 'do not have any practical understanding of the care of MS' often missing simple changes to the care regime that would have made a considerable difference; and the 'terrible problem of (finding) good respite care'. There were good things, a caring social worker who helped gain access to the Independent Living Fund, useful help from homeopathy and very useful aids for the home and wheelchair (*Way Ahead* 1999: 16). But the vision of a well-equipped and well-prepared service for MS is far away as one reads of the experiences still occurring at the end of the century. Of course neither we nor the editors of *Way Ahead* would deny that good experiences can also be found, or that this example is representative. Its typicality is not the point; rather, the existence of experiences like those recounted by the anonymous correspondent set the challenges any system that is concerned with standards or responsiveness have to respond to. We find in this account, and in others we have reported, problems in structures of care and in the process of delivering services. As well as appropriate resources there is a need to use what is available in ways that better meet the needs identified by the people who really appreciate the challenges of living with MS – that is, those living with the condition and those most intimately caring for them. We do not see great evidence of these voices being appropriately privileged in planning or evaluation.

But as well as looking at care this chapter has also been concerned with seeking to understand the nature of the lived experience of MS both at a social and at an individual level. Not least we have been concerned to ask if a user involvement agenda is ipso facto in the best interests of people with MS.

There is something potentially controlling and hierarchical about an imperative to be informed, to have to have a view, to have to play a part in planning and evaluating services. The space for someone to say, 'I don't want to know, I just want to be looked after, I don't want to face that now,' is disappearing, at least as a socially approved or accepted space. If we wanted to locate this in a theoretical schema we could look to Foucault's observations that areas of social practice are controlled not by excluding talk of them but by wrapping them in words. In Foucault's terms, we shape them into a 'discourse' (see Foucault 1978). He uses the example of sex and describes how we scrutinise sexuality more than ever and make a science out of sex. But it is a science devoted to the analysis of desire rather than the increase of pleasure. It serves those who act in ways consistent with the discourse and not those who seek their own way. If we borrow his approach we can examine how the imperative to know gives legitimacy to the structures that allow or encourage it and does not necessarily increase the sense of autonomy the individual feels he or she may have.

Allied to what we might call a variety of 'repressive tolerance of service users' views' is a problem in having room to 'rail' against it all. When you are not only expected to live with MS but also take responsibility for your own care, and the care of others like you, there is not much space left for being angry or being different. The sociologist Goffman looked at people who lived with the tensions this can foster. The temptation to create one's own identity by manipulating the domain of one's behaviour in a socially disapproved of way can be very great. This does not have to be grand rebellion, although it can be. Rather it often is in little things where one takes charge of one's identity. In so doing one can manage to recreate something of one's own, rather than just conforming to the expectations of others (see Goffman 1968). These are areas that have been considered, specifically in relation to MS, by Stewart and Sullivan (1982) and Robinson (1988a).

The extent to which the experience of MS is like that of other conditions and how far it is to be understood around a defining construct of uncertainty that is peculiar to MS and a very few other conditions that might share the usually lengthy diagnostic process, the variation in progression, and the (largely) absent treatments of established efficacy has been explored by Robinson and colleagues, drawing on the Brunel Archive. The archive also allows for an evaluation of the impact of self-help and voluntary-sector groups, in the way they can offer some sense of identity and control over the illness (see Robinson 1988a: see also Quin 1996).

A part of this sense of identity and control is explored in Williams (1993). He considers the way that illness faces individuals with moral imperatives and engages them in 'the pursuit of virtue'. That is, the sick individual will show that their position is legitimate and that they are worthy by displaying, say, independence and self-affirmation. Williams, in presenting the experience of a woman with rheumatoid arthritis, contrasts the world of contingencies – the everyday world in which the individual interacts with others and experiences successes and failures – and an attempt to enact a story about herself as she wishes to be understood, to be seen as a particular sort of person. It is in the everyday world that individuals continue to enact and express themselves. Coping strategies, everyday self-enactment, are moral practices in the sense that Oakeshott identifies: 'a moral practice is, in part, a language of self-enactment; that is, a language in which conduct may be recognised in terms of its "virtue" and an agent may recognise himself in terms of his "virtuousness"' (Oakeshott 1975: 75).

But, as Williams has demonstrated, there is far more to coping with chronic illness than the instrumental management of symptoms. He places this self-management alongside other interconnected influences, including the enactment of stories and the evolution of a lived biography. To stress the importance of this gestalt he quotes MacIntyre: 'the unity of a virtue in someone's life is intelligible only as a characteristic of a unitary life, a life that can be conceived and evaluated as a whole' (1981: 191).

We will return to a consideration of the extent to which we can think of continuity, of a unitary life, in situations of illness where that illness is life threatening and incurable when we look at living with MND. Here what we have been seeking to do is consider if the language of user involvement has been included in the characteristic language of self-enactment of people with MS, and if its pursuit is considered a concomitant 'virtue'. Is to be unconcerned about addressing the needs of MS in general as opposed to one's own needs to be unvirtuous, are we being bullied into altruism and into a complicity with the state and the professions? In so doing are we compromising our resort to redress, our freedom to invoke the language of rights? Are we limited if we are being directed towards involvement as opposed to 'railing against the dying of the light' or seeking some sort of detachment into the contemplation of the moment, or of the spiritual?

Notes

1 For this and the subsequent two sections we have drawn on material published by the MS Society and the MS Research Trust. It is this that is widely available to people with MS, to those caring for them and to a wide range of the professional and public with an interest in MS.

2 This is a saying attributed to many people; we chose to believe it came from Martina Navratilova talking about her success as a tennis player.

5 Motor neurone disease

'Just a little bit of hope'

As with MS, one of the defining characteristics of living with motor neurone disease (MND) is uncertainty. But, although there are some similarities, we have uncertainty of a different order. We will see how the problems of diagnosis are widespread, as they are with MS, how there is some variation in patterns of progression and how life expectancy can vary. But, overall, there is a much more predictable outcome. That outcome is premature death. A second defining characteristic for many people is MND's speed of progression. This presents both the person with MND, and their carers, with great challenges.

If premature death is a predictable outcome how far is uncertainty a justifiable way of framing the MND experience? There are exceptions to the predominate patterns that exist with MND and the very existence of exceptions allows a person with MND some psychic space. They might say, 'If some people (however few) do not decline quickly and die early then perhaps I will be one of them.'

While the existence of exceptions justifies the use of uncertainty, for the majority it might be appropriate to reframe a resort to a reliance on uncertainty as something we can more appropriately describe as denial. Beresford (1995) sees denial as a response to serious situations to which we may all resort. With MND, it may come and go, and 'This can help the patient live with the possibility of death and an uncertain future.' However, 'Continuous denial can be destructive if it persists, since it may block attempts by others to provide help as the disease progresses and the person becomes weaker' (Beresford 1995: 66). Robinson and Hunter (1998) quote a Canadian report in which they contrast two sorts of denial. One is an unhelpful strategy and one acts positively as 'a protective coping mechanism that helps a person who has received a terminal diagnosis retain psychological equilibrium' (ALS Society of Canada 1994: 9). We can suppose that either a prevalent assumption of uncertainty, or denial, will impact on future orientation and user involvement.

We have interviewed six people with MND with their six carers. In addition we have had meetings and discussions with a range of professional service providers. We have also had discussions with Motor Neurone Disease Association (MNDA) staff both at central office and regionally. In this chapter, we hope to use the insights so gained to help us evaluate the research data and we will do so, in the main, by shaping the chapter around many of the concerns people with MND and their carers discussed and by using their own words as much as possible.

As with other interviews we have presented there is not a strong theme of overt engagement with user involvement as a discreet policy and practice agenda. Direct questions about the person's stance vis-à-vis the user involvement agenda are not productive. Such issues appear not to have yet entered the popular lexicon of health concerns and care needs. That is not to say people are unconcerned about user involvement but rather that these concerns have to be elicited out of the lived experience of their illness. That lived experience is placed in the context of the disease characteristics of MND and the normal configuration of care for people with MND in the sections that follow.

What is motor neurone disease?[1]

We will see in what follows that there is frequently an absence of knowledge as to what MND is and what forms it can take. This absence is near universal in those people newly diagnosed, but it is also widespread in those people the newly diagnosed come into contact with. Simple information about what a person faces with MND therefore becomes a prerequisite to user involvement. As we shall see in subsequent sections so too does a knowledge of what services could be of benefit in responding to the manifestations of the disease. We offer then not a handbook on MND and its care but the essential framework of knowledge as to the physical impact of the disease and the services that might be available to set up the possibility for a debate about user involvement.

MND is a progressive degenerative disease affecting the motor neurones in the brain and the spinal column. Characteristically there is a progressive loss of function of limbs and weakness or wasting of the muscles of the trunk and neck. Speech and swallowing often become increasingly difficult. About 80 per cent of people with MND will have their speech affected. What begins with first signs like stumbling, a weakened grip, cramps or a hoarse voice can progress to a state of total dependence in activities of daily living and a loss of functional speech.

It is likely that life will be severely shortened. Death usually follows the weakening of the respiratory system and occurs either because of an infection or the deterioration of the muscles that make breathing possible.

There are three different, although often overlapping, forms of MND. The most common, which affects about 66 per cent of people with MND, is amyotrophic lateral sclerosis (ALS). ALS usually begins in people over 55, males are more affected than females, a ratio of three to two, and average length of time from diagnosis to death is three to four years. ALS is characterised by muscle weakness, spasticity, hyperactive reflexes and emotional lability. Progressive muscular atrophy (PMA) affects 7.5 per cent of people with MND. Onset is usually in people under 50 with males five times more likely to be diagnosed. The majority of people with PMA survive beyond five years from diagnosis. PMA is predominantly lower motor neurone degeneration. It causes muscle wasting and weakness (often starting with the hand), loss of weight and muscle twitching. The third form of MND, progressive bulbar palsy (PBP), makes up about 25 per cent of diagnoses. It mostly occurs in older people and is slightly more common in women. Survival from onset of symptoms is usually between six months and three years. PBP is particularly characterised by speech and swallowing difficulties. Speech is thick and slurred and deteriorates to the point where the person with this form of MND has to communicate by writing or by using other communication aids. Swallowing difficulties cause choking on food, pooling of saliva and dribbling. Feeding by tube may be necessary. Many people with PBP continue to walk throughout, but muscles in the upper body may become progressively weaker.

Onset of all forms is invidious, with the initial speed and pattern of progression varying widely. It is common for there to be a considerable time lag between the onset of symptoms and diagnosis. O'Brien *et al.* (1992) identified a mean time of 13.5 months, but other studies report longer times. Calculations such as these are difficult in that they rely on retrospective accounts of what may have, at the time, been symptoms readily explained in other ways.

> I found that my left hand, I could not control it, and then I found that my arms were weaker, both arms and after a month or two I knew that something was wrong so I went to my doctor. I went to a consultant, not a neurologist. The consultant I saw realised it was a neurological disease and made an appointment at the hospital. He said, 'I'll have you an appointment in three weeks'. That was early February 1995. By that time my arms weren't working and I could not control finger movement. They told me they thought I had motor neurone disease. They put me on some drugs that seemed to help: I could move my arms better. But, by July, I was in hospital again and I was worse. I could not raise my arms, my fingers, and my voice was shaky.
>
> (Mr H, age 44)

Mr and Mrs J discussed the shift from symptom to diagnosis in Mr J's case:

> February 1991 he was diagnosed. He started to be ill twelve months before that, little tell-tale signs … weakness in his knee and he thought it was an old football [injury], he used to have water on the knee. Anyway things got worse, he wasn't steady walking, as if he was drunk, stumble. He got a stick. I said, 'You should go to the doctors'. He has not been one to go to the doctors. It had been fifteen years since he had gone.

He did go to his GP and from there went to the hospital, to a specialist, for a brain scan at another hospital then to another specialist at a third hospital:

> All the tests were negative. But there had to be something. He [the hospital specialist] said all they could do was the same tests in six months and get some physiotherapy in the mean time. But then they called back early and we were told by [the doctor] that 'It's motor neurone'.
>
> (Mrs J)

Mr K was diagnosed a few months prior to our meeting. He and his wife told of the events that led to it. As with many of our interviews, the lead in telling the story was the carer. The speech difficulties of the person with MND meant they were looked to in order to voice agreement, or offer a different emphasis, rather than direct the narrative.

> For two years or so he would come in from golf complaining of his legs. [He also] said, 'My mouth is like pudding'. He said this to the GP who thought he might have had a slight stroke. His speech had changed – but it was not really noticeable. He went to hospital, they thought it was arthritis in the knees. He had other tests. Then at work his feet felt really heavy. We had never heard of MND, we were thinking it was a trapped nerve or something like that. CT scans were negative, we moved from orthopaedics to neurology.
>
> (Mrs K)

After diagnosis, the remorseless progression was described by Mr M:

> I found that every two months, approximately, a new situation would develop that I would loose the ability to do something else. First of all it was to grip anything or to lift my hand above my head. In roughly two-month periods I would feel the weakness develop but it would take two months to become prominent, so that I knew I had lost that ability. It was gradual, all the time. Legs first, then a loss of use in arms. I had crutches, then a wheelchair.

Although three types of MND can be identified, there is some overlap and within each form considerable variation. For example, people with PMA, in time, develop upper motor neurone involvement and in PMA and ALS most people eventually experience speech and swallowing difficulties. For some people, death occurs before they have experienced the usual range of symptoms, others experience plateaux, of weeks or months, when no further deterioration occurs.

The variation hidden within average statistical presentations is well illustrated by survival figures. While average lengths of time from diagnosis to death are indicated above, what this hides is the estimate that, taking all forms of MND, 40 per cent survive five years, 10 per cent survive ten years and a small number have lived over twenty years.

Onset, progression and outcome are indeed then characterised by uncertainty. It is also a characteristic of all forms of MND that not all parts of the body are directly affected. Intellect and memory generally remain intact, although in about 5 per cent of cases some cognitive impairment has been reported. But the ability to communicate or to effect some control over one's environment is considerably compromised and intense frustration can result. Fatigue is also common and can reduce concentration span: some people can only read or watch TV for limited periods, for example. Bowel and bladder functions are not directly affected, although there may be some disturbance of bowel function in later stages. There may also be problems of constipation caused by immobility or a low liquid intake because of swallowing difficulties. Sexual function remains, in many people, until a late stage although movement problems may require some discussion of the best way to facilitate sexual activity. The senses remain unimpaired and eye movement remains when all other movements have been lost. Indeed eye pointing can be used as a means of communication if all else fails.

Incidence, cause and treatments

There is some uncertainty about precise figures for incidence and prevalence. But there is agreement that UK incidence is of the order of one per 50,000 per year (about the same as multiple sclerosis) and prevalence is thought to be between eight and ten per 100,000. Multiple sclerosis prevalence is about fifty per 100,000, reflecting its chronic rather than life-shortening characteristics. Although MND is not a hereditary condition, there does appear to be a familiar tendency in about 5 per cent of cases. There are about 6,000 people with MND at any one time in the UK, with three people dying daily from its effects.

The cause of MND is not known. A number of theories are actively being pursued by researchers in studies of both the disease process and the way motor neurones function. Areas of research include metabolic and cellular biology and biochemistry. Attempts are being made to isolate a relevant virus, to look at genes, to consider the neuro-toxic effects of heavy metals and trace elements and to identify any other significant environmental triggers.

There are also specific drug treatments that offer some prospect of extending life or extending the time before mechanical ventilation is needed for breathing. For example, Riluzole has been marketed in the UK since 1996 and trials have indicated some improvement in survival (Chilcott *et al.* 1997).

While there is no treatment for MND itself, any summary that suggests 'nothing can be done' is far short of the truth (Barby and Leigh 1995). There is a wide repertoire of treatments to address symptoms and some considerable success in effecting improved comfort and well-being. Symptoms can be held steady, or the decline resulting from the progress of the condition can be slowed (Oliver 1995). In essence the intention of treatment is palliative.

Contemporary palliative care concentrates on two guiding principles: first, a focus on quality of life and its maintenance; second, a multidisciplinary approach designed to offer 'total care for total pain' in Dame Cicely Saunders' renowned phrase (see Summers 1981). Examples of intervention designed to maintain as good a quality of life as possible and respond effectively to complex symptoms with multidisciplinary work include responding to weakness with careful positioning and nursing and using physiotherapy to prevent deformity and maintain remaining movements and mobility.

Although sensory nerves are not affected by MND, about 40 per cent of patients report pain (Saunders *et al.* 1981). Some of that pain is caused by stiff joints or by skin pressure when a person has difficulty shifting position. Nursing care, advice to partners and carers at home about how and when to turn the person, physiotherapy and drugs – perhaps an opiate analgesic or anti-inflammatory drugs or even a local anaesthetic are all facets of the multidisciplinary response such a symptom requires. Other sorts of pain include emotional and spiritual, or existential, pain. These of course can be experienced by all those touched by MND, not just the person so diagnosed.

Studies of MND patients living in the community have identified a wide range of problems, many of which would have been amenable to palliative care interventions. One study of respite care found a considerable number of problems on admission: 77 per cent of patients reported pain. Constipation was a problem for 86 per cent. Insomnia troubled 64 per cent and was often the main reason for exhaustion in both patients and carers, and was the factor precipitating requests for respite care. Pressure sores were surprisingly common; depression and anxiety affected a third of patients, and weight loss and anorexia 27 per cent. Seventy-seven per cent had swallowing difficulties but only one was fed by a nasogastric tube and none had been referred for gastrostomy feeding. The authors comment: 'That these patients had not been referred for symptom control is curious, and may reflect a lack of awareness from their primary care physicians as to the palliative treatments available' (Hicks and Corcoran 1993: 149). While receiving respite care in a hospice, these people were treated such that it was nearly always possible to eliminate pain, constipation and insomnia.

There is also published evidence that feeding by tube may improve mood and energy as well as nutritional status (Park *et al.* 1992), although there are likely to be emotional barriers to moving towards a wider use of this treatment. Feeding by tube is described in the medical literature as involving a simple technique: 'The placement of a gastrostomy feeding tube can be performed under local anaesthetic; the procedure takes on average twenty minutes and causes minimal distress to the patient' (Ellershaw *et al.* 1993: 52).

But it is a technique associated by patients with a sense of how bad things might become. It can be seen to be at odds with the sense that many people with MND have that what they need is hope. For many people with MND the reality they live with is one in which they have to balance the possible gains from medical intervention with the wish to preserve their bodily integrity and their sense of self control.

At this point, we can record the observations of the Patients' Patron of the MND Association Professor Stephen Hawking who, in the 1993/4 MND Association Annual Review, encompasses hope, science and activism:

> Being diagnosed with motor neurone disease is pretty shattering, as many of those who read this will know. But, as I can testify, it need not mean that one has to give up hope. The Motor Neurone Disease Association is doing a tremendous job in helping those with the condition and in providing support and backup for their families. It is also sponsoring research into the cause of the condition. In the last year or so there has been exciting progress linking, at least some forms, to a lack of anti-oxidants. It does not seem unreasonable to hope that this will led to a cure, or at least a way of stopping it getting

worse. Motor neurone disease strikes as often as multiple sclerosis but is much less well known. We need the MND Association to fight our battles and win us public recognition.

Hawking (1994: 2)

Multidisciplinary teams

Characteristically, people with MND are likely to encounter at least nine different professions, and sometimes several different sorts of speciality within a profession. For example, they may be nursed by a general nurse, a district nurse and a Macmillan Nurse. They will see a general practitioner and a neurologist: they may have seen other specialists during the process of diagnosis and may see a palliative physician towards the end of their lives.

General practice

The general practitioner is likely to be the first person consulted as initial symptoms become manifest and cause concern to the patient. But that GP is unlikely to have had any frequent contact with the diagnosis and subsequent treatment of MND. This, together with problems of identifying what may be relatively minor problems as suggestive of a potential MND diagnosis, may mean the initial phase is drawn out. The continuing relationship with the GP varies greatly. A significant variable appears to be the extent to which the GP follows the progression of symptoms by seeking out new information in collaboration with the patient. The GP is likely to be at the heart of continuing care and so plays a key role in the multidisciplinary response that evolves. As we have commented elsewhere this is a position that has been enhanced by the changing organisation of health care towards a service led by primary care (Department of Health 1997a).

Our interviewees had variable experiences of GPs.

Mrs J described her family doctor as:

> A waste of space. He doesn't know anything. He never comes near. He used to come when [my husband] had to have a sick note. These days you don't need a sick note so he doesn't come. I suppose if we needed him he would come but I don't know what use he would be.

Others have found their GP's:

> Very good, with both of us because I was in a state as well ... They were help [at the time of diagnosis]. I don't think they knew a lot themselves but they gave us both hope.

(Mrs K)

The GP is honest about it. All they give you is painkillers. But I'm not in pain, I'm in discomfort ... I asked (local MNDA) to send information to the GP practice.

(Mrs L)

Senior Clinical Medical Officer for Physical Disability

Community Trusts may have a Senior Clinical Medical Officer for Physical Disability. He or she has special responsibility for the care of the physically disabled in the area. Some Trusts utilise this post imaginatively. For example in Scunthorpe Community Health Care NHS Trust the role of the post holder involves: overseeing the development of services; developing a database; making an initial visit to assess the needs of the patient and family. It also involves the establishment of a Clinical Review Forum to be held on a regular basis to co-ordinate services and facilitate the sharing of information and problems. Everyone involved is invited, including the patient and carers.

Neurology

Neurologists can sometimes diagnose after taking a detailed history and carrying out a clinical examination. Sometimes they need to refer for neurophysiological investigations. These involve testing conduction in peripheral nerves with small electrical impulses and looking for spontaneous activity by placing a needle directly into muscles.

As with GPs, neurologists are likely to have a wide-ranging case load – although they are more likely to be familiar with diagnosing MND and making recommendations as to its ongoing treatment. As we have discussed in the chapter on multiple sclerosis, there are fewer than 300 neurologists in the UK and only a very few of them would consider MND their primary interest.

As well as small numbers, and varied interests, there may be problems in persuading neurologists to operate as part of a multidisciplinay team. Boggild characterises his fellow neurologists as 'not naturally team players'. He suggests the neurological role may be sidelined if they do not look to the contribution of other professions. They need to change their pattern of work if they want 'to remain on the team rather than find themselves on the bench' (Boggild 1998). We will argue that the way the diagnosis and immediate prognosis is communicated, usually by the neurologist, sets a pattern likely to be perpetuated in terms of the relationship between the person with MND and the medical profession. After many years of concern with how the medical profession communicates bad news, at the very least neurologists ought to meet the expectation that they will discuss the diagnosis with honesty and sympathy.

While there are examples of good practice, there has also been, over many years, severe criticism of the contribution of doctors and especially neurologists in this area. In 1985, Norris and colleagues wrote that 'Motor neurone disorders, particularly the most malignant – progressive bulbar palsy and amyotrophic lateral sclerosis – provide an astonishing example of therapeutic ignorance or nihilism in modern medical practice' (Norris *et al.* 1985: 259).

Seven years later Norris's message had not fundamentally changed:

> Many doctors and especially neurologists (90 per cent in our experience) continue to offer no care to patients suffering from this fatal paralysis, as though the lack of a cure is somehow equated with the absence of any treatment. This is curious because patients with many other fatal diseases receive supportive care or palliation from their doctors (including neurologists). Yet a paralysed patient with motor neurone disease is often neglected despite the availability of many symptomatic treatments.
>
> (Norris 1992: 459)

Nursing

Nurses are likely to encounter people with MND in hospital and the community. The emotional impact of diagnosis and a progressive loss of capabilities will make demands on the nurse, as will a series of more specific problems the nurse can take a lead in responding to. The need to advise the best way to achieve comfort when sitting or lying – both in terms of technique and equipment – help with pain control, respiratory care and nutrition and hydration as well as sensitively supporting people as they accept the need for communication aids are all part of a repertoire of nursing care. Many of these tasks are done in collaboration with other professions, and all involve the need to consult closely with carers. One district nurse, Sue Thomas, has described how she set about learning about the nature of need and multidisciplinary responses to it and, on subsequent home visits to people with MND, had many of the people she saw say to her:

> You are the first nurse I've met who knows what my problems are'. It must be very distressing to patients to think they are suffering from a disease that little is known about and to be reliant for care on professionals with limited knowledge of their needs.
>
> (Thomas 1991: 43)

A study from New Zealand (Carter *et al.* 1998) compared the responses of health professionals caring for both people with MND and MS. The study found responses that were more negative in relation to the MND patients. Specifically, this negativity related to the amount they felt able to offer and to their ability to convey hope. An ability to convey hope contributes to supportive care (Kim 1989). It may also contribute to future orientation and mobilisation of involvement in one's own care.

Physiotherapy, occupational therapy and speech therapy

The physiotherapist can respond to the problems caused by altered muscle tone, problems in maintaining an erect posture while standing or sitting, loss of mobility, respiratory problems and problems with swallowing and talking. The latter problems can also involve speech therapists whose remit is to help with encouraging and advising the patient on the best way to use damaged and deteriorating mechanisms. It is a role best achieved if referral is early and if there is some continuity of care. A sense of familiarity with the specific problems of one patient, of the emotional resonance of deteriorating speech and the extent of the person with MND's openness to communication aids is not something easily achieved. For example, how far will setting exercise regimes depress the patient because they are likely to record deterioration, or how far will a patient accept means of communication other than oral ones?

Occupational therapists (OTs), like many other professionals, have to plan with the knowledge that the progression of MND varies considerably in different patients. An occupational therapist may be well used to working with people who have neurological illness, and many of the needs will be similar. But what is not so familiar will be this sense of progression that is difficult to predict. For example, does the OT recommend installation of removable equipment, a vertical lift, a shower cabinet and so on, rather than recommend building an extension onto a house? Practically, suggesting removable equipment may well be good advice but it invokes a sense of the temporary, that the person with MND will be not be alive long enough to 'justify' major building work and as such this advice may have an emotional impact, or a cost in terms of morale. There are also potential problems in recommending particular aids or adaptations that are appropriate to the current level of ability but may not be so appropriate in the near future. The OT, like the rest of the multidisciplinary team, operates in the area of the management of uncertainty.

Other professions involved can include dieticians, social workers (for both emotional help for the patient and family and also advice on accessing local services and seeking appropriate welfare benefits.) The MND Association also provides practical help and advice as well as offering forums for mutual support.

Mrs N was living in a Cheshire Home when she was interviewed. She felt that the daily physiotherapy she received was:

> keeping me going. I have a sense of achievement. They help me to actually stand up two or three times a week. Yesterday I managed to open an envelope and read the letter without any help. That's me, if I can do one thing I try and do something else.

A contrasting picture comes from Mrs L who finds her OT:

> Hopeless. They are all right with strokes and arthritis and that's the only way they know how to treat me. They don't always listen to what I say. The point is they might have had training but they have never had the complaint. They wanted to fit things so that I could open the curtains, put the light on. I don't need that because I couldn't be here on my own anyway. If I hadn't got my husband I would have to go away.

Speech therapists generally appeared much approved of. The ability to communicate and to be understood is so important. Mrs J's description of the speech therapist appeared to put her in the centre of her network of support:

> The speech therapist is super. We go to the hospital to see her. If there is anything you want, physiotherapist, hospital, she will get in touch.

Like many of our interviewees, there was a sense that help was forthcoming when it was requested. But within the context of this positive impression there were problems in timing. The experience of Mr and Mrs H is typical:

> We had asked the social services for advice on changing the doors. That was in September and in the time it has taken for us to discuss it with them he has deteriorated and so couldn't handle opening the doors even if they changed them ... In the early stages the OT brought gadgets for opening bottles, tipping kettles and so on. But now [my husband] has lots of trouble doing things even with them. Things have been adequate at that time. Obviously, if [he] is deteriorating we get things [so] that we can manage for three months and then they are redundant.

Care regimes

While there is an apparent consensus between service providers, people with MND and their carers that the sort of care regime being looked for should be characterised by patient management and not crisis management, and that its configuration should be determined by the views of the patients themselves, this consensus is not often realised in practice. In part, this is due to the problem of reconciling the practical benefits of planning ahead with the emotional reluctance to anticipate decline. In part, it is due to a problem in justifying the allocation of scarce resources before need is acute. For example, offers of help in the form of equipment, aids or short-term respite care have to be made in anticipation of further decline of functions if these services are to be in place at the point at which skills are still sufficient to benefit from them. If these forms of help arrive late, when the relevant physical capacity they are designed to augment is lost, there impact is very demoralising: arriving too early, when they seem unnecessary, can lead to them being rejected. In terms of service planning, one can see the benefit of the continuity of care: for example, if someone develops speech problems, it is much easier to work with him or her if a relationship has already been established. It is both easier practically for the worker – comprehension is more likely – and emotionally for the patient who will not have the challenge of establishing a new relationship without one of the skills they would have most relied on in the past. But, given scarce resources, it is not always possible to plan ahead by offering help when need is not so great, in anticipation of future benefits when problems escalate.

As well as these challenges to planning there is also the reality of MND presenting a clear example of high-need, low-incidence care. This is a characteristic it shares with a wide range of other conditions and the policy relevance of this within the modern welfare state has been considered in our introduction and will be revisited in our conclusion. Suffice to say, here, that this feature of MND presents challenges for both individual health practitioners and for planning systems of care. For example, incidence and prevalence figures mean that a typical GP will only rarely encounter a person with MND and a health authority will only have a small number of people within its area as it seeks to set targets within its health improvement plan. MND presents a community of interests or needs and not a geographic community and as such risks being marginalised in a health and social care planning system based on locality.

Many of the problems of service provision are brought into close focus by diagnosis and by end-of-life care. We will consider each of these crucial stages. They are also stages that highlight the emotional impact of the disease and that illustrate challenges to effecting user involvement.

Diagnosis

The debate about the benefits of frank discussion about diagnosis and prognosis has been present for many years. Research evidence about the efficacy of such frankness has been accumulating since the 1970s. There are a number of published biographical accounts that consider diagnosis and disclosure. Henke (1968) writes:

> I am very glad that the doctor answered my questions fully and honestly, even to the point of telling me that I would need to be with people who were prepared to do everything for me. Being told that the disease was a progressive one enabled me to do things while I could and not leave them in the hope that I would soon be feeling better.
>
> (Henke 1968: 765)

Carus, in 1980, adopts a similar attitude: 'I could not live a lie ... I have never regretted telling [my wife] because we have always been able to discuss any problems and work things out together' (Carus 1980: 455).

Research on people with cancer (Hinton 1979) found that they were least anxious and depressed where communication was frank and where they were given answers to their questions. But, as Saunders *et al.* (1981) point out, the trajectory of even terminal cancer has occasional unexpected upturns. Sometimes 'final' attempts at treatment have a marked impact. A doctor who has worked in a hospice

> will have a number of such patients to quote if it seems right to add hope and optimism to a poor prognosis. At best, motor neurone disease may have a temporary remission during which time the disease ceases to progress, but

this is rare. Many doctors believe that such a prognosis is too bleak to be contemplated in full by anybody.

(Saunders *et al.* 1981: 133)

Johnston *et al.* (1996) found that with MND, as with other incurable diseases, patients were in favour of having information rather than being protected from distressing news.

> Unconfirmed fear does not seem preferable to having the diagnosis, even when the prognosis is as poor as in MND ... it is possible to overvalue the impact of an 'incurable' or 'terminal' diagnosis and to undervalue the impact of uncertainty.
>
> (Johnston *et al.* 1996: 31)

The value of the diagnosis 'lay primarily in labelling the condition and facilitating coping efforts ... suggesting the importance of a label in developing a representation of a disease which would then give a target for coping efforts' (Johnston *et al.* 1996: 31).

Johnston *et al.*'s study found, also, that patients preferred the diagnosis to be given in a direct, empathic style while someone else was present. They wished to be able to ask questions and wanted to receive information on what to do. There was no evidence that poor communications were associated with later mood disturbance. What the study did not show was how far information was given clearly and how far its implications were understood. Rather, the study showed how far people thought these things had happened.

In our interviews, each person had a detailed story to tell of his or her diagnosis and of the information received then, or shortly after. None had any significant degree of prior knowledge about MND. It is our contention that the point of diagnosis represents a major status passage and that the possibilities inherent in the new identity a person enters into are influenced by the way the diagnosis is given. At the very least it defines the doctor as a positive or negative influence and shapes the sense of any capacity for the individual to effect any control over what is happening to them now, and what may happen in the future.

Mrs N was told she had MND by her neurologist eight months before our interview:

> I asked, 'What's that?' He said, 'It's premature ageing of the nerve endings attached to your muscles. You can sit there and be a cabbage or you can fight it. The only way you can fight it is via physiotherapy. It's up to you.' I said, 'Knowing me, I'm going to fight it'. He said, 'I thought you would'.

Mrs N's brother was her closest family carer and spoke to the consultant at the diagnosis:

> A lot of doctors believe people don't want to know what the trouble is, they only want to know the good news and I think from the consultant's point of

view, when he told me he definitely misled me. Because I said, 'Will she be able to drive her car' and he said 'Oh yes,' he said 'No reason why she shouldn't.' Well, there was no chance she was going to drive a car. I got the impression that the physios were going to come round more or less every day … or at least three or four times a week. When you come to look at what happened that was absolutely impossible. But he was concerned with getting the bed and with getting us out as happy as we could be. I can understand them not telling people how bad they are likely to get. But at the end of the day we wanted to know what she needed at home. I wanted to get things organised. But they don't spell it out to you … They tell you virtually as if it was a cold you've got, gives you the impression, I imagine if someone is told in the early stages, they would say, 'Right, I'm going to work this off.' I can imagine people getting that impression.

This sense of underplaying the significance was not what Mr M experienced when he was given his diagnosis by a neurologist in 1994:

I was in (hospital) having final tests to confirm it. I was in a room on my own. He just came in and said, 'I'm afraid you have got a disease that is, will continue to deteriorate and there is nothing we can do for you.' And that just left me totally stunned and at a loss, not knowing what is going to happen next … At that time I still considered myself to be able bodied and I fully believed that I was, before he told me, that they would find out what it was and put it right. I was in a total state of shock … I've thought about this a lot and perhaps there isn't a good way to tell anyone, I just don't know … The consultant came in with four other people, I don't know who they were, and they just stood over me. And then I was just left on my own. I walked out and went onto the main ward. I just had to tell somebody. I went up to one chap and he wasn't interested and then another and he listened to me. He said, 'While the problems are still down there you keep on top of them,' and that is what I have tried to do. That came from another patient.

Mr M's wife adds that, at this point, nobody had actually mentioned MND, he still didn't know what he had got. Indeed, it was only after his discharge and subsequent appointment with his GP that the diagnosis was given. Mr M again:

When I was walking through the ward I heard the nurses saying, 'Mr M has been told but he hasn't been told that yet.' And I thought, 'Oh what else?' At the time I thought of cancer. We had a terrible night of wondering what it was until we went to the doctor the next day.

Mrs W experienced her husband's diagnosis as something that became part of the problem, not something helpful. He was told in hospital by the neurologist eight months before our interview. Mrs W was not there when the diagnosis was given. But she speaks of the events as ones that made her feel ill and hopeless:

He was told, 'You have got MND'. 'What's that?' 'There's no cure'. That was it. I've no complaint with the way they found out, they just have to eliminate things and particularly with this it would have made no difference if they had found out on day one. But being told, he was so matter of fact. I don't know what I expected him to be really … I know they can't wrap things up. But it would have made such a difference. Because for two months I was just so ill. I think they were more worried about me than about [my husband]. I never thought I would feel right again. And the difference that could have made, I think, just in the way we were told. I'm not saying we would have walked out of the hospital laughing. But the difference in how our doctor [GP], tried to, and did, get us out of this hopeless feeling just with what they said. And people, friends, who knew somebody who had not had MND but had cystic fibrosis and how she had dealt with it. But the difference that could have been made, we just came out of that hospital and we felt as though we hadn't got any hope at all, and [it's the same] every time we have been back to the hospital since.

By contrast Mrs L, diagnosed eighteen months before we saw her and then aged 70, reported the diagnosis as having been handled well. She, however, did regret the delay from the arrival of her first symptoms to finding out:

The doctor who told me was very nice. He sat on the bed. He waited until my husband was there. He held my hand and brought a woman with him, I didn't know who she was. He was very good. He said, 'Any questions?' Well, you can't think can you at the time. Then he came the next morning before nine and still asked me if I had any questions, but you can't think what to ask.

Mr L comments:

At her first appointment, after she started tripping, they just got her a walking stick, no tests.

Mrs L continues:

If something had happened then and I'd have known I could have done things I had in my dreams. The Orient Express I never got on, things like that while I could walk. I just wish he had said. It would have made a difference to my life for a year.

Members of the same research team who looked at diagnosis (Johnston *et al.* 1996) have also studied how people cope with motor neurone disease (Earll *et al.* 1993). In their sample of fifty people with MND almost all are identified as knowing they have got MND and that there was no cure. But, beyond that, there was considerable variation. For example their expectation of the progress of the disease showed that less than a half expected to be worse in six months, the remainder either did not know what to expect or expected they would be about the same. One person expected to be better. Whilst most in the sample saw the disease as serious only half of them rated it as very serious. Overall representation of the condition seemed linked to objective problems of daily living and not things like the severity of symptoms or speech or swallowing problems. The vast majority had done something to try and understand their condition and 20 per cent had tried alternative therapies. Eighty per cent thought that they were coping quite, or very, well and people were more likely to think they were doing well if they had made some coping effort, seeking either alternative remedies or information.

Our interviewees spoke of how they experienced being left alone to cope after the diagnostic period. None of them knew anything substantial about the disease and their wish to find out showed a variation not just between individuals with MND but between the priorities of those of their carers.

After the diagnosis of MND was given to Mr H he was told:

> There wasn't a great deal they could do … all they could do was manage the problems that arise and so continue at the outpatients every three months. But after that I felt that they were leaving me on my own … They told me I had got motor neurone disease without telling me what it was, what would happen. They told me what it was but not what would happen to my body … The only thing I knew about it was that it was incurable and that Don Revie had died from it, and that was all. [My wife] tried to find out about it but I was happy to go along. I knew that I would get worse and that sooner or later I might never move. But [my wife] went all over getting information.[2]

Mrs H adds:

> I went to [the local] reference library and found out as much as I could on MND. I photocopied a lot of information and brought it home but I found it very difficult to understand. It was out of medical reference books and was, obviously had terminology. Then I contacted the [hospital] library and asked for information, obviously there was a charge for it, but I got that and then we got information from the MND Association. [My husband's] sister phoned them. For us who don't know medical terminology the information we got from them, for [my husband] and I, it was much more beneficial. It was in simple terms. It covered all the different areas, problem areas, who you had to talk to, drugs available and it was all written in clear precise English while the other things had gone over my head.

Mr J, at his diagnosis, asked:

> 'What's this?' [and the neurologist replied]: 'It's a wasting away of the muscles.' I asked if there was treatment, he said, 'There is none. All we can do is keep the muscles you have got as strong as we can.'

Mrs J added:

> They said there was no cure for it at the moment. There were trials going on and hopefully there would be and all they could do was keep the muscles as strong and give help when it was needed. But nothing else.

Mr and Mrs J had only heard about Don Revie, they did not know of anyone else with MND.

> When we joined the MND Association they sent us loads of booklets. I read them and when I said to him 'Look at this', he said, 'No, I don't want to know'. Now they send us *Thumb Print* (Newsletter of the MNDA) I think every quarter. I read it and I point out anything in it that's of interest to him, that's good, you know. But, other than that, he has never wanted to know.
>
> (Mrs J)

Mr and Mrs M did 'not really' know about MND at diagnosis although Mrs W's sister had a friend who had it. Apart from that, they knew about David Niven and Don Revie but 'didn't know how it developed'. They didn't consider that they got information at the time.

> A social worker's help was offered at the time [the neurologist] was telling me this. I thought: 'Well does he mean a counsellor, or someone who is going to give me some encouragement?' But when it worked out it seemed the social worker was coming to tell me of all the benefits a disabled person could get.
>
> I wanted to get in touch with the MND Association. I had to find that out for myself. I wasn't directed. I didn't really want to know to what extent the disease could develop. I needed to be able to cope with it as it developed and not be worrying about what might, or might not, happen two years down the road. That's how I have looked at it. So I've coped with each new situation as it developed. That is still how I do it.
>
> (Mr M)

There is a need to understand that giving information is something that contributes to the sense a person has about the autonomy they might enjoy while living with the illness. Further, the way that information is given can give a presentiment of the developing relationship the person will have with the professions they will encounter. Information is not neutral, it can be empowering or disabling:

> The speech therapist, when he came at last, for a reason best known to himself, said, 'Eventually you will have respiratory problems, in the ability to expand your chest.' I thought, 'Well, thank you very much.' It probably will develop but at the moment I'm all right. But it's at the back of my mind. Now, I

think, if for some reason I can't breathe properly I think, 'Oh heck, this is the next phase.' It may not be.

(Mr M)

We know all there is to know and we don't want to know anything else that isn't positive. We know it all and you just need just some, just a little bit of hope. That's what you need.

(Mrs K)

Many of our respondents spoke of information that they had been given that was not helpful. The most common example related to swallowing. Ostensibly we can hypothesise that professionals, in giving information about swallowing, are seeking to offer reassurance. Perhaps they see a concern with swallowing as something they can readily alleviate. But, when this information is given, often very early after diagnosis, it conjures up a degree of disability and need that is alien to the way people were choosing to cope with their new illness status.

The [hospital staff] told me about the swallowing and about my arms but they didn't tell me about some of the other things that can happen. It can be blooming degrading the illness really. You can do nothing for yourself. Perhaps, they didn't want to tell me too much. He [the doctor] said 'If it comes to that we can keep you living with tubes in your stomach'. I said, 'I hope I die before that comes'.

(Mrs L)

As people came along to see me, especially specialists like the speech therapist or the doctor who came to examine me for the use of the POSSUM (an electronic environmental control system) they would say, 'If your swallowing deteriorates we will put a tube in your stomach.'

(Mr M)

Mrs M adds,

'They came out with it just like that!'

The tube was not mentioned to Mrs N. Here the absence of information was a problem:

In the hospital I was told to eat well, drink well and talk a lot and if I was in any difficulty to call my doctor. He [the GP] said, 'Well if you can't swallow the best you can do is dial 999 because you won't be breathing'.

(Mrs N)

Her brother, Mr N, added:

He said 'Don't ring me, ring the ambulance'. Now I wasn't very happy about that.

Mrs N completed their comments on this subject by saying:

It ruins confidence really.

End-of-life care

In this section we will consider just two aspects of end-of-life care that, together, illuminate areas of major concern, the physical circumstances associated with death and the place of care.

The Motor Neurone Disease Association produces a booklet for professionals on death and dying and encloses within it a booklet written with patients and carers in mind titled 'How will I die?' The summary guidance on the front of the patients and carers booklet is instructive:

At some point everyone with MND realises that death is inescapable sooner or later. This leaflet has been given to you because you have asked the question directly or indirectly. If you don't want to think or talk any further about this matter put the leaflet aside now.

The booklet, like the professionals' one, recognises the social, practical and spiritual context of dying – talking about it, involving one's family, making a will, perhaps consulting a spiritual adviser – and it also looks at specific fears of the process of dying the person with MND may have. A specific area of fear is that of choking to death, and the leaflets are reassuring about the capacity to prevent this.

Attacks of breathlessness or choking can sometimes indicate that an end-of-life stage is approaching. MND is rarely, itself, a specific cause of death. However, death usually follows the weakening of the respiratory system, itself caused by MND, either because of an infection or the deterioration of the muscles that make breathing possible. Addressing both the fears and the actuality of choking is therefore central to end-of-life care.

A study of care in a hospice included data on 124 patients with MND of whom 113 died in the hospice. Most had been initially referred for nursing care (56 per cent). Others had gone for respite care (20 per cent) or symptom control (15 per cent). Only 8 per cent had initially been referred specifically for terminal care. Of those that died, 40 per cent of people deteriorated suddenly and died within twelve hours, a further 18 per cent died within twenty-four hours. Four per cent died within three days and 17 per cent died within seven days. However, although the most typical clinical picture preceding death is one of sudden and rapid deterioration due to respiratory failure, no patient in this study choked to death. The authors conclude that: 'The term choking is an emotionally charged one and does not accurately describe the cause of death in motor neurone disease. Its use must be abandoned' (O'Brien *et al.* 1992: 473).

The experience of the MND Association is that most people with MND prefer to die at home, a preference widely shared in other diagnostic groups. However, the terminal phase of the disease may include an escalation of health care needs alongside the likelihood that family and other carers will be tired from the accumulating burdens, both physical and emotional, of responding to the demands consequent upon the illness. This is a time in which co-ordination between services is paramount if the person's wishes are to be supported. But it is a time which, even if anticipated, often occurs suddenly. Advance planning is required, but as we have seen this is not easy, for both practical and emotional reasons. Some of the likely problems of terminal care planning are replicated in the problems of providing appropriate respite care.

A study of respite admission to a hospice (Hicks and Corcoran 1993) found that, although the majority of respite admissions were planned more than a week in advance, a significant number of requests were for admission within a few days. This, the authors suggest, demonstrates a breakdown in community support and a lack of awareness as to the gravity of the situation until a crisis point is reached. It is carer exhaustion, or at least the perceived need by the GP for the carer to have a break, rather than the physical deterioration of the patient which is given as the reason for admission to respite care. But well-co-ordinated community care might have prevented such urgent requests.

> Some patients and carers feel that respite care is best provided in their own homes, where familiar surroundings are coupled with appropriate equipment, and have even suggested that professionals should offer a full-time domicilary service for two weeks so that carers can take a holiday. The cost of such a scheme is beyond the reach of most people although it could be seen as an ideal.
>
> (Hicks and Corcoran 1993: 148)

While there are very good reasons for a move to institutional care in some cases, some fundamental questions need to be addressed before the decision is made. First, is it possible to put in place help that would allow home care to continue if this is what the patient wants? Second, what sort of institution would offer best care? Third, and allied with this, what is the priority for the patient? Moore (1993) contrasted patients who died at home with those who died in hospital. The former had

> a greater sense of self determination in a setting that offered them a sense of belonging, and that the families who provided support felt more comfortable assisting the patient in his decision to die at home ... As one patient stated, 'I can ... experience the familiar smells of my wife's cooking or perfume. I can direct, discipline and watch my children play baseball. I can run my business and financial affairs, I can refuse a treatment or medication, have a beer or order a pizza. In other words, be in control.'
>
> (Moore 1993: 66–7)

In contrast, in this Canadian study, patients who died in hospital usually had decisions about care and the approach to dying imposed upon them by professionals. 'Quite often, invasive procedures, untimely medications, or aggressive nursing techniques contributed to a loss of patient dignity and control' (Moore 1993: 66).

Contact with other people with MND

We were concerned to see how far people had contact with others in similar situations. Any collective expression of needs, or strategic user involvement, seems predicated on a pooling of such experiences. There are clearly practical problems to the achievement of this: the geographic dispersal of people with MND, the problems in communication associated with its development (speech difficulties would make telephone contact problematic, loss of manipulative skills would inhibit the use of computer-based networks). In addition, there is the speed of deterioration in many people and the burden of symptoms. Our interviewees identified a number of other inhibiting factors when we asked if they had, or wished to have, contact with others with MND. (We will comment on their specific thoughts about the role of the MNDA in a subsequent section.) Not surprisingly there is a difference in emphasis, even in overall agendas, between people with MND and their carers.

In contemplating the future after her husband was diagnosed Mrs H says that meeting others

> was something we thought about in the early stages. I mean certainly from my point of view I wanted to know more about it and I certainly could have met someone just to see what was ahead of me and how it was going to progress … [Now] … I don't feel the need to talk to someone with motor neurone is the answer. It may be beneficial but I don't think it is the answer, it's not such a priority as it was in the beginning.
>
> (Mrs H)

Mr H arrived at the same conclusion but for different reasons:

> I don't think I would like that (meeting other people with MND) because I feel, if they were worse than me by seeing them I may feel worse.

Mr and Mrs J had met someone with MND. Although the meeting appeared to be unproblematic at the time, subsequently it did raise uncertainties:

> Another chap from [nearby] had come down with the same disease and the speech therapist asked 'Would you meet him?'
>
> (Mr J)

Mrs J continued:

It's all right speaking to a doctor but it's not the same as speaking to someone with the same illness. So yes, he did, and within a year he had died and this is why I ask, 'Is there a slow process?' Everybody is really happy with his [the husband's] progress.

Mrs K, who was caring for her husband, viewed suggestions that she should attend group meetings as implying criticism of her actions:

One doctor at hospital said he thought it would be a good idea for me to go to groups because 'It seems to me the poor chap who has got this is coping quite well and it's you that is not'. We came out and just sat on that bench outside and we, well I did, cried.

Mr M's position had changed:

Initially I didn't want to know what, eventually, the disease leads to. I just wanted to cope with what developed ... [Now] one of the things I want to do is use my situation to make people aware of the difficulties of this disease and try to press for more research and so I wrote to the *Yorkshire Post* (regional daily newspaper) and they did an article on me.

Self-help groups: the MND Association

The UK MND Association was set up in 1979, the Scottish MNDA two years later and the Irish three years after that. The context of the UK MNDA's establishment was a perceived lack of scientific interests and a prevalent medical defeatism in relation to MND. The achievements of the Associations, in a wide range of areas, have been considerable. There is a network of Regional Care Advisers, a wide range of practical supports for people with MND and their carers, over 100 local branches and groups, centres bringing together care and research, research studies funded or supported, an annual international symposium, and lobbying and education – sometimes collaboratively with over forty other international associations and sometimes in collaboration with other UK groups, for example via the Neurological Alliance.

What began as self-help organisations, literally of well-meaning amateurs, have become focal points for advances in research, medicine and therapeutics ... they are acquiring a distinctive professionalism and expertise in areas ranging from the daily life of people with ALS/MND to the organisation of public education and the strategic management of research.

(Cardy 1993: 5)

One area of concern to the Association is the extent to which they can offer a particular perspective on how research progresses. Specifically, while an aim common to both the MNDA and drug companies might be to find both treatments and cure, the Association has priorities in how people with MND are used, and a remit to speak up for their interests if they appear to be at odds with the tactical decisions that drug companies might choose to make. For example, there is a need to protect from over-exploitation the relatively small population of people with MND willing, and able, to participate in research.

Pharmaceutical companies will want to maintain confidentiality during drug development and maximum publicity when viable compounds are produced. But they are operating in a rapidly changing environment. The speed with which information can be communicated and the wider access to such information via the Internet is a major factor. Not only can people challenge what was previously sequestered expert knowledge but they can also seek alliances and exert pressure. We have seen in relation to HIV/AIDS research a wish to shift the established protocols of drug trials. This has been done by arguing for there being no placebo group or other sorts of blinding or double blinding. Organised and knowledgeable patient and carer groups have argued that the established guidelines are not adequate for incurable and often rapidly deteriorating conditions where the length of orthodox trial protocols might be longer than some patients' life expectancy, or certainly long enough to see a very major deterioration in their functioning. Indeed HIV/AIDS groups shared information about studies specifically to negate the protocols of the drug company and the health administration (Kramer 1995: 379–82; Gray *et al.* 1995). This is an area we have commented on in both our MS and CF chapters. Here we can reiterate that information technology offers a particular appeal in areas of contested knowledge, expert doubt and prognostic uncertainty. It also offers a particular appeal for those challenged in terms of mobility and orthodox communication, and to those geographically isolated.

Cardy's review of the role of the MNDA also includes a recognition that technological advance and continually refined treatment regimes, for example ventilator developments and changes in feeding techniques, may mean people can be kept alive longer. Such possibilities raise questions about patient autonomy, carer views (given they may not always be the same as those of the person they are caring for), and medical possibilities. The developments involve questions about quality of life as well as duration of life and necessitate engaging with the continuing debate about choosing to bring forward the time of one's death.

In the context of a maturing Association and a developing culture of patient and carer involvement in many areas of health and social care Cardy comments:

> The time is past when these issues could be settled solely by medical professionals. Patients and care givers themselves, and patient associations will have an increasingly important part to play in pushing out the boundaries of ethico-legal frameworks, as they have already begun to do in the context of patient choice over the modest interventions now available.
>
> (Cardy 1993: 7)

But choice is a sophisticated construct that needs information and understanding. It is likely to be exercised, in this context, in times of great stress for patient and carer and to be in an area about which people are unlikely to have prior knowledge or experience. There is also likely to be little by way of a cultural context within which to understand or make choices outside of that context that can be shaped by the MNDA nationally and locally (see King 1993 on the cultural context of HIV knowledge).

One area in which the accumulated experience of the MNDA, in terms of its familiarity with the views of people with MNDA, their carers, professionals, the research community and policy makers can become evident, is in seeking to establish agreed standards of care. The document they have drawn up (MNDA 1997) identifies speed of progression as the key feature of the disease and informed choice for people with MND as the guiding principle for responding to it.

> The key feature of the disease is the speed of progression which poses huge problems of adjustment for people who have MND; an escalating burden on carers and families; and a challenge to those (purchasers and providers) who are involved in meeting the variable and complex needs across agency boundaries.
>
> It is essential that people with MND be enabled to make informed choices about living with the disease and achieving quality of life.
>
> (MNDA 1997: 1)

These features and principles translate to standards about speed in acquiring the correct diagnosis, its sensitive communication, subsequent planning and continuity and co-ordination of support and care. There should be 'planning and management of the disease determined by the needs and wishes of the person with MND, their family and carers'.

Our interviewees' responses to the role of the MNDA were very positive. Perhaps this is not surprising in that we contacted people to interview via the good offices of the regional MNDA representative and so recruited a particular sub-set of the overall population of people with MND. What was clear was the wide range of activity looked to from the MNDA. We have seen how Cardy describes the nuanced and developing relationship of the MNDA as it negotiates a role in relation to the many agendas and interests that intersect the field. Here we reflect some of them in the comments of our interviewees.

Putting people in touch with one another and providing information is one important activity. After hearing her husband's diagnosis, Mrs H wanted to know more about the MNDA.

> We spoke to the MNDA about it and asked if there were any meetings, groups, which we could go along to. From my point of view, it was to talk to other people to find out how they coped with a certain situation because if I could learn from that that was going to help both of us. There was a group that met in [nearby town], which wasn't really a problem, on a Friday. But they weren't really meeting for that purpose. They were meeting to initiate fund-raising. Now I work and felt I just didn't have time to get involved in anything like

that. So that's about as far as we ever got ... From my point of view I feel I know more now than I did in the early stages and I've learnt now if I am finding something a problem then I can speak to someone in social services or to the care adviser for the MND for the region. There are people you can speak to help overcome these problems.

(Mrs H)

Mr and Mrs J hadn't met anybody else with MND:

But that's our fault. [the local branch] sent us invitations to go to meetings, but we never have done. There's also always a big congress in Birmingham and they send and ask if we want to go, but we haven't. The trouble is getting there, no transport is provided.

Others are clearer that they don't want to attend groups:

We have been in touch with the MNDA and spoken to people but I didn't feel I wanted to go to any groups. I'd love to be able to help someone come round from this. But I don't want to go to any of the groups.

(Mrs K)

Mr M approached contact differently:

I've not cut myself off from people with MND. I've been to meetings of the local group, met other people, talked with them and I know pretty well now what, eventually, the disease leads to.

If there is some difference of opinion about the benefits of group membership there is a very warm welcome for the MNDA's provision of aids and adaptations:

The MNDA have been fantastic ... all we have had to do is open our mouth and it has been there.

(Mr J)

I've received every help I have asked for and sometimes even things I didn't know I was able to get, like the POSSUM

(Mr M).

We can see, in the range of views we have encountered, how there can be problems in achieving informed choice if people do not want information in advance of need and if there is a reluctance to actively participate in groups. But there is also a sense in some people's interviews of the benefits to themselves that can accrue from the knowledge and experience of others. There is also a sense that organisations like the MNDA offer a way to influence services and help others like themselves.

Social attitudes and MND

We have considered the views of a small number of people with MND and those caring for them and have put this alongside a critical reading of the literature. Those we interviewed often had general views as to what was needed and comments to make on the social position of those with MND. Mr N, for example, speaking about his sister's experience of having MND, concluded that:

> You have got to fight for assistance. This is the problem in today's society. If you haven't got somebody fighting for you then you never get anything. And I think if people were made more aware of what they have to do, of what can be done and can't be done they will be a lot better off.

Mr M had a generally positive experience:

> When they are with me people seem to behave as they always have done. I don't know what they are like when they are out of my company. There are certain friends who don't want to see me because they don't want to see me like this. I understand that and I just wait until they feel they can. But generally people have just accepted me as I used to be. That's how I feel anyway. People have been more attentive, more caring, and that has been a development in this situation. I have felt that from them.
>
> (Mr M)

Mr H's experience had not been so positive:

> I find socially that my old mates won't say hello to me, and not talk to me anymore, either because they don't know what to say or that they are shocked at seeing me, how I am.

Mrs H felt that:

> The more people that know, or are aware, then things might happen.

But Mrs K wanted a certain sort of social reaction:

> It's just the simple things that people say. You just need hope. If you meet someone in the street and they say, 'What has [your husband] got?' and you say, 'MND,' they say, 'Oh,' and my stomach would drop. And then you bump into somebody and they say, 'I know someone with that, nine years ago, and he struggles but is still walking,' that is what you want to hear.
>
> (Mrs K)

In considering the overall experience of those closest to this condition, people with MND, current carers and recent past carers, we can look to a survey which gathered data from 641 in the first group, 501 in the second and 232 in the third

(Birch *et al*. 1995). The majority of people with MND were diagnosed by a consultant neurologist (515 people) and were given the diagnosis in a hospital. Four hundred and eleven people felt the diagnosis was given sensitively and 189 said it was not. There appeared to be a shift in that more people diagnosed in the previous two years reported sensitivity than those diagnosed five or more years ago, but there was still a very large minority reporting negatively. Many people were told when they were alone, in a blunt manner and without explanation or an opportunity to discuss what future help might be available. A considerable majority of current and past carers experienced the diagnosis as a negative experience in which their needs were not adequately considered and in which sufficient information was not given.

As Birch and colleagues well understand, these sorts of results are problematic because we do not know what people are comparing their experiences with. Likewise, when people are asked to rate how good the services they receive are, we have to consider their replies alongside any narratives of the experience we can elicit to help us see the evidence on which they base their conclusions.

We also have to consider a consistent puzzle in attempts to elicit estimates of satisfaction with care in the UK: recipients of health services report high levels of satisfaction with care even in situations where the stories they tell would seem to indicate poor service or where objective measures (how long they were kept waiting, how little continuity of staff there was and so on) would seem to suggest all is not well. Birch *et al*. (1995) found that most people rated services highly and considered them well co-ordinated: 473 people with MND (out of 609 replies) rated services good or very good. Current and past carers were also positive (382 out of 477 current and 174 out of 216 past carers).

Thoughts about priorities showed all groups putting 'more research into MND' as top (as with MS and CF surveys). Increased knowledge amongst the public was ranked second amongst people with MND while carers put the way diagnosis was given second and past carers wanted an increase in knowledge amongst professionals as their second priority.

The three groups identified different things as top problems: people with MND said reliance on others; carers said psychological adjustment and past carers identified physical burden/total reliance as the main problem. Such differences underline the complexities of seeking user involvement, not least because they show that using carers as proxy voices for people with MND is likely to distort priorities. Carers have needs services should respond to. But when they look back on their experience they are likely to have a different sense of what was needed than the ones they had when in the midst of providing care.

Biographical accounts

There has been publicity associated with the deaths of well-known figures from MND: David Niven, Leonard Cheshire, Jill Tweedie, Don Revie and Joan Lestor (and internationally, Dimitri Shostakovich). There is also the high profile of Stephen Hawking with his continued contribution to not only his academic discipline but also to the MNDA. A number of people with MND have written about the disease and their insights help illustrate some of the points made above. Some biographical accounts talk about the impact on themselves: 'It's a lot like going from being 37 to being 90 in six months' (Whitehurst 1995). Others talk of its impact on those around them. Sandra Fordham writes about her 6-year-old son: 'Our parent/child relationship has been turned upside down. I'm unable to help him put on his school uniform but he helps me when I'm struggling with jumpers and is good at scratching my ear' (Fordham 1996: 72).

The comedian Zed sums up many of the oft-reported features in a newspaper interview where he describes the speed of progression of his MND by saying that last August he was playing football, after Christmas he needed help to walk and by May he was confined to a wheelchair. 'I can't keep up with the disease any more. Every day I find something new I can't do.'

He identifies the biggest blow as being the impairment of his speech: 'people assume I've nothing worth saying. They exclude me from conversation, or talk over me, or are too embarrassed to ask me to repeat myself.'

He continues:

> It's difficult to maintain any dignity. I burp all the time now, as the back of my throat's always open. And I need to use a finger to move food around my mouth, as my tongue doesn't work properly. If I'm at a restaurant, people laugh or call me a retard. They don't realise the disease only affects your body and not your mind.
>
> (Quoted in Batty 1998: 13)

There are resonances in this description of that distinction between impairment and disability discussed in previous chapters. It is the reaction to the physical manifestations of the illness that cause, or confound, many of the problems. These reactions certainly add to the practical difficulties with mobility and speech that, in themselves, can create challenges to involvement. A social attitude that assumes a specific form of speech as a *sine qua non* of intelligence will be very detrimental to the chances of people with MND maintaining their place in society, let alone shaping their care.

Future orientation

We would argue that prerequisites for user involvement include a sense of future orientation and a belief that some things are changeable.[3] These prerequisites underpin the more specific practical problems and emotional challenges to bringing people together. Our interviewees offered some specific thoughts on policy and practice, but also contributed more general summaries of the way this small group of people saw their life with MND, or their life caring for someone with MND.

Mrs L, who lives in a small town surrounded by countryside for many miles, is concerned with the lack of specialist knowledge of those who come to help her. She suggests:

They could do something like Macmillan Nurses, somebody like that, a specialist. If they had only one trained then she could train the others.

She is concerned as to what will happen if she is not able to stay at home being cared for by her husband (he is now 76 years old):

> What would be of help is that someday, unless I die, I will have to go away. I mean he has done very well but ... No one can tell you where. I mean there are homes around here but they aren't trained, they don't know anything about it. They talk about hospice but say they will only have you in for a week or so. But I just wonder where I will end up. It would be nice to know that ... If I won the lottery I would open a home, with staff who knew what they were doing. There must be people, apart from me, who wonder what is going to happen to them.

After being diagnosed, Mr M's attitude was:

> I thought, well, I've got to get on with the rest of my life and I didn't know what that meant in terms of life span or whatever.

A specific practice change he would recommend links with the diagnostic process:

> What would be of great help at diagnosis is if the consultants could say that a person from MNDA would be available to come to talk to you. Instead of like I had to do, wait a month or two before I even knew the organisation existed.

A part of future orientation for some people includes not thinking too much about what might have been. Mr and Mrs J had to give up the family business and now neither of them works. Mrs J says:

> I've resigned myself to not doing anything now.

But there is still a need to plan ahead with changes in the house or to go on an outing or a holiday:

> Life has to go on so you have got to have things working for you to help you. Struggle enough, life, isn't it ...? Things could be a hell of a lot worse, so we just get on with it.

Mr J added:

> We're OK really.

Mrs K's attitude is of the 'making-the-most-of-it' school:

If it comes to his having to have a wheelchair all the time, we are hoping it won't, but if it does, well you can still have a good life in a wheelchair can't you?

Conclusion

This last quote from Mrs K sums up many of the things we have discussed above. In thinking about the lived experience of the disease, and the exercise of user involvement in relation to it, we have to consider its physicality. We have to look at moral agency, at the elements of an ethical life with illness and the capacity to say yes to life. We also have to consider the presence or absence of a future orientation. We included in the title of this chapter the words of one of our interviewees saying that what was needed was 'just a little bit of hope'. Hope combines expectation with desire. It is, then, a particular sort of future orientation. The experience of MND can cause a rift between the two components of hope. For some this is a spur to action, for others it negates the imperative for future orientation. User involvement intrudes pragmatism into the encounter between expectation and desire. The two can only come together through action. For some people with MND, committing to that action, or facing the dislocation between expectation and desire, is too much.

Notes

1 For these opening sections we have drawn on material published by the MND Association. They produce detailed guidance on a range of aspects of MND in leaflets targeted at professionals, people with MND, their carers and children.

2 We carried out interviews for this chapter in Yorkshire. The person whose MND was most well known was Don Revie, former manager of Leeds United Football Club. Cardy makes the important point that, 'The disease, if known at all, has only a little folklore, that being thoroughly dreadful in character' (1993: 7).

3 The publication of figures about increasing class inequalities in cancer and heart disease in the first months of 1999 was attributed to poverty, a lack of health care facilities and lifestyle factors. David Player, formally of the Health Education Council, linked a class variable in making choices about smoking and healthy eating to a lack of future orientation (BBC Radio 4, 28 April 1999). People on estates, he argued, don't have a sense of the future in the same way as the middle classes do. They don't see why they should do things now to benefit later life – their preoccupation is more immediate. While this reading of the figures is problematic, in that it presupposes that different social classes express future orientation in the same way (a way defined by one particular class), it does link with our observations about user involvement and future orientation.

6 Cystic Fibrosis

'As normal a life as possible'

Cystic fibrosis is a genetic condition that affects people from birth. Since the 1960s, when people with this condition rarely lived beyond their teens, life expectancy has steadily increased and many people are now living into their twenties and thirties. Although the disease is caused by mutation of a single gene, there are over 600 different mutations and the severity of symptoms varies widely from mild chest complaints and infertility to serious illness. Most people are diagnosed soon after birth but those with mild disease may not be diagnosed until later in life. The disease exhibits a great variety of symptoms (Duncan-Skingle and Foster 1991) and its severity varies not only between individuals but also over the course of the lifespan. In consequence, people with cystic fibrosis often have widely differing needs, depending on the severity of symptoms, and these needs fluctuate during the course of their lives.

Cystic fibrosis causes the body to produce abnormally thick mucus which blocks air passages in the lungs and becomes the site of recurrent bacterial infections. The mucus obstructs the pancreas and blocks the passage of digestive enzymes to the small intestine, thus impairing absorption of nutrients. As a result, it is often difficult for a person with cystic fibrosis to maintain an adequate weight.

People with cystic fibrosis can spend up to eight hours each day on various treatments and therapies in addition to dietary and other considerations that can interfere with a 'normal' lifestyle. Most undergo a daily regime of physiotherapy to loosen mucus from the lungs, often preceded by the inhalation of bronchodilators and/or antibiotics. Pancreatic enzymes must be taken before each meal and many people also take vitamin and other nutritional supplements. As pulmonary damage increases, with corresponding decrease in lung function, complications, including hemoptysis (spitting or coughing up of blood), diabetes and colonisation by resistant bacteria may develop. The frequency of hospital visits is likely to increase, as will the need for surgical intervention to treat hemoptysis, nasal polyps, nutritional deficits and for the insertion of central intravenous catheters to administer medicines. For some people, intravenous therapy, which can be administered in the patient's own home, has reduced the necessity for frequent hospital visits but remains a considerable restriction to lifestyle. Nocturnal nasogastric or gastrostomy feeds may be introduced to maintain body weight and aggressive antibiotic treatment, pulmonary toilet and use of oxygen and measures to control pain become increasingly necessary as breathing becomes more difficult.

As life expectancy has improved and people with cystic fibrosis are increasingly surviving into adulthood, two distinct groups have emerged: children and adults. Teenagers, who can largely be expected to make their own decisions about treat-ment and lifestyle but still remain under the legal jurisdiction of their parents, inhabit uneasily the middle ground. The emergence of distinct age groups can be attributed, in part, to the administrative separation of hospital services into children's and adults' services and to the fact that, historically, cystic fibrosis was almost exclusively a disease of childhood. The distinction is also reflected in the two national organisations which represent the interests of people with cystic fibrosis: the Cystic Fibrosis Trust, whose main constituency consists of children with cystic fibrosis and their parents, and the Association of Cystic Fibrosis Adults. Deaths among young children have become increasingly rare but, although most teenagers now survive into adulthood, some will die. Others will be experiencing seriously deteriorating health at the point of transition from children's to adult ser-vices and this has implications both for their care and for the aftercare of families.

The course of disease is rarely predictable. Although it is possible to predict that, as people become progressively more ill, they are likely to be entering a terminal phase, some people who are seriously ill do recover and the prospect of a heart-lung transplant offers hope of recovery and the prolongation of life. Over the past twenty years, there have been considerable advances in treatment for cystic fibrosis and the prognosis for sufferers has improved dramatically (Bell and Shale 1993; Dinwiddie 1993). People with cystic fibrosis are now both fitter and are living longer. The likelihood that the prognosis will continue to improve (Dinwiddie 1993) overshadows the knowledge that cystic fibrosis is still a life-limiting condi-tion. As the prospect of an early death recedes for the group as a whole, it becomes less easy for individuals to predict the likely span of their own lives and to confront the prospect of their own early death. A post from a 40-year-old contributor to a CF online chat group (CYSTIC-L) neatly encapsulates this dilemma:

> I have celebrated the 30th anniversary of my 'last' birthday. The docs let me go home 30 years ago to die.
>
> Well, I'm still here, with a wife of 17 years, 7-year-old son (no CF), and 15 years at the same company.
>
> Because I was raised with the 'You gonna die soon', I didn't set any goals, didn't learn how to manage money, and other important life skills.
>
> My advice: plan a normal life. Normal people die at all ages every day. Yes, as CF individuals we are at a disadvantage but let's not handicap ourselves with an attitude to boot. Focus on life and having fun: focusing on your upcoming death is about as fun and as useful as cleaning up bird poop.

Such optimism has been fuelled by the development of gene therapy, although the initial euphoria about a 'miracle cure' which was 'just around the corner' has been replaced by more realistic and quieter optimism. Although cystic fibrosis remains a progressive and ultimately fatal disease (Smith and Stableforth 1992), many of those interviewed for the present study believed that it is now a realistic prospect that cystic fibrosis may cease to be terminal and will become, instead, a managed condition.

The nature of the disease places heavy demands on health services, especially the acute hospital sector. A specialist clinic in Ireland found that length of hospital stay for patients with cystic fibrosis was more than double the average and that the cost of antibiotics was between five and twenty times greater than that for the average patient (Mulherin *et al*. 1991). The authors point out that, while paediatric hospitals are accustomed to treating patients with cystic fibrosis, this is 'a relatively recent development for an adult general hospital'. As the prognosis for the disease improves and people are living longer, the demands on the health care system are likely to increase. A brief survey of health service planners in one English health region found that, already, some were beginning to question the disproportionate use of resources by cystic fibrosis patients (Rhodes 1996). Paradoxically, the improved prognosis for cystic fibrosis patients leads to greater visibility within the health care system and potentially greater vulnerability as health service planners begin to consider questions of service priority and the opportunity costs of maintaining or increasing current levels of provision. It is therefore all the more important for people with cystic fibrosis to have a voice in the planning and delivery of their own health care.

Overview

This chapter addresses both empowerment at the individual level, and the potential for the development of a collective 'voice'. A central plank of official rhetoric has been the extension of consumer choice to the patient. Important areas of choice are choice in relation to individual treatment decisions and choice about who provides treatment and care and where. Two of the most significant choices for cystic fibrosis patients are when to commence palliative care and where to choose to die. A brief review of some of the options for patient choice in the treatment of cystic fibrosis is followed by a discussion of the options for palliative care. The chapter ends with a discussion of the extent to which people are presented with or offered choices about their treatment and care and their manner of living as they approach the ends of their lives and, secondly, of the ways in which people confronted with these various choices may experience them as empowering or disempowering. The analysis draws heavily on the work of Marion Barnes and David Prior (1995).

The interviews

During the course of the study, five specialist hospital centres for the treatment of cystic fibrosis, two Barnardo's projects and a children's hospice were visited, and a range of professionals were interviewed, including specialist medical and nursing staff, physiotherapists and social workers. Interviews were also carried out with members of the two national organisations serving the interests of people with cystic fibrosis, the Cystic Fibrosis Trust and the Association of Cystic Fibrosis Adults. Interviews with service users included both children and adults with cystic fibrosis and families and carers. People were contacted through the nurse specialists, at clinic sessions, through the national organisations, local groups and word of mouth. The interviews with professionals were conducted in their places of work. Those with patients and their relatives and carers were carried out on the wards, at clinic sessions or in their own homes. Three were telephone interviews. Most of the interviews and discussions were tape-recorded and later partially transcribed. In total, seventeen professional staff and seven people with cystic fibrosis were interviewed. Discussions were also held with four others, including three children under the age of 16, and with twelve family members.

Having a say

At the level of individuals, people with cystic fibrosis are usually actively involved in decisions about their own treatment and care. Unlike people in the late stages of multiple sclerosis or motor neurone disease, they are rarely so ill that they cannot communicate, although increasing breathlessness may limit their ability to carry on long conversations. They also tend to be a younger group. Thirdly, they usually have a long history of involvement with the health services and are familiar with the environment and staff and able to negotiate their way around 'the system'. They are often very knowledgeable both about their condition and about the treatments available and described themselves as highly vocal and assertive. In the words of one adult patient:

> Cystic fibrosis people are very outgoing and quite often achieve what they want.

This assertiveness was born from the familiarity which comes with long usage:

> You feel as if you are very much part of a team; almost at home with them all. You become very relaxed with them. Because you have known them a while, you are often on first-name terms, therefore you can talk about things that you think are wrong without fear of putting staff backs up and, usually, they will listen to you.
>
> (Woman with cystic fibrosis)

> Cystic fibrosis patients demand a lot more, unlike a lot of other patients. They are less intimidated by the health services, perhaps because they have been involved since a very young age.
>
> (Man with cystic fibrosis)

Despite this, treatment options and approaches often seemed to be determined more by the approach of consultants than by individual patients' wishes. A culture of consultant autonomy and professional rivalry was perceived to be far more influential in determining clinic practice than any views patients might have, either individually or collectively. An active member of the Association for Cystic Fibrosis Adults (ACFA) explained:

> Through my work with cystic fibrosis, I deal with a number of different consultants in different clinics and they all have different views about how treatments should be done. So, even if you get something done in one clinic, there is no guarantee that another doctor will think it is a good idea and do it in a different clinic. That is even without the involvement of patients. Patients always seem to come, not even second, but third down the line.

An area of some contention between patients and staff was intravenous (IV) antibiotic treatment administered in the patient's own home. The young people who were interviewed for the present study strongly supported home IV for themselves because it gave them greater autonomy and control over their lives, although they were aware that it was not necessarily the best option for everyone. Home IV can place extra burdens on the patient and increase the sense of isolation from others with the disease as well as from the support of the hospital multidisciplinary team (Catchpole 1989). Some nurses interviewed were afraid that it would be pushed in consideration of cost above patients' needs. Their fears are endorsed by the comments from respondents to a survey of cystic fibrosis adults who felt under pressure to accept this form of treatment when they were not happy to do it or with the back-up they received (Walters 1994).

The issue of failing to comply with treatment posed a more difficult problem, especially for teenagers. Many seem to value their chosen lifestyle over the possibility of an improved prognosis through adherence to an arduous daily treatment regime. Staff, who believed that some young people were jeopardising their future health, had difficulty in allowing them to exercise this choice. Although staff recognised that they often had little influence over adults, teenagers were generally considered too immature to be trusted with the choice.

Typically, parents assume responsibility for ensuring that their children's treatment regimes are followed but, as they enter adolescence, it is generally expected that young people will begin to take responsibility for themselves (Pounceby 1997). Yet, as Pounceby notes, parents may be reluctant to relinquish this role and there may be differing expectations between paediatrician and adult physician (*ibid.*).

The link between compliance with treatment and progressive disease, however, is inconclusive (Abbott *et al.* 1994). Teenagers, who may be enjoying reasonably good health, for whom the threat of ill health may seem a distant possibility and who may have seen others become ill despite strict adherence to treatment (Wynn-Knight 1996), may be unwilling to follow complex and time-consuming regimes which, at best, have an uncertain payback. The notion of health care advice ignores the fact that between health professional and patient there may be a significant clash of agendas, with professionals preoccupied by the potential benefits of treatment for the patient, while the latter is weighing up the personal costs of carrying it out (Abbott *et al.* 1994). In a survey of young people with cystic fibrosis between the ages of 13 and 24, Pounceby found that almost a quarter thought the doctor had no understanding of how treatment affected their lives and a similar proportion thought their doctor's approach was so rigid that they could not contemplate discussing treatment difficulties with him or her. 'For a substantial minority of people a traditional medical model prevailed, with little notion of a partnership or therapeutic alliance within which a shared agenda regarding the management of the treatment regimen could develop' (Pounceby 1997: 234; cf. Nuttall and Nicholes 1992). For teenagers, questions of independence and autonomy may compound tensions with parents and with health professionals, which crystallise around the issue of adherence to treatment. Issues of patient autonomy and user involvement may be confused with conflicting expectations relating to the transitional status between childhood and adulthood.

One area where people did seem to have genuine choice was in the decision whether or not to opt for an organ transplant, usually of the lungs and/or heart. Even here, family dynamics can raise complicated ethical questions over whether or not the person has real choice. By the time a transplant is considered, the chances of long-term survival are slim. Even if the transplant is successful, the future prognosis is by no means certain (Dinwiddie 1993). Many patients were thought to opt for a transplant for the sake of their families and instances where patients decide against a transplant are often a source of familial tension. The situation with children could become even more complex, with both staff and parents assuming the right to act on behalf of the child, sometimes from different perspectives.

Respondents complained that, whereas in the past doctors may have been over-optimistic in their portrayal of the risks of organ transplant, their current approach was too bleak. Whether or not it was a case of people not wanting to hear information which might dampen their hopes, or of doctors erring on the side of caution, people felt that they were not always receiving objective information.

The majority of people with cystic fibrosis have little choice of where treatment is provided or who provides it. For most, the choice is between a specialist centre, to which they may have to travel up to 100 miles, and their local district general hospital, where services and treatments are likely to be less good. In areas without a specialist centre, the local hospital is often the only option. Fear of being labelled a 'trouble-maker' or of not being accepted back was said to prevent people from changing to a different centre. Outside London, distance and the refusal of health authorities to pay for treatment outside their area were also major deterrents. Although it was widely accepted that specialist centres generally offer better services, centres can vary widely in their policies (Pounceby 1997) and the approach and standards of service of a single centre can affect a large number of people.

For some people, the role of the GP was pivotal; for others, the major part of their treatment and care was managed through specialist centres, with the GP fulfilling only a marginal role. The role of GPs, however, is likely to become more important in the future as the NHS moves further towards a primary-care-led service (Department of Health 1998a).

Respondents stressed the importance of 'having a good GP', both as a provider of services and as a gatekeeper to other services. An essential quality of a 'good GP' was the ability to listen and the most valued relationship was one of partnership. However, for many cystic fibrosis patients and their families, there seems to be little option of changing GP if they are not satisfied. Although the Cystic Fibrosis Trust (CFT) knew of cases where people had been struck off GP lists, it was more common for people to have difficulty in finding a GP who would accept them when they moved. People's sense of powerlessness came through in their use of words like 'lottery' and 'luck' to describe their experiences.

Palliative and terminal care

One of the areas in which people seemed to have some of the greatest opportunities to influence their own care was palliative and terminal care. Although, as they become progressively more ill, they are likely to be entering a terminal phase, the prospect of a heart-lung transplant offers hope of recovery. Most people, offered the possibility, opt for a transplant. The decision not to have a transplant almost inevitably means entering a palliative phase which will ultimately end in death. Even for those who choose to have a transplant, the likelihood of surviving long enough for suitable donor organs to become available is low and most will die while on the waiting list. Aggressive antibiotic treatment in order to keep the patient well enough to remain a candidate for transplant is usually continued to the point when it becomes obvious that the patient has become too ill or asks for it to be stopped. In consequence, aggressive treatment is often continued until near death. There is often only a short palliative phase and the decision to cease active treatment can be highly traumatic for both patients and their relatives (Cottrell 1991). In consequence, terminal care for people with cystic fibrosis has been, perhaps, less well developed than for people suffering from other conditions such as cancer.

One nurse specialist suggested that many young people with cystic fibrosis choose the option of a heart-lung transplant because they fear a lingering death:

> Their big fear is ending up on the wards for a long time without the freedom to go home, a long deterioration. They see people going through that and they are very frightened of it, and opting for a heart-lung transplant is a way of avoiding that.

The prospect of a transplant generates hope which, in many cases, will be unrealistic and may impede the patient and family from coming to terms with declining health and an early death. Although some staff spoke of the cruelty of a hope which was unlikely to be fulfilled, for many people it seemed to offer a means of coping. One mother, for example, described her feelings:

> I think that is how you get, how you cope with things in different ways. I do (deny it) to a certain extent. I don't feel, perhaps, [she'll die] tomorrow. If I

did, I would probably end up going mad, because you do. You have to take each day at a time because you can't look too far ahead because it would just frighten you to death. And, if you do feel, and that's what I was doing, thinking too far ahead at that time when K [my daughter] decided to come off [the waiting list for a lung transplant], I was thinking that was it. All we had aimed for was this transplant and then there was nothing there left or the end, you know, sort of thing to me, because it was going to be deteriorate and deteriorate and deteriorate. And I've seen her friends do that and I didn't want that for K. You just want a chance, don't you?

Admission to the waiting list for a transplant signals a rite of passage. For most, it marks officially the beginning of a decline which will ultimately end in death. Consequently, this can be a very distressing and traumatic time, both for patients and for families (Wynn-Knight 1996).

Staff spoke of the difficulty of preparing somebody for the possibility of rejection and death when transplant is a time of great hope and the emphasis is on the maintenance of good health through the pursuit of aggressive treatment. The change from aggressive to palliative treatment was rarely gradual but often sudden and traumatic. In some professionals' view, there is a tendency for active treatment to be continued for longer because the condition affects children and young adults than would be the case if patients were older. This was certainly an issue which concerned staff at the children's hospice visited.

The extent to which children have an independent voice was a matter of some debate. In one doctor's opinion, families are not always the best advocates for the child and are often prepared to 'try one last chance' in pursuing painful and invasive treatment which has little chance of success. In such cases, children's wishes or rights seemed to be indistinct from those of parents. Staff were at pains to stress that they always considered children's wishes to be paramount but, as one nurse admitted,

> Below a certain age, parents seem to have complete decision-making powers over what happens to their child.

Even where children were older, the child's rights were often confused: either the child would be too ill or would opt for treatment for the sake of parents. In the adult centres, staff were equally concerned about the pursuit of inappropriate aggressive treatment when people were admitted to accident and emergency or onto other wards.

One of the most delicate issues which professionals have to confront is the potential for patients and relatives to hold conflicting views. First, there is the difficult question of the extent to which children are able or allowed to have an independent voice. Second is the problem of determining the extent to which patients' expressed views are their own or reflect those of their families, partners or carers. All those professionals interviewed believed that some young people opt for a heart-lung transplant less in accordance with their own wishes than to please their parents or partners. A vivid example of the emotional tension within families which can accompany these life or death decisions was revealed in the anguish of the parents of a teenage boy who was seriously ill but refusing the option of a transplant.

Death in hospital

Surveys of bereaved relatives of people who have died of cancer suggest that the majority of people had wanted to die at home (Seale and Cartwright 1994; Addington-Hall and McCarthy 1995a; Addington- Hall 1998). Staff interviewed for the present study, however, reported that most patients with cystic fibrosis choose to die in hospital. In 1991, a survey of seventeen major cystic fibrosis centres in the United Kingdom and Ireland found that, of the 378 deaths which had taken place over the previous eight years, only sixteen (4 per cent) had occurred at home. Seven centres had experienced no home deaths (Cottrell 1991). Yet, two years later, a review of terminal care in cystic fibrosis stated:

> Many patients will die comfortably at home and the role of domiciliary nursing and physiotherapy services, and a close liaison with a general practitioner, are particularly important. Parents and families have usually been involved in management from an early age and, where possible, should be involved in discussion of the nature of end-stage care.
>
> (Bell and Shale 1993: 49)

As Cottrell's study showed, the overwhelming majority of cystic fibrosis deaths occur in hospital rather than at home or in a hospice or nursing home. There are probably several reasons for this. As one specialist nurse pointed out, specialist centres have little tradition of patients dying at home. One consequence is that staff have little knowledge of how to manage death in the community or how to access community services and their inexperience may inhibit them from suggesting a home death. A second reason is that patients with cystic fibrosis usually have a long history of involvement with a particular hospital, know the staff by first names and feel more secure among familiar faces and surroundings.

> Over the years, they become more like friends than patients. The children, and as they grow up, young adults learn to trust the staff and often confide in the nurses, particularly at night, telling them their innermost thoughts and fears – often about death.
>
> (Cottrell 1992: 28)

Conversely, many patients may have no relationship with the GP or district nurse as they have always gone directly to the hospital and may fear that insufficient or inexperienced support may result in mismanagement (*ibid.*). The availability of appropriate technical support and expertise was also thought to give patients a greater sense of security. A comment, from a nurse specialist for adults, reflected the general view:

> Most die in hospital. They want to be here because they are used to having so much treatment and support. They know the staff; they know oxygen is available and so on. They feel safer here.

In her opinion, it was largely patients' preference which dictated unit practice:

> A few patients we would love to get home but, whenever we mention it, they just say, 'No'. They feel safer here and don't want to leave.

Cystic fibrosis patients in specialist centres often have single rooms and facilities, which are not generally available to patients on other wards, and, in this sense, are more privileged than others. For some, there may also be a final desperate hope that a new treatment may become available. As one nurse explained:

> ... from what they've said to me, it's just because they feel that, if anything comes along that might help them, then they're more likely to get it in hospital; they feel they may be forgotten at home. And, when I've mentioned hospices, you know, if anything comes along that's new and wonderful, whilst they're in hospital, they might get it; they feel that.

Others may be motivated by a desire to protect their families or partners from the distress of having to manage their dying at home (cf. Cottrell 1991), not wanting their families to see them die (Quin 1996), or a fear of their families' reactions during the dying phase. As one nurse interviewed for this study explained,

> A cystic fibrosis death is quite frightening... Patients prefer to die in hospital and that's also true of the adults ... The patients need the reassurance and familiarity of hospital.

We know from studies of cancer patients that people's preferences can change over time and as the threat of death looms nearer (Hinton 1996). It was only in the last few days of life, when imminent death became a certainty, that some patients would opt for a hospital death.

> I think if you asked most of the patients, 'Where would you like to die, would it be at hospital or at home?' I think most of them would say, 'At home.' But, I think, when it actually comes to it ... most of them do want to be in hospital, they feel safer.
>
> (Specialist nurse, adults' unit)

> But, when the time is leading up to that, a lot of them they like the security of being in hospital, because when they get these breathless attacks they

become very anxious and they like the security. They know the doctors are going to be there, they know what to do about switching up the oxygen. We haven't had many deaths at home, we've had one or two, one of which has been planned and has gone OK. And a couple of times we've tried to plan it that they die at home but they've usually come back in because they've not coped at home because of the breathless attacks, because of the anxiety, they're frightened.

(Specialist nurse, adults' unit)

Sometimes, it seemed to be the families or carers who had made the decision because they felt unable to cope, rather than the patients themselves.

Death at home

The lack of familiarity with community services on the part of hospital staff was, perhaps, nowhere so clearly illustrated as by their inexperience when confronted by the prospect of a home death. Nurses gave vivid accounts of the emotional and physical toll in managing their first death at home:

It was a completely new experience. I didn't really know what to do. The problem was that I didn't really know whom to go to and I learned a lot from it in terms of what you can and cannot do in the community.

(Nurse, adults' unit)

All the home deaths described had been supported by a specialist cystic fibrosis nurse. In two instances, the specialist nurse reported difficulty enlisting the help of community staff on the grounds that they already had heavy workloads and lacked experience of patients with cystic fibrosis.

A home death could involve the nurse in intensive support, which was expensive in time, energy and emotional strain, especially if the patient lived a long distance from the hospital. As one nurse explained, supporting a patient to die at home could take her away from other work to the detriment of her other responsibilities:

I spent an awful lot of time on the motorway in that week and a half, and very much to the detriment of my other workload.

Considerations of staff time and resources may be one of the factors weighed in the balance when the option of a home death is presented to patients.

Staff described situations in which families had refused specialist palliative care services because of their association with death and dying, a problem which has been reported elsewhere (Shaw *et al.* 1998). Families' hostility to the involvement of Macmillan nurses, for example, as well as preventing access to specialist palliative care services, may have been a factor which militated against a home death. In one case, staff were partially able to circumvent this difficulty by using informal contacts. Access to the Macmillan service, however, was limited. As one nurse (children and adults) explained:

> It seems to be this view that the Macmillans are for cancer only.

In part, this is a legacy of the development of palliative care which is intimately linked with the care of cancer patients (Fordham, Dowrick and May 1998). In interviews with GPs, Field (1996, 1998) found that the majority still equate terminal care with the care of cancer patients. Even where they have been defined as 'terminally ill', people with non-malignant conditions may be deemed ineligible for the services of palliation and terminal care routinely extended to patients dying from cancer (*ibid.*).

In the survey of home deaths referred to above (Cottrell 1991), only three of the sixteen families had had the support of a visiting Macmillan nurse. Community nursing support was only present in a minority of cases, with only six families receiving support from a district nurse. In six families, there was no involvement of the GP, although all appear to have received continuing support from the hospital. Significantly, mothers were the main caregivers for all the patients who had died at home, even those older patients who were married (*op cit.*). People with cystic fibrosis often have a very close relationship with their mothers stemming from the heavy caring responsibilities they have borne since birth (Bluebond-Langner 1996). For those without this maternal support, the option of a home death may be less of a possibility.

Hospice care

Some people had to travel up to 150 miles to their nearest specialist unit. The costs to families in terms of travel, accommodation expenses, time and disruption could be considerable but, although a local hospice which could offer both respite and terminal care might well have eased the burden, hospice care was a little-used resource among the units visited. In part, this was a reflection of hospices' own admissions policies and reluctance to take patients with non-malignant diseases (Fordham *et al.* 1998; Eve *et al.* 1997).

One children's unit, however, had begun to refer a few patients to their local children's hospice, although this was a recent innovation.

> If you had asked me two years ago, I would have said there is no place for cystic fibrosis children in hospice care but now we have a 16-year-old lad awaiting a heart-lung transplant – he has been on the waiting list since he was 11 – and he goes as respite care. There are a lot of boys his own age with muscular dystrophy, so there are a lot of boys there with whom he has something in common.
>
> (Nurse specialist, children's unit)

Even here, hospice care was unlikely to be considered for any but a minority of patients. In this minority of cases, the hospice was seen as having a potential role in providing: respite care and involvement of a home care team in specific cases; family therapy; bereavement support; a place where families and children can talk about terminal illness without feeling they have to keep denying it; support for the dying patient at the end, if this ties in with ongoing support. It is a matter of debate whether these services would be provided more appropriately within a hospice setting than in-house within the ambit of specialist cystic fibrosis provision. Perhaps for this reason, some nurses believed that the most valuable contribution which hospices could make was as a teaching resource.

Although some staff saw a potential role for hospices, the perceived disadvantages were generally considered to outweigh the advantages. The issue of age was mentioned by several people. A nurse explained:

> The unit here is very geared up for young people. We have a pool table, videos, and television. In the hospice there were all old people in the bays who were dying. I couldn't see our 22-year-old patients being happy there.

Staff referred to the familiarity of the hospital staff and surroundings as a reason why patients preferred to die in hospital and, conversely, to the unfamiliarity of the hospice as the reason why it was not more often considered. One of the few who had any experience of using hospice services explained:

> Last year we had several children who died on the ward but hospice was not an option, but we could have used them if the children had known them first. It wouldn't have been appropriate to transfer them to somewhere they didn't know.
>
> (Nurse specialist, children's unit)

Continuity was one of the most important considerations, especially at a time of great stress.

> They're at quite a sticky position when we start looking at withdrawing antibiotics and putting morphine and other comforting measures in. They don't feel that they want to sort of move from one establishment to another at that time. It's more than they can cope with.
>
> (Nurse specialist, adults' unit)

In the view of a children's nurse, one way round the problem was for hospices to extend their services to incorporate more of an outreach approach and to change their policy so that families could make contact at an earlier stage, even though their child might not be eligible for inpatient admission.

> Maybe if the hospice had more of a home outreach service which did home assessments just so that the children and families could know who they are. In that case of the children whom we referred recently, it would have helped if the hospice could at least have done a home assessment so that the family

could have got to know them. Even if they had then refused to admit them, at least they would have known who they are.

A further obstacle was the popular association of hospice care with terminal care (*cf.* Shaw *et al.* 1998). This discouraged families from using not only hospice services but also the services of palliative care teams more generally. In the view of one specialist children's nurse, it was this association which was the primary deterrent. She was one of the few from a unit which had made referrals to a hospice and who saw a potential, though limited, role for hospice care. As she explained:

> Parents are not conditioned to think of cystic fibrosis and hospice care. The word 'hospice' is very unfortunate.

The dilemma for staff was that the point when hospice care might be considered was also the point when the prospect of a heart-lung transplant offered the greatest hope. In the words of one nurse:

> It is too late to bring them (hospice services) in at the end. At the point when children need heart-lung transplants, when they are severely affected by the cystic fibrosis, we could perhaps refer them to the hospice. Many children on the heart-lung waiting list die before an organ becomes available. But the heart-lung transplant means hope and hospice means dying, so you can't refer a family to the hospice because you can't take away that hope.

Part of the explanation for why the units visited did not make greater use of hospice and other palliative support services may have been their lack of knowledge of and experience in using them. Custom and practice, however, seemed to vary between centres. Prior experience and personal contacts were important in shaping practice and expanding the range of services offered. A nurse from an adult unit, for example, commented on the different approach adopted by another unit:

> In [another hospital], I know they have used hospices quite successfully. The cystic fibrosis nurse there is an ex-palliative care nurse, so she got into it from that direction. She had a different experience. We are maybe lacking knowledge in that area.

In another instance, a children's unit had begun to make increasing use of a local respite home because staff knew personally the nurse who ran it. However, there is little evidence that these variations form part of any coherent strategy which has been widely discussed among professionals, or even within units. Nor do they necessarily herald a more general change in approach to terminal care for cystic fibrosis patients.

Informed choice

A critical dimension of the consumer model of choice is adequate information on which to base choices. Initially, most information about the disease is filtered through parents. The amount of information shared depends on how much parents have been told or understood and how comfortable they feel in sharing this information. Many parents keep the terminal nature of the disease hidden from their children for as long as possible (Quin 1996). By the time they reach late adolescence, information is more likely to be given directly by medical staff (*ibid.*). In a study of cystic fibrosis adults in Northern Ireland, Quin found that one of the areas least likely to be openly discussed was male infertility. Some people preferred not to know and tried to limit the extent to which they would have to confront negative information by not seeking it out: 'The doctor asked me would I have it (sperm test) done and I said no. I said I'd rather not know unless I really had to find out ... What you don't know, you know, you always have a bit of hope' (*ibid*: 76).

Such responses challenge the simple assumption underlying the consumer model that the provision of information is both a necessary and sufficient condition for the exercise of choice. When the right to know becomes an imperative to be informed it can lead to demoralisation and the destruction of hope. A strategy of avoidance in relation to information-seeking behaviour in order to minimise distress and to sustain hope for as long as possible, even in the face of seemingly overwhelming odds, was one of the main ways in which people coped. The people we interviewed sought to manage information flow in ways which they felt able to handle. The choice not to be informed or to be informed in ways and at a pace which suited them was one of the most difficult areas of their lives which they had to manage.

People with cystic fibrosis feared an early death but their greatest fear was of a long preliminary lingering period and then a protracted final experience of dying (*cf.* Pounceby 1997; Quin 1996). Yet, they had difficulty projecting themselves into a future when they are seriously ill. Thus, although people with cystic fibrosis may be generally knowledgeable about their condition, information about options for palliative care is not always readily available and accessible, either practically or psychologically. Potential sources of information were identified as: professionals; experience at second hand through seeing other people who need palliative care; word-of-mouth and informal networks; local groups; and national organisations. Each of these will be examined in turn. Although the media – radio and television, magazines and newspapers – might have been included in this list, people who took part in the study did not mention them.

Professionals

Discussing death

Much of people's treatment takes place in hospital and, by the time they are approaching death, much of their time will probably have been spent in hospital.

Yet the emphasis on active treatment and life-prolonging interventions creates an atmosphere of optimism and hope where it can be difficult for either staff or patients and their families to broach the subject of death or dying and which leaves little space or opportunity to talk about psychological and spiritual needs or issues concerned with palliative care. This was especially so in the children's units visited where death is encountered less frequently and, since most children are now living into adulthood, is likely to be experienced as even more of a failure of medical care. The following comment from one nurse specialist echoed the general view:

> We tend to take a very positive attitude here and we're talking about living and maintaining normality so it is difficult, both for us and for the families, to talk about the child dying. (Nurse specialist, children's unit)

It was difficult to strike a balance between the promotion of a positive attitude and a realistic acceptance of the possibility of prolonged ill health and an early death.

> We try to get them to live as normal a life as possible. We don't want them to live every day thinking that they have a chronic, terminal illness.
> (Nurse, adults' unit)

Staff were unhappy about discussing death when the disease was so unpredictable. The dilemma, as one of the paediatric nurses explained, was that:

> At the point when the children need a heart-lung transplant, they are severely affected; their quality of life is low but they are not necessarily terminally ill. Most of the children die waiting because there are not enough organs available, and some gradually get worse, or rapidly get worse and do die, but others recover, so they are not necessarily terminally ill.

Nor did they always feel able to cope with the emotional burden or competent to raise issues which they might then be unable to handle. As one nurse commented:

> Personally, I am wary of discussing those issues with patients because I am afraid of opening up issues which I would then not be able to deal with. I do not feel that I am skilled enough. I would be afraid of opening up all sorts of cans of worms.
> (Nurse specialist, adults' unit)

For others, it was also a matter of culture and tradition. Broaching these subjects was not within their practice repertoire and they lacked the support of more experienced colleagues.

> Because of the way the unit was set up and run, it's a question of breaking down barriers and traditions. We need experience to have the confidence to

do it and to discuss it with the patients. If you haven't got that knowledge, you are less likely to discuss it or to raise it, plus it depends what support service you have got.

(Nurse, adults' unit)

In another unit, on the other hand, staff appeared more confident:

And that's the difficult thing, we're always keeping on going, and then, when it gets to a stage, I mean, they've been in hospital for quite a few weeks and they're not getting over the infection, and they know themselves:'I'm not getting any better, am I?' you know, 'Do you think I'm going to die?' And they're very frank about talking about dying; they're very open about it. And, again, I presume that's from having a life that, you know, knowing all along your life that you've got a life-threatening condition, that you're not going to have a normal lifespan. So we can talk, they are very open about talking about death and dying.

(Nurse, adults' unit)

These comments suggest that it may be a matter of giving patients permission to talk. Patients may be inhibited not so much by their own reluctance as by staff's own fears and sense of inadequacy: in other words, both patients and staff may be constrained by mutual fears and uncertainty about each other's reactions. Cottrell (1991) describes the practice in the clinic in which she worked of offering patients a questionnaire in which they could write down, well in advance, their wishes for when they are in the terminal stages. The questionnaire contained such questions as:

- Are you afraid of dying?
- Where would you like to die?
- How much would you like to be told if your health deteriorates?
- Who would you like to be with you?
- Would you like to be buried or cremated?
- What would you like to happen to your personal belongings?

In Cottrell's view, 'it is extremely important for patients to express their wishes, as it allows them to feel that they are in full control until the last moment' (1991: 28).

It was in this sphere that some staff saw a potential role for hospices. Hospice staff, they believed, would be better equipped to compensate for the shortcomings of their own service which they recognised but felt unable to address themselves. The problem was especially acute for the children's unit:

When we are looking after terminally ill children, we are also looking after children who are well and children who have been newly diagnosed so it is difficult to, perhaps, help the children come to terms with a terminal diagnosis. At a hospice, all their children are terminally ill. It is much easier for them.

This lack of openness is vividly described by a contributor to the online handbook of the US Cystic Fibrosis Foundation:

> On occasion I read the letters written back and forth between my doctors – 'end stage', 'not expected to live more than 2 years', 'severe obstruction' etc, etc. (of course, no one says these things to my face) – and it's hard not to wonder if I'm living in some self-created fantasy world in which I'm convinced that I 'can' in fact hang on for 2 years on my own without a transplant.
>
> (Trueworthy 1999: Chapter 33)

The difficulties experienced by staff were matched by some patients' apparent reluctance to discuss or confront their likely prognosis. Both staff and patients labelled this attitude 'denial' and would speak of patients and families who were 'in denial'.

'Denial'

The pressure to be like others leads many children to pretend that they do not have cystic fibrosis and, typically, they do not tell their friends or classmates about their condition. In her survey of 104 young people with cystic fibrosis, Pounceby found that a third had difficulty telling friends that they had the disease for fear of not being socially accepted, of exciting sympathy, or of having their identity reduced simply to the fact of their cystic fibrosis (Pounceby 1997). One young woman summed up the general attitude when she said:

> It's being different and people finding out. I don't want to be treated like some kind of charity case or have people thinking ' I'd better be kind to her because she's got cystic fibrosis' ... I don't like advertising or fundraising; I don't want posters plastered all over the place about what I've got.
>
> (Pounceby 1997: 101)

Similarly, in Quin's study of twenty-five young people with cystic fibrosis, 40 per cent said that they would avoid telling others about their condition as far as possible and a further 40 per cent said that they would not discuss it with others at all (Quin 1996).

The emphasis on leading a 'normal life', both at hospital and at home (Wynn-Knight 1996), encourages families to collude in this 'denial', especially if their children are healthy. McCracken (1984) referred to a collusive denial within the family of the potential hazards of the disease, with the mutual desire to protect each other, of both the young person and parents inhibiting a potentially supportive sharing of fears. Such an approach is inherently fragile: not only is it constantly vulnerable to the intrusion of events but it can lead to resentment and anger when children find out that they have been misled (Wynn-Knight 1996: 143). It also leaves parents in a continuous state of apprehension that their children may discover potentially distressing information from other sources. The following is an extract from a communication to the online support group CYSTIC-L from the mother of an eight-year-old child with cystic fibrosis:

> As she grew older, when death affected those around us, we discussed it openly. But, we never told her that her disease was a terminal one. She knows she is different, that she takes medicines, etc. I am afraid that now she is older, and researching other things, she will look cystic fibrosis up and read it by herself and be devastated.

During their teenage years, the pressure to conform can lead some young people to neglect their health so that, when they become ill or see their friends becoming ill, they can find themselves confronted by the potential seriousness of their condition for the first time.

> We have a lot of teenagers who go through a lot of problems because they see their friends die with cystic fibrosis. They have lived with denial and their families have lived with denial, and then they begin to see their friends die.
> (Specialist nurse, children's unit)

> They see friends die of cystic fibrosis and sometimes the cystic fibrosis gets worse in their teenage years and that can be very frightening, and death looms much closer.
> (Specialist nurse, adults' unit)

One young person explained:

> I think a lot of people, when they are teenagers, don't want to admit they have got cystic fibrosis and avoid any possible mention or reminder of it. I would go to the doctor and I wouldn't listen to a word he was saying. Then suddenly I woke up one day and realised the implications of actually having cystic fibrosis because I knew it was going to kill me.
> (Woman with cystic fibrosis)

Respondents described this as a 'stage' which teenagers typically go through as part of the process of growing up with cystic fibrosis:

> Like anything, like telling a child not to put its finger in the fire, people have got to learn for themselves. A lot of teenagers pretend they haven't got cystic fibrosis, don't tell any of their friends, don't look after themselves properly – I went through that stage – and, suddenly, they get ill and that brings it home.
> (Man with cystic fibrosis)

Many people carry this attitude into adult life. A nurse, for example, recalled a patient, who for years didn't tell anyone she had cystic fibrosis. She didn't tell anyone at work. Eventually, when she got ill, she did tell them.

Both patients and staff used the word 'denial' as convenient shorthand to describe this attitude:

> I always said that I would never let it rule my life or prevent me from doing anything. I didn't tell anyone at school that I had it so, if you call that 'denial' … I never told anyone about it. I still don't accept that … well, I mean, I've been on the transplant list for two-and-a-half years and I still don't accept that I need it. So, I suppose, yeah … I know that I am ill but I still don't think that I am.
>
> (Woman with cystic fibrosis)

Although some people took it to the extreme and, as far as they were able, told no one about their condition, such distancing was a common reaction which enabled people to cope with their lives. The approach adopted by the young man quoted below was typical:

> A lot of people cope with it by not seeking it out, as I have done for many years. I have totally ignored it. You push it away. If it doesn't intrude on my life, I don't want to think about it. People can't go round thinking about it all day.

The transition from children's to adult services can be a time of emotional crisis, when people find themselves confronted, often for the first time in their lives, with the prospect of dying and the realisation that they have a terminal illness. Pounceby (1997) found that young people's fears about moving to adult services were compounded not simply by the loss of familiarity and sense of safety but by symbolic fears of growing older and nearer to death. As a nurse specialist interviewed for the present study explained,

> Previously, the question of death and dying used to be addressed when they were much younger. Now it can come as quite a shock when they come to the adult unit and people are dying.

Amongst teenagers, two main responses were described: either a hopeless fatalism in which the young people adopted the attitude: 'I'm going to die anyway, so why bother?' or a failure or refusal to associate distressing information about cystic fibrosis with their own situation. Some, for example, managed to distance themselves from the ill patients they saw on the ward and did not see them as having any relevance to their own situation. Psychologically, they were able to bracket off distressing or uncomfortable information (Bury 1991).

Interviewer: What was it like coming on to the adult unit when you had never actually been in hospital before?

Respondent: It was really hard work at first – the routine and having IVs and stuff ... It was a bit of a shock. Well, I never really saw them (other patients) as me. I mean, I thought I am not going to get like that – not for years. So, I didn't really think I would get like that – not for a long time anyway. So ... I didn't really think I'd get like that. So, it never really upset me. I just felt bad for them and stuff.

Similarly, a contributor to the *CYSTIC-L Handbook* describes meeting a child who was waiting for a double lung transplant:

> ... seeing him there, with his wry smile and slight slouch, a real, palpable, dying boy, intrigued me beyond my ability to restrain myself. We were linked somehow: he had what I had. Despite the huge, obvious differences that I believed would forever separate us; there was no denying that somehow we were linked.

> ... Stories like his are why I stayed as far away from clinic as possible. The whole place, with its sick and wounded, was like some kind of spook house where, if I wasn't careful, I would touch something horrible, catch something visible, become something altogether undeniable.

(Curtis 1997)

Some people would try to avoid this confrontation by refusing to look around the adult unit when they were first introduced. Sometimes, however, it was families who were even more frightened of facing up to these issues than the young people themselves.

> For example, we had one boy who moved over from the paediatric unit. They tried to tackle some of the issues about the possibility of declining health, male infertility and so on before the boy moved over here but the father went mad and he wrote saying they were not trying to avoid the issues at home but would deal with them in their own time. The father was afraid that he would not be included in consultations with his son. He attends every consultation; he won't let his son see us on his own; he won't look around the ward because he says his son will never need to come here. We get that quite a lot. People won't look around the ward because they say, 'I won't be coming in'. They are frightened to see someone who is sick; they don't want to face up to that. It's a big problem of denial, especially if the child is well.

(Specialist nurse, adult unit)

Another aspect of 'denial' has been referred to as 'blunting' (Miller and Green 1984) or 'minimisation' (Boyle *et al.* 1976); in other words, a tendency to play down symptoms and ill health. Studies of people with cystic fibrosis have found significant differences between doctors' and people's own views of disease severity (Abbott, Dodd and Webb 1995; Pounceby 1997), with patients consistently under-rating severity compared with doctors' assessments. Abbott, Dodd and Webb

(1995) suggest that the difference might be due, in part, to people viewing their own illness from a broader perspective, encompassing all aspects of their lives. In the view of Kellerman *et al.* (1980), young people who have grown up with a chronic illness have learnt to live with frequent life disruption and to tolerate heightened stress and may therefore be inclined to perceive only a severe exacerbation of their illness as a major event. On the other hand, it may also be a means of emotional protection or of minimising the threat of the disease.

Professionals were concerned that those who chose to conceal their disease were not allowing themselves to face up to the implications of having a terminal illness and, as a result, would be poorly prepared for the ill health which would almost inevitably overtake them. However, they also recognised that, for many people, this attitude could be an effective means of coping.

> Cystic fibrosis is a chronic terminal illness that a lot of families live with by denial and I would say it is healthy denial. I know the text books would say that this is pathological and they ought to be confronting and coming to terms with the knowledge that the illness is terminal, but that isn't necessarily always the best approach.
>
> (Specialist nurse, children's unit)

Mador and Smith (1988: 141) suggest that 'the degree of denial should not truly or consistently distort the patient's real understanding of his or her disease, but rather provide some reprieve from a demoralising awareness of its effects'. Other studies (Aspin 1991; Moise *et al.* 1987) have found less psychological distress and higher self-esteem among those with an avoidance response. Zeltzer *et al.* (1980), for example, distinguish between 'adaptive denial' as a strategy enabling people to live with hope and 'maladaptive denial' which may lead to non-compliance with treatment. Other studies have observed correlations between optimism and positive coping strategies (Venters 1981; Pounceby 1997).

The dilemma for people with cystic fibrosis is that a general orientation towards promoting optimism and sustaining hope leads to tension where it collides with the realities of disease progression. The various strategies for managing this tension – denial, avoidance, minimisation or compartmentalisation – are constantly vulnerable to the intrusion of events. Staff were aware of the delicate path they were treading between encouraging a positive attitude to life and preparing people to cope with serious ill health and eventual death.

As a means of coping, strategies of avoidance or denial were fragile and could break down at any point. A person could be managing successfully for many years before suddenly feeling overwhelmed by the realisation that he or she has a terminal illness. Typically, this realisation seemed to come in the teens or early twenties but it could occur at any time. As one person remarked:

> With cystic fibrosis, it could hit you at any time. People develop emotionally at different rates and have different life experiences.

The emotional impact of such a realisation could be highly traumatic, as the same person, now in her mid-twenties, recounted:

> Perhaps it is a bad thing because, when you are diagnosed as a baby, by the time you get to your teens, everybody is aware and knows you have got cystic fibrosis and you are just expected to get on with it. No-one ever says, ever asks how it feels, how you feel about it. If it was something like cancer or some terminal illness where the diagnosis comes later in life, it is very much treated as a life-shaping event … whereas, with cystic fibrosis, it has been around for so long that you are expected to get on with it and I think that is quite difficult. You start thinking, 'Why the hell should I put up with it? Why should I go along with everything?' It's almost like a grieving process that you are going through.

For those diagnosed in early childhood, there is no dramatic point of diagnosis but, as the quotation above demonstrates, this does not necessarily negate the notion of ontological break, a dramatic disruption of a person's biography which comes with the realisation of the implications of living with a life-limiting illness. Yet, there may be little in the way of psychological support to help manage this crisis. As the young woman quoted above explained:

> You need to have somewhere where you can talk about it and come to terms with it.

Yet, there was

> no obvious place to turn to for emotional help.

In hospital, the emphasis had been on the treatment of physical symptoms, with little attention to psychological and social needs (*cf.* Pounceby 1997):

> All the emphasis is on the physical, you know: 'How far can you walk? Can you run without getting breathless?' … I think that is, perhaps, slowly changing but it is a long time coming.

Her parents had attempted to shield her since babyhood and she had felt unable to talk to them. By contrast, most of the respondents in Pounceby's study (1997), on the other hand, reported that they were able to talk to their parents about the illness, although they did not necessarily do so. But, 'while the degree of open communication was greater than often previously found in families of children with chronic illnesses, this does not necessarily mean feelings about the illness itself were openly expressed' (*ibid*: 121).

Uncertainty

However they might try to ignore it, the threat of ill health hangs over all those with the disease and the uncertainty of not knowing when it might strike could be highly stressful. In one woman's view:

> Being well with cystic fibrosis can be almost as damaging mentally as being very ill with cystic fibrosis. You are told about this horrendous disease. I used to grow up thinking I probably wouldn't be here by the age of twenty. Yet, you might be really well with it and you think, 'Well, why am I not ill?' ... You think, 'Well, maybe it can happen tomorrow' or 'When is something going to happen?'. It plays on your mind almost as much if you are very well as if you are very ill because, if you are very ill, you know.

Such views were echoed in Pounceby's study where almost a quarter of respondents worried about the long-term uncertainties of the illness. Koocher (1984) cited uncertainty as the single greatest stress for people with cystic fibrosis, with disruptions to normal activities resulting from symptoms and treatment and unexpected exacerbation or gradual progression interrupting or forestalling college, career, marriage and family plans.

As we have seen, for many people, the sudden realisation that they have a progressive, terminal illness is likely to be both precipitated and exacerbated by the transfer from children's to adults' services. When people are, perhaps, most in need of continuity and the security and trust which comes from familiar faces and surroundings, they are not only expected to take over responsibility for their treatment from their adult carers but also forced to transfer to a new professional team in an unfamiliar environment. Teenagers struggling with emotional difficulties, who may have had little cause for frequent hospital visits during their childhood, are unlikely to have formed relationships of sufficient trust with members of staff which would encourage them to confide in them.

In two of the areas visited, the children's charity, Barnardo's, had employed social workers to set up projects specifically to help young people with cystic fibrosis with emotional and relationship issues as well as with practical problems in obtaining benefits, mortgages, insurance and so on. Parents, too, had turned to them for emotional support in times of stress. A mother, whose daughter was refusing to go on the waiting list for a transplant, recounted how she had turned to a Barnardo's social worker for support:

> Just, it's basically somebody to listen and not to actually say anything. He tried to put J's [my daughter's] point of view, but objectively – which I couldn't see because, when you're a mum, you are blinkered. You can't see any other [point of view] because all you want is the best for her because you can see how you would relate to how J would see it. But she was coming to it completely differently. She was frightened. So was I but in a different way.

Paradoxically, perhaps, parents had least contact with other parents of children with cystic fibrosis when they might have been most likely to need it. As their adult children grew older, their health was more likely to deteriorate and, in the absence of a transplant, to continue to decline. Yet parents of young adults were less likely to be active members of local groups than those with younger children. As families move away and their children grow up, groups fold. In the words of one mother:

> Some of them have passed away now … The main ones, they've all moved away; they've grown up; they are [my son's] age [22] and older. Apart from K, who comes to this clinic now, and the lad who died, there is no group anymore.

They were also less likely to meet other parents or staff at clinics because, as adults, their children attended the hospital independently. Thus, at the time when they were most likely to need emotional support and advice, their resources were often depleted.

Seeing others

In hospital, other patients could be a valuable source of support:

> I am friendly with a good few of them. We spend time with each other, like we go in each other's rooms and stuff because it gets boring. There are a lot of elderly on. It's mainly elderly … We can talk about what's going on with us, with our lungs, and how we feel and stuff. But, we are advised not to see each other all the time because, obviously, if one's got an infection, that'll pass it around. But it is good to talk to people who are the same situation as you and how they're dealing with it and stuff – that's good.
>
> (Young woman with cystic fibrosis)

However, as the comment above illustrates, staff sometimes discouraged young people from socialising for fear of cross-infection.

Improvements in treatment have meant that people with cystic fibrosis may have experienced little ill health before their transfer to an adult unit and they may continue to maintain good health and have little cause for frequent hospital visits. Contact with people who are seriously ill or dying may therefore be minimal. As one nurse explained:

> We now have young people with cystic fibrosis who are now very well when they come to the adult unit, whereas, in the past, they may have been more ill; plus they have home IV treatment, so they don't see people with cystic fibrosis. They don't see sick patients or people who die, so it's possible for them to avoid the issue very well.

Two recent developments have further helped to reduce social mixing in hospital. The first has been the introduction of home intravenous treatment; the second has been the emergence of a particularly virulent bacterium.

Intravenous antibiotic therapy, which can be administered in the patient's own home, has reduced the necessity for hospital visits and, thus, further insulated people from confrontation with the implications of having a terminal disease by reducing their opportunities for meeting other people with cystic fibrosis. From a nursing point of view, hospital visits serve an important educational function in helping both parents and children come to terms with the prospect of ill health:

> The children need the education so that they can see other children with cystic fibrosis and it helps them to face it, to come to terms with it.
>
> (Specialist children's nurse)

As a nurse explained, many families seem to cope with the condition by compartmentalising their lives into 'normal life' and hospital. Far from incorporating hospital visits into the general routine, they were treated as a separate sphere which was allowed to impinge on 'normal life' as little as possible (*cf.* Bluebond-Langner 1996; Bury 1991).

The emergence of a particularly virulent bacterium *Burkholderia cepacia* has had an even more dramatic impact on nursing practice: at the time of the study, many hospitals had introduced segregation policies whereby infected patients were nursed separately on general wards. This usually meant that they were isolated not only from other cystic fibrosis patients but from people of their own age. Facilities in the cystic fibrosis wards tend to be better than those in general wards, which meant patients were left feeling stigmatised and isolated. One nurse described how segregation had affected ward life.

> Once the new unit opened, there were problems with cepacia. Patients with cepacia felt that they were not getting the same facilities ... Even when the research fellow here left, we had to have two leaving parties – one for cepacia patients and one for non-cepacia.

Patients both described themselves and were described by others as 'lepers'.

> It's really awful. I know we're not supposed to pass infection on but, sometimes, if you get to clinic a bit early like and there's still non-cepacia patients there, you are made to go and sit in a room and you feel like a leper or something – because I've got this bug and they haven't, you're split off.
>
> (Patient with B. cepacia)

The impact of a positive sputum test on an individual's life can be catastrophic, as the case of the two brothers described below vividly demonstrates:

> We had a case of two brothers with cystic fibrosis and eventually they decided not to see each other because one of them had cepacia. He was clear of it for

a while but it did come back. It always seems to come back so it does seem to be a life-long thing. It is very isolating.

(Specialist nurse, adult unit)

Not only can people become stigmatised and isolated, social networks disrupted and friendships lost but they are confronted with a life-threatening agent which they can pass on to others and which is likely to remain with them for the rest of their lives.

Initial fears, however, have begun to subside as people are learning to live with the new risks of cross-infection. Not all specialist centres, for example, have adopted the rigid segregation policy described above. A recent telephone survey of 350 adults with cystic fibrosis found that 11 per cent of respondents attended a hospital where there appeared to be no segregation policy and a further 35 per cent were unsure about their hospital's policy (Gallup 1996).

Informal networks

Clinics as meeting places

Hospital visits provided one of the main opportunities for meeting other people with cystic fibrosis and friendships were formed which, for some, were renewed only on subsequent visits but, for others, were extended into their lives outside hospital. As one person remarked:

Going to a clinic is more of a social event than anything else.

Another commented:

It is very rare that I don't meet someone I know. You get to know other cystic fibrosis adults, especially if you are in hospital together. The smaller the hospital, the better because you get to know people better'.

(Man with cystic fibrosis)

A few people seemed to have built up quite strong networks and friendships amongst other people with cystic fibrosis and their families. Often these were friendships of long standing. Relationships between families and children, who had first met each other while visiting the children's service, would continue into adulthood when, as teenagers, the young people moved to the same adult unit. These friendships could incorporate whole families, although parental contact tended to drop off as children moved into adulthood. Where people spent some time on the ward as inpatients, strong friendships could be formed which persisted beyond the hospital walls. However, the fact that people attended centres with large geographical catchments meant that it was often difficult for them to maintain contact with each other outside the hospital.

Quin (1996) found that the situation in which death was most openly discussed was amongst the cystic fibrosis adults who were in regular contact with each other. In the words of one of her respondents: 'I've talked to them (CF informal group) about dying and they've talked to me about dying and it's great, because outside CF I'd never talk to anybody about dying. We're all in this together' (Quin 1996: 86). This group was also the most likely to have friends die and these deaths had had a profound effect on the anticipation of their own death. Fears about the dying process were linked with the experience of seeing and hearing about the deaths of others.

People measured their own progression in relation to the perceived condition of others. As long as they felt healthy, this could be a helpful strategy but, once they began to slip behind, it could become demoralising and emotionally difficult to handle, as this contribution to an online chat group demonstrates:

> I don't wish to be someone else, I just wish to live a long life and do all the many things I want to do. I want to marry [my boyfriend] … I want a child to call me Mommy, I want to touch lives, and I want to do something to be remembered. But all that is a big maybe. I'm 21 and I am supposed to be making out a will. I go and sit in a waiting room at a transplant centre and I'm the youngest one there by far.
>
> I hate that there are other cfers healthier than me. I want to be healthy again too. I used to be called one of the healthy cfers when I was a teen, now I can tell in the staff's faces when they talk to me that they think I'm end stage.
>
> (Contributor to CYSTIC-L discussion group
> http:/cf-web.mit.edu/info-zone/faq/)

Partly for these reasons, many people choose not to associate with others with the disease and have no contact beyond the occasional hospital visit. Pounceby (1997) found that almost 70 per cent of her respondents reported that they had no friends with cystic fibrosis. Even within hospital, some people resisted mixing with other people with the disease. One woman, interviewed for the present study, observed:

> It is possible to isolate yourself in hospital. Cystic fibrosis patients have single rooms. You can just shut your door and only talk to the nurses and doctors. So, you can isolate yourself in hospital just as easily.

Others were able to compartmentalise their friendships, as in other areas of their lives, into cystic fibrosis and not cystic fibrosis. When asked whether she chose to have cystic fibrosis friends, one young woman replied:

> No, I never see them other than in hospital. It's just chance that we come in at the same time. When I'm in, there's not always the same ones in at the same time, so you do meet different ones. But, lots of times, ones that are pretty ill like me and come in every month or so, we do meet up quite often. But we never see each other out of hospital … We're in here for two weeks so

we have a natter for two weeks and stuff and then we say, 'See you next time,' and that's it.

Community networks

Outside hospital, people could feel more isolated. Often, they were unable to discuss the issues which concerned them within their own families because they were too emotionally involved. Friends, who had no experience of cystic fibrosis, could offer only limited support. Only 35 per cent of the young people interviewed in Pounceby's study (1997) said they would turn to friends for support. Parents, similarly, could feel isolated. As one mother explained,

> My friends are very good but they are not living with him [my son] so it's very difficult to talk to them ... It's very difficult for you to know who to talk to.

Although there may have been a tendency for respondents to exaggerate the extent of social mixing which occurred prior to the emergence of B. *cepacia*, it has clearly had a significant effect on socialising between people with cystic fibrosis, both at the formal and informal level. When first confronted with the existence of a new 'killer bug', the cystic fibrosis population reacted with a fear which amounted to, what one person described as, 'near hysteria'. People were afraid to mix socially, official gatherings were cancelled and local groups disintegrated. Although the initial 'hysteria' has given way to a calmer approach, many local groups have failed to recover their former strength. Meetings and conferences are still held but participants may be asked to produce a recent sputum test. For most people, the impact on social life appears to have been less dramatic. The Gallup survey of adults with cystic fibrosis led the authors to conclude that 'the occurrence of *cepacia* amongst the cystic fibrosis community appears to have had little or no effect on social life ... Only 2 per cent of those interviewed say it has greatly reduced their social activities' (Gallup 1996: 23). Nevertheless, people who have become infected have often found themselves isolated, shunned by cystic fibrosis acquaintances and segregated from other cystic fibrosis patients in hospital. One might surmise that those whose social lives had been most affected were among the small minority (only 4 per cent in Pounceby's study) whose main friendships were with other people with cystic fibrosis.

Ill health

Ill health could also be an isolating factor within the cystic fibrosis population. It was hinted that people who are the most ill may be among those most likely to become isolated from others with the disease not simply because they are physically unable to socialise but because they may be actively shunned. Respondents suggested that people feared confrontation with their own mortality and the fragility of their own health through contact with an ill person.

> There is certainly a feeling that it is not talked about in the cystic fibrosis community that, if someone is very ill with cystic fibrosis, there is a sense that you are wanting to keep away from it ... Because it is a case of 'There but for the grace of God go I' sort of feeling. And I think, if you can hide from that feeling and those images ... that you hear and see when you talk to those sorts of people, the better it is.
>
> (Man with cystic fibrosis)

On the other hand, people with cystic fibrosis were not thought to be victims of the general social ostracism experienced by people with conditions believed to be infectious. Nor were they socially stigmatised and forced into the closed social networks of many sufferers from HIV/AIDS. The weakly developed associations and networks observed among people with cystic fibrosis seemed to result more from internally generated factors than from external forces.

The death of friends

It is the death of a friend, however, which most exposes the fragility of the social networks in the cystic fibrosis community and subjects them to the greatest strain. A committee member of the Association for Cystic Fibrosis Adults described the impact which the death of one of its members had on the rest of the group:

> We lost our ex-chairperson about two months ago. She died very unexpectedly. She wasn't very ill and no one expected it. And that made a big gap. That made us all kind of think, 'Well, hang on. Is it a good idea getting close to people with cystic fibrosis?' Because, you know, it does hurt. Even after it has happened a few times – and I've got a few friends who have died – you think it will be easier but it never gets easier. And you think, 'Well, should I actually be making friends among people who have cystic fibrosis who, you know, are probably going to die?' It made us all sit back and think a while.

The death of a close friend not only caused the group to question the wisdom of forming friendships with other people with cystic fibrosis and, in so doing, risk the inevitable pain of bereavement when they died, but gave them the opportunity to discuss issues concerning mortality and dying which they had previously been afraid to broach:

> It wasn't an issue which we actually talked about. After [X] died, we talked about it more, probably, than we had done all our previous years, which we find was a lot healthier.

Although the young people interviewed in this study generally valued their friendships with other people with cystic fibrosis, as this person's experience demonstrates, such friendships could prove to be double-edged swords. The immediacy of friends dying made death more real: simply knowing in the abstract was not enough. As Quin observes, the impact is felt on a number of levels: the loss of a friend or acquaintance, a foreshadowing of their own deterioration and deaths, the cumulative impact of successive deaths, and the sense of loss of control and powerlessness over the disease which comes when they see others die who seemed healthy for long periods or who stuck dutifully to their treatment regimes (Quin 1996).

National organisations

Apart from hospital visits, one of the main ways of finding out about cystic fibrosis and of contacting other people with the disease is through the two national organisations representing the interests of people with cystic fibrosis: the Association for Cystic Fibrosis Adults (ACFA) and its parent body, the Cystic Fibrosis Trust (CFT).

Both the CFT and ACFA produce their own newsletters: *CFNews* and *Input*, respectively. Although 86 per cent of those interviewed for the Gallup survey said they received the Association newsletter *Input*, less than half could recall what it was called. A minority (14 per cent) appeared to be unaware of its existence. For 77 per cent, the newsletter was their only contact with ACFA but only 53 per cent said they would miss it if it were no longer published. Many respondents seemed to confuse *Input* with *CFNews* and it was not always clear to which publication they were referring. However, 69 per cent found it 'interesting' and 63 per cent claimed to read every issue. The primary areas of interest were advances in medical treatment and 'good news stories'.

One person, who had previously had the job of editing the newsletter, explained how difficult it was to select material which would appeal to such a disparate and wide-ranging readership:

> The trouble is that there are so many varying degrees of cystic fibrosis, from people who barely have it to people who are extremely debilitated by it. It is very difficult to cater for everyone because you have to cover such a broad spectrum. It is very difficult to have an organisation that caters for such a wide market and to know how to pitch articles to cover such wide extremes.

In her view, many people, especially teenagers, were likely to be put off simply because it was a newsletter aimed at people with cystic fibrosis:

> I think a lot of people when they are teenagers don't want to admit that they have got cystic fibrosis and avoid any possible mention or reminder of it.

For others, it was, perhaps, less a question of denial than of fear:

> People are, perhaps, wary of reading about people who are seriously ill and those who are seriously ill don't want to be reminded of it. If the person who is writing is, maybe, more ill than they are, they think, 'Maybe that can happen to me.' I think some people don't read the magazine for that reason.

This view was strongly endorsed by respondents to the Gallup survey (1996). The following comment was cited as typical:

> It is always so dull and boring and quite depressing … There are people with cystic fibrosis with terrible problems, I know that … but I don't know that it should be here for all the rest of us to get depressed about.
>
> (Gallup 1996: 40)

The desire for 'good news stories' also came through in the interviews for the present study, where the concern was not just to offset 'depressing' reminders of ill health but to counteract the negative portrayals of cystic fibrosis in the media. In one hospital visited, the patients had established their own notice board for 'good news stories' to counterbalance what was perceived to be a medical fixation with ill health. Nearly all claimed to read regularly either the ACFA newsletter *Input* or the CFT publication *CFNews*, yet, when asked where they would go for information, none said that they would turn to either organisation as their first choice.

Conventional methods of communication, such as written materials and audiotapes, are unlikely to reach everybody. In addition, as a member of the CFT explained, active members like himself tend to be white and middle class and their concerns and approach reflect this. Other groups are poorly represented. The prevalence of cystic fibrosis amongst the Afro-Caribbean population is low and it is even lower among Asians and, in consequence, these groups form a very small minority of people with cystic fibrosis. Their views and needs are not merely poorly reflected by the national organisations but largely untapped, although there is, perhaps, a slow but growing recognition that they cannot simply be assumed to be identical to those of the majority of members.

The appointment of professionals to the CFT has provoked an ongoing debate not only about whether or not professionals are the best qualified to run an organisation like the CFT but whether people with cystic fibrosis are always the best qualified to give fellow members support and advice. In one person's view:

> … there is a tendency to think that, when you have a condition, you are the expert on that condition because you know how it feels. If you are asking for a personal view, then that is the ideal place you can come to but, sometimes, I don't know whether people who actually have the condition are the best qualified to comment on the condition in an overall sense. You are just too close to it, I think, and that is a problem. (Man with cystic fibrosis)

He went on to explain that an important element of empathy is shared experience, something difficult to achieve, given the variability between people in symptom severity and the unpredictability of the illness:

> For example, someone having a bad time with cystic fibrosis might phone up someone who is very mildly affected. And it is difficult to have empathy with that person because you are not suffering the same problems.

Not only could it be difficult to empathise but emotionally damaging:

> It is very depressing to see someone who is much worse than you are because you start thinking that, at any time, it might be you.

Again, the theme emerges of both psychological and physical distancing as a form of self-protection against the fear and depression which people were aware could destroy them just as surely as their disease. In one person's words, 'Coping with it is in your head as much as anything else'.

The Internet

At the time of writing, neither of the two UK national organisations had a website on the Internet, although the possibility had been discussed and this is an area where, generally, there is rapid development. None of those we asked thought that the Internet would be an effective means of communication with the majority of members. As one man explained, few members have access to email or the Internet and those who have access through their work might be reluctant to use it for fear of disclosing their cystic fibrosis to colleagues. For those who have private access, the advantage of computer-mediated communication is the privacy it affords and the opportunity to discuss anonymously subjects which it would be difficult to raise in face-to-face conversations. More importantly, perhaps, computer-mediated communication enables its users to conceal information about themselves, specifically information about their state of health.

By contrast, the Cystic Fibrosis Foundation (CFF) of the United States has an extensive website (www.cff.org) providing a comprehensive range of information about cystic fibrosis and related issues, including updates on advances in research and clinical trials, public policy issues and answers to frequently asked questions. Its services to members include Cystic Fibrosis Services Inc., which acts as 'a patient advocate' by persuading insurance companies and managed care organisations to cover therapies for people with cystic fibrosis. The CFF also offers a one-stop pharmacy for all CF medication needs which claims to offer 'the lowest prices on CF medications'. The role of email support groups, specifically CYSTIC-L, will be discussed below.

Collective organisation

The email support group straddles the boundary between empowerment at the level of the individual and collective empowerment. Among the CF population, there are a number of potential opportunities for individuals to meet together and to present their views and opinions collectively, on the grounds that a chorus of voices is likely to be more effective than the lone voices of individuals. These include: national organisations, local groups, specialist centres and informal networks in addition to the computer-mediated communication and chat groups introduced above.

National organisations

National organisations can enhance the collective voice of people with cystic fibrosis in a number of different ways: providing aggregated information collected about individual members, for example from requests for help or questionnaires and surveys; providing a national pool of people with cystic fibrosis and their families and carers from which other agencies can draw; advocacy on behalf of individual members; campaigning on behalf of members as a group; organising direct action, such as demonstrations or co-ordinated boycott of services; providing an opportunity for members to get in touch with people in the same situation and form their own networks. The effectiveness of these various approaches will depend, in part, on the extent to which the organisation is perceived to be representative of people with cystic fibrosis and their families and on the extent to which it can be said to represent their interests and views.

The Cystic Fibrosis Trust

The CFT was established primarily as a fundraising organisation for medical research. Since its inception, however, it has experienced a number of changes which have resulted in a gradual change in approach. First, survival rates for cystic fibrosis have improved and the membership of the Trust has expanded to include a growing number of adults with cystic fibrosis. These adult members are not only able to speak for themselves and become their own advocates but bring with them a new set of needs and concerns. Where, for example, further education and training for a future career were considered irrelevant to teenagers who were not expected to survive into adulthood, they are issues of concern to many young people with cystic fibrosis today. In addition to medical services and treatments are practical concerns about discrimination in employment, difficulties in obtaining a mortgage or insurance and so on, and emotional needs in the area of relationships, marriage and family (Walters 1994). Secondly, as people with cystic fibrosis have been able to remain healthier for longer, they have been able to lead more 'normal' lives and the medical emphasis on illness and disease has become less relevant. Related to this has been the change in thinking about chronic illness and disability among disabled people generally. Conceptions of chronic illness and disability which emphasise 'individual tragedy' have been rejected in favour of a more positive emphasis on ability and achievement and the medical focus on the negative aspects of impairment has been superceded by a 'social model of disability' which stresses discriminatory and environmental impediments to autonomy and participation (Barnes and Mercer 1996). A further change has been in the charity sector itself. Financial constraints and resultant reductions in statutory services have meant that charities and voluntary organisations have increasingly moved in to fill the gaps. With the introduction of the internal market in health and social services, which separated commissioning and purchasing from provider functions, many charities and voluntary organisations have developed new or enhanced roles as service providers. The requirement of health authorities to conduct assessments of needs for services has also encouraged some groups to adopt a more proactive role in articulating the needs for services of their members.

A marker of these changes has been the establishment by the CFT of the Family and Support Service (FASS). Although there is still a strong emphasis on raising money for medical research, the Trust is now providing more practical and social services to members, including advocacy on behalf of members – both on an individual basis and on behalf of the collective; the provision of practical and financial help and advice; information about the disease and about services; and a limited counselling and befriending service. The image of the sick child, which underpinned the Trust's fundraising efforts, has been criticised by many of its adult members for conveying to the public a misleading message and for presenting an overly negative portrayal of cystic fibrosis which fuels the discriminatory attitudes they confront in their daily lives. Yet, as a paid employee of the Trust admitted and many members themselves accepted, it is this image which is most likely to attract donations.

The changing focus of the CFT has resulted in tension between its two main functions: fundraising and providing services to members. Although the possibility of setting up two separate organisations has been discussed, the proposal was rejected on the grounds that a second organisation would be unlikely to succeed without the funds which the parent organisation is able to attract. However, it was tensions such as these, together with a belief that their needs were not being adequately addressed, which encouraged some members to set up their own organisation specifically for adults with cystic fibrosis, the Association for Cystic Fibrosis Adults.

A further change has been the appointment of paid professionals to take over the main tasks of running the organisation. Such changes have been controversial and the process of transition has not always been smooth. The issue was not simply one of high salaries but of the potential alienation of a large part of the membership. As one member remarked, there was an unfortunate irony about this situation:

> When it was first set up, it was primarily set up for those people [ordinary members] and they brought in the odd professional and now it has sort of been taken over by the professionals. They've sort of grabbed hold of it and said, 'We're the professionals, we know what's best'. Certainly, for the parents of cystic fibrosis children out there involved in jumble sales etc., they feel at a distance from the Trust.

In some respects, then, professionalisation of the national organisation has been accompanied by a distancing from its grassroots. Such concerns, however, were generally balanced by a realistic appraisal of the changing context in which charities operate.

The Cystic Fibrosis Trust undertakes advocacy both on behalf of the membership collectively and on behalf of individuals. Examples of the former include giving evidence to the House of Commons Select Committee on Children's Health and producing information for hospitals. Examples of the latter include challenging clinical decisions, such as the refusal of home IV treatment, and financial issues.

An issue of particular concern was the practice of hospitals to charge relatives for accommodation. Families could not insure against such charges because cystic fibrosis is a pre-existing condition and many people were reluctant to ask for help. As an employee of the Trust explained,

> They are so grateful for this wonderful place called Harefield or Papworth or whatever and this wonderful surgeon called Yacoub or whoever, they don't want to be thought of as trouble-makers or ungrateful. And they are so vulnerable at this time; they are absolutely dependent.

In such situations, the Trust would try to act as advocates on behalf of individuals but were often hindered by families' unwillingness to make a fuss. It was for reasons such as these that some Trust members saw a need for collective advocacy:

> This is why we need a collective voice and it is not left to individuals.

However, people's reluctance to complain publicly meant that they were not easy to mobilise as a group, making it difficult to mount a campaign and accumulate sufficient evidence on which to base a case. The Trust was therefore forced to try other routes by taking it out of the local arena and trying to raise it as an issue for national policy:

> Rather than ask families if they want to make a fuss, we use other opportunities: for example, when giving evidence to the House of Commons Select Committee on Children's Health, we inserted it there.
>
> (Employee of the CFT)

This issue highlights a general difficulty of campaigning in this area. Even people's gratitude may have hidden dimensions. A public expression of gratitude may stem from a fear of upsetting staff at a time when people are dependent on their good will. In one nurse's view, at times of great stress, people's gratitude may spring more from their need to believe that their relative is receiving the best possible treatment and care than from the actual service provided:

> They are grateful because they have no option but to be grateful because it would be too painful to think of not getting a good service.

Fear and gratitude may, thus, be complexly intertwined. As one trust member observed:

> It is at times like this that you are least likely to start asserting your rights.

The relationship between the CFT and the specialist centres for the treatment of cystic fibrosis was variably described, depending on the perspective of informants. Workers in the Trust generally thought that the Trust's financial support to centres enabled it to exert an influence over policy:

The CFT have produced their own advice to hospitals about what patients want. The centres usually listen to us because they often get quite a lot of money from us to support their clinical work.

Staff in the centres that were visited, on the other hand, maintained a distant connection and, in some instances, relationships were somewhat strained. One respondent suggested that there was a tendency for health service trusts to marginalise the CFT because they perceived it to be primarily a fundraising organisation.

The Association for Cystic Fibrosis Adults

The Association for Cystic Fibrosis Adults (ACFA) was set up as an offshoot of the CFT. The growing number of adults with cystic fibrosis felt that the Trust was too strongly oriented towards parents and children and that the portrayal of cystic fibrosis as a disease of children not only masked their own existence but meant that their needs and concerns were not adequately addressed. All adults with a diagnosis of cystic fibrosis become automatic members and, at the time of writing, there were some 15–16,000 names on the mailing list for the Association newsletter *Input*. There are no membership fees or subscriptions. Active membership, however, was found to be confined to a small group. The Committee was aware that they were not representative of cystic fibrosis adults in general. The very desire to become involved set them apart. Both Pounceby's study (1997) and a Gallup poll (1996) commissioned by the CFT confirmed a general antipathy to involvement in collective activities organised around cystic fibrosis.

Lack of continuity and disruption caused by illness and death were a constant hazard. As we have seen, the impact of the death of a member of this small, fairly close-knit group could be devastating, especially if the death was unexpected. Not only could it cause some to question whether it was wise to become so committed to ACFA and close to other members but it could lead to serious disruption of the programme.

The majority of members, however, show little interest in active participation. Most people, it was suggested, are too busy leading their own lives and many adults keep their cystic fibrosis hidden and avoid any public association with the disease.

People with cystic fibrosis are busy being 'normal' and busy discarding the label. Therefore, something which attempts to identify them in terms of their disease is something that will be resisted.

(CFT employee)

In addition, people who are well may not see the relevance of an organisation which they perceive 'is for sick people'. One Committee Member explained:

I think a lot of people think that members of the committee and at conferences just sit around and talk about cystic fibrosis … and they don't want to get involved in that. They don't want to be reminded they've got cystic fibrosis and think there is nothing worse than being cooped up in a room with other people with cystic fibrosis.

The main explanation for the lack of development, however, was the advent of the bacterium *Burkholderia cepacia*. As one person remarked:

Cross-infection has really put the lid on ACFA.

As a nurse recalled,

They had a lot of social gatherings and conferences, a lot of branch meetings as well. Now, there are quite strict rules about cross-infection. Every cystic fibrosis adult who mixes with other cystic fibrosis adults knows they are putting themselves at risk.

Yet not all agreed that fear of cross-infection was the sole or even the most important reason for the decline:

Some people are not going to participate no matter what we do.

Others were optimistic that the Association would grow stronger once people's initial fear had subsided.

In an effort to elucidate some of these factors with a view to revitalising the Association, the CFT commissioned the market research organisation, Gallup, to conduct the telephone survey adults mentioned earlier (Gallup 1996). The survey found that only 77 per cent of those interviewed had already heard or seen anything about ACFA prior to the interview and few were interested in becoming active members. When asked to state what, in their view, the Association does, almost 50 per cent of respondents to the Gallup survey referred to information about cystic fibrosis and medical breakthroughs; 24 per cent mentioned the publication of a newsletter but only 15 per cent saw it as a 'forum' or 'communication channel', acting as a 'voice' for members and keeping people in touch with each other's views. Few (12 per cent) regarded it as a support network for people with cystic fibrosis and even fewer (2 per cent) saw it as a pressure group. Nonetheless, it was through its campaigns that Committee members thought that the organisation was primarily identified. It was certainly the campaign for free prescriptions which received the greatest support (93 per cent) among respondents to the Gallup survey. Other issues which were important to respondents were: helping people to obtain medication and treatment; providing information; promoting a more positive image of cystic fibrosis, namely that people with the condition can lead full and active lives; raising the profile of cystic fibrosis amongst the general population; lobbying for more specialist centres in hospitals; helping people obtain state benefits; improving the supply of donor organs; getting the CFT to do more to meet the needs of cystic fibrosis adults; providing a counselling service; providing funding for the provision of community physiotherapists; help for travel costs to hospital; obtaining funding for fertility treatment (*ibid.*).

The CFT is typical of many national charities of its kind and conforms more closely with the disability movement's characterisation of an organisation 'for' disabled people than to that of an organisation 'of' disabled people (Oliver 1996a). In part, this is an inheritance of the culture of the time in which it was set up; in part, it reflects a failure to keep pace with advances in the treatment of cystic fibrosis which have meant that many more people are now surviving into adulthood. Although recent changes have included the development of a greater advocacy and campaigning role and the provision of more practical and inform-ational support services to members, it is still the 'medical' model of disability which dominates its promotional literature. The ACFA, on the other hand, is not a fundraising organisation and conforms more nearly to the characterisation of an organisation 'of' disabled people. However, it relies heavily on the CFT to provide financial and other resources and its ability to adopt an independent or confrontational stance is inevitably compromised. The problem for ACFA is that, although it is an organisation which does, at least potentially, enable people with cystic fibrosis to have a 'voice' and fulfils the requirements of an organisation set up by members for members, it provides an opportunity which most adults with cystic fibrosis seem unwilling to take.

Neither of the two national organisations can be considered fully representative of their members. Both are dominated by a white, middle-class perspective and only a minority of members is active. Those who adopt the leading role are not necessarily representative of the majority. This clearly has implications for the extent to which these organisations can be considered to represent the interests of members collectively, especially the small number of families from minority ethnic groups, whose views are likely to be submerged by the more vocal, white, middle-class majority. In some senses, then, people with minority interests can be disempowered by the dominance of the more powerful majority. Even the majority may find themselves disempowered when they do not have a major say in the way in which the organisation is run. The Cystic Fibrosis Trust has become increasingly professional in its approach and has appointed a number of profess-ional employees. In consequence, some grassroots members have felt distanced from the national executive; this has had knock-on effects for ACFA. In common with the experience of many similar organisations, questionnaires and surveys of members have achieved only limited response rates, a notable exception being the surveys carried out by Walters (1991, 1994).

Local groups

The vigour of local branches of the CFT seemed to be largely dependent on the commitment and enthusiasm of a few individuals. One such person, who had watched her local branch fold after she and her husband left, observed:

> Parents need initial support but only a minority are interested in continued involvement.

Another commented:

> If their children are not ill both parents and children want to get on with living a normal life and to dissociate themselves from anything to do with cystic fibrosis.

A specialist children's nurse explained:

> The new parents don't particularly want to join that group because they can pretend that their child hasn't got cystic fibrosis because of the advances in treatment and, to attend the group, means that they *know* that their child's got cystic fibrosis. It sounds really strange but I talk to them about living with a chronic, life-threatening disease and the majority say: 'I don't have to have it here' [tapping her forehead], 'I can have it … you know' [tapping the back of her head], because they know about it but, if they had to live with that knowledge on a daily basis, then they'd not be in a mental state to cope.

In some instances, people ceased their involvement when their children became ill or died. One person explained that she had been unable to face people whose children were still alive and healthy and thought that this would have made them embarrassed and reticent about trying to offer support. Another woman, whose child was well, confessed that she had not known what to say to a woman whose own child had died.

For agencies wishing to engage in local consultations with people with cystic fibrosis, local groups provide only a limited means of access. The emphasis on fundraising is known to deter some people from joining and few adults with cystic fibrosis are active members. Active membership was variable and focused on fundraising rather than campaigning on issues of common concern to members. This is encouraged by the Trust which publishes annual league tables of the amounts raised by each group. Moreover, people seemed to need the support of local groups more at certain times: at the time of the initial diagnosis; when their child first started school and began to catch infections; and, later, when the child started secondary school.

The Barnardo's projects, which had been established in two of the areas visited to help young people with cystic fibrosis with social, financial and practical problems, were another potential forum for collective action. The projects were mainly concerned with giving advice about benefits, housing and employment issues. As with other collective activities, opportunities to meet in groups had been severely curtailed since the advent of B. *cepacia*. One project had ceased all collective activities after losing six people in twelve months.

Specialist centres

Although people with cystic fibrosis considered themselves to be a generally vocal group and to possess an assertiveness bred from long familiarity with the staff and setting, there was little evidence of collective organisation among patients within the hospital centres. None of those visited had an organised patient group. One hospital had attempted to run groups in the past but these had foundered through lack of support. In part, this could be attributed to the large catchment area served by the centre. As the social worker at the centre explained,

> We tried to have patient groups but they were not very well attended. People with cystic fibrosis had problems getting in from work or from college and many lived quite a distance away.

Some centres, however, were better at taking account of patients' views than others. At one, which operated a strict segregation policy for patients infected with B. *Cepacia*, patients with *cepacia* felt that they were not getting the same facilities. The social worker attached to the centre contacted all the *cepacia* patients and invited them to a meeting to find out what they wanted. This discussion was ongoing. The same centre had recently won an award which had included a financial component, and patients had been consulted about how the money should be spent. The areas in which patients' views were allowed to exert an influence, however, tended to be confined to what have been termed 'the hotel aspects of health care' (Pound *et al.* 1994), as the following comment from a nurse specialist (adults) reflected:

> We have a very verbal group of patients here who make it known to us what they want and don't want. The way the unit has developed here, putting fridges in the rooms and television, a pool room etc., has really been in response to patients. The suggestions have really come from them.

Yet there is a danger of underestimating the importance of these aspects. It is the little things which can often make a large difference to the way in which people experience their care.

There was some evidence of attempts to organise collectively initiated by members of ACFA, although these tended to be short-lived and dependent on the enthusiasm of individuals. In one centre, which had recently moved to a new site, for example, a patient who was a member of ACFA had taken it on herself to write to every patient to seek his or her views about the move.

Some people suggested that hospital clinics might prove a fruitful recruiting ground for health authorities seeking the views of people with cystic fibrosis, although they warned that many people would not want to participate in any sort of consultative exercise. A general cynicism about 'talking shops', where much was said but little action resulted, emerged from the interviews with patients, as did the repeated warning that those who consented to participate were generally unrepresentative of the majority of people with cystic fibrosis.

> You usually find that people involved in any particular health groups or organisations are very committed people and very passionate about what

they believe in. But, sometimes – we certainly found it in ACFA – you tend to get very polarised views. You tend to get people with very strong views about certain things but who don't necessarily represent their full members' needs and wants.

(Committee member of ACFA)

Informal networks

We have already noted that the strength of informal networks was variable. Most families need additional support at particular times during the course of their children's growing up and there was a tendency for people to dip in and out of networks, depending on their needs. The risks of their children catching infections from each other meant that it was unwise for them to spend too much time in each other's company and this further discouraged the formation of enduring attachments between families. Existing networks appeared to serve social and support functions rather than as vehicles for the development of a collective voice on issues of common concern. Any collective activity tended to centre on fundraising organised by the local groups. Nevertheless, informal networks were important mechanisms for the exchange of information. When their children transferred to adult services and began to attend clinics on their own, networks which had included parents tended to disintegrate.

Among adults, some people had strong social ties with other people with cystic fibrosis, others had only tenuous links. The emergence of B. *cepacia* had disrupted existing networks and obstructed the formation of new ones. Hospital visits provided one of the main opportunities for people to meet and to form their own informal networks. Here, people were able to compare experiences and treatments and sometimes suggestions might be passed on to staff. Staff receptivity, however, was variable, as one man explained:

For example, someone who says one of their friends has said, 'Oh, we do this in our clinic'. Even if you had a mechanism where you could go to a doctor and say, 'This would be a good idea for us to do this in the clinic', you have got the problem (a) of whether or not he is going to listen to you anyway and (b), even if he thinks it is a good idea, there is a certain amount of professional antagonism between them, so that, you know, he might give it a try or he might not.

It was in those aspects of service provision marginal to the main work of the clinics where staff appeared to be most receptive to patients' views. The wide geographical catchments served by the specialist centres and the desire of many people to compartmentalise their lives into hospital and 'normal life' meant that networks were often not sustained outside hospital. Many people attend the same centre throughout their lives, which means that opportunities to meet and talk with people who attend different centres and for the cross-fertilisation of ideas are limited.

Computer-mediated communication and chat groups

As we discussed above, problems of isolation and distance can sometimes be overcome by the technologies of computer-mediated communication. The technology also offers the potential for a co-ordinated approach to an agenda of user involvement. For example, the CFT's counterpart in the United States of America, the Cystic Fibrosis Foundation, is overtly political in its intentions and organises a Public Policy Alliance which describes itself as 'a grassroots network to educate our legislators'. It acts as a political pressure group, co-ordinating collective action and advising members on effective lobbying in 'an effort to orchestrate an insurmountable power on the political front'. Members can join via the enrolment form which is provided on the CFF website.

CYSTIC-L

CYSTIC-L is an email support group for people with cystic fibrosis and their friends, families, and health care providers. It includes both casual banter about the varied impact that cystic fibrosis has on people's lives as well as technical and medical information exchanges. It is the first Internet mailing list devoted to cystic fibrosis and was founded in February 1994 by a graduate student with cystic fibrosis at the University of Yale. Archives for CYSTIC-L, beginning in June 1994, can be accessed at CF-WEB (http://www.cf-web.org/). Current membership is about 600 and consists mostly of parents and patients and some health care professionals. The majority of subscribers are in the USA, with the remainder mainly from countries where English is the primary language. Current traffic levels run around twenty to fifty messages a day.

CYSTIC-L produces a comprehensive, online *Handbook* that contains general information and opinions intended to provide a general orientation to cystic fibrosis. The forty-four chapters deal with issues ranging from basic information about cystic fibrosis, through diagnosis, treatment options, alternative medicine, lung transplantation, insurance, benefits and financial matters to neonatal

Table 6.1 Contributions to on-line CF chat group (CYSTIC-L) between 24 February and 3 March 1999.

Contributors	No. of contributors		No. of contributions	
Mothers	44	(34%)*	122	(41%)
Fathers	5	(4%)	10	(3%)
Other relatives	5	(4%)	11	(4%)
Women with CF	40	(31%)	79	(26%)
Men with CF	18	(14%)	48	(16%)
Women (not known)	12	(9%)	27	(9%)
Men (not known)	4	(3%)	4	(1%)
Total	128	(100%)	301	(100%)

* percentages do not add up to exactly 100 as a result of rounding

screening and pregnancy. It includes chapters on 'Finding a physician', 'Dealing with medical persons', 'Coping with the diagnosis' and 'Coping with death'.

A brief analysis of contributions to the List during the week beginning 24 February 1999 revealed that the largest group of contributors were mothers of children with cystic fibrosis (34 per cent): only five (4 per cent) contributors identified themselves as fathers. Women with cystic fibrosis (31 per cent) formed the second largest group, outnumbering men by more than two to one. Overall, female contributors to the List outnumbered male contributors by more than three to one. The overwhelming majority of participants came from the US, although two Canadian and two European (English) contributors were identified.

The List has enabled people to communicate over long geographical distances (in the case of the European contributors, over continents) and has opened communication channels between people who would otherwise have had no contact with each other. It was clear that many participants were regular contributors and there were several references to the idea that List contributors constituted a form of surrogate 'family'. Many people commented on the value of the social contact which their participation in the List afforded. Active participation, however, was variable, with some people dropping out of the List for long periods and rejoining at a later date. Over the week, several contributors reintroduced themselves with an explanation of their absences. Ill health and hospitalisation were major reasons for absences. List contributions usually ended with conventional identifications, including the age, sex and status of the contributor. Apart from these conventions of etiquette, contributors used abbreviations and expressions which were unlikely to be in widespread use outside the List and which identified participants as a community. Hospitalisations, for example, were referred to as 'going to the club'.

During the week, there were 128 contributors and 301 contributions to the mail group (excluding fourteen housekeeping messages from the List holder), giving an average of 2.4 messages per contributor. The largest number of messages was from two women engaged in an acrimonious debate about the merits and demerits of a new treatment, who posted fifteen messages between them. The main topics of discussion were treatment and medication issues and diagnosis (especially late diagnosis), followed by personal news items (birthdays, marriages etc.) and non-medical topics.

The List served as both a repository of information and a network for information exchange on medical and health-related topics. Participants compared symptoms and experiences of medications and treatments, passed on information and answered queries based on their own experiences, and introduced List subscribers to new treatments and the results of new research. They also gave advice about how to manage relationships with health professionals – in two instances, the advice was to change doctors – and how to assess the quality of information given by comparing it with the advice given to other contributors. Comparisons were made between different specialist centres and different hospitals in their treatment of people with cystic fibrosis. There was discussion about the best treatments for particular symptoms and about what constitutes good quality care. In this way, subscribers to the List were empowered not just by access to information but by the knowledge that others were experiencing similar symptoms and shared similar experiences, that they could draw on the experiences of others and could count on their support in their dealings with health professionals.

The List also served as a mechanism for sharing practical advice on a range of non-medical issues related to CF, including: obtaining health and life insurance, comparing different schemes and different providers; work-related issues, such as how to manage prolonged and repeated absences through ill health, employment law, managing IVs while at work, and home working; educational issues, such as absences from school and home tuition; advice about disability and other state benefits; environmental issues, including how to deal with relatives who smoke and advice about household heating; disclosure – specifically, how to tell prospective partners that you have CF and how to tell a child that the disease may be terminal. Contributors provided each other with information and with practical and moral support: for example, in the exchanges concerning relatives who smoked, people compared experiences and suggested different ways of dealing with the problem as well as giving moral support for a chosen course of action.

The fact that the largest group of contributors consisted of parents of children with cystic fibrosis mirrors the experience of the Cystic Fibrosis Trust of the United Kingdom where the bulk of the active membership of local groups is made up of parents. People's need for information and for social and moral support is different at different times: as contributors to the present study observed, it is often high around the time of diagnosis and while parents are relatively inexperienced in the management of the disease. The preponderance of mothers might be explained by the fact that it is usually mothers who assume the greatest responsibility for their children's care. This does not, however, explain the preponderance of women overall, especially as it is men who usually have greater access to the technologies of computer-mediated communication. Many of the female contributors were using their male partner's email address. This is a phenomenon which needs further investigation and verification by analysis of a longer time period and which, if substantiated, clearly has implications for the use of online chat groups and mailing lists as a vehicle for user involvement.

One of the most important functions of the List was as a network of support and information exchange for carers of people with cystic fibrosis. We know from our own study that carers and those they care for often have different information needs, with those cared for often less concerned to know about the details of disease progression than about how to make the most of their day-to-day lives. The high participation by carers may act to suppress use of the List by people who actually have the disease themselves and the mixed audience may mean that some topics are less likely to be discussed. On the other hand, the lower participation rates of people with cystic fibrosis may simply reflect their desire to get on with their lives without dwelling on their cystic fibrosis.

The overall tone of contributions was positive. One can speculate, perhaps, that the high proportion of parent contributors, who do not want to think of their children dying at this early stage, may have skewed the emphasis towards optimism. Many parents clearly believed that a cure would be found during their children's lifetimes. There seemed almost to be a collective, unspoken agreement to sustain the general optimism by avoiding reference to dying or death. One contributor, for example, prefaced her message, bringing to the attention of subscribers a mailing list for parents who have lost a 'special needs' child, with the words: 'I know this is a sad subject but …'.

The post from a contributor with cystic fibrosis whose health was failing and who was clearly depressed sounded a discordant note in the otherwise optimistic tenor of communications. This post generated several responses and revealed the potential of the List to provide both emotional support, in terms of messages of empathy and support, and practical support, in terms of advice about anti-depressants and other practical measures. We do not know the number and content of personal communications which did not appear on the List.

Users of the List not only have access to medical information but to a wealth of anecdotal experiences and lay perceptions and opinions. It is debatable whether this produces a better informed and more assertive group of patients or, alternatively, people who are more confused and uncertain, who have lost faith in both the skills and goodwill of professionals but who do not feel competent themselves to navigate the sea of information which threatens to engulf them. This brief excursion into the world of the Internet chat group suggests that it is the first scenario which is the more likely, with participants helping to guide each other through the Information Sea. Contributors acted collectively as their own policemen and guides, monitoring the quality of information posted to the List and drawing participants' attention to other sources of information. However, the warning which accompanied every message, 'Consult a trusted doctor before ANY change to your treatment', although a necessary caveat, could be read, per-haps, as a collective abdication of responsibility and begs the question of situations where the doctor is not trusted.

The List empowered its members through its function as a network of social interchange, information exchange, and emotional and practical support. It served as a vehicle for highlighting inconsistencies in practice and monitoring treatment and care, and as a forum for the collective discussion of good practice. However, there were no formal mechanisms for communicating directly with service providers. Any impact on the delivery of services was likely to be exerted in interactions between individual List subscribers and health service practitioners. The List was also used more directly as a means of co-ordinating collective action through publicising fundraising activities and co-ordinating the setting up of a club for children. During the week of investigation, however, there was no evidence that it was used in any more strategic or political way as a lobbying or pressure group. Nevertheless, the potential is there for direct political action through, for example, co-ordination of mass lobbying or demonstrations, boycott of services or providers, non-participation in or sabotage of clinical trials, collection of online signatories to petitions, and co-ordination of demands for particular treatments or approaches to care.

Discussion

People with cystic fibrosis are encouraged to construct their identities around their similarity to other people and their ability to live 'normal' lives. Many actively conceal their cystic fibrosis from others. For people living under the shadow of life-limiting illness, the desire to avoid thinking about it and to concentrate on the here and now seems to be a powerful means of coping. In consequence, people do not actively seek out information which may distress them, avoid situations where they may be confronted with it, and may fail to assimilate it when they are. Information given at an inappropriate time or when people feel unequal to handling it may be demoralising and emotionally traumatic. At worst, it can be experienced as an act of unwitting, or even deliberate, cruelty when it leads to the elimination of hope. Managing information flow in ways and at a pace which they feel able to handle is one of the main ways in which people tried to cope with living with a life-limiting disease. There is a tendency for professionals to regard the giving of information as a means of educating patients and the act of communication as an event (Robinson *et al.* 1996). For patients, on the other hand, the issue was not simply one of ignorance and the supply of information but of receptivity and resistance and the communication of information less an event than a process.

Information about palliative care and services for those who are dying may not always be easily available. Improvements in treatment and the introduction of home-based therapies have reduced the number of hospital visits and inpatient stays. The opportunities for people to experience dying at second hand by seeing others, to learn what options may be available and to discuss their fears with staff and with other patients are therefore fewer. For people who have become infected with B. *cepacia* and who are segregated within hospital from other cystic fibrosis patients, these opportunities may be even more restricted. In the community, families and carers looking after a sick relative often become socially isolated. The interviews revealed a tendency to avoid contact with others who were seriously ill out of embarrassment and fear.

Paradoxically, perhaps, as people with cystic fibrosis have become healthier, their opportunities to acquire the relevant information to enable them to make informed choices in this area are likely to have decreased. People do not need to go into hospital so often and are therefore less likely to meet others with the disease, be part of social networks or take part in activities organised around cystic fibrosis.

One can speculate that, as the outlook for the cystic fibrosis population as a whole improves, those diminishing few who suffer early complications and ill health and who die young may come to be regarded almost as 'pariahs', almost as if they are being blamed for failing to live up to the new expectations. Their misfortune threatens the general optimism and they and their families become, quite literally, 'dangerous' to associate with. In this way, families can become socially isolated, both before and after the death of their child.

People not only seem to actively avoid those situations where they are most likely to acquire information about terminal care and managing death but the knowledge gained through experience tends to remain locked away within individual families rather than circulated through community networks. Families whose children have died appear to become excluded or, in some cases, to exclude themselves from networks of families of children with cystic fibrosis. Families become excluded not only because their experience threatens the general optimism but because it foreshadows the worst fears of other members.

A children's nurse described the situation when a child died in the unit:

> The majority of people come on a four-weekly or a six-weekly clinic appointment, so they see the same people as the kids are growing up and they get to know one another and they talk to one another, and they care about each other's children. You know, it's very much that sort of a close-knit family. But, when one dies, the other cystic fibrosis families back off, because what they are looking at is what they're going to feel like when their child actually dies of cystic fibrosis. And it's quite strange because it's as if they don't want to put themselves through it and their own child through it. And, if you're close to a cystic fibrosis family, you're grieving each time another child dies, but you're not actually grieving that child, you're grieving your own child. And they [the families] feel guilty about that.

A tendency to shun people who have been bereaved has been reported in other studies (e.g. Rhodes and Shaw 1998). Some bereaved parents seem to sense this intuitively and to shun local fundraising groups after the death of their child. They also tend to drop out of local groups and cystic fibrosis networks through a desire to dissociate themselves from anything to do with cystic fibrosis which might excite painful memories. For some families, this process of disassociation seems to be an important element of the bereavement process. In consequence, there appears to be little repository within the community for the experiential knowledge of bereaved families and few mechanisms for sharing or passing it on. Support groups for bereaved carers may enable some families to share their experiences and emotions but the information remains confined within the closed group.

The main repository of knowledge seems to be the specialist hospital centres but it is the knowledge of medical and nursing staff rather than the knowledge of people who have lost a close family member. Although staff may act as a conduit of information, the communication is not direct from family to family: rather, it is passed through a professional filter and, in the process, perhaps loses some of its immediacy and relevance.

The chief, and often the only, contact most people have with the national organisations representing the interests of people with cystic fibrosis is through their newsletters. The newsletters may be one of the most successful means through which to convey information but even they are likely to have limited effectiveness. Evidence from both the current study and the Gallup survey suggest that members may be resistant to receiving information about these matters via this route and that some may even be put off from reading the newsletters altogether. As in other areas of their lives, people are likely to shun any discussion of terminal care needs. The provision of individual advice and information in response to telephone enquiries may be a more productive channel, although whether people would use this service to seek this type of information and whether the information provided would be adequate to meet their needs remains an open question.

One of the most profitable approaches is likely to be through the Internet, although, even here, there may be a reluctance to confront issues around death and dying. As we have seen, people with cystic fibrosis do not always want to hear from others with the disease. Moreover, only a minority of people have access to the Internet. The discussion group CYSTIC-L seems to be a resource more widely used by carers than people with cystic fibrosis themselves and limited mainly to subscribers in the United States. Nevertheless, to those who have access, the Internet offers a powerful means of empowering them to take a more active role in their own treatment and care. By offering opportunities for the sharing of information and experiences, it breaks down people's sense of isolation and gives them the confidence of knowing others in similar situations. The Net serves as a repository for both lay and professional knowledge and gives people the information and confidence with which to challenge professional opinion so that relationships come to conform more closely to those of genuine partnership.

Choice

The provision of information about services and treatment options, however, is no guarantee of choice for users. Knowing that there may be better services provided elsewhere is no consolation when people have no option of moving to an alternative provider. On receiving advice to change doctors, a contributor to the online mailing list (CYSTIC-L) replied: 'Thanks for your responses. I agree, and I would love to find another doc. Unfortunately, this doctor is the only CF doc in the area'.

In welfare services, the nature of the relationship between service producer and consumer or user, as Barnes and Prior (1995) note, is 'complex and shifting' and 'the service itself is produced in an interaction which cannot always be predicted. Choices will be exercised on both sides of the relationship, but these will often be the result of negotiation and debate about options to which both parties must contribute' (1995: 58).

The importance to people of continuity, familiarity, confidence, security and trust were persistent themes throughout the interviews for the present study. Often, these seemed to be more highly valued and more relevant to people's circumstances than the opportunity for choice.

For people with cystic fibrosis, death in hospital appears to be the preferred option. Advantages included familiar surroundings, staff in whom patients felt confidence and trust, and the security of technical back-up support. However, patients and their families have little or no knowledge or experience of other options. The decision to cease curative treatment is usually made within a short time of death, often only days.

> And because, perhaps, the end does come so quickly, although it's happening over a long period of time, the actual turning point is very short at the end when we say: 'Right, that's it, we've done as much as we possibly can and you're not getting any better'.
>
> (Specialist nurse, adults unit)

Patients are usually already in hospital and a decision to die at home entails an active decision to leave as opposed to a passive decision to stay. A decision to leave involves other people in making arrangements for the journey home and for the support the patient will need while he or she is there. Without previous discussion and pre-planning, such a move may not be feasible.

Surveys of bereaved relatives and carers of people who died from cancer reported that most of those cared for had wanted to die at home, although only a minority had actually done so (Seale and Cartwright 1994; Addington-Hall and McCarthy 1995a). This apparent mismatch between people's reported wishes and their actual place of death, however, may be misleading. Unpacking the details of the circumstances of individual deaths would throw greater light on what has become an emotive issue which, in some instances, has been used crudely in support of arguments for the transfer of resources from inpatient to community palliative care services. Staff interviewed for the present study reported that, although many patients with cystic fibrosis state an initial preference for a home death, they opt for hospital as death becomes more imminent. Nurses recounted instances where patients had chosen to go home but had later returned to hospital, often as emergency admissions, because their families had been unable to cope.

The choice of where to die may be a highly complex decision which changes over time and with the imminence of death, and which is negotiated between the patient, family members and hospital staff. The surveys of bereaved relatives and carers, referred to above, reported differences between the dead person's and carers' and relatives' views about appropriate care on a number of dimensions (Seale and Cartwright 1994; Addington-Hall and McCarthy 1995a). Similarly, conflicts of interest and differences of opinion between professionals and patients with cystic fibrosis have been widely discussed (e.g. Pounceby 1997; Abbott, Dodd and Webb 1995). How these differences are managed and whose opinions actually hold sway will vary between cases.

Hospitals not only fail to match the intimacy and familiarity of the home environment but are often located at considerable distances from people's homes, especially the specialist centres which many cystic fibrosis patients attend. However, it was suggested that, for some people, this very separation of hospital from home helped in coping with the poignancy of death and pain of parting. Yet families face the inconvenience and expense of long journeys and the 'hotel charges' which some hospitals levy for their accommodation while they are there. Hospitals are rarely able or prepared to accommodate whole families and the accommodation provided is often located at some distance from the ward, although single put-up beds in the ward are sometimes available. The potential for choice could, perhaps, be enhanced or made more attractive if some of the characteristics of the hospital which patients seem to value could be provided in alternative settings.

One of the main reasons why people opted for a hospital death seemed to be a fear of inadequate symptom control at home, suggesting that better symptom control provided in the home environment might encourage more people to choose to die at home. Better liaison and shared care between hospital and community staff at an earlier stage in the illness would encourage the familiarity with community staff which people valued in staff in hospital. It would also both enhance the skills and confidence of community staff and reduce the costs of a home death in terms of specialist nursing input. The appointment of specialist cystic fibrosis nurses in the community could lead to improved care for people in the late stages of illness, as has been demonstrated in other areas, for example for people with end-stage chronic obstructive pulmonary disease (Skillbeck *et al.* 1997) or diabetes (Diabetes Specialist Nurse, personal communication).

Hospice services could, perhaps, be extended to provide more outreach services in the community, day and respite care, in addition to therapies and psychological support which would benefit people at earlier stages in their illnesses. This would go some way towards counteracting their image as places in which to die rather than as resources upon which people can draw as and when they need. Greater provision specifically for people with cystic fibrosis and care shared with hospital services may help to familiarise people with hospice staff and surroundings at an earlier stage.

The need for fewer hospital visits and inpatient stays may lead to a reduction in the level of dedicated secondary care services for people with cystic fibrosis in the future. In consequence, hospitals may become less familiar and, perhaps, less comfortable places, and may cease to hold some of their current attractions as a choice of location in which to die. Hospices or nursing homes for younger people, by expanding their expertise and widening their intake to include a wider variety of diseases, may emerge as alternative options. The expansion of respite and outreach community care may encourage more families to opt for a home death. Staff will gain greater confidence in managing death in the community and the example of others may encourage patients to see it as a genuine choice.

The dimensions of choice

The people with cystic fibrosis who were interviewed for the study presented themselves as unusually vocal and assertive patients, described their relationship with medical and nursing staff as generally good, and thought that, on the whole, treatment decisions were discussed with them and that they had some influence over the care and treatment they received. Yet it is in the later stages of their illness that they are, perhaps, likely to feel least empowered. Barnes and Prior (1995) suggest that the extent to which people find choices empowering or disempowering will depend on the way in which the dimensions of coercion, predictability, frequency, significance and participation are combined in any particular instance. This analysis may help us better to understand the situation of people with cystic fibrosis who are approaching the ends of their lives.

Coercion

People with cystic fibrosis who may be entering a terminal stage in their illness may face little in the way of overt coercion in terms of treatment and care. Yet the evidence from the present study suggests that they may be subject to considerable subtle manipulation. A complex mix of family and professional pressures may sometimes obliterate any sense of personal choice. As with people dying from other terminal diseases, there may be a conflict of interest between patients and relatives and carers over the place of death. Studies of bereaved carers have shown that people may often be admitted to hospital to die in the last few days or even hours of their lives. In some cases, this is because carers are no longer able to cope or are afraid of being alone when the death occurs or of living in the same house in which a person has died (Rhodes and Shaw 1998). Alternatively, patients themselves may pre-empt such fears by choosing to spend their last days and hours in hospital in order to spare relatives and partners.

The decision to opt for an organ transplant may be especially traumatic and many staff believed that some people would opt for a transplant for the sake of their parents or partners rather than for their own sake. The time when the option is first presented is simultaneously a time of hope and of desperation. Although the prospect of a transplant offers hope of a new lease of life, it also marks official recognition that the illness has become terminal. The way in which options are presented, and by whom, can affect both the choice and the way in which the choice is perceived. In the past, doctors were reticent about presenting the risks of a transplant and the problems of obtaining a suitable organ. The present more 'realistic' approach to discussions of the possible outcomes may not have affected the choices patients make but it is likely to have affected the ways in which the implications of these choices are perceived.

Although the possibility of a suitable donor organ becoming available may be remote, the decision to opt for a transplant may mean continuing aggressive treatment for longer than might have been the case, sustaining hope for longer and postponing coming to terms with the likelihood of an early death. Those for whom a transplant is no longer an option and who have entered a palliative phase may find themselves coerced into accepting aggressive or invasive treatments and, thus, sacrificing comfort and dignity for the possibility of prolonging life, however small.

The pace of medical advance and the possibility of organ transplants in a sense create their own climate of coercion: although giving people with cystic fibrosis and their families the strength of hope, at the same time they can distract them from those concerns which might help them to plan for declining health and a foreshortened lifespan. Improvements in therapy over the past twenty years, with the average life expectancy more than doubling, have created a sense of optimism which leads some families to forget that their child has a terminal disease. People extrapolate from past success into a future characterised by continued medical progress. The possibility of medical advance holds out hope of discovery of a 'cure' which, for many people with cystic fibrosis, has removed the certainty of an early death. Whereas twenty years ago few people survived beyond their teens, some are now living into their forties and beyond and it is predicted that the average lifespan for those born in the 1990s will be forty years (Bell and Shale 1993). The prospect of continued medical advance, supported by the evidence of past progress, is therefore more realistic than a similar sense of hope would have been twenty, or even ten, years ago. It is easy to convince oneself that one does not have, or one's child does not have, a serious debilitating condition which may eventually prove fatal. Although people claim to 'live one day at a time', they may simultaneously adhere to an optimistic vision of the future which precludes more pessimistic outcomes. In this climate, it is difficult to anticipate a future of declining health and early death and people may find themselves entering the last part of their lives with little preparation and little knowledge of the choices they may have available to them.

Predictability

The unpredictable nature of the disease makes forward planning difficult. People with cystic fibrosis may face the immediacy of death not once but many times as the disease progresses (Quin 1996). The expected death, however, is a hospital death. As far as is possible without personal experience, it is familiar and 'known'. By comparison, death at home is an unknown. Neither staff nor patients and their families are likely to have experience of managing death in the community. They do not know what to expect in terms of either services or quality of care. They have no prior knowledge or standards on which to base judgements. Patients may have little relationship with their general practitioner or district nurse as they have always gone directly to the hospital for their treatment (Cottrell 1991). Given that much of their experience is likely to have been with specialist staff, they may have little confidence in generalist staff, whom they fear have insufficient experience in catering for their particular needs (*ibid.*). They may doubt their own ability or that of their family to cope as their condition deteriorates. Relatives may similarly doubt their own capabilities, not having been in this situation before or met others who have experienced it.

Frequency

As death approaches, families may be forced to make decisions with little prior knowledge or information to guide them. They are likely to choose the familiar over the unfamiliar. Death in hospital for people with cystic fibrosis is not an unfamiliar occurrence. Staff, in adult units especially, will have experienced it many times before, whereas death at home is likely to be a first occurrence. In hospital, there is a routine procedure for managing death; at home, there are no precedents, no formal procedures or designated roles; neither patient nor family members know how they will or should react or how they will manage.

Significance

A further complicating factor for many people with cystic fibrosis is the compartmentalisation of their lives into 'normal life' and 'hospital'. Some people seem to have managed their lives by maintaining a rigid separation between hospital and home in an effort to retain a sense of normality by restricting the intrusion of the hospital into the home (*cf.* Bluebond-Langner 1996). It is a way of containing the disease. In the same way that some people attempt to maintain a separation between their home and their place of work, some families attempt to confine the cystic fibrosis within the realm of the hospital. Hospital is the place of ill health and treatment and it is, perhaps, unsurprising that it is also the place of death. With the introduction of more home-based therapies, however, this separation is becoming increasingly difficult to sustain.

We know from studies of bereaved families that some families cannot face the prospect of their relative dying in their home (Rhodes and Shaw 1998). The fear of death polluting the domestic space may be even stronger among families who have lived with cystic fibrosis and attempted to manage its intrusion by compartalisation and there is some evidence that reasons such as these may influence some people's choice of a hospital death. Cottrell (1991), for example, recounts the case of an adolescent patient who did not want his room at home as a reminder of his death. By exerting some control over the place and manner of their dying and deaths, people attempt to influence the legacies and memories they leave behind them.

Participation

In hospital, the role of the family may be more that of bystanders than participants. At home, their role is more likely to be that of active carers. But, although they may have been caring for a person for many years, they may never have been in the role of caring for someone who is dying and may never have witnessed a death. In addition, much of the care over the past few months will probably have been in hospital and family members may not have had to care for the patient when he or she has been seriously ill. They may doubt their own abilities and capacity to cope both physically and emotionally. In hospital, on the other hand, they can be reassured that the patient will be cared for by experienced staff.

Conclusion

As we have seen, empowering people to take control over the last stages of their lives is not simply a matter of supplying information on which to base choices about different options, although this can be an important element. The giving of information is not an event but a process. This process is especially complex where managing information flow is one of the main ways of coping with living with a chronic and life-limiting illness. Many people adopted a strategy of avoidance in relation to information-seeking behaviour in order to minimise distress and to sustain hope for as long as possible. The dilemma for people with cystic fibrosis is that a general orientation towards promoting optimism and sustaining hope leads to tension where it collides with the realities of disease progression and is constantly vulnerable to the intrusion of events. People tread a precarious path between adopting a positive attitude to life and preparing themselves to cope with serious ill health and eventual death.

Secondly, the unpredictable course of the disease makes forward planning difficult and encourages an approach of living day to day. It also leaves room for hope. In Armour's words, 'Uncertainty is both a curse and a blessing but it has taught us some skills in balancing on a tightrope between hope and despair' (Armour 1991: 120). These difficulties, compounded when the rapidity of medical advance is added to the vagaries of disease progression, are vividly described in the email letter quoted at the beginning of this chapter: 'I have celebrated the 30th anniversary of my "last" birthday. The docs let me go home 30 years ago to die'.

Thirdly, it is difficult to acquire relevant information about possible choices and about how to plan end-of-life care. This is a reflection, in part, of the medical emphasis on curative treatments; in part, of both a public and private reluctance to discuss these issues. Much relevant information is experiential in nature and cannot be passed on adequately by professionals, yet opportunities to acquire experiential information about palliative care are limited. The nature of needs means that many palliative care services are services unlikely to be used more than once and death, by its very nature, denies the possibility of communication of the experience. Even assuming adequate information, opportunities for choice will be few where options are limited. Even where options may theoretically be open, there may be little or no opportunity for choice: a home death for many people with cystic fibrosis, for example, may be little more than a theoretical possibility.

Many of the same inhibitory factors are operating at the collective level. Two issues which bedevil attempts to facilitate involvement are a reluctance to associate publicly with the disease and an apparent reluctance or inability to consider future needs and unwillingness to engage in discussion.

Computer mediated communication (CMC) offers, perhaps, the greatest challenge to conventional forms of organisation. It enables people to communicate with others with cystic fibrosis and to maintain contact with the wider world at times when they are most ill. The impersonal, disembodied character of CMC may help to cut through the inhibitions which discourage communication by creating a shield which protects people from confrontation with the bodily evidence of illness and decline in others and masks their own physical state. Through comparing experiences with others, people may come to recognise common interests and concerns. The democratic nature of the Internet enables networks to be permeated by new ideas and perspectives, and exposure to more politicised self-help and advocacy groups may lead to a heightened political consciousness. This can lift people out of the realm of the personal into a wider collective world and can shift the focus from a narrow concentration on medical research as the agent of deliverance and cure towards a broader, strategic perspective. This would encourage a move away from the need to identify oneself as someone with cystic fibrosis to a wider political identity shared with others in a range of circumstances and with a range of illnesses and impairments. Discussion of topics may become easier by moving them from the level of the personal to the level of the collective. Through dilution of their personal immediacy, a certain protective distance is created which mitigates their emotional impact.

This is a consideration which health authorities seeking to involve local people in decision making might do well to heed. Rather than treating palliative care as a separate issue, it would, perhaps, be better to view it as an integral component of a comprehensive package of treatment and care throughout the lifespan so that discussions about palliative care become part of more general discussions about services.

7 Conclusions

We have seen common themes emerging in the preceding chapters. The illnesses on which we have chosen to concentrate have a number of shared features. But there are also significant differences. We begin our conclusion by summarising some of these themes and highlighting their varying manifestations in relation to the specific circumstances of either MS, MND or CF. We then go on to look at the more general impact of illness in terms of biographical disruption and we put this in the context of our changing society. After considering specific aspects of user involvement in relation to end-of-life care, we look at some of the processes currently in place for consultation and consider additional or alternative ones. We finish with an overview of policy in this area. In consequence, our conclusion covers the three principal areas of concern addressed in the book: narratives of illness, the meaning of user involvement and the policy context in which it is pursued. In so doing it reiterates some of the descriptions and analysis presented in more detail in the preeceding chapters. As we said in our introduction some of our readers may have concentrated on those parts of the book that look at the illness closest to their personal or professional concerns. Here we offer a brief overview to help them locate individual chapters in the overall topography of our argument.

Themes and variations

Living with uncertainty

Uncertainty is present in all three illnesses to varying degrees. It is particularly evident in diagnosis and in patterns of progression. With MS and MND there is often prolonged uncertainty. There is no definitive test, diagnosis proceeds by a process of elimination. It is often difficult to get doctors to take early symptoms seriously. We have recorded examples of symptoms being misdiagnosed as depression or trivial physical complaints. Alternatively, symptoms have been characterised as malingering or, in one example, as drunkenness! With CF, most people are diagnosed within the first few months of life and there is a definitive test, therefore this stage of the illness is not usually one where we see uncertainty. However, progression in CF does vary, although the most evident determining factor is age. For most people with CF, health will begin to deteriorate after their teens. With medical advances, this deterioration has been delayed longer and longer for people with CF as a whole. But, for some, problems come much earlier. Each relapse may herald further deterioration. But it may also be followed by recovery and this recovery may occur even after serious illness. Even in the terminal phase, the prospect of an organ transplant offers hope of prolonged good quality life. But a scarcity of suitable donors means that most will die while on a waiting list, while those that have the operation still find their prospect of recovery fraught with uncertainty. The rapid pace of medical advance in CF, which has led to dramatic improvements in life expectancy for the group as a whole, continues and new developments following the ability to isolate genes, and the prospects of gene therapy this offers, present a real hope of a cure.

With MS, progression and prognosis is uncertain. Relapses can occur suddenly with little warning. MND sees a much greater certainty and speed of progression and a bleaker prognosis. Speed of progression is often so rapid that people cannot keep pace with new symptoms, either in organising practical aspects of their lives or in making adjustments to self-perception. While there appear many potentially interesting advances in treatment, we do not see the prospect of cure being discussed in the same way as we see in CF.

Hope

Uncertainty is one of most difficult aspects of illness to cope with for all three groups. But if things are uncertain there remains room for hope. In each illness the grounds for hope are different. With MS, the hope is that it may not be too severe and may not lead to a shortening of life. People hope that medical advances may lead to a cure during their lifetime and to the more effective treatment of symptoms in the shorter term. Medical advances give those with CF hope that progress will continue. There is a general sense that a cure is just around the corner. With MND, where treatment optimism is not so evident, the basis of hope seems to be located in quality-of-life terms. People hope that things won't get too bad.

What is evident in all three conditions is the stress of living with alternating hope and disappointment – improvements in health followed by relapses, over-optimistic reports of new drugs/treatments, symptoms recurring despite treatment and so on. We have noted people with MS finding out they cannot be treated with particular drugs, either because they have the 'wrong sort of MS', or because the drugs are being rationed on cost grounds (e.g. beta interferon). With CF, for those on the transplant list, there might be a failure to find suitable donors. Or there might be the discovery that one has become too ill to be considered for transplant.

Uncertainty, hope and the experience of disappointment do not necessarily preclude user involvement. But they do frame the experience of the person with the illness and their carers. Not least, they make many demands on a person's time and emotional energy, with the consequent impact on the space for other things.

In our discussions of illness experience, we have sought to understand the scope for user involvement and its possible place in an individual's life. In so doing, we wish to reframe user involvement and consider how it might be seen from the bottom up, rather than see it as a policy initiative, from the top down. However firm a government commitment or a professional orientation might be, it is the extent to which such a commitment resonates with the individual's life that ensures how far it marks a widespread shift in the biography of illness.

Social invisibility/exclusion

That illness is lived in a social context is evident from all we have presented. Social structures and attitudes impact on the scope for user involvement. With MND, the relatively low incidence contributes to people's isolation. But there is also a general tendency to avoid illness and misfortune. This is manifest in the general population but also in people with illness themselves. We have talked about the context of liminality, that is of living outside the conventional structures when ill, but there is also a chosen route some take to not meet with others in the same situation. This is particularly poignant in relation to CF where we see parents of living children avoiding parents of children who have died. It is not surprising that people attempt to maintain a 'normal' lifestyle for as long as possible. But this helps maintain a sense of invisibility that allows policy makers and planners to sideline those who are most ill. The practical difficulties of involvement should be a spur to imaginative thinking, rather than be accepted as an adequate excuse for inaction.

Information and organisation

We have seen how the giving of information can be seen as both empowering and disempowering at various stages in the illness career. Individuals develop their own strategies for managing the flow of information: at times they may seek it out; at other times they might avoid it or bracket it off in a discreet and contained area. There is clearly a differential need for information at different stages of illness and often conflicting needs between people with the illness and their carers. This ambiguous role of information is most clearly displayed in the family where a child has CF. The parents may wish to hide information from the child. Specifically, we have presented the example of a letter from a mother terrified that her child will find out that CF is considered to be a terminal illness. Bluebond-Langner's work offers a poignant context for these concerns in that she identifies the sense that children with CF develop about their own condition and its prognosis. They often 'protect' their parents by pretending not to be aware of the seriousness of their illness. The children with CF in her study do not so much compare themselves with other terminally ill children as they do with the world of healthy children and with themselves in the past. The reality of what our category of future orientation means in practice is summed up by one child who says, 'They're not buying me a coat to grow into this winter' (Bluebond-Langner 1989: 7).

Parents of children with CF will often have had a long history of contact with health services and consequently have both considerable knowledge and impres‐ sive advocacy skills, as will their growing children. This, together with the emo‐ tional appeal of an illness of children and the impact of a prevalent treatment optimism, means we see a relatively well-resourced specialist service. Obtaining adequate care appears to be seen as requiring less of a fight than it does in relation to MS and MND. As with CF, the diagnosis takes those involved by surprise. But people with MS or MND and their carers are unlikely to have built up knowledge and advocacy skills before the demands of day-to-day care drive out the space for other priorities. There is a sense of vulnerability or powerlessness in people who feel they cannot fight on their own but are also ambivalent about seeking the support of others.

We have reported a wide range of fears: of confrontation with one's own mortal‐ ity, a fear of progression, of losing friends, of forming relationships with people who might die, of being seen as unwelcome and unhelpful by those with the same diagnosis but less developed symptoms, and so on. These fears vary according to the individual's circumstances, particularly the stage of illness, and they are fears less manifest in carers. That carers are often more keen to meet others for support and to find out information means that we need to be wary of the domination of organisations by carers' agendas.

Organisations for people with MS, MND and CF are generally enthusiastically supported in our accounts. With MS and CF, they have the challenge of encomp‐ assing wide variation in degrees of illness and impairment, while in MND they have rapid progression, demanding symptoms and a generally older cohort to respond to. All have a relatively low level of membership in local branches and national organisations. There are many possible reasons for this:

- emphasis on normality discourages mixing with others with same disease
- rejection of disease identity
- fear of seeing others in worse health
- fear of causing distress to others in better health
- not wanting to find out discouraging information
- emphasis on fundraising
- fear of cross-infection (CF)
- low incidence
- mobility, communication difficulties

Such factors will be well known to organisations with small memberships but raise questions about their legitimacy and representativeness if they are to be used as proxy voices for wider user constituencies.

User involvement and social power

An interest in user involvement does not mean that traditional conflicts between service providers and users go away. Two examples can illustrate long-standing tensions.

Conflicts have occurred between mothers and health visitors as mothers became more confident in the months following giving birth and, in so doing, felt that health visitors were not taking sufficiently into account their views. This suggests that professional support for user involvement might be limited if it begins to impinge on their sense of expertise and judgement. User involvement is only welcome when it conforms with what the professional wants to hear (Pearson 1995: 106–20).

Many people see the community they live in as hostile and dangerous. It is a mistake to assume that the community is seen as benign. It is certainly not the place many people would choose to look for support. Here we must equate community with both the geographical area and the community of interest. Sometimes the relationship with the professional is more comfortable. In that relationship with professionals there is a complex nexus encompassing access to resources, power and independence. Some users strategically manipulated the health system in order to increase their access to scarce resources, often at the price of increasing dependency (Heyman 1995: 7).

As well as the power differences with professionals the experience of living with illness is shaped by long-standing social divisions. A Canadian study reported the experiences of immigrant Chinese women and Anglo-Canadian women with diabetes living in Canada. An initial reading of the data suggested styles of managing the illness that related to the ethnicity of the women. But the authors report that, when the circumstances of women's lives are examined, styles of managing illness that could be related to ethnicity become recognisable as pragmatic ways of dealing with the harsh realities of material existence. It is argued that the trends towards individualising social problems, and shifting the responsibility for caretaking from the state to the individual, obfuscate the social context of illness, and exclude the socially disadvantaged from adequate health care (Anderson *et al.* 1991: 101). This study reminds us of the need not to forget the material circumstances of a person's life even when that life is being lived with an illness that we might assume is all encompassing.

Biographical disruption

We have considered the impact of diagnosis and subsequent illness experience on a person's sense of self. In doing this we have been able to draw on a rich source of data in existing published studies. This corpus of work has highlighted how 'illness, and especially chronic illness, is precisely that kind of experience where the structures of everyday life and the forms of knowledge that underpin them are disrupted' (Bury 1982: 169). This disruption to everyday life calls for major restructuring of self – the perception of who one is and what one is able to do. In other words, the individual has to 'reconstruct a sense of order from the fragments produced by chronic illness' (Williams 1984: 177). Restructuring of life is an ongoing and reflexive process influenced by the ups and downs of the illness course and the events of everyday life. That is, it occurs within a complex nexus of personal, social and political factors (Kleinman 1987).

This biographical disruption and reconstruction goes on in times where there is a reassessment of the sorts of society we live in. In particular, we have looked at postmodernism and at the Foucauldian idea of a shift in disciplinary power in society.

Frank distinguishes between pre-modern times before popular experiences were overtaken by technical expertise, modern where there is a dominance of a medical narrative (a dominance that drives its practitioners away from the experience of illness), and postmodern where the capacity to tell one's own story is reclaimed (Frank 1995; see also Kleinman 1988). It was the alliance between the human sciences, both medical and social, that established the subjective patient, the patient's view and, more recently, the 'consumer perspective'. A user involvement agenda just might mean a shift in the relationship of power/knowledge, new disciplinary power becomes dominant – the subjective person disciplines him- or herself (Nettleton 1995: 236).

User involvement and the end of life

The process of dying and manner of death may give shape to a person's entire life (Dworkin 1993; see also Garrard 1996). By retaining some degree of control over their dying and deaths, people are able to influence the legacies and memories they leave behind. The concept of user involvement, as we have interpreted it, comprises not only giving people the opportunity to take control over the ends of their lives but the opportunity to extend this legacy by influencing services for others after they have died.

Problems arise where opportunity is translated into obligation and user involvement comes to be regarded as a condition of receipt of services and, more widely, of responsible citizenship. An expectation that people will co-operate in a programme of user involvement moves from an agenda of empowerment to one of moral coercion. This form of coercion may be especially inappropriate when people are approaching the ends of their lives, have little time left to them and may have alternative goals to which they wish to devote their remaining energies.

Official consultation

The services likely to be needed by people with chronic or terminal illnesses are provided by a range of different agencies, including health and social services, independent and voluntary providers. These services may or may not be identified as specifically for people in one diagnostic group or one particular stage of their lives.

Services provided by social service agencies, such as home care, short-term breaks, equipment and adaptations are usually considered part of generic provision. Consultations with users will be dominated by the largest or best organised groups and, in the main, will reflect the needs that arise from those with a largely stable physical condition. The main interest and lobbying groups, including Help the Aged, Age Concern, disability groups and umbrella bodies like the Council for

Voluntary Services (CVS), similarly reflect the numerical dominance of this group as opposed to the needs of those with changing, and often deteriorating, health.

By contrast, health services for people who are terminally ill are usually separately identified. Palliative care services, for example, tend to be seen by health service providers as exclusive to people who are in the late stages of terminal illness, and services are dominated by provision for people with cancer. Similarly, voluntary provision is dominated by the cancer charities. The needs of people with other diagnoses tend to be either neglected or subsumed into a service specifically orientated towards cancer care.

If services for people who are terminally ill are not widely recognised as a social services concern, the only route for consultation will be the health service route and a considerable area of legitimate need will be unavailable for user involvement. A survey of social services departments in the Trent region revealed that services for people with palliative care needs were not generally seen as a social services responsibility. If they did appear in community care plans, this was more as an afterthought than an indication of genuine commitment (Rhodes 1996).

Different agencies have their own approaches and perspectives on both the need to consult and the means of consultation. From the perspective of service users or potential users, there is no single, clear route for consultation and the situation is fragmented and confused. Agencies' failure to engage in a collaborative approach runs the twin risks of duplication of effort and the commandeering of the time and energy of people who may have little of both left to them.

There is, therefore, a need for:

- joint recognition of people with chronic and terminal illnesses who are approaching the ends of their lives as a distinctive group
- joint recognition that the issues which concern this group straddle agency boundaries
- the development of machinery for joint consultation with service users and potential users of services

Some progress towards this has already begun with the establishment of joint palliative care strategy groups and joint consultations in the drawing up of social services community care plans and continuing health care policies. However, the extent of joint consultations and joint working varies considerably between agencies and there is little evidence of the involvement of service users in these exercises. The focus on palliative care, although it has achieved much in highlighting the needs of people who are dying in the context of health services, may distract attention from the need to view service provision for this group as an issue of wider interagency concern.

Engaging people in discussion

A major problem identified in the study is how to engage people in discussion when:

- there is a general reluctance or inability to anticipate future needs for services
- the numbers of people in any local population with a specific illness or condition are likely to be very low

One way forward might be to raise these issues on a more general level by encouraging a debate about palliative care as more than just terminal care. Another would be to generate general discussion in a wider arena than single condition groups, either through alliances between groups, such as the Neurological Conditions Alliance or the Long Term Medical Conditions Alliance, or through disability organisations. The latter, in particular, not only have well-developed networks and a comprehensive remit serving people with a wide range of conditions but a history of success in challenging the medical account of disability and promoting both national and local discussion of the meaning of disability.

Within the movement of disabled people as a whole, there is a strong antipathy towards emphasis on single interest or disease groups on the grounds that it leads to fragmentation and a focus on differences rather than those issues which disabled people share in common. Neither cystic fibrosis organisations, the CFT nor ACFA, for example, have strong associations with the movement of disabled people, although individual members of ACFA have been involved in campaigning for disability rights.

Alliances have the advantage of strength in numbers. However, there is a danger that a focus on common concerns will give little opportunity for discussion of members' particular interests and needs. The presentation of a consensus view can result in the suppression of minority interests and the issuing of bland statements which neither satisfy nor are truly representative of anyone. On the other hand, the presentation of multiple viewpoints risks giving an impression of fragmentation and lacks the force of a single message, backed up by the weight of majority opinion.

It may be that a reluctance to talk about future needs is an authentic choice and, as such, should be respected. Alternatively, it may be that people's reluctance stems more from the fact that they are not currently given appropriate opportunities or because the issues are raised in contexts and in ways which inhibit discussion. It may also be a consequence of unsatisfactory encounters with service providers in the past. We have looked at how the process of communicating a diagnosis in MS and MND sets up, in some people, a lasting antipathy to doctors. We would suggest that the findings we offer here are best followed up by further study into different approaches which might encourage greater user involvement.

The means of consultation

A further problem for agencies wishing to engage in local consultations is how to consult with people whose needs are likely to be great but whose numbers in any local area are likely to be low. Although one possible solution might be to approach the national organisations which represent the interests of people with the particular illness or impairment, it could rightly be objected that consultation at the national level disregards the exhortation contained in *Local Voices* to consult locally and to tailor services to local needs.

Aside from the question of the extent to which such organisations can be said to be fully representative of the views of their members, most seem to be more concerned with the latest medical advances than issues concerning palliative and terminal care. Children's organisations have been, perhaps, more progressive in this area, with the establishment of the generic Rainbow Trust and ACT.

An alternative is to try to approach people locally. However, as this study has demonstrated, local community networks are likely to be weak and poorly developed. It may be possible to build on and to strengthen existing networks or to create new networks for the purposes of consultation. An example of this approach would be the Fife experiment with panels of older people. While the Fife project brought people together to discuss issues, a different approach would be to visit people in their own homes. This would, of course, lose the advantage of providing a forum for the exchange of ideas and enabling of social contacts between people who are likely to have few opportunities for socialising. A third approach, which would go some way towards overcoming this shortcoming, would be to establish some form of technological link-up through telephone or computer networks.

Given people's apparent reluctance to engage in debate about the provision of specifically targeted palliative and terminal care services, another approach could be to pursue more generic consultation. One person interviewed was a member of a panel of representatives from the general public who were sent periodic questionnaires by the local health authority to elicit their views about priorities for health service commissioning. Occasionally, they were invited to public meetings or seminars. A specific questionnaire on palliative and terminal care, sent out as part of this routine exercise, may prove a more effective vehicle for tapping the views of some people than more specifically targeted approaches. The model could, perhaps, usefully be replicated on a smaller scale amongst specific groups of service users or potential users.

A problem for any organisation seeking to engage the public in this way is the gap in information and understanding which has to be bridged before any meaningful discussion can take place. The interviews conducted for the present study revealed that even people familiar with health service provision were still largely unaware of, or confused by, the radical upheaval following the reforms of the health and social services. A more stable period for services and meaningful freedom of information legislation would aid the process of user involvement, in this and in other areas.

A final word on policy

The wish to pursue user involvement can be located alongside more general trends in public sector organisation, most notably a new model of public management which sees the benefits of establishing partnership and collaboration. In pursuit of this, there are mechanisms in place to involve organisations from different sectors to combine in devising policy and implementation strategies. In health policy, Health Improvement Programme Boards reflect a recognition that address-ing the health needs of an area requires the involvement of the local authority, the voluntary sector and others. There are now posts with a specific remit to co-ordinate across institutions. Thus we see, in regulation and legislation, a duty to co-operate emerging in the public sector. It is this context that frames the develop-ment of a range of public participation and user involvement initiatives: citizens' juries, panels, stakeholder conferences and so on (see Hogg 1999b).

We have seen how these changes in part reflect a shift more generally in society. The postmodern ethic of our time is 'an ethic of voice, affording each a right to speak her own truth, in her own words' (Frank 1995: xiii). But what user involve-ment there is has also been won, it has not just emerged or been given. It has been won by the politicisation of the self-help movement (Zola 1987). It is the achievement of women's health groups, of alliances around childbirth and childcare, and subsequently breast cancer groups; it has been won by the continuing struggle of the disability movement and by HIV/AIDS activists. It is the product of many years of effort by groups responding to the shortcomings of the mental illness services and to the efforts of minority ethnic groups. It is not the product of an enlightened government, although the moves to recognise and respond to the shortcomings activists have raised should raise at least one cheer.

In health policy there has been an historic lack of democratic accountability, save through one's MP and hence Parliament. Attempts to draw in the voice of service users, through, say, Community Health Councils, have had a very limited scope and impact (Rose 1975). Now there is a shift towards a public participation model but, as we have said in a number of places above, this is not the same as user involvement. When the public have health needs and become service users, their focus changes. User involvement and public participation have to be run side by side, without assuming they will always be in harmony. There will need to be some mechanism to reconcile the inevitable differences. User involvement and equity may well be at odds if strong sectional voices can effect a redistribution of resources in their own interests and to the potential detriment of, say, an agenda focused on tackling inequalities (Hogg 2000). We have spoken above of the profound questions raised when utilitarianism encounters sectional need. Is it the greatest number or the greatest need that should be privileged?

The summaries of user involvement and the accounts of life with our chosen illnesses have illustrated that, to be effective, user involvement has to be seen as an integral part of both a health care delivery system and as part of the world view of those people living with illness. It does not work if it is grafted on. Much of the user involvement so far put in place is best seen as an artifact. It is there either to serve the needs of the health care system as it seeks new routes by which to claim legitimacy in the context of enhanced consumerism in the welfare state and the challenge to the historical authority of experts – itself a manifestation of late, or post, modernity – or it is a device to stave off a more rights-based approach to health care entitlement and delivery. Milewa *et al.* (1999) describe community participation in health planning as occurring in the context of the democratic deficit of the NHS and hence generating active management rather than active citizenship. Thus, user involvement should not be assumed to be a 'hurrah-word' (sic). Its pursuit is not all good. One should not conflate consumerism and empowerment. We have looked at how one can be bullied into involvement by social expectations, including the powerful means of the creation of moral precepts for being successfully ill. User involvement can interfere with altruism, it can distort priorities by giving the more able and more organised privileged access and, consequently, it is not necessarily egalitarian.

But user involvement can, if effective, positively shape the lives of people receiving services in many and varied ways. We can see its benefits in the overall design of care systems and can appreciate both how it can make the fit between what is available and what is needed on an individual level so much better, both practically and emotionally. It can empower and give a sense of dignity and worth to people whose experience of care can, and often does, put these under severe challenge. We have shown, in our accounts of illness, how one has to look for user involvement in the minutiae of lives with illness, in the giving of information, in the way help is offered. An ethic of user involvement must frame all encounters the ill person has and inform the perspective of the care provider. It has to grow in and through structures, practices, expectations and responsibilities. It is a philosophy and not a procedure. In this, it is like democracy or justice, although it sits, conceptually, between these two. It is about privileging the voice of those most effected by ill health and saying that it is just so to do.

Bibliography

Abberley, P. (1987) 'The concept of oppression and the development of a social theory of disability'. *Disability, Handicap and Society* 2, 1: 5–19.

Abbott, J., Dodd, M., Bilton, D. and Webb, A.K. (1994) 'Treatment compliance in adults with cystic fibrosis'. *Thorax* 49: 115–19.

Abbott, J., Dodd, M. and Webb, A.K. (1995) 'Different perceptions of disease severity and self care between patients with cystic fibrosis, their close companions, and physician'. *Thorax* 50: 704–96.

ACHCEW (1993) *NHS Complaints Procedures: A Submission to the Complaints Review Committee.* London: ACHCEW.

Action (1998) 'Assisting carers using telematic interventions to meet older persons' needs'. European Commission DGX111 Telematics Applications Programme, Disabled and Elderly Sector. Website: http://www.hb.se/action/

Addington-Hall, J., Lay, M., Altmann, D. and McCarthy, M. (1997) 'Community care for stroke patients in the last year of life: results of a national retrospective survey of surviving family, friends and officials'. *Health and Social Care in the Community* 6, 2: 112–19.

Addington-Hall, J.M. (1998) *Reaching out: Specialist Palliative Care for Adults with Non-Malignant Diseases.* London: National Council for Hospice and Specialist Palliative Care Services and Scottish Partnership Agency for Palliative and Cancer Care.

Addington-Hall, J.M., Anderson, H.R., Macdonald, L.D. and Freeling, P. (1991) 'Dying from cancer: the views of bereaved family and friends about the experience of terminally ill patients'. *Palliative Medicine* 5: 207–14.

Addington-Hall, J. and McCarthy, M. (1992) *Regional Study of Care for the Dying.* London: University College London.

Addington-Hall, J. and McCarthy, M. (1995a) Regional Study of Care for the Dying: methods and sample characteristics. *Palliative Medicine* 9: 27–35.

Addington-Hall, J. and McCarthy, M. (1995b) 'Dying from cancer: results of a national population-based investigation'. *Palliative Medicine* 9: 295–305.

Adonis, A. (1998) 'Transforming Democracy: involving the public in decision-making, the public involvement programme. Website: http://www.pip.org.uk/opinion.htm

Age Concern (1997) *Helping Hand. A Newsletter for Local People* 4: 4. Age Concern, Wakefield,

Age Concern (2000) *A Right to be Heard: Report of the Talk-Back Project.* London: Research and Development Unit, Fieldwork Division, Age Concern England.

Ahmad, W.I.U. (2000) *Ethnicity, Disability and Chronic Illness.* Milton Keynes: Open University Press.

Ahmad, W.I.U. and Atkin, K. (eds) (1996) *'Race' and Community Care*. Buckingham: Open University Press.

Ahmedzai, S., Morton, A., Reid, J.T. and Stevenson, R.D. (1988) 'Quality of death from lung cancer: patients' reports and relatives' retrospective opinions', in Watson, M. Greer, S. and Thomas, C. (eds) *Psychosocial Oncology*. Oxford: Pergamon Press.

ALS Society of Canada (1994) *Resources for Health Care Society*. Toronto: ALS Society of Canada.

Anderson, J.M., Blue, C. and Lau, A. (1991) 'Women's perspectives on chronic illness: ethnicity, ideology and restructuring of life'. *Social Science and Medicine* 33, 2: 101–13.

Armour, S. (1991) 'Andrew' In Cooper A. and Harpin V. (eds) *This is our child*. Oxford: Oxford University Press, pp. 120–31.

Arnstein, S.R. (1969) 'A ladder of citizen participation'. *Journal of the American Institute of Planners* 35: 216–24.

Aspin, A.J. (1991) 'Psychological consequences of cystic fibrosis in adults'. *British Journal of Hospital Medicine* 45: 368–71.

Atkinson, D. (1999) *Advocacy: A Review*. Brighton: Pavilion Publishing.

Audit Commission (1997) *Finders, Keepers: The Management of Staff Turnover in NHS Trusts*. Abingdon, Oxfordshire: Audit Commission Publications.

Ballard, C.G. (1990) 'Psychiatric in-patient audit: the patient's perspective'. *Psychiatric Bulletin* 14: 674–5.

Barby, T.F.M. and Leigh, P.N. (1995) 'Palliative care in motor neurone disease'. *International Journal of Palliative Nursing* 1, 4: 183–8.

Barnard, S. (1998) 'Consumer involvement and inter-agency collaboration in clinical audit'. *Health and Social Care in the Community* 6, 2: 130–42.

Barnes, C. (1991) *Disabled People in Britain and Discrimination: A Case for Anti-Discrimination Legislation*. London: Hurst and Company.

Barnes, C. (1992) *Disabling Imagery and the Media: An Exploration of the Principles for Media Representation of Disabled People*. Ryburn Publishing and BCODP British Council of Organisations of Disbaled People

Barnes, C. and Mercer, G. (eds) (1996) *Exploring the Divide: Illness and Disability*. Leeds: The Disability Press.

Barnes, M. (1997) *Care, Communities and Citizens*. Harlow: Addison Wesley Longman Ltd.

Barnes, M. (1999) 'International developments in multiple sclerosis'. MS: Meeting the Need. Third Annual Conference of the MS Research Trust's MS Nurse Forum. Royal Hotel York 10–12 October.

Barnes, M. (1999) 'Users as citizens: collective action and the local governance of welfare', *Social Policy and Administration* 33, 1: 73–90.

Barnes, M. and Bennett-Emslie, G. (1996) *'If they would listen …' An Evaluation of the Fife User Panels Project*. Edinburgh: Age Concern Scotland.

Barnes, M., Cormie, J. and Crichton, M. (1994) *Seeking Representative Views from Frail Older People*. Edinburgh: Age Concern Scotland.

Barnes, M. and Prior, D. (1995) 'Spoilt for choice? How consumerism can disempower public service users'. *Public Money and Management* July–September: 53–8.

Barnes, M. and Shardlow, P. (1996) 'Effective consumers or active citizens? Strategies for user influence in health and social care services and beyond'. *Research, Policy and Planning* 14, 1: 33–8.

Barnes, M., Thompson, A.J., Bates, D., Campion, K., Cullen, D.M., Fuller, K. (1999) *Basics of Best Practice in the Management of Multiple Sclerosis*. London: Multiple Sclerosis Society of Great Britain and Northern Ireland and MS Research Trust.

Barnes, M. and Walker, A. (1996) 'Consumerism versus empowerment: a principled approach to the involvement of older service users'. *Policy and Politics* 24, 4: 375–93.

Barnes, M. and Wistow, G. (1992) *Researching User Involvement*. University of Leeds: Nuffield Institute for Health Studies.

Barton, L. (ed.) (1996) *Disability and Society: Emerging Issues and Insights*. Harlow: Longman.

Batty, D. (1998) 'No laughing matter'. *The Guardian* 26 May: 13.

Bauman, Z. (1978) *Hermeneutics and Social Science*. London: Hutchinson.

Bauman, Z. (1992) *Mortality, Immortality and Other Life Strategies*. Stanford: Stanford University Press.

Beaver, K., Luker, K. and Woods, S. (1999) 'Conducting research with the terminally ill: challenges and considerations'. *International Journal of Palliative Nursing* 5, 1: 13–17.

Begum, N. and Fletcher, S. (1995) *Improving Disability Services*. London: King's Fund Centre.

Bell, S. and Shale, D. (1993) 'Terminal care in cystic fibrosis'. *Palliative Care Today* 2, 4: 48–9.

Benn, M. (1997) 'Live and let die'. *Community Care* 31 July–6 August: 16.

Benz, C. (1988) *Coping with Multiple Sclerosis*. London: Optima.

Beresford, P. and Campbell, J. (1994) 'Disabled people, service users, user involvement and representation'. *Disability and Society* 9: 315–25.

Beresford, P. and Croft, S. (1993) *Citizen Involvement: A Practical Guide for Change*, Basingstoke: Macmillan.

Beresford, S. (1995) *Motor Neurone Disease*. London: Chapman and Hall.

Berger, P.L. and Luckmann, T. (1967) *The Social Construction of Reality*. London: Allen Lane.

Bernat, J.L. (1997) 'The problem of physician-assisted suicide'. *Seminars in Neurology* 17, 3: 271–9.

Bewley, C. and Glendinning, C. (1994) *Involving Disabled People in Community Care Planning*. York: Community Care/Joseph Rowntree Foundation.

Billings, J.A. (1996) 'Slow euthanasia'. *Journal of Palliative Care* 12, 4: 21–30.

Birch, P., Ferlie, E. and Gritzner, C. (1995) *Report on the Views and Experiences of People Affected by Motor Neurone Disease*. Northampton: MNDA.

Blaxter, M. 1976. *The Meaning of Disability: A Sociological Study of Impairment*. London: Heinemann.

Blaxter, M. (1990) *Health and Lifestyles*. London: Tavistock/Routledge.

Blaxter, M. (1993) *Consumer Issues Within the NHS*. Discussion Paper, Leeds: NHS Executive.

Blaxter, M. (1996) 'Whose fault is it? People's own conceptions of the reasons for health inequalities'. *Social Science and Medicine* 44, 6: 747–56.

Bluebond-Langner, M. (1989) 'Worlds of dying children and their well siblings'. *Death Studies* 13, 1: 1–16.

Bluebond-Langner, M. (1996) *In the Shadow of Illness: Parents and Siblings of the Chronically Ill Child*. Princeton, NJ: Princeton University Press.

Blyth, A. (1990) 'Audit of terminal care in general practice'. *British Medical Journal* 300: 983–6.

BMA (1998) British Medical Association Annual Meeting, Cardiff, 8–11 July.

Boggild, M. (1998) 'Multi-disciplinary working: a neurologist's perspective'. *Way Ahead: News from the MS Nurse Forum* 5, January: 2.

Boseley, S. (1998) 'BMA moves on suicide. Doctors to hold conference on assisted deaths'. *The Guardian* 8 July: 9.

Bower, H. (1999) 'Open wide and say @h'. *The Guardian: Society* 12 January: 14.

Bowling, A. (1993) *What People Say About Prioritising Health Services*. London: King's Fund Centre.

Bowling, A. (1996) 'Health care rationing: the public's debate'. *British Medical Journal* 312: 670–4.

Boyd, K. (1993) 'Short terminal admissions to a hospice'. *Palliative Medicine* 7: 289–94.

Boyle, I.R., di Sant Agnese, P.A., Sack, S., Millican, F. and Kulczycki, L.L. (1976) 'Emotional adjustment of adolescents and young adults with cystic fibrosis'. *Journal of Pediatrics* 88, 2: 318–26.

Bradburn, J. and Maher, J. (1995) 'The growth of advocacy groups for cancer patients in Europe and the USA'. *Oncology Today* 12: 14–17.

Bradburn, J., Maher, J., Adewuyi-Dalton, R., Grunfeld, E., Lancaster, T. and Mant, D. (1995) 'Developing clinical trial protocols: the use of patient focus groups'. *Psycho-Oncology* 4: 107–12.

Bradburn, J., Maher, J. and Young, J. (1995) *Experts Speaking: How Establishing Links Between Local Cancer Support Groups and a Regional Specialist Cancer Hospital Led to Increased Patient Involvement*. London: Lynda Jackson MacMillan Centre for Cancer Support, Mount Vernon Hospital.

Bradburn, J., Maher, E.J., Young, J. and Young, T., (1992) 'Community-based cancer support groups: an undervalued resource?' *Clinical Oncology* 4: 377–80.

Braye, S. and Preston-Shoot, M. (1995) *Empowering Practice in Social Care*. Milton Keynes: Open University Press.

Brewin, T. (1996) *Relating to the Relatives*. Abingdon: Radcliffe Press.

Brindle, D. (1999a) 'Charities quit forum over disability cuts'. *The Guardian*, May 13.

Brindle, D. (1999b) 'Charityfair 99. Time to address the big ideas'. *The Guardian: Society*, 21 April: 23.

Brody, D.S., Miller, S.M., Lerman C.E., Smith D.G. and Caputo G.C. (1984) 'Patients' perception of involvement in medical care: relationship to illness attitudes and outcomes'. *Journal of General Internal Medicine* 4: 506–11.

Brody, H. (1987) *Stories of Sickness*. New Haven: Yale University Press.

Brookes, H. and Barton, A. (1994) 'Consent to treatment', in Powers, M.J. and Harris N.H. (eds) *Medical Negligence*. London: Butterworth (2nd edition).

Brosnan, M. (1998) *Technophobia: The Psychological Impact of Information Technology*. London: Routledge.

Buck, D. (1996) 'What are the net costs?' *Health Service Journal* 12 September: 20.

Buckinghamshire Health Authority (1997) *Buckinghamshire Citizens' Jury Report, March 1997, Should Buckinghamshire Health Authority Fund Treatment from Osteopaths and Chiropractors for People with Back Pain?* Buckingham: Buckingamshire Health Authority and Kings Fund.

Buckley, M. (1997) 'Industrious resolution'. *Health Service Journal* 107, 5558: 32–3.

Buckman, R. (1996) 'Talking to patients about cancer – no excuse now for not doing it'. *British Medical Journal* 13: 699–700.

Burnfield, A. (1985) *Multiple Sclerosis: A Personal Exploration*. Guernsey: Condor.

Burnfield, A.(1989) 'Multiple sclerosis: the case for telling the truth'. MS Society, Information Sheet.

Bury, M. (1991) 'The sociology of chronic illness: a review of research and prospects'. *Sociology of Health and Illness* 13: 451–68.

Bury, M. (1982) 'Chronic illness as biographical disruption'. *Sociology of Health and Illness* 4: 167–82.

Bury, M. (1996) 'Defining and Researching Disability: Challenges and Responses', in Barnes, C. and Mercer, G. (eds) *Exploring the Divide: Illness and Disability*. Leeds: The Disability Press.

Butler, P. (1999) 'My way'. *Health Service Journal* 7 January: 10.

Calman, K. and Hine, D. (1995) *A Policy Framework for Commissioning Cancer Services*. London: Department of Health and Welsh Office.

Calnan, M. (1988) 'Lay evaluation of medicine and medical practice: report of a pilot study'. *International Journal of Health Services* 18: 311–22.

Cambridge, P. and Brown, H. (1997) 'Making the market work for people with learning disabilities: an argument for principled contracting'. *Critical Social Policy* 17, 2: 27–52.

Cameron, H. (1998) 'The sponsorship of research by the pharmaceutical industry – why and how?' Biomedicine and Health Conference, University of Sheffield, 30 October.

Campbell, J. and Oliver, M. (1996) *Disability Politics: Understanding our Past, Changing our Future*. London: Routledge.

Campling, J. 1981. *Images of Ourselves: Women with Disabilities Talking*. London: Routledge and Kegan Paul.

Cancerlink (1990) *Declaration of Rights of People with Cancer*. London: Cancerlink.

Cancerlink (1998) *Directory of Cancer Self Help and Support*. London: Cancerlink.

Cardy, P. (1993) 'Research and the associations: an era for partnership'. *Palliative Medicine* 7 (suppl. 2): 3–9.

Carers National Association (1997) *Still Battling? The Carers Act One Year On*. London: Carers National Association.

Carr-Hill, R. (1992) 'The measurement of patient satisfaction'. *Journal of Public Health Medicine* 14: 236–49.

Carr-Hill, R. (1995) 'Measurement of user satisfaction', in Wilson, G. (ed.) *Community Care: Asking the Users*, London: Chapman and Hall.

Carter, H., McKenna, C., MacLeod, R. and Green, R. (1998) 'Health professionals' responses to multiple sclerosis and motor neurone disease'. *Palliative Medicine* 12: 383–94.

Carter, R.E. (1984) 'Family reactions and reorganization patterns in myocardial infarction'. *Family Systems Medicine* 2: 55.

Cartwright, A. (1992) 'Social class differences in health and care in the year before death'. *Journal of Epidemiology and Community Health* 46: 54–7.

Carus, R. (1980) 'Motor neurone disease: a demeaning illness'. *British Medical Journal* 1: 455.

Catchpole, A. (1989) 'Cystic fibrosis: intravenous treatment at home'. *Nursing Times* 85, 12: 40–2.

CCUF LINK (1993) CCUF LINK, *The Bulletin of the Community Consultation and User Feedback Unit*, NHS Cymru, Wales. March (1).

Cella, D.F. and Yellen, S.B. (1993) 'Cancer support groups', *Cancer Practice* 1: 56–61.

Chan, M. (1994) 'Breaking barriers', *Health Service Journal* 104, 5428: 33.

Charmaz, K. (1991) *Good Days, Bad Days. The Self in Chronic Illness and Time*. New Brunswick: Rutgers University Press.

Chesler, M.A. (1991) 'Mobilising consumer activism in health care'. *Research in Social Movements, Conflicts and Change* 13: 275–305.

Chilcott, J., Golightly, P., Jefferson, D., McCabe, C.J. and Walters, S. (1997) *The Use of Riluzole in the Treatment of Amyotrophic Lateral Sclerosis. Guidance Notes for Purchasers,*

97/03. Trent Institute for Health Services Research, Universities of Leicester, Nottingham and Sheffield.

Clarke, D. (1994) 'Whither the hospices?' in Clarke, D. (ed.) *The Future for Palliative Care: Issues of Policy and Practice*. Buckingham: Open University Press, pp. 167–77.

Clark, D. and Haldane, D. (1990) *Wedlocked?* Oxford, Polity.

Clarke, M. and Stewart, J. (1998) *Community Governance, Community Leadership and the New Local Government*, York: York Publishing Services.

Coiera, E. (1996) 'The Internet's challenge to healthcare provision: a free market in information will conflict with a controlled market in healthcare'. *British Medical Journal* 312, 7022: 3–5.

College of Health (1994) *Consumer Audit Guidelines*. London: College of Health.

Comaroff, J. and Maguire, P. (1981) 'Ambiguity and the search for meaning. Childhood leukaemia in the modern context'. *Social Science and Medicine* 158: 115–23.

Cooper, L., Coote, A., Davies, A. and Jackson, C. (1995) *Voices Off: Tackling the Democratic Deficit in Health*. London: Institute for Public Policy Research.

Coote, A. (1996) 'The democratic deficit', in: Marinker, M. (ed.) *Sense and Sensibility in Health Care*. London: BMJ Publishing, pp. 173–97.

Coote, A. and Lenaghan, J. (1997) *Citizens' Juries: Theory into Practice*. London: Institute for Public Policy Research.

Copperman, J. and Morrison, P. (1995) *We Thought We Knew ... Involving Patients in Nursing Practice*. London: King's Fund.

Corbin, J. and Strauss, A.L. (1987) 'Accompaniments of chronic illness: change in body, self, biography and biographical time', in Roth, J.A. and Conrad, P. (eds) *The Experience and Management of Chronic Illness*. Greenwich, Conn: JAI Press.

Cornell, S. (1996) *The Complete MS Body Manual*. P.O. Box 1270, Chelmsford, CM2 6BQ.

Cottrell, J. (1992) 'The role of the cystic fibrosis nurse specialist in terminal care and bereavement care', in T.J. David (ed.) *Role of the Cystic Fibrosis Nurse Specialist*. Proceedings of a meeting held in London, 21 November, Abingdon: The Medicine Group (Education) Ltd pp. 26–31.

Coulter, A. (1998) *Informing Patients: An Assessment of the Quality of Patient Information Materials*. London: King's Fund.

Coulter, A., Peto, V. and Doll, H. (1994) 'Patients' preferences and general practitioners' decisions in the treatment of menstrual disorders', *Family Practitioner* 11: 67–74.

Court, J.M. (1991) 'Outpatient-based transition services for youth'. *Paediatrician* 18: 150–6.

Cowley, S. (1990) 'Who qualifies for terminal care?' *Nursing Times* 86, 22: 29–31.

Craig, G. and Manthorpe, J. (1996) *Wiped Off the Map: Local Government Reorganisation and Community Care*. Hull: Social Research Publications.

Craig, P. (1997a) 'Death knell should be sounded for CHCs'. *Health Service Journal* 19 June: 23.

Craig, P. (1997b) 'CHCs deserve to face the axe – and soon'. *Health Service Journal* 107, 5539: 18.

Crail, M. (1998) 'Of debatable value'. *Health Service Journal* 5 February: 13.

Croft, S. and Beresford, P. (1990) 'A sea change'. *Community Care* 4 October: 30–1.

Croft, S. and Beresford, P. (1992) 'The politics of participation'. *Critical Social Policy* Autumn 35: 20–44.

Crow, L. (1992) 'Renewing the social model of disability'. *Coalition* July: 5–9.

Crow, L. (1996) 'Including all of our lives: renewing the social model of disability', in Barnes, C. and Mercer, G. (eds) *Exploring the Divide: Illness and Disability*. Leeds: The Disability Press.

Curtis, M. (1997) 'When illness is a secret'. *CYSTIC-L Handbook*. CF-Web Online Information about Cystic Fibrosis. Website: http://www.cf-web.org/

Cystic Fibrosis Foundation (1999) CF-Web Online Information about Cystic Fibrosis. Website: http://www.cf-web.org/

Dakof, G.A. and Taylor, S.E. (1990) 'Victims' perceptions of social support: what is helpful from whom?' *Journal of Personality and Social Psychology* 9: 118.

Davies, A.R., Doyle, M.A.T. and Lansky, D.J. (1993) *A Guide to Establishing Programmes for Assessing Outcomes in Clinical Settings*. London: Joint Commission on the Accreditation of Healthcare Organisations.

Davies, M.L. (1997) 'Shattered assumptions: time and the experience of long-term HIV positivity'. *Social Science and Medicine*. 44, 5: 561–71.

Davis, A., Ellis, K. and Rummery, K. (1998) *Access to Assessment: Perspectives of Practitioners, Disabled People and Carers*. Bristol: Policy Press.

Davis, H. and Daly, G. (1995) 'Codes of conduct are not enough'. *The IHSM Network 2*, 4: 3.

Davis, K. (1993a) 'The crafting of good clients', in Swain, J., Finkelstein, V., French, S. and Oliver, M. (eds) *Disabling Barriers – Enabling Environments*. London: Sage, with Open University Press.

Davis, K. (1993b) 'On the movement', in Swain, J., Finkelstein, V., French, S. and Oliver, M. (eds) *Disabling Barriers – Enabling Environments*. London: Sage, with Open University Press.

De Conno, F. and Martini, C. (1997) 'Video communication and palliative care at home'. *European Journal of Palliative Care* 4, 5: 174–7.

Department of Health (1989a) *Working for Patients*. London: HMSO.

Department of Health (1989b) *Caring for People*, Cm 849; London: HMSO.

Department of Health (1991) *The Patient's Charter*. London: HMSO.

Department of Health (1993a) *Clinical Audit: Meeting and Improving Standards in Health Care*. London: HMSO.

Department of Health (1993b) *Consumer Participation in Community Care: Action for Managers*. London: NHS Training Directorate/King's Fund Centre.

Department of Health (1994a) *Being Heard: report of the Wilson Committee's Review of NHS Complaints Procedures*. London: Department of Health.

Department of Health (1994b) *The Framework for Local Community Care Charters in England*. London: Department of Health.

Department of Health (1995a) *Acting on Complaints*. Leeds: NHS Executive.

Department of Health (1995b) *NHS Responsibilities for Meeting Continuing Health Care Needs* HSG (95) 8/LA (95) 5. Leeds: NHS Executive.

Department of Health (1996) *A Policy Framework for Commissioning Cancer Services: Palliative Care Services*, EL (96) 85. Leeds: Department of Health.

Department of Health (1997a) *The New NHS: Modern, Dependable*. Cm 3807. London: HMSO.

Department of Health (1997b) *NHS Priorities and Planning Guidance 1998/99*, EL (97) 39. Leeds: Department of Health.

Department of Health (1997c) *Involving Patients: Examples of Good Practice*. London: Department of Health.

Department of Health (1998a) 'Patients and their GPs to get access to information on local clinical performance. New clinical audit proposals – speciality by speciality – unveiled for the NHS'. Speech by Frank Dobson, Secretary of State for Health, Tuesday 9 June 1998, Department of Health 98/227, London.

Department of Health (1998b) *In the Public Interest: Developing a Strategy for Public Participation in the NHS*. London: Department of Health.

Department of Health (1998c) *Research: What's in it for Me?* Report from the Standing Advisory Group on Consumer Involvement in NHS Research. London: Department of Health.

Department of Health (1999) *Performance Tables for Social Services to be Introduced*. Press release 1999/0101. London: Department of Health.

Department of Health and Welsh Office (1995) *A Policy Framework for Commissioning Cancer Services* (Calman/Hine Report). London: HMSO.

Department of the Environment, Transport and the Regions (1998) *Modern Local Government: In Touch with the People*, Cm 4014, London: The Stationery Office.

de Raeve, L. (1994) 'Ethical issues in palliative care research'. *Palliative Medicine* 8, 4: 298–305.

Devins, G.M., Sealand, T.P. and Edworthy, C.M. (1993) 'Social handicap of MS'. *The Journal of Nervous and Mental Disorders* 181: 377–81.

Dillner, L. (1997) 'I've got a complaint'. *The Guardian* 4 March: 16.

Dinwiddie, R. (1993) 'Clinical advances: new therapies for cystic fibrosis'. *Paediatric Respiratory Medicine* 1, 2: 22–5.

Dixon, P. (1993) 'Some issues in measuring patient satisfaction' *CCUF LINK, the Bulletin of the Community Consultation and User Feedback Unit*. NHS Cymru, Wales December (3): 6–7.

Dolan, J.G., Bordley, D.R. and Miller, H. (1993) 'Diagnostic strategies in the management of acute upper gastrointestinal bleeding: patient and physician preferences'. *Journal of General Internal Medicine* 8: 525–9.

Donahue, J.M. and McGuire, M.B. (1995) 'The political economy of responsibility in health and illness'. *Social Science and Medicine* 40, 1: 47–53.

Donaldson, L. (1995) 'The listening blank'. *Health Service Journal* 21 September: 22–4.

Doyal, L. and Gough, I. (1991) *A Theory of Human Need*. London: Macmillan.

Duncan-Skingle, F. and Foster, F. (1991) 'The management of cystic fibrosis'. *Nursing Standard* 5, 21: 32–24.

Dunlop, R., Davies, R. and Hockley, J. (1989) 'Preferred versus actual place of death: a hospital palliative care support team experience'. *Palliative Medicine* 3: 97.

Dunning, M. and Needham, G. (eds) (1994) *But Will It Work, Doctor?* Report of a conference about involving users of health services in outcome research. London: Consumer Health Information Consortium.

Dworkin, R. (1993) *Life's Dominion*. London: Harper Collins.

Dyer, C. (1996) '"Vegetative" patient wakes up after seven years'. *The Guardian* 16 March.

Earll, L., Johnston, M. and Mitchell, E. (1993) 'Coping with motor neurone disease – an analysis using self-regulation theory'. *Palliative Medicine* 7, suppl. 2: 21–30.

Edgar, H. and Rothman, D.J. (1991) 'New rules for new drugs: the challenge of AIDS to the regulatory process, in Nelkin, D., Willis, D.P. and Parris, S.V. (eds) *A Disease of Society: Cultural and Institutional Responses to AIDS*. Cambridge: Cambridge University Press, pp. 84–115.

Ell, K. 1996. 'Social networks, social support and coping with serious illness: the family connection'. *Social Science and Medicine* 42, 2: 173–83.

Ellershaw, J., O'Gorman, B. and Deeson, A. (1993) 'Motor neurone disease – part two'. *Palliative Care Today* 2, 2: 52–3.

Ellis, K. (1993) *Squaring the Circle: User and Carer Participation in Needs Assessment*. York: Joseph Rowntree Foundation.

Etherington, S. (1999) 'Flight from the centre'. *The Guardian* 2 June: vi–vii.

Eve, A. and Smith, A.E. (1996) 'Survey of hospice and palliative care inpatient units in the UK and Ireland'. *Palliative Medicine* 10, 1: 13–21.

Eve, A., Smith, A.M. and Tebbitt, P. (1997) 'Hospice and palliative care in the UK 1994–5, including a summary of trends 1990–5'. *Palliative Medicine* 11: 31–43.

Fakhoury, W.K.H., McCarthy, M. and Addington-Hall, J. (1997) 'Carers' health status: is it associated with their evaluation of the quality of palliative care?' *Scandinavian Journal of Social Medicine* 25, 4: 296–301.

Fallowfield, L.J., Hall, A., Maguire, P., Baum, M. and A'Hern, R.P. (1994) 'Psychological effects of being offered choice of surgery for breast cancer'. *British Medical Journal* 309: 448.

Fallowfield, L.J., Baum, M. and Maguire, G.P. (1987) 'Do psychological studies upset patients?' *Journal of the Royal Society of Medicine* 80: 59.

Faulkner, A. (1992) *Effective Interaction with Patients*. Edinburgh: Churchill Livingstone.

Faulkner, A. (1995) *Working with bereaved people*. Edinburgh: Churchill Livingstone.

Faulkner, A. (1996) 'When the News is Bad'. *Oncology Today* 13: 14–17.

Faulkner, A. (1998) 'Communication with patients, families, and other professionals'. *British Medical Journal* 316: 130–2.

Ferguson, I. (1997) 'The impact of mental health user involvement'. Paper presented to 25th Annual Meeting of the Social Services Research Group, Citizens, Participants or Consumers? Edinburgh, April.

Ferriman, A. (1998) 'Trials and error. Are doctors being forced to inflict unwanted information on patients?' *The Guardians' Society* 13 May: 8.

Field, D. (1996) 'Awareness and modern dying'. *Mortality* 1: 255–65.

Field, D. (1998a) 'Special not different: General practitioners' accounts of their care of dying people'. *Social Science and Medicine* 46, 9: 1111–20.

Field, D. (1998b) 'Multiple Sclerosis: Expanding palliative care beyond present boundaries'. Paper given at Multiple Sclerosis: Frontiers in Science and Patient Care and Disease Management Conference, Birmingham, 6 May.

Field, D., Douglas, C., Jagger, C.D. and Dand, P. (1995) 'Terminal illness: views of patients and their lay carers'. *Palliative Medicine* 9: 45–54.

Fildes, S. (1994) (ed.) *Eating and MS – Information and Recipes*. London: Multiple Sclerosis Resource Centre.

Fitzgerald, G. and Briscoe, F. (1996) *Recipes for Health for MS*. Wellingborough: Thorsons.

Forbes, J. and Sashidharan, P. (1997) 'User involvement in services – incorporation or challenge? *British Journal of Social Work* 27: 481–98.

Ford, R. and Rose, D. (1997) 'Heads and tales'. *Health Service Journal* 6 November: 28–9.

Fordham, S. (1996) 'The last days of my life'. *New Woman* June: 72–3.

Fordham, S., Dowrick, C. and May, C. (1998) 'Palliative medicine: is it really specialist territory?' *Journal of the Royal Society of Medicine* 91: 568–72.

Forsythe, E. (1979) *Living with Multiple Sclerosis*. London: Faber & Faber.

Forsythe, E. (1988) *Multiple Sclerosis: Exploring Sickness and Health*. London: Faber & Faber.

Foucault, M. (1978) *The History of Sexuality*. Harmondsworth: Penguin.

Foucault, M. (1982) 'The Subject and Power', in, Dreyfus, H.L. and Rabinow, P. (eds) *Michel Foucault: Beyond Structuralism and Hermeneutics*. Brighton: Harvester Press.

Frank, A.W. (1995) *The Wounded Storyteller*. Chicago: University of Chicago Press.

Frank, A.W. (1997) 'Illness as moral occasion: restoring agency to ill people'. *Health* 1, 2: 131–48.

Frankenberg, R. (1986) 'Sickness as cultural performance: drama, trajectory, and pilgrimage'. *International Journal of Health Services* 16, 4: 603–26.

Frankenberg, R. (1987) 'Life: cycle, trajectory or Pilgrimage? A social production approach to Marxism, metaphor and mortality', in, Bryman, A., Bytheway, B., Allatt, P., Keil, T. (eds) *Rethinking the Life Cycle*. London: Macmillan, pp. 122–38.

Frankl, V. (1984) *Man's Search for Meaning*. New York: Washington Square.

Franks, A. (1997) 'Breaking bad news and the challenge of communication'. *European Journal of Palliative Care* 4, 2: 61–5.

Freeman, J., Johnson, J., Rollinson, S., Thompson, A. and Hatch, J. (1997) *Standards of Healthcare for People with MS*. London: Multiple Sclerosis Society of Great Britain and Northern Ireland and the Neurorehabilitation and Therapy Services Directorate of the National Hospital for Neurology and Neurosurgery.

French, S. (1993) 'Disability, impairment or something in between'. *Disability: A Social Challenge or an Administrative Responsibility*, in, Swain, J., Finkelstein, V., French, S. and Oliver, M. (eds) *Disabling Barriers – Enabling Environments* London: Sage, pp. 17–25.

Fulton, G., Madden, C. and Minichiello, V. (1996) 'The social construction of anticipatory grief'. *Social Science and Medicine* 43, 9: 1349–58.

Gallup (1996) *Survey Amongst CF Adults*. New Malden: The Gallup Organisation.

Garrard, E. (1996) 'Palliative care and the ethics of resource allocation'. *International Journal of Palliative Nursing* 2, 2: 91–4.

George, R. and Sykes, J. (1997) 'Beyond Cancer?' in, Clark, D., Hockley, J. and Ahmedzai, S. (eds) *New Themes in Palliative Care*. Buckingham: Open University Press.

George, M. (1998) 'Homeward Bound'. *Community Care* 8–14 January: 18–19.

Gerhardt, U. (1996) 'Narratives of normality: end stage renal failure patients' experience of their transplant options', in, Williams, S. and Calnan, M. (eds) *Modern Medicine: Lay Perspectives and Experiences*. London: UCL Press, pp. 139–66.

Gilbert, H. (1995) *Redressing the Balance: A Brief Survey of Literature on Patient Empowerment*. London: NHS Executive.

Gilbert, J. (1996) 'The benefits and problems of living wills (advance statements about medical treatment) in cancer patients'. *Progress in Palliative Care* 4, 1: 4–6.

Giroux, L. (1995) *Recycled – A Story of Hope*. Canada: Fenix Ryzing Associates.

Goffman, E. (1968) *Stigma*. Harmondsworth: Penguin.

Goss, S. and Miller, C. (1995) *From Margin to Mainstream*. York: Joseph Rowntree Foundation.

Gott, M., Stevens, T., Small, N. and Ahmedzai, S.H. (2000) *User Involvement in Cancer Care. Exclusion and Empowerment*. Bristol: Policy Press.

Graham, J. (1982) *Multiple Sclerosis: A Self-Help Guide*, 2nd edition. London: Thorsons (2nd edition).

Grande, G.E., Todd, C.J. and Barclay, S.I.G. (1997) 'Support needs in the last year of life: patient and carer dilemmas'. *Palliative Medicine* 11: 202–8.

Gray, J.N., Lyons, P.M. and Melton, G.B. (1995) *Ethical and Legal Issues in AIDS Research*. Baltimore: Johns Hopkins University Press.

Hallett, C. (1987) *Critical Issues in Participation*. Newcastle: Newcastle Association of Community Workers.

Ham, C. (1986) *Managing Health Services: Health Authority Members in Search of a Role*. SAUS Study No 3. Bristol: School for Advanced Urban Studies, University of Bristol.

Ham, C. (1993) 'Priority setting in the NHS: reports from six districts'. *British Medical Journal* 307: 435–8.

Hamilton-Gurney, B. (1993) *Public Participation in Health Care Decision-Making*. University of Cambridge: Health Services Research Group.

Hansell, R. (1995) 'The role of the General Medical Practitioner in the management of MS'. *MS Management* 2, 2: 19–24.

Hares, T., Spencer, J., Gallagher, M., Bradshaw, C. and Webb, I. (1992) 'Diabetes care: who are the experts?' *Health Care* 1: 219–24.

Harris, L. (1990) 'The disadvantaged dying'. *Nursing Times* 86, 22: 26–9.

Harrison, S., Barnes, M. and Mort, M. (1997) 'Praise and damnation: mental health user groups and the construction of organisational legitimacy'. *Public Policy and Administration* 12: 4–16.

Harrison, S., Hunter, D., Marnock, G. and Pollitt, C. (1992) *Just Managing: Power and culture in the National Health Service*. London: Macmillan.

Harrison, S. and Pollitt, C. (1994) *Controlling Health Professionals*. Buckingham: Open University Press.

Hawking, S. (1994) *Motor Neurone Disease Association Annual Review 1993/4*. Northampton: MNDA.

Health Care UK (1996/7) *The King's Fund Review of Health Policy*. London: King's Fund Publishing.

Health Service Journal (1997) 'News focus: white Christmas'. 10 December: 10–13.

Henke, E. (1968) 'Motor neurone disease – a patient's view'. *British Medical Journal* 2: 765.

Henwood, M. (1996) *Continuing Health Care: Analysis of a Sample of Final Documents*. Leeds: Nuffield Institute for Health, Community Care Division.

Heritage, Z. (1994) *Community Participation in Primary Care*. London: Royal College of General Practitioners (Occasional Paper 64).

Heslop, J. (1995) 'Palliative care needs assessment: incorporating the views of service users'. *Progress in Palliative Care* 3, 4: 135–7.

Heyman, B. (1995) *Researching User Perspectives on Community Health Care*. London: Chapman and Hall.

Hicks, F. and Corcoran, G. (1993) 'Should hospices offer respite admissions to patients with motor neurone disease?' *Palliative Medicine* 7: 145–50.

Higginson, I. and Priest, P. (1996) 'Predictors of family anxiety in the weeks before bereavement'. *Social Science and Medicine* 43, 11: 1621–25

Higginson, I., Priest, P. and McCarthy, M. (1994) 'Are bereaved family members a valid proxy for a patient's assessment of dying?' *Social Science and Medicine*, 38, 4: 553–7.

Higginson, I., Wade, A. and McCarthy, M. (1990) 'Palliative care: views of patients and their families'. *British Medical Journal* 301: 277–81.

Hinton, J. (1979) 'Comparison of places and policies for terminal care. Occasional survey'. *Lancet*, I: 29.

Hinton, J. (1994) 'Which patients with terminal cancer are admitted from home care?' 8: 197–210.

Hinton, J. (1996) 'Services given and help perceived during home care for terminal cancer'. *Palliative Medicine* 10: 125–34.

Hirschman, A. (1970) *Exit, Voice and Loyalty: Responses to Decline in Firms, Organisations and States*. Harvard: Harvard University Press.

Hitch, P.J., Fielding, R.G. and Llewelyn, S.P. (1994) 'Effectiveness of self-help and support groups for cancer patients: a review', *Psychology and Health* 9: 437–48.

Hoffenberg, R. (1992) 'Rationing'. *British Medical Journal* 304, 6820: 182.

Hogg, C. (1995) 'Beyond the Patient's Charter: working with users'. London: Health Rights.

Hogg, C. (1999a) 'Looking for a common interest'. *Health Matters* 37: 12–13.

Hogg, C. (1999b) *Patients, Power and Politics*. London: Sage.

Hogg, C. (2000) 'The customer isn't right'. *Health Matters* 39: 18–19.

Holmes, J., Madgwick, T. and Bates, D. (1995) 'The cost of multiple sclerosis'. *British Journal of Medical Economics* 8: 181–93.

Hon, J. (1994) 'Bad news, I'm afraid' *Nursing Standard* 8, 32: 52–3.

Hopkins, A. (1996) 'Clinical audit: time for a reappraisal?' *Journal of the Royal College of Physicians of London* 30, 5: 415–25.

Hornquist, J.O., Hansson, B., Akerlind, I. and Larsson, J. (1992) 'Severity of disease and quality of life: a comparison in patients with cancer and benign disease'. *Quality of Life Research* 1: 135–41.

Hospice Information Service (1996) *1996 Directory of Hospice and Palliative Care Services in the United Kingdom and the Republic of Ireland*. London: St Christopher's Hospice.

House of Commons Health Select Committee (1996) *Long Term Care: Future Provision and Funding*. London: HMSO.

Hoyes, L., Jeffers, S., Lart, R., Means, R. and Taylor, M. (1993) *User Empowerment and the Reform of Community Care*. Bristol: School for Advanced Urban Studies.

Hughs, A. and Bradburn, J. (1996) 'Only human. Involving consumers in audits of breast cancer services highlights problems and provides valuable feedback'. *Health Service Journal* 1 February: 30.

Hugman, R. (1991) *Power in Caring Professions*. Basingstoke: Macmillan Educational Ltd.

Hunter, D.J. and Harrison, S. (1997) 'Democracy, accountability and consumerism', in, Iliffe, S. and Munro, J. (eds) *Healthy Choices: Future Options for the NHS* London: Lawrence and Wishart.

Hyppönen, H. (1997) *So many questions … All InClusive*, the newsletter of the InClude project 4: 1.

Ignatieff, M. (1984) *The Needs of Strangers*. London: Chatto and Windus.

Illman, J. (1997) 'Facing up to a sickly state of mind'. *The Guardian* 25 February.

IPPR (1996) *Improving Palliative Care in Walsall, Walsall Citizens' Juries, August 1996*. London: Institute of Public Policy Research.

IPPR (1998) The Public Involvement Programme. London, Institute for Public Policy Research. Website: http://www.pip.org.uk/

Ivers, V. (1994) *Citizen Advocacy in Action: Working with Older People*. Stoke on Trent: Beth Johnson Foundation (in association with the European Commission).

Jackson, E. (1997) 'The reality of patient choice'. *European Journal of Palliative Care* 4, 1: 4.

James, N. and Field, D. (1992) 'The routinization of hospice: charisma and bureaucratisation'. *Social Science and Medicine* 34: 1363–75.

Jarman, F. (1995) 'Communication problems: a patient's view'. *Nursing Times* 91, 18: 30–1.

Jochemsen, H. and Keown, J. (1999) 'Voluntary euthanasia under control? Further empirical evidence from the Netherlands'. *Journal of Medical Ethics* 25, 1: 16–21.

Johnson, J. and Lane, C. (1993) 'Role of support groups in cancer care'. *Support Care Cancer* 1: 52–6.

Johnston, M., Earll, L., Mitchell, E., Morrison, V. and Wright, S. (1996) 'Communicating the diagnosis of motor neurone disease'. *Palliative Medicine* 10: 23–34.

Jones, D.E. and Vetter, N.J. (1984) 'A survey of those who care for the elderly at home: their problems and their needs'. *Social Science and Medicine* 19: 511.

Jordan, J., Dowswell T., Harrison, S., Lilford, R.J., and Mort, M. (1998) 'Whose priorities? Listening to users and the public'. *British Medical Journal* 316: 1668–70.

Joule, N. (1992) *User Involvement in Medical Audit*. London: Greater London Association of Community Health Councils.

Kahssay, H.M., Taylor, M.E. and Berman, P.A. (1998) *Community Health Workers: The Way Forward*. Geneva: World Health Organisation.

Kellerman, J., Zeltzer, L., Ellenberg, L., Dash, J. and Rigler, D. (1980) 'Psychological effects of illness in adolescence. I: anxiety, self-esteem, and perception of control'. *Journal of Paediatrics* 97, 1: 126–31.

Kellehear, A. (1990) *Dying of Cancer: The Final Year of Life*. Chur: Harwood Academic Publishers.

Kellehear, A. and Fook, J. (1991) 'Dying of cancer: implications for professionals'. Paper presented to the Third International Conference, Grief, Bereavement and Contemporary Society. Sydney, Australia, June–July 1991.

Kelly, M.P. and Field, D. (1996) 'Medical sociology, chronic illness and the body'. *Sociology of Health and Illness* 18, 2: 241–57.

Kelson, M. (1995) *Consumer Involvement Initiatives in Clinical Audit and Outcomes*. London: College of Health.

Khan, U. (1998) 'Up and ATAM'. *Health Service Journal* 30 April: 32–3.

Kim, T. (1989) 'Hope and a mode of coping in amyotrophic lateral sclerosis'. *Journal of Neuroscience Nursing* 6: 342–7.

King, E. (1993) *Safety in Numbers*. London: Cassell.

Kingsley, P. (1981) 'Foreword', in, Graham, J. (1982) *Multiple Sclerosis: A Self-help Guide*. London: Thorsons, pp. 11–12.

Klein, E. (1984) *Gender Politics*. Cambridge, MA: Harvard University Press.

Kleinman, A. (1987) 'Illness meanings and illness behaviour', in, McHugh, S., Vallis, M. (eds) *Illness Behaviour: A Multidisciplinary Model*. New York: Plenum Press.

Kleinman, A. (1988) *The Illness Narratives*. New York: Basic Books.

Koocher, G.P. (1984) 'Terminal care and survivorship in paediatric chronic illness'. *Clinical Psychology Review* 4: 571–83.

Kramer, L. (1995) *Reports from the Holocaust*. London: Cassell.

Lasagna, L. (1970) 'Special subjects in human experimentation', in Freund, P.A. (ed.) *Experimentation with Human Subjects*. New York: George Braziller.

Layton, A. (1993) 'Planning individual care with protocols'. *Nursing Standard* 8: 32–4.

Layward, L., Dytrych, L. and Beresford, A. (1998) 'Symptoms in MS: patients' perspectives'. Paper presented at MS: Frontiers in Science and Patient Care and Disease Management Conference, Bimingham, 5–6 May.

Layzell, S. and McCarthy, M. (1993) 'Specialist or generic community nursing care for HIV/AIDS patients?' *Journal of Advanced Nursing* 18: 531–7.

Lenaghan, J., New, B. and Mitchell, E. (1996) 'Setting priorities: is there a role for citizens' juries?' *British Medical Journal* 312: 1591–3.

Lewis, C. (1996) 'Deadly dilemma'. *The Guardian: Society* 16 March: 3.

Lewis, J. and Glennerster, H. (1996) *Implementing the New Community Care*. Buckingham: Open University Press.

Lewthwaite, J. (1996) 'The Patients Influencing Purchasers (PIP) Project'. *Purchasing in Practice* 8: 18–19.

Liddle, B. (1991) *Caring Principles, Personal Service Initiative Guidelines*. Sheffield: Trent Regional Health Authority.

Lifton, R.J. (1968) *Death in Life: Survivors of Hiroshima*. New York: Random House.

Lindow, V. (1991) 'Sources of invalidation of health service users'. *Changes* 9: 124–34.

Lindow, V. (1994) *Self-Help Alternatives to Mental Health Services*. London: MIND.

Lindow, V. and Morris, J. (1995) *Service User Involvement*. York: Joseph Rowntree Foundation.

Lindsay, M. (1997) *Balancing Power: Advocacy Services in One Scottish Health Board Area*. Strathclyde: University of Strathclyde.

Linn, M., Linn, B. and Stein, S. (1982) 'Beliefs about causes of cancer in cancer patients'. *Social Science and Medicine* 16: 835–9.

Loder, C. (1996) *Standing in the Sunshine*. Shoreham-by-Sea, Sussex: Century.

Lupton, C. and Taylor, P. (1995) 'Coming in from the cold'. *Health Service Journal* 16 March: 22–4.

Lupton, D., Donaldson, C. and Lloyd, P. (1991) 'Caveat emptor or blissful ignorance? Patients and the consumerist ethos'. *Social Science and Medicine* 33, 5: 559–68.

McCarthy, M., Addington-Hall, J. and Altmann, D. (1997) 'The experience of dying with dementia: a retrospective study'. *International Journal of Geriatric Psychiatry* 12, 3: 404–9.

McCarthy, M., Addington-Hall, J. and Lay, M. (1996) 'Dying from heart disease'. *Journal of the Royal College of Physicians of London* 30, 4: 325–8.

McCracken, M.J. (1984) 'Cystic fibrosis in adolescence', in, Blum, R. (ed.) *Chronic Illness and Disabilities in Childhood and Adolescence*. New York: Grune & Stratton.

MacIntyre, A. (1981) *After Virtue: A Study in Moral Theory*. London: Duckworth.

McIver, S. and Meredith, P. (1998) 'There for the asking. Can the government's planned annual surveys really measure patient satisfaction?' *Health Service Journal* 19 February: 26–7.

McKee, L. (1999) 'A little click, a lot of clout'. *The Guardian*, 12 January: 13.

McLean, S. (1996) 'A real choice'. *Community Care*, 30th May–6 June: 18.

McLeod, E. (2000) *Facing it Together: Older Women, Secondary Breast Cancer and Self-Help Support Groups*. Birmingham: Age Concern.

McNamara, B., Waddell, C. and Colvin, M. (1994) 'The institutionalisation of the good death'. *Social Science and Medicine* 39: 1501–8.

McNamara, B., Waddell, C. and Colvin, M. (1995) 'Threats to the good death: the cultural context of stress and coping among hospice nurses'. *Sociology of Health and Illness* 17: 222–44.

McSherry, W. (1996) 'Reflections from a side ward'. *Nursing Times* 92, 33: 29, 31.

Mador, J.A. and Smith, D.H. (1988) 'The psychosocial adaptation of adolescents with cystic fibrosis: a review of the literature'. *Journal of Adolescent Health Care* 10, 2: 136–42.

Manero, E. (1997) 'Community Health Councils exist to service their communities not the NHS – or anyone else'. *Health Service Journal* 107, 5547: 17.

Mannion, R. and Small, N. (1999) 'Postmodern health economics'. *Health Care Analysis* 7: 255–72.

Marsh, E. (1996) *Black Patent Shoes*. Canada: Sideroad Press.

Maslow, A.H. (1968) *Towards a Psychology of Being*. Princeton: Van Nostrand.

Matthews, B. (1978) *Multiple Sclerosis: The Facts*. Oxford: Oxford University Press (1st edition; 1993: 3rd edition).

Meredith, C., Symonds, P. and Webster, L. (1996) 'Information needs of cancer patients in West Scotland: cross-sectional survey of patients' views'. *British Medical Journal* 313: 724–6.

Milewa, T., Valentine, J. and Calnan, M. (1999) 'Community participation and citizenship in British health care planning: narratives of power and involvement in the changing welfare state'. *Sociology of Health and Illness* 21, 4: 445–65.

Miller, D. (1993) 'Deliberative democracy and social choice'. in, Held, D. (ed.) *Prospects for Democracy*. Cambridge: Polity Press.

Miller, N. (1995) 'An overview of performance indicators', in, Black, S., McNeely, T. and Kendrick, A. (eds) *Performance Indicators in Social Work*. Dundee: Social Services Research Group, Scotland.

Miller, S.M. and Green, M.L. (1984) 'Coping with stress and frustration: origins, nature and development', in, Lewis, M. and Saarni, C. (eds) *The Socialisation of Emotions*. New York: Plenum Press.

Mills, M. Davies, H. and Macrae, W. (1994) 'Care of dying patients in hospital'. *British Medical Journal* 309: 583–6.

MNDA (1997) *Standards of Care*. Draft. Northampton: Motor Neurone Disease Association.

Moise, J.R., Drotar, D., Doweshuk, C.F. and Stern, R.C. (1987) 'Correlates of psychosocial adjustment among young adults with cystic fibrosis'. *Developmental and Behavioural Paediatrics* 8, 3: 141–8.

Monette, P. (1988) *Borrowed Time*. London: Collins Harvill.

Monks, J. and Frankenberg, R. (1995) 'Being ill and being me: self, body, and time in multiple sclerosis narratives', in, Ingstad, B. and Reynolds Whyte, S. (eds) *Disability and Culture*. Berkeley: University of California Press.

Montbriand, M.J. (1995) 'Alternative therapies as control behaviours used by cancer patients'. *Journal of Advanced Nursing* 22, 4: 646–54.

Moore, M.K. (1993) 'Dying at home: a way of maintaining control for the person with ALS/MND'. *Palliative Medicine* 7, suppl. 2: 65–8.

Moore, W. (1996) 'And how are we feeling today?' *Health Service Journal* 28 March: 30–2.

Moore, W. (1997) 'High price of silence'. *The Guardian: Society* 12 February.

Moore, W. (2000) 'Health Report. Patient Power'. *The Observer Magazine*, 19 March.

Morgan, G. (1997) 'Involving users in the planning and provision of mental health services'. Citizens, Consumers or Users? 25th Annual Meeting of the Social Services Research Group, Edinburgh, 9–11 April.

Mount, B.M., Cohen, R., Macdonald, N., Bruera, E. and Dudgeon, D.J. (1995) 'Ethical issues in palliative care research revisited' (Letter). *Palliative Medicine* 9: 165–6.

Mount, B.E.M. (1996) 'Morphine drips, terminal sedation, and slow euthanasia: definitions and facts, not anecdotes'. *Journal of Palliative Care* 12, 4: 31–7.

MS Matters (1998) 'Who does the buck belong to?' 18, March/April: 12–13.

Mulherin, D., Ward, K., Coffey, M., Keoghan, M.T. and Fitzgerald, M. (1991) 'Cystic fibrosis in adolescents and adults'. *Irish Medical Journal* 84, 2: 48–51.

Murphy, R.F., Scheer, J., Murphy, Y. and Mack, R. (1988) 'Physical disability and social liminality: a study in the rituals of adversity'. *Social Science and Medicine* 26, 2: 235–42.

Myers, F. and MacDonald, C. (1996) 'Power to the people? Involving users and carers in needs assessments and care planning – views from the practitioner'. *Health and Social Care in the Community* 4, 2: 86–95.

National Cancer Alliance (1996) *Patient Centred Cancer Services? What patients say*. London: NCA.

Neale, B. (1991) *Informal Palliative Care: A Review of Research on Needs, Standards and Service Evaluation*. Occasional Paper No. 3. Sheffield: Trent Palliative Care Centre.

Nettleton, S. (1995) 'From the hospital to community health care: Foucauldian analyses', in, Heyman, B. (ed.) *Researching User Perspectives on Community Health Care*. London: Chapman and Hall.

Neuling, S.J. and Winefield, H.R. (1987) 'Social support and recovery after surgery for breast cancer: frequency and correlates of supportive behaviors by family, friends and surgeon'. *Social Science and Medicine* 27: 385.

NHS Executive (1994a) 'Purchasing for Health: involving local people'. Speech by Brian Mawhinney. Leeds: NHS Executive.

NHS Executive (1994b) *The Patient's Charter: Hospital and Ambulance Services Comparative Performance Guide 1993–94*. Leeds: NHS Executive.

NHS Executive (1995) *Consumers and Research in the NHS*. London: Department of Health.

NHS Executive (1996) *Patient Partnership: Building a Collaborative Strategy*. London: Department of Health.

NHS Executive (1998) *Health Research: What's in it for Consumers? Report of the Standing Advisory Group on Consumer Involvement in the NHS Research and Development Programme*. London: Department of Health.

NHS Management Executive (1992) *Local Voices: The Views of People in Purchasing*. London: National Health Service Management Executive.

Nocon, A. (1994) *Collaboration in Community Care in the 1990s*. Sunderland: Business Education Publishers Limited.

Nocon, A. (1997) 'Satisfaction surveys: a note of caution'. *Community Care Management and Planning* 5, 1: 32–4.

Nocon, A., Baldwin, S., Jones, L. and Stuart, O. (1995) *The Social Support Needs of Physically and Sensory Disabled Adults: A Literature Review, Social Services Inspectorate*. Belfast: Department of Health and Social Services.

Norris, F.H. (1992) 'Motor neurone disease: treating the untreated'. *British Medical Journal* 304, 22 February: 459–60.

Norris, F.H., Smith, R.A. and Denys, E.H. (1985) 'Motor neurone disease: towards better care'. *British Medical Journal* 291, 27 July: 259–62.

Nuttall, P. and Nicholes, P. (1992) 'Cystic fibrosis: adolescent and maternal concerns about hospital and home care'. *Issues in Comprehensive Paediatric Nursing* 15: 199–213.

Oakeshott, M. (1975) *On Human Conduct*. Oxford: Clarendon Press.

Oakley, A. (1980) *Women Confined: Towards a Sociology of Childbirth*, Oxford: Martin Robertson.

O'Brien, T., Kelly, M. and Saunders, C. (1992) 'Motor neurone disease: a hospice perspective'. *British Medical Journal* 304, 22 February: 471–3.

Oliver, D. (1995) *Motor Neurone Disease. A Family Affair*. London: Sheldon Press.

Oliver, M. (1990) *The Politics of Disablement*. Basingstoke: Macmillan and St. Martin's Press.

Oliver, M. (1996a) *Understanding Disability: From Theory to Practice*. Basingstoke: Macmillan.

Oliver, M. (1996b) (In Barton, L.) (ed.) *Disability and Society: Emerging Issues and Insights*. Harlow: Longman.

Oliver, M. (1996c) 'Defining impairment and disability: issues at stake', in, Barnes, C. and Mercer, G. (eds) *Exploring the Divide: Illness and Disability*. Leeds: The Disability Press.

Oliver, S. and Buchanan, P. (1997) *Examples of Lay Involvement in Research and Development*. London: EPI Centre, Social Science Research Unit, London University Institute of Education.

OLR, IPPR (1996) *Cambridge and Huntington Health Authority's Citizens' Jury, May 1996. Rationing Health Care*. London: Opinion Leader Research, Institute of Public Policy Research.

Ong, B.N., Jordan, K., Richardson, J. and Croft, P. (1999) 'Experiencing limiting long-standing illness'. *Health and Social Care in the Community* 7, 1: 61–8.

Ortega y Gasset, J. (1953) 'In search of Goethe from within', in, Phillips, W. and Rahv, P. (eds) *The New Partisan Reader*. New York: Harcourt Brace.

Osborn, A. (1992) *Taking Part in Community Care Planning*. Leeds/Edinburgh: Nuffield Institute for Health/Age Concern Scotland.

Øvretveit, J. (1992) *Health Service Quality*. Oxford: Blackwell Scientific.

Øvretviet, J. (1995) *Purchasing for Health*. Buckingham: Open University Press.

Oxenham, D. and Boyd, K. (1997) 'Voluntary euthanasia in terminal illness', in, Clark, D., Hockley, J. and Ahmedzai, S. (eds) *New Themes in Palliative Care*. Buckingham: Open University Press.

Park, R.H.R., Allison, M.C., Lang, J. Spence, E., Morris, A.J., Danesh, B.J.Z., Russell, R.I. and Mills, P.R. (1992) 'Randomised comparison of percutaneous endoscopic gastronomy and nasogastric tube feeding in patients with persistent neurological dysphasia'. *British Medical Journal* 304: 1406–9.

Parker, G. (1993) *With This Body: Caring and Disability in Marriage*. Buckingham: Open University Press.

Parker, S. (1997) 'More than a silent witness'. *Nursing Times* 93, 12: 38.

Parkes, C.M. (1995) 'Guidelines for conducting ethical bereavement research', *Death Studies* 19: 171–81.

Parsons, I. and Newell, C. (1996) *Managing Mortality: Euthanasia on Trial*. Geelong: Villamena Publishing Service.

Parsons, T. (1951) *The Social System*. London: Routledge and Kegan Paul.

Payne, S.A. (1996) 'Perceptions of a "good" death: a comparative study of the views of hospice staff and patients'. *Palliative Medicine* 10: 301–12.

Peace, G. (1994) 'Sensitive choices'. *Nursing Times* 90, 8: 35–6.

Pearson, P. (1995) 'Client views of health visiting', in, Hyeman, B. (ed.) *Researching User Perspectives on Community Health Care*. London: Chapman and Hall.

Peckham, S. (1993) 'Community participation and the NHS: users, consumers or people power?' Paper presented at the Political Studies Association Annual Conference, Leicester, April.

Perry, S. (1994) *Living with Multiple Sclerosis. Personal Accounts of Coping and Adaptation*. Aldershot: Avebury.

Philpot, T. (1998) 'Let history judge'. *Community Care* 3–9 December: 18–20.

Pickard, S., Williams, G. and Flynn, R. (1995) 'Local voices in an internal market: the case of community health services'. *Social Policy and Administration* 29, 2: 135–49.

Pollock, A. and Pfeffer, N. (1993) 'Doors of perception'. *Health Service Journal* 2 September: 26–8.

Pounceby, J. (1997) *The Coming of Age Project: A Study of the Transition from Paediatric to Adult Care and Treatment Adherence Amongst Young People with Cystic Fibrosis*. London: Department of Health/Cystic Fibrosis Trust.

Pound, P., Bury, M., Gompertz, P. and Ebrahim, S. (1994) 'Views of survivors of stroke on the benefits of physiotherapy'. *Quality in Health Care* 3: 69–74.

Povey, R., Downie, R. and Prett, G. (1997) *Learning to Live with MS*. London: Sheldon Press.

Price, L.J. (1995) 'Life stories of the terminally ill: therapeutic and anthropological paradigms. *Human Organisation* 54, 4: 462–9.

Public Involvement Programme (1998) *Choosing the Right Models: Determining the Purposes of Public Involvement, Seminar to launch the Public Involvement Programme*. London: Institute of Public Policy Research. Website: http://www.pip.org.uk/

Quin, S. (1996) *Uncertain Lives, Untimely Deaths. Experiences and Psychosocial Needs of the Young Adult with Serious Chronic Illness*. Aldershot: Avebury.

Radford, I. and Trew, K. (1987) *A Survey of Multiple Sclerosis Sufferers and Their Carers in Northern Ireland*. Belfast: Queens University and MS Action Group.

Radley, A. (1993) *Worlds of Illness*. London: Routledge.

Ramsay, N. (1995) 'Sitting close to death: observation on a palliative care unit'. *Group Analysis* 28, 3: 355–65.

Rashid, A., Forman, W., Jagger, C. and Mann, R. (1989) 'Consultations in general practice: a comparison of patients' and doctors' satisfaction'. *British Medical Journal* 299: 1015–16.

Raudonis, B.M. (1992) 'Ethical considerations in qualitative research with hospice patients'. *Qualitative Health Research* 2, 2: 238–49.

Rawles, J. (1972) *A Theory of Justice*. Oxford: Oxford University Press.

Redmayne, S. (1995) *Re-Shaping the NHS*. Birmingham: NAHAT.

Review Committee on NHS Complaints Procedures (1994) *Being Heard: The Report of a Review Committee on NHS Complaints Procedures*. London: HMSO.

Rhodes, P. (1996) *Purchasing for Palliative Care Services: Survey of Health and Social Service Purchasers in the Trent Region*. Unpublished study. Sheffield: Trent Palliative Care Centre.

Rhodes, P. (1999) 'Palliative care: the situation of people with chronic respiratory disease'. *British Journal of Community Nursing* 4,3: 131–36.

Rhodes, P. and Nocon, A. (1998) 'User involvement and the NHS reforms'. *Health Expectations* 1, 2: 73–81.

Rhodes, P. and Nocon, A. (forthcoming) 'User involvement and public participation in the modern welfare state: a commentary on the NHS and Social Services white papers'.

Rhodes, P. and Shaw, S. (1998) 'Informal care and terminal illness'. *Health and Social Care in the Community* 7, 1: 39–50.

Ridley, N. (1997) 'The unkindest cut of all'. *Community Care* 2–8 October: 8.

Rigge, M. (1994) 'Involving patients in clinical audit'. *Quality in Health Care* 3, Supplement S2–S5.

Rigge, M. (1995) 'Does public opinion matter?' *Health Service Journal* 105, 5469, 7 September: 26–27.

Rigge, M. (1997a) 'Dr who?'. *Health Service Journal* 107, 5577: 24–2.

Rigge, M. (1997b) 'Keeping the customer satisfied'. *Health Service Journal* 107, 5570: 24–26.

Robinson, I. (1988a) *Multiple Sclerosis*. London: Routledge.

Robinson, I. (1988b) Reconstructing lives: negotiating the meaning of multiple sclerosis, in, Anderson, R. and Bury, M. *Living with Chronic Illness*. London: Unwin Hyman.

Robinson, I. and Hunter, M. (1998) *Motor Neurone Disease*. London: Routledge

Robinson, I., Hunter, M. and Neilson, S. (1996) *A Despatch from the Frontline: The Views of People with Multiple Sclerosis About Their Needs*. University of Brunel: Brunel MS Research Unit.

Robson, P., Locke, M. and Dawson, J. (1997) *Consumerism or Democracy? User Involvement in the Control of Voluntary Organisations*. York: Policy Press/Joseph Rowntree Foundation.

Rodgers, J. (1994) 'Power to the people'. *Health Service Journal* 24 March: 28–9.

Rogers, A. and Pilgrim, D. (1991) '"Pulling down churches": accounting for the British mental health users' movement'. *Sociology of Health and Illness* 13: 129–48.

Rose, H. (1975) 'Participation: the icing on the welfare cake?' in, Jones, K. and Baldwin, S. (eds) *The Yearbook of Social Policy in Britain*. London: Routledge and Kegan Paul.

Rosenblatt, P.C. (1995) 'Ethics of qualitative interviewing with grieving families'. *Death Studies* 19: 139–55.

Rossiter, D. and Thompson, A. (1995) 'Integrated Care Pathways and their role in the clinical audit of rehabilitation for people with Multiple Sclerosis'. *MS Management* 2, 3: 1–18.

Russon, L. (1997) 'The implications of informed consent in palliative care'. *European Journal of Palliative Care* 4, 1: 29–31.

Rust, A. (1997) 'Involving disabled users in service planning and delivery: Shropshire case study based on two national projects'. Citizens, Consumers Or Users? 25th Annual Meeting of the Social Services Research Group, Edinburgh, April 9–11.

Saltman, R. (1994) 'Patient choice and patient empowerment'. *International Journal of Health Services* 24, 2: 201–29.

Sandy, O., Rajan, L., Turner, H. and Oakley, A. (1996) *A Pilot Study of 'Informed Choice' Leaflets on Positions in Labour and Routine Ultrasound* CRD Report No.7. York: NHS Centre for Reviews and Dissemination, University of York.

Sang, B. (1999) 'The customer is sometimes right'. *Health Service Journal*. 19 August: 22–3.

Saunders, C., Walsh, T.D. and Smith, M. (1981) 'Hospice care in motor neurone disease', in, Saunders, C., Summers, D.H. and Teller, N. (eds) *Hospice: The Living Idea*. London: Edward Arnold, pp. 126–47.

Savage, R. and Armstrong, D. (1990) 'Effect of a general practitioner's style on patients' satisfaction: a controlled study'. *British Medical Journal* 302: 968–70.

Schapiro, R. (1994) *Symptom Management in Multiple Sclerosis*. New York: Demos.

Seale, C. and Cartwright, A. (1994) *The Year Before Death*. Aldershot: Avebury.

Segal, J. (1994). *Emotional Reactions to MS*. Stanstead: Multiple Sclerosis Resource Centre.

Service First Unit (1999) *Involving Users: Improving the Delivery of Health Care*. London: Cabinet Office.

Seymour, J.E. and Ingleton, C. (1999) 'Ethical issues in qualitative research at the end of life'. *International Journal of Palliative Nursing* 5, 2: 65–73.

Shakespeare, T. (1992) 'A Response to Liz Crow'. *Coalition* September: 40–42.

Shakespeare, T. (1993) 'Disabled people's self organisation, a new social movement?' *Disability and Society* 8, 3: 249–64.

Shakespeare, T. (1996) 'Disability, identity, difference', in, Barnes, C. and Mercer, G. (eds) *Exploring the Divide: Illness and Disability*. Leeds: The Disability Press.

Shaw, S., Rhodes, P. and Noble, W. (1998) *An Assessment of Needs for Palliative Care Services in Rotherham*. Sheffield: Trent Palliative Care Centre/University of Sheffield.

Shearer, A. (1991) 'A silent and unnecessary desperation'. *Search* 9 May: 21–3.

Sibley, W. (1996) *Therapeutic Claims in Multiple Sclerosis*. New York: Demos (4th Edition).

Siegler, M. and Osmond, H. (1979) *Patienthood*. New York: Macmillan.

Sikora, K. (1994) 'Engraged about radiotherapy'. *British Medical Journal* 308: 188–9.

Simms, A., Radford, J., Doran, K. and Page, H. (1997) 'Social class variation in place of cancer death'. *Palliative Medicine* 11: 369–73.

Skilbeck, J., Matt, L., Page, H. and Clark, D. (1997) 'Nursing care for people dying from chronic obstructive airways disease'. *International Journal of Palliative Nursing* 3, 2: 100–6.

Smaje, C. (1995) *Health, 'Race' and Ethnicity: Making Sense of the Evidence*. London: King's Fund Institute.

Small, N. (1993) *AIDS: The Challenge*. Aldershot: Avebury.

Small, N. (1998a) 'The story as gift: researching AIDS in the welfare market place', in, Barbour, R. and Huby, G. (eds) *Meddling with Mythology*. London: Routledge.

Small, N. (1998b) 'Death of the authors'. Mortality 3, 3: 215–28.

Small, N., Rice, N., Ashworth, A., Coyle, D., Hennessy, S., Jenkins-Clarke, S. and Ahmedzai, S. (1995) 'The use of proxies in palliative care'. Barcelona: Fourth Congress of the European Association for Palliative Care.

Smith, D.L. and Stableforth, D.E. (1992) 'Management of adults with cystic fibrosis'. *British Journal of Hospital Medicine* 48, 11: 713–23.

Smith, K. and Dickson, M. (1998) 'Silent majority'. *Health Service Journal* 17 December: 33.

Snell, J. (1998) 'When the going gets tough'. *Health Service Journal* 108, 5593: 28–30.

Social Work Services Inspectorate for Scotland (1996) *Population Needs Assessment in Community Care: A Handbook for Planners and Practitioners*. Edinburgh, Scotland: SWSIS.

Sofka, C.J. (1997) 'Social support "internetworks", caskets for sale, and more: thanatology and the information superhighway'. *Death Studies* 21: 553–74.

Sone, K. (1997) 'What would you do for a quiet life?' *Community Care* January: 18–19.

Spence, F. (1984) 'The value of life in geriatric patients'. Unpublished MSc thesis, University of Manchester.

SSI/SWSG (1991) *Care Management and Assessment: Practitioners' guide*. London: HMSO.

SSRG (1997) Citizens, Consumers or Users? 25th Annual Workshop, April. Edinburgh: Social Services Research Group.

Standing Medical Advisory Committee and Standing Nursing and Midwifery Advisory Committee (1992) *The Principles and Provision of Palliative Care*. London: HMSO.

Stewart, D. and Sullivan, T. (1982) 'Illness behaviour and the sick role in chronic disease, the case of multiple sclerosis'. *Social Science and Medicine* 16: 1397–404.

Stewart, J. (1996) 'Innovation in democratic practice in local government'. *Policy and Politics* 24: 29–41.

Stewart, J., Kendall, E. and Coote, A. (1996) *Citizens' Juries*. London: IPPR.

Stuart, M. (1994) 'Living positively'. *Hospice Bulletin* 22: 1–2.

Sullivan, S. (1994) *Involving the Public in Health and Social Care Planning*. Discussion paper (unpublished), East Dyfed Health.

Summers, D. (1981) 'The caring team in motor neurone disease', in, Saunders, C., Summers, D.H. and Teller, N. (eds) *Hospice: The Living Idea*. London: Edward Arnold, pp. 148–55.

Sykes, N.P., Pearson, S.E. and Chell, S. (1992) 'Quality of care of the terminally ill: the carer's perspective'. *Palliative Medicine* 6: 227–36.

Taylor, M., Hoyes, L., Lart, R. and Means, R. (1992) *User Empowerment in Community Care: Unravelling the Issues*. Bristol: School for Urban Studies.

Taylor, R. (1984) 'Alternative medicine and the medical encounter in Britain and the United States', in, Salmon, W. (ed.) *Alternative Medicines: Popular and Policy Perspectives*. London: Tavistock.

Teff, H. (1994) *Reasonable Care*. Oxford: Clarendon Press.

The Guardian (1998a) 'A patient's right to know. More details are needed'. Editorial, June 11: 23.

The Guardian (1998b) 'GP charged with murder of cancer sufferer'. June 11: 8.

The Guardian (1998c) 'Deadly dilemma for doctors'. Letter, June 17.

The Guardian (1999) 'Kevorkian jailed for 10–25 years'. April 14.

Thomas, R. (1995) *Multiple Sclerosis – The Natural Way*. Shaftesbury: Element.

Thomas, S. (1991) 'Motor neurone disease'. *Community Outlook* 1, 9: 42–6.

Thomas, S. (1996) 'On the right track'. *Health Service Journal* 106, 5500: 31.

Thompson, A. (1997) 'The jury's out'. *Health Service Journal* 22 February: 22–3.

Thompson, A., Johnston, S., Harrison, J., Sheil, R. and Burnard, S. (1997) 'Service delivery in multiple sclerosis. The needs for co-ordinated community care'. *MS Management* 4, 1: 11–18.

Thorne, S.E. (1993) *Negotiating Health Care: The Social Context of Chronic Illness*. London: Sage.

Thornton, P. and Tozer, R. (1994) *Involving Older People in Planning and Evaluating Community Care: A Review of Initiatives*. York: Social Policy Research Unit, University of York.

Thornton, P. and Tozer, R. (1995) *Having a say in change. Older people and community care*. Community care into practice series. York: Joseph Rowntree Foundation.

Thorpe, G. (1993) 'Enabling more dying people to remain at home'. *British Medical Journal* 307: 915–18.

Tillich, P. (1952) *The Courage to Be*. New York: Yale University Press.

Townsend, J., Frank, A., Fermont, D. (1990) 'Terminal cancer care and patients' preferences for place of death: a prospective study'. *British Medical Journal* 301: 415–7.

Trueworthy, R. (1999) (ed.) *CYSTIC-L Handbook*. Online information about cystic fibrosis. Website: http://www.cf-web.org/

Turner, V. (1974) *Drama, Fields and Metaphors*. Ithaca: Cornell University Press.

Twigg, J., Atkin, K. and Perring, C. (1990) *Carers and Services: A Review of Research*, London: HMSO.

Twigg, J. and Atkin, K. (1994) *Carers Perceived: Policy and Practice in Informal Care*. Buckingham: Open University Press.

Twycross, R. (1996) 'Jack Kevorkian: a medical hero? Better palliative care is the answer'. *British Medical Journal* 313, 7051: 227.

Tyler, P. (1994) 'A group growing into adulthood'. *Linkup* 37: 6–8.

UPIAS (1976) *Fundamental Principles of Disability*. London: Union of the Physically Impaired against Segregation.

Urben, L. (1997) 'Self-help groups in palliative care'. *European Journal of Palliative Care* 4, 1: 26–8.

van den Berg, J.H. (1972) *The Psychology of the Sickbed*. New York: Humanities.

van der Maas, P.J., van der Wal, G., Haverkate, I. (1996) 'Euthanasia, physician-assisted suicide, and other medical practices involving the end of life in the Netherlands, 1990–1995'. *New England Journal of Medicine* 335, 22: 1699–705.

van Overstraten, A.R. (1999) 'The patient's role in the improvement of care'. *Multiple Sclerosis* 5, 4: 302–5.

Venters, M. (1981) 'Familial coping with chronic and severe childhood illness: the case of cystic fibrosis'. *Social Science and Medicine* 15A: 289–97.

Vidal, J. (1999) 'Global conflict@Internet. Anatomy of a very nineties revolution'. *The Guardian: Society*, January 13: 4.

Walker, G., Bradburn, J. and Maher, J. (1996) *Breaking Bad News*. London: King's Fund.

Walter, T. (1993) 'Modern death: taboo or not taboo', in, Dickenson, D. and Johnson, M. (eds) *Death, Dying and Bereavement*: Buckingham: The Open University Press, pp. 33–44.

Walters, A. (1995) 'A hermeneutic study of the experiences of relatives of critically ill patients'. *Journal of Advanced Nursing* 22: 998–1005.

Walters, S. (1991) *Association of Cystic Fibrosis Adults: First National Survey 1990–1991*. Birmingham: Institute of Public Health, University of Birmingham.

Walters, S. (1994) *Association of Cystic Fibrosis Adults (UK): Survey 1994 Analysis and Report*. Birmingham: Institute of Public Health, University of Birmingham.

Warren, S., Greenhill, S. and Warren, K.G. (1982) 'Emotional stress and the development of multiple sclerosis: case-control evidence of a relationship'. *Journal of Chronic Disability* 35: 821–31.

Warren, S., Warren, K.G. and Cockerill, R. (1991) 'Emotional stress and coping in multiple sclerosis (MS) exacerbations'. *Journal of Psychosomatic Research* 35: 37–47.

Way Ahead (1999) 'MS: A carer's perspective'. *Way Ahead* 3, 4: 16.

West, P. (1990) 'The status and validity of accounts obtained at interview: a contrast between two studies of families with a disabled child'. *Social Science and Medicine* 30: 1229–39.

White, C. (1996) 'Capturing local representation? The use of citizens' juries as a research tool'. *Social Research Association News* August 1996: 1, 4.

White, P. (1999) 'Invalid criticism?' *The Guardian: Society* April 21: 9.

Whitehead, M. (1992) 'Is it fair? Evaluating the equity implication of the NHS reforms', in, Robinson, R. and LeGrand, J. (eds) *Evaluating the NHS Reforms*. London: King's Fund Institute.

Whitehurst, A. (1995) 'When the motors fail'. *Nursing Times* 91, 1 February: 48–9.

Williams, B. (1994) 'Patient satisfaction: a valid concept?' *Social Science and Medicine* 38, 4: 509–16.

Williams, B. and Grant, G. (1998) 'Defining "people-centredness": making the implicit explicit'. *Health and Social Care in the Community* 6, 2: 84–94.

Williams, G. (1984) 'The genesis of chronic illness: narrative reconstruction'. *Sociology of Health and Illness* 6, 2: 175–200.

Williams, G. (1993) 'Chronic illness and the pursuit of virtue in everyday life', in, Radley, A. (ed.) *Worlds of Illness. Biographical and Cultural Perspectives on Health and Disease*. London: Routledge.

Williams, G. (1996) 'Representing disability: some questions of phenomenology and politics', in, Barnes, C. and Mercer, G. (eds) *Exploring the Divide: Illness and Disability* Leeds: The Disability Press.

Williams, S.J. (1998) 'Health as moral performance: ritual, transgression and taboo'. *Health* 2, 4: 435–57.

Willis, J. (1999) *Consultation: A Myth or a Reality?* Wakefield: Age Concern.

Wilson, J. (1994) *Two Worlds: Self-Help Groups and Professionals*. Birmingham: Venture Press, with the British Association of Social Workers.

Winkler, F. (1987) 'Consumerism in health care: beyond the supermarket model'. *Policy and Politics* 15: 1–8.

Wired Welfare? (1999) Wired Welfare? The Internet Support Research Project. Website: http://www.york.ac.uk/res/vcc

Wistow, G. (1993) 'Democratic deficit'. *Community Care* 30 September: 29.

Wood, J. (1999) 'Laying it on the line over the disparate expectations of PCG board members'. *Health Service Journal* 109, 5637: 18.

World Health Organisation (1978) *Primary Health Care*. Geneva: World Health Organisation.

Wynn-Knight, S. (1996) 'Social and psychological perspectives, in, Shale, D. (ed.) *Cystic Fibrosis*. London: BMJ Publishing Group.

Young, M. and Cullen, L. (1996) *A Good Death. Conversations with East Londoners*. London: Routledge.

Zeltzer, L., Kellerman, J., Ellenberg, L., Dash, J. and Rigler, D. (1980) 'Psychological effects of illness in adolescence. II: impact of illness in adolescence – crucial issues and coping styles'. *Journal of Paediatrics* 97, 1: 132–8.

Zola, I.K. (1987) 'Self-help enters a new era. The politicisation of the self-help movement'. *Social Policy* 18: 32–3.

Index

Abberley, P. 66, 77
Abbott, J. 64, 159, 160, 175, 204
accountability 25, 29, 30–1, 220
acquired immune deficiency syndrome
    (AIDS) 2, 49, 59, 79, 81, 86, 87, 183;
    drug availability issues 105; palliative
    care 77; research 147
Action 87
Addington-Hall, J. 56, 60, 70, 71, 72, 74,
    75, 163, 204
Adonis, A. 42
advance directives 63
advocacy 14, 22, 53; Cystic Fibrosis Trust
    189–90; self-advocacy groups 82–4
Age Concern 84, 85, 86, 92, 216
Age Concern Scotland (ACS) 84–5
Ahmad, W.I.U. 22
alliances 77–9, 218
amyotrophic lateral sclerosis (ALS) 126,
    128; see also motor neurone disease
Anderson, J.M. 215
Andrew 209
antibiotic treatment, cystic fibrosis 156, 159
aphasia 7
Armour, S. 209
Armstrong, D. 49
Arnstein, S.R. 19
arthritis 14
ASH 14
Aspin, A.J. 176
Association for Children with Terminal
    Conditions (ACT) 79, 219
Association for Cystic Fibrosis Adults
    (ACFA) 156, 158, 184, 185–6, 189,
    191–3, 196, 218
Atkin, K. 22, 64, 65
Atkinson, D. 14
audit 38–9, 55, 112; consumer audit 40, 55;
    user involvement 39
Audit Commission 25
Australian Consumer Association 34

Avon Health 45

Ballard, C.G. 49
Barby, T.F.M. 129
Barclay, S.I.G. 65, 73
Barnard, S. 39, 55
Barnardo's 178, 194
Barnes, C. 65, 66, 77, 79, 188
Barnes, M. 21, 22, 24, 28–9, 32, 33, 34, 35,
    49, 52, 54, 57, 60, 64, 65, 68, 70, 71, 72,
    73, 76, 84, 85, 92, 105, 122, 157, 203,
    205
Barton, L. 6
Batty, D. 152
Bauman, Z. 1, 10
Beaver, K. 62, 63
Begum, N. 22
Bell, S. 156, 163, 207
Benz, C. 105
Beresford, P. 21, 50–1, 53, 54, 125
Berger, P.L. 1
Bernat, J.L. 63
beta interferon 101; availability of 4, 101
Bewley, C. 49, 52
Billings, J.A. 63, 75
biographical accounts: motor neurone
    disease 151–2; multiple sclerosis 95–6
biographical disruption 6–8, 215–16
Birch, P. 151
Blaxter, M. 7, 32, 35, 96
Bluebond-Langner, M. 7, 63, 67, 166, 180,
    208, 213
Blyth, A. 73
body 5–6; disembodiment 89–90, 209
Boggild, M. 109, 111, 132
Boseley, S. 36, 58, 75
Bower, H. 37
Bowling, A. 43, 46
Boyd, K. 63, 74
Boyle, I.R. 175
Bradburn, J. 15, 55, 82, 83

Bradford Health Authority 45
Braye, S. 21
breaking 'bad news' 72–3
breast cancer 15, 49, 80; focus groups 55;
    National Breast Cancer Coalition
    (NBCC) 83
Brindle, D. 27, 52
Briscoe, F. 105
Bristol and District Community Health
    Council 45–6
British Liver Trust 14
British Medical Association (BMA) 36
Brody, D.S. 35
Brody, H. 6
Brosnan, M. 37
Brown, H. 49
Buchanan, P. 41
Buck, D. 33, 90
Buckinghamshire Health Authority 88
Buckley, M. 40
Burkholderia cepacia 180, 182, 192, 194, 195,
    196, 201; *see also* cross infection
Burnfield, A. 95, 106
Bury, M. 6, 174, 180, 215
Butler, P. 27

Calman Hine Report 15, 57
Calman, K. 15, 57, 70
Calnan, M. 60
Cambridge, P. 49
Cameron, H. 102
Campbell, J. 50–1, 53, 54, 77
Campling, J. 96
cancer 2, 3, 73; breast cancer 15, 49, 55, 80;
    carer relationships 117; groups 14, 55,
    78–9; lung cancer 80; palliative care 57,
    59–60, 61, 72, 77, 217; self-advocacy
    groups 82–3; self-help groups 79, 80,
    81–2; services 15, 41, 57, 217;
    treatment 6
Cancerlink 15, 79, 80, 81, 83
CancerNet 86
cannabis, therapeutic use 102
Cardy, P. 64, 67, 68, 71, 87, 89, 100, 121,
    146, 147, 148
care management 28
carers 14, 115, 117, 199, 214; as proxies
    65–6; death and 208; information
    services 87, 199; loss of earnings 116;
    needs of 151, 199; stress 117; *see also*
    respite care
Carers (Recognition and Support) Act
    (1995) 65, 115
Caring for People (White Paper) 27, 28
Carr-Hill, R. 27, 40

Carter, H. 133
Carter, R.E. 117
Cartwright, A. 74, 163, 204
Carus, R. 136
Catchpole, A. 159
CCUF LINK 49
Cella, D.F. 79
Chan, M. 22
charities *see* organisations; *see also specific*
    charities
Charmaz, K. 7
Chesler, M.A. 82
Chilcott, J. 129
childbirth 14
children's rights 162–3
choice 24, 29, 32–4, 53, 68, 92, 147–8;
    ceasing treatment 75–6; constraints on
    32–3, 71–4; cystic fibrosis patients 157,
    159–60, 169–85, 203–8, 209; dimensions
    of 68–74, 205–8; empowerment and
    33–5, 68–74; information and 33, 35, 69,
    71, 169; place of death 74–5, 204–5
Choice in Dying 88
chronic fatigue syndrome (CFS) 86
citizens' juries 46–8; online 88
Clark, D. 95
Clarke, M. 30
clinical audit *see* audit
clinical governance 39
clinical guidelines 37
clinical indicators 39
clinical trials 104–5, 147; *see also* research
co-polymer-1 101
coercion 68–9, 206–7
College of Health 14, 40, 41, 55
Commission for Health Improvement 27, 39
commissioning of healthcare 42–3; joint
    commissioning groups 52
communication 82, 136; collective
    organisation 88–9; electronic 82, 89–90,
    197–9, 209, 219; *see also* breaking 'bad
    news'; denial; information and
    communication technologies (ICTs)
community care: palliative 57; user
    involvement 27–9
Community Care Charters 28
community care plans 62, 86
community health councils (CHCs) 45–6,
    48, 220
community issues groups 48
competition 32
complaints 40–1
compliance 49, 159–60; *see also* treatment;
    cystic fibrosis

computer-mediated communication 82, 86, 89–90, 197–9, 209, 219
consensus conferences 48
consent 36
consequentialist thinking 12
constipation 130
consultation 18, 23, 24, 28, 216–19; engaging people in discussion 217–18; joint consultative committees (JCCs) 51–2; means of 218–19; proactive 49; reactive 48–9; and self-help groups 80
consumer audits 40, 55
Consumer Congress 14
consumerist approach 20–1, 22, 24, 27, 29, 54, 82, 169; complaints and 40–1; compromising circumstances 71–4; criticisms of 32–4; patients as consumers 35–42
consumers 20; patients as 35–42
Consumers Advisory Group on Clinical Trials 15
Consumers Association 14
Consumers in NHS Research 42
continuing healthcare policies 58, 62
Cooper, L. 24, 42, 46
Coote, A. 23, 46, 47, 51
Copperman, J. 55
Corbin, J. 5, 8
Corcoran, G. 60, 130, 144
Cormie, Joyce 85
Cornell, S. 105
Cottrell, J. 161, 163, 164, 166, 171, 207, 208
Coulter, A. 37
Council for Voluntary Services (CVS) 216–17
counselling, multiple sclerosis and 118–19
Cowley, S. 70
Craig, G. 53
Craig, P. 46
Crichton, M. 85
Croft, S. 21, 54
cross infection 179–80, 192, 194, 195
Crow, L. 67, 79
Cullen, L. 70, 71, 73
Curtis, M. 175
cystic fibrosis (CF) 2, 155–210, 213–14; choice issues 157, 159–60, 169–85, 203–8; compliance with treatment 159–60; computer-mediated communication 197–9, 209; cross infection 179–80, 192, 194, 195; denial 172–7; discussion about death 169–72, 181–2; family life 7; ill health 183–4; informal networks 181–5, 196; information 201;

local groups 178, 193–4; meeting others 179–83; national organisations 185–7, 188–93; newsletters 185–6, 191, 202; palliative care 157, 161, 165–6, 168; prognosis 156–7, 206; respite care 205; specialist centres 190, 194–6, 202, 204; terminal care 161–8, 203–5; treatments 155–6, 158–60, 206–7; uncertainty 6, 178–9, 207, 209, 211–12; *see also* families
Cystic Fibrosis Foundation (CFF), US 187, 197
Cystic Fibrosis Trust 156, 158, 161, 185–6, 188–91, 192–3, 199, 218; Family and Support Service (FASS) 189
CYSTIC-L (online chat group) 172, 174, 182, 187, 197–200, 202, 203

Dakof, G.A. 117
Daly, G. 24
Davies, A.R. 38, 39
Davies, M.L. 9, 11
Davies, R. 74
Davis, A. 28
Davis, H. 24
Davis, K. 22, 31, 64, 66
De Conno, F. 91
de Raeve, L. 62
death: at home 74–5, 144–5, 165–6, 204–5, 207, 208; discussion about 169–72, 181–2; in hospital 163–5, 203–5, 207, 208; of friends 184–5
DeathNet 88
decibel diplomacy 49
deliberative opinion polls 48
democratic deficit 30
demyelination 97
denial 63, 73, 172–7
Department of Health 21–2, 27, 28, 30, 33, 38, 39, 40, 46, 55, 58, 110, 131, 160
Department of the Environment, Transport and the Regions 30
depression 130
Devins, G.M. 116
diabetes 117, 205
diagnosis: motor neurone disease 127–8, 136–43, 151; multiple sclerosis 97–9, 121
Dickson, M. 27
dietetics: motor neurone disease 134; multiple sclerosis 113
Dillner, L. 40
Dinwiddie, R. 156, 160
disability 5–6, 77, 79, 96, 152; medical model of 65, 68, 193; social model of 64–5, 66–7, 78, 81, 188; *see also* illness

disabled-run organisations 53, 66
Dixon, P. 40
Dodd, M. 64, 175, 204
Donahue, J.M. 34
Donaldson, L. 44, 45, 46, 54
Dowrick, C. 166
Doyal, L. 13
drug availability 4, 101–2, 105
drug trials 104–5, 147
Duncan-Skingle, F. 155
Dunlop, R. 74
Dunning, M. 38, 39
Dworkin, R. 63, 70, 216
Dyer, C. 35

Earll, L. 139
Edgar, H. 101, 105
Ell, K. 117
Ellershaw, J. 130
empowerment 20–1, 27–8, 58, 68, 76, 92;
    choice and 33–5, 68–74; collective
    empowerment 76–86; computer-
    mediated communication 200, 209;
    health professionals 26; ladder of 19;
    principles of 21
equal opportunities 13
Etherington, S. 52
euthanasia 58–9, 63, 75
Eve, A. 60, 75, 104, 166
exit 20, 74
experience goods 70
expert patient programme 14

Fakhoury, W.K.H. 71
Fallowfield, L.J. 35, 94–5
families, cystic fibrosis and 7, 160, 162–3,
    164, 168, 175, 178, 194, 202
Faulkner, A. 72
Ferguson, I. 22
Fermont, D. 74
Ferriman, A. 36
Field, D. 5, 65, 104, 166
Fife Users Panels Project 84–5, 92, 219
Fildes, S. 105
Fitzgerald, G. 105
Fletcher, S. 22
Fook, J. 72
Forbes, J. 52, 53, 54, 84
Ford, R. 55
Fordham, S. 79
Fordham, Sandra 152, 166
Forsythe, E. 96
Foster, F. 155
Foucault, M. 123
frail older people 84–6

Frank, A. 74
Frank, A.W. 2, 3, 4, 6, 8, 10–11, 96, 216, 220
Frankenberg, R. 3, 7–8, 63
Frankl, V. 9
Franks, A. 72
Freeman, J. 121
French, S. 67, 79
frequency of service use 70, 207
Fulton, G. 72, 79, 80–1
future orientation 8–9; motor neurone
    disease 152–4; multiple sclerosis 94, 107

Gallup 68, 180, 181, 183, 186, 191, 192, 202
Garrard, E. 70, 71, 216
gastrostomy feeding: cystic fibrosis 155;
    motor neurone disease 130
gene therapy, cystic fibrosis 156
general practitioners (GPs): choice of 33;
    cystic fibrosis and 160–1, 163, 207;
    motor neurone disease and 131–2;
    multiple sclerosis and 109–11
George, M. 118–19
George, R. 57, 60, 72
Gerhardt, U. 7
Gilbert, H. 18, 20, 22, 24, 27, 28, 32, 33,
    35–6, 38, 39, 40, 41, 42, 45, 48, 74
Giroux, L. 96
Glendinning, C. 49, 52
Glennerster, H. 28
Goffman, E. 123
Goss, S. 19, 28
Gott, M. 14, 15, 80
Gough, I. 13
Graham, J. 95, 104
Grande, G.E. 65, 73
Grant, G. 33, 34, 49–50
Gray, J.N. 80, 147
Green, M.L. 175

Haldane, D. 95
Hallett, C. 19, 20
Ham, C. 43, 52
Hamilton-Gurney, B. 18
Harris, L. 70
Harrison, S. 23, 24, 25, 26, 32, 37, 50–1, 54
Hawking, Stephen 130–1, 151–2
Health Action Zones 26
Health Care UK 25
Health Improvement Programmes 25, 43
Health Improvement Programme Boards
    220
health professionals: as proxies 64–5;
    empowerment 26; *see also* general
    practitioners (GPs)
heart disease 117

heart-lung transplant, cystic fibrosis 156, 160, 161–2, 163, 206, 212
Help the Aged 216
Henke, E. 136
Henwood, M. 58
Heritage, Z. 64
Heyman, B. 215
Hicks, F. 60, 130, 144
Higginson, I. 65
Hine, D. 15, 57, 70
Hinton, J. 63, 74, 136, 164
Hirschman, A. 20
Hitch, P.J. 81
Hockley, J. 74
Hoffenberg, R. 43–4
Hogg, C. 14, 24, 220
Holmes, J. 116
home care 118–19
home-based techniques 73; cystic fibrosis 159
hope 87, 161, 169, 201, 206, 209, 212–13
Hopkins, A. 38
Hornquist, J.O. 8
hospice care 71, 75, 79; access to services 49, 56–7, 59–60, 75; cystic fibrosis patients 166–8, 205; hospice movement 56, 59–61, 65, 104; multiple sclerosis patients 103–4; respite care 144
House of Commons Public Accounts Committee 39
Hoyes, L. 19
Hugman, R. 31
human immunodeficiency virus (HIV) 6, 9, 14, 79; research 147
Hunter, D.J. 23
Hunter, M. 125
hyperbaric oxygen therapy 102
Hyppönen, H. 87

identity, sense of 124
Ignatieff, M. 10, 11, 13–14
Illman, J. 63, 67, 68, 72
illness 10, 50, 79; body's role in 5; control over 124; disruption of life course 6–8; sick role 10–11; *see also* disability
InClude web server 87
inclusion 12
incontinence helpline 90
infertility, cystic fibrosis patients 169
information 72, 92, 94–5, 213; access to 35–6; choice and 33, 35, 69, 71, 169; CF patients/carers 201–2; Internet and 36–7, 86, 90, 102, 105, 147; motor neurone disease patients/carers 136–7,

140–2; multiple sclerosis patients/carers 105–8; stress and 117
information and communication technologies (ICTs) 86–91; cautions and challenges 90–1; collective organisation and 88–9, 200, 209; computer-mediated communication 82, 86, 89–90, 197–9, 209, 219; and disembodiment 89–90; treatment literacy and 87–8, 198, 200; user involvement and 88; *see also* Internet
informed consent 36
Ingleton, C. 62
insomnia 130
Institute for Public Policy Research (IPPR) 24, 42, 46, 47
integrated care 30; multiple sclerosis 111–12
International Alliance of ALS/MND Associations 86
International Cancer Information Centre 86
International Federation of Multiple Sclerosis Societies 105, 121
Internet 86–7, 89, 187, 203, 209; access to 91; information and 36–7, 86, 90, 102, 105, 147; online services/support groups 86; service provision and 91; *see also* information and communication technologies (ICTs)
Internet-related chat (IRC) services 86
intimate bodily care 6
intravenous therapy, cystic fibrosis 155, 159, 179
involvement 18; *see also* user involvement
Ivers, V. 84

Jackson, E. 68
James, N. 65
Jochemsen, H. 75
Johnson, J. 79
Johnston, M. 137, 139
joint commissioning groups 52
joint consultative committees (JCCs) 51–2
Joint Palliative Care Strategy Groups 62
Jones, D.E. 117
Jordan, J. 24, 50, 54
Joule, N. 39

Kahssay, H.M. 15
Kellahear, A. 72, 73
Kellerman, J. 176
Kelly, M.P. 5
Kelson, M. 39
Kendall, E. 46

Keown, J. 75
Khan, U. 23, 31–2, 51
Kim, T. 133
King, E. 148
King Lear conundrum 11
King's Fund Nursing Development Unit 55
Kingsley, P. 104–5
Kirklees and Calderdale Health Authority 45
Klein, E. 78
Kleinman, A. 4, 215, 216
Koocher, G.P. 178
Kramer, L. 147

ladder of citizen participation 19
Lane, C. 79
Lasagna, L. 62
Layton, A. 111
Layward, L. 96
Layzell, S. 77
Leary, T. 86
Leeds Health Authority 45
legal redress 35, 74
legitimacy 23, 30, 55, 58
Leigh, P.N. 129
Lenaghan, J. 47, 51
Lewis, C. 63, 65–6
Lewis, J. 28
Lewthwaite, J. 55, 68
liability 35
Liddle, B. 20
life course, disruption of 6–8, 215–16
Lifton, R.J. 9
liminality 7–8
Lindow, V. 49, 51, 54, 81
Lindsay, M. 22
Linn, M. 3
living wills 63
local authority representation 23, 24
Local Voices (NHS Management Executive) 22–4, 48, 54
Loder, C. 105
Long-Term Medical Conditions Alliance (LMCA) 14, 48, 79, 218
Luckmann, T. 1
Luker, K. 62, 63
lung cancer 80
Lupton, C. 42, 44, 45, 53
Lupton, D. 34

McCarthy, M. 56, 65, 71, 77, 163, 204
McCracken, M.J. 172
MacDonald, C. 28
McGuire, M.B. 34
McIver, S. 27

McKee, L. 87, 89
McLeod, E. 14, 15
Macmillan nurses 165–6
McSherry, W. 60
McTaggart, L. 37
Mador, J.A. 176
Maher, J. 82, 83
Manero, E. 46
Mannion, R. 12
Manthorpe, J. 53
markets 12, 32–3
Marsh, Eva 96
Martini, C. 91
Maslow, A.H. 12
Matthews, B. 106
May, C. 166
mediococentrism 8
MENCAP 14
mental health 14
Mercer, G. 65, 66, 77, 79, 188
Meredith, C. 35
Meredith, P. 27
Milewa, T. 220
Miller, C. 19, 28
Miller, D. 26–7
Miller, N. 27
Miller, S.M. 175
Mills, M. 60
MIND 14
Mindlink 14
Modernising Social Services 29–32, 51
Moise, J.R. 176
Monks, J. 3, 7–8, 63
Montbriand, M.J. 73
Moore, M.K. 144–5
Moore, W. 14, 38, 39, 40, 48, 53
moral agendas 10–11
Morgan, G. 22
Morrison, P. 55
Moss, Catti 37
Motor Neurone Disease Association (MNDA) 125, 130, 134, 143, 144, 146–9
motor neurone disease (MND) 2, 125–54; care regimes 135–6; contact with other patients 145–6; diagnosis 127–8, 136–43, 151; end-of-life care 143–5; future orientation 152–4; multidisciplinary care teams 131–5; nature of 126–9; pain 129–30; palliative care 129–30; prevalence 129; social attitudes and 150–2; treatments 129–30; uncertainty 125, 128, 211–12
Mount, Balfour M. 62, 75
Mount Vernon Hospital 83
Mulherin, D. 157

multiple sclerosis (MS) 2, 94–124; benign
MS 99; bridging gaps between services
111–12; costs of 116; counselling
118–19; diagnosis 97–9, 121; drug
availability 4, 101; end-of-life care
103–4; information 105–8; medical
needs 109–11; meeting others 108–9;
nature of 96–7; nursing services 112;
prevalence 96–7; progressive MS
99–100; respite care 115–16; social work
113–15; stress and 116–18; symptoms 97;
treatments 100–3, 105; uncertainty 6,
97, 99–100, 104–5, 211–12; user vs
professional views 119; variation 6, 8
Multiple Sclerosis Society 105, 108,
111–12, 120, 121
Murphy, R.F. 7
Muscle Power 53, 82
Muscular Dystrophy Society 53
Myers, F. 28

narrative 2–4; key features of 4–11
nasogastric tube feeding: cystic fibrosis 155;
motor neurone disease 130
National Breast Cancer Coalition (NBCC)
83, 84
National Cancer Alliance 41, 83
National Consumer Council 14
National Disability Information Project 87
National Institute for Clinical Excellence
27
Neale, B. 56
Needham, G. 38, 39
needs 11–14, 25, 105; assessment 58; of
carers 151, 199
Nettleton, S. 1, 216
Neuling, S.J. 117
Neurological Alliance 79, 146, 218
neurologists 109, 110, 111, 132–3
Newell, C. 63
NHS 58; *The New NHS: Modern,
Dependable* 24–7, 51, 57, 64; user
involvement 25–7, 28
NHS and Community Care Act (1990) 28
NHS Executive 28, 39, 41, 42, 48
Nicholes, P. 160
Nicholson, R. 121
Nocon, A. 20, 21, 25, 26, 27, 29, 30, 31, 40,
51, 53, 54
Norris, F.H. 132–3
North Bedfordshire Health Authority 45
North Thames Regional Health Authority
41
nursing services: motor neurone disease 133;
multiple sclerosis 112

Nuttall, P. 160

Oakeshott, M. 124
O'Brien, T. 127, 143
occupational therapy: motor neurone
disease 134; multiple sclerosis 113
Oliver, D. 129
Oliver, M. 5, 10, 66, 67, 77, 80, 96, 193
Oliver, S. 41
OncoLink 86
Ong, B.N. 7
online support groups 86
open awareness 72
Opinion Leader Research 47
opinion polls 48
organ transplant, cystic fibrosis 73, 156,
160, 161–2, 163, 168, 206, 212
organisations 77–9, 214, 218–19; as proxies
66–8; disabled-run organisations 53, 66,
192; partnership 51–3; *see also specific
organisations*
Ortega y Gasset, J. 9
Osborn, A. 54
Osmond, H. 106
Øvretveit, J. 42, 43
Oxenham, D. 63

pain control 56; motor neurone disease
129–30
palliative care 38, 49, 56–63, 70, 73, 77–9,
217; access to 72, 75; AIDS 77; cystic
fibrosis 157, 161, 165–6, 168; definition
of 56; information 35; motor neurone
disease 129–30; multiple sclerosis
100–1; self-help groups 79; service
provision 59–60, 61, 70, 77; significance
of 70–1; user involvement 57–9, 71; *see
also* hospice care; terminal care
Park, R.H.R. 130
Parker, G. 6
Parker, S. 63, 69, 72, 75
Parkes, C.M. 62
Parsons, I. 63
Parsons, T. 10
participation 12, 18–20, 22–4, 42–8, 55,
220; citizens' juries 46–8; community
health councils 45–6; community issues
groups 48; consensus conferences 48;
deliberative opinion polls 48; in
healthcare policy 25–6; in palliative care
services 71, 208; ladder of citizen
participation 19; standing/interactive
panels 45; *see also* user involvement
partnership 18, 51–3
paternalism 13, 31, 35, 53

Patient Partnership Strategy 42
Patients Association 14, 48
Patient's Charter 22, 27, 28, 53–4
Patients Influencing Purchasers Project 48, 55, 68
Patients' Representatives 40
Patients' Subgroup of the Clinical Outcomes Group 42
Pearson, P. 215
Peckham, S. 19
performance targets 38
Perry, S. 96
personal accounts: motor neurone disease 151–2; multiple sclerosis 95–6
personal responsibility 10, 29, 34
Pfeffer, N. 43
Philpot, T. 31
physiotherapy: cystic fibrosis 155; motor neurone disease 133–4; multiple sclerosis 113
Pickard, S. 32
policy 1, 4, 58, 219–21; social policy 12; user involvement in healthcare policy 21–32
Pollitt, C. 24, 25, 37
Pollock, A. 43
Pounceby, J. 64, 159, 160, 169, 172, 174, 175, 176, 177, 178, 182, 183, 191, 204
Pound, P. 38, 195
Povey, R. 105
power 19–20; *see also* empowerment
predictability of service effects 70, 207
premature death 4; motor neurone disease 125; multiple sclerosis 100
pressure groups *see* organisations
pressure sores 130
Preston-Shoot, M. 21
Price, L.J. 7
Priest, P. 65
Primary Care Groups/Trusts 26, 27, 33, 39, 43, 110
primary health care 18
Prior, D. 32, 33, 34, 35, 68, 70, 71, 72, 73, 76, 157, 203, 205
priority setting 28, 42–3, 47
professional practice 1
progressive bulbar palsy (PBP) 127; *see also* motor neurone disease
progressive muscular atrophy (PMA) 126, 128; *see also* motor neurone disease
provisional existence 9
proxies 63, 64–8; carers as 65–6; organisations as 66–8; professionals as 64–5
public consultation *see* consultation

public engagement 19
Public Involvement Programme 42
public participation *see* participation

quality assurance 38–40, 48
quality of life 8, 38, 64, 73, 75, 76, 147
quality standards *see* standards
Quin, S. 68, 124, 164, 169, 172, 181–2, 185, 207

Radford, I. 95
Radiotherapy Action Groups Exposure (RAGE) 15, 83
Rainbow Trust 219
Ramsay, N. 60
Rashid, A. 49
rationing 24, 43–4, 88; and palliative care 56–7
Raudonis, B.M. 62
Rawles, J. 13
Redmayne, S. 45
redress 35, 74
remyelination 101
representativeness 47, 50–1, 194
research 146–7, 151; AIDS/HIV 77, 147; panels 45; user involvement 41–2; *see also* clinical trials
resource allocation 13, 42, 47, 115, 116; cystic fibrosis 157
respiratory failure, motor neurone disease 126, 143
respite care 64, 144; cystic fibrosis 205; motor neurone disease 144; multiple sclerosis 115–16
rheumatoid arthritis 124
Rhodes, P. 21, 25, 26, 27, 29, 30, 31, 51, 53, 54, 56, 57, 62, 70, 74, 157, 202, 206, 208, 217
Ridley, N. 115
Rigge, M. 38, 39, 48, 55
right to die: cases 35; organisations 88; *see also* euthanasia
Riluzole 129
Rivermead Hospice 112
Robinson, I. 36, 64, 66, 68, 73, 94, 95, 96, 119, 123–4, 125, 201
Robson, P. 50
Rodgers, J. 28
Rose, D. 55, 220
Rosenblatt, P.C. 71
Rossiter, D. 111
Rothman, D.J. 101, 105
Russon, L. 63, 72
Rust, A. 22

St Christopher's Hospice 56
Saltman, R. 20, 22, 32, 44
Sandy, O. 35
Sang, B. 14
Sashidharan, P. 52, 53, 54, 84
Saunders, Dame C. 129, 136–7
Savage, R. 49
Schapiro, R. 105
Scunthorpe Community Health Care NHS
    Trust 132
Seale, C. 163, 204
search goods 70
Segal, J. 105
self 215–16; postmodern 10
self-advocacy groups 82–4
self-help groups 48, 79–82, 91; cancer 79,
    80, 81–2; online 86
Senior Clinical Medical Officer for Physical
    Disability 132
Service First Unit 15
Seymour, J.E. 62
Shakespeare, T. 65, 67, 77, 78
Shale, D. 156, 163, 207
Shaw, S. 56, 57, 70, 71, 74, 165, 168, 202,
    206, 208
Shearer, A. 90
Sibley, W. 105
sick role 10–11
Siegler, M. 106
significance of services 70, 207–8
Sikora, K. 15
Simms, A. 74
Skilbeck, J. 70, 73, 205
slow euthanasia 75
Smaje, C. 22
Small, N. 2, 3, 6, 12, 95
Smith, A. 12
Smith, A.E. 104
Smith, D.H. 176
Smith, D.L. 157
Smith, K. 27
Snell, J. 25
social contract 13
social exclusion 12, 213
social policy 12
social services: *Modernising Social Services*
    29–32, 51; motor neurone disease and
    134; multiple sclerosis and 113–15;
    palliative care 57, 61; user involvement
    28, 29–32
Social Services Inspectorate 28
Sofka, C.J. 86, 88
Sone, K. 65
speech difficulties, motor neurone disease
    126, 127, 152

speech therapy: motor neurone disease 134,
    135; multiple sclerosis 113
Spence, F. 64, 76
spoiled identity 50
Stableforth, D.E. 157
standards 38; motor neurone disease care
    148; multiple sclerosis care 121–2; user
    involvement and 122
Standing Medical Advisory Committee 59
Standing Nursing and Midwifery Advisory
    Committee 59
standing panels 45
StartHere 87
steroids, multiple sclerosis treatment 100,
    101, 102–3
Stewart, D. 123
Stewart, J. 30, 45, 46, 47, 48, 51
Strauss, A.L. 5, 8
stress 116–18
Stuart, M. 79
suicide, assisted 59, 63, 75, 88; *see also*
    DeathNet
Sullivan, S. 19, 43, 48
Sullivan, T. 123
Summers, D. 129
support groups 80–1, 202; online 86; *see also*
    CYSTIC-L
surveys 95; satisfaction surveys 27, 29, 40
survivor politics 83
Survivors Speak Out 14
swallowing difficulties, motor neurone
    disease 126, 127, 130
Sykes, J. 57, 60, 72
symptom relief 65, 73, 74, 75; home-based
    techniques 73; pain control 56

'Talk Back' Project, Wakefield 85–6, 92
Taylor, M. 19, 20
Taylor, P. 42, 44, 45, 53
Taylor, R. 33
Taylor, S.E. 117
Teff, H. 35
telephone conferences 82
temporal orientation 9
terminal care 57, 60–1, 217; cystic fibrosis
    161–8, 203–5; motor neurone disease
    143–5; multiple sclerosis 103–4;
    obtaining views by proxy 63, 64–8;
    obtaining views in advance 63–4; user
    involvement 60–1, 63–8, 216; *see also*
    hospice care; palliative care: terminal
    illness 58–9
The New NHS: Modern, Dependable 24–7,
    51, 57, 64
Thomas, R. 105

Thomas, S. 40
Thomas, Sue 133
Thompson, A. 47, 48, 111
Thorne, S.E. 96
Thornton, P. 82, 84
Tillich, P. 9
time 8–10
Todd, C.J. 65, 73
Townsend, J. 74
Tozer, R. 82, 84
transplants *see* organ transplant
treatment: cancer 6; ceasing treatment
    75–6; compliance 159–60; cystic fibrosis
    155–6, 158–60, 206–7; motor neurone
    disease 129–30; multiple sclerosis
    100–3, 105
treatment literacy 64, 87–8
Trew, K. 95
trials, clinical 104–5, 147
Trueworthy, R. 172
Turner, V. 7
Twigg, J. 64, 65
Twycross, R. 63
Tyler, P. 82

UK Advocacy Network 14
UK Citizens Online 88
UK Central Council for Nursing, Midwifery
    and Health Visiting (UKCC) 69
uncertainty 4, 6, 211–12; cystic fibrosis 6,
    178–9, 207, 209, 211–12; motor neurone
    disease 125, 128, 211–12; multiple
    sclerosis 6, 97, 99–100, 104–5, 211–12
Urben, L. 79, 80, 81–2
user involvement 1–2, 55, 92, 152, 220–1;
    agenda 4–5, 10; in clinical audit 39; in
    community care 27–9; in healthcare
    policy 21–32; in palliative care 57–9, 71;
    in social services 28, 29–32; in terminal
    care 60–1, 63–8, 216; information
    technology and 88; narrative 2–4; nature of 18–21;
    research 41–2; social power and 214–15;
    standards and 122; user group activity
    14–15; *see also* participation
users 19–20, 31, 54, 55; categories of 19;
    partnership 51–3; representativeness
    50–1; responsibility of 29; role of
    48–55
utilitarianism 12–13

van den Burt, J.H. 9
van der Maas, P.J. 75
van Overstraten, A.R. 105
variation: multiple sclerosis 6, 8; services
    30
Venters, M. 176
Vetter, N.J. 117
Viagra 102
voice 20
voluntary organisations *see* organisations

Wade, A. 65
Walker, A. 21, 22, 24, 28–9, 32, 49, 52,
    60, 65, 68, 72, 76, 84, 85, 92
Walker, G. 41, 72
Walters, S. 159, 188
Walton MS Centre, Liverpool 111
wants 11–13
Warren, S. 116
Webb, A.K. 64, 175, 204
welfare provision 12, 30, 54, 203
West, P. 3
White, H. 90
White, M. 111
White, P. 52, 68
Whitehead, M. 23
Whitehurst, A. 152
Williams, B. 33–4, 40, 49–50
Williams, G. 2, 124, 215
Williams, S.J. 10
Willis, J. 85, 93
Wilson, J. 80, 81
Winefield, H.R. 117
Winkler, F. 22, 32, 33, 35
Wired Welfare 89
Wistow, G. 23, 33, 54, 57, 64
women's movement 78
Wood, J. 27
Woods, S. 62, 63
Working for Patients (White Paper) 27, 28
World Health Organisation 18
Wynn-Knight, S. 36, 159, 162, 172

Yellen, S.B. 79
Young, M. 70, 71, 73

Zed 152
Zelter, L. 176
Zola, I.K. 80, 220